LOST HARBOR

LOST

The Controversy over

WARREN L. HANNA

HARBOR

Drake's California Anchorage

University of California Press, Berkeley, Los Angeles, London

University of California Press
Berkeley and Los Angeles, California
University of California Press, Ltd.
London, England

© *1979 by* *The Regents of the University of California*

ISBN 0 – 520 – 03785 – 5
Library of Congress Catalog Card Number: 78 – 64456
Printed in the United States of America

1   2   3   4   5   6   7   8   9

To my wife Frances

whose understanding, patience, and encouragement have been an inspiration

Contents

List of Illustrations   xi
Preface   xv

Part I. The Controversy

1. The Great Drake Mystery   3
2. The Circumnavigation   13
3. The California Sojourn   25
4. The Kingdom of Nova Albion   33
5. The Elizabethan Visitors   45
6. The Anchorage Sleuths   66

Part II. The Evidence

7. "The Famous Voyage"   85
8. *The World Encompassed*   96
9. Other Early Accounts   103
10. Contemporary Maps and Charts   113

Part III. The Debate

11. A Format for Review and Analysis   137
12. The Approach   142
13. The Latitudes   152
14. The White Cliffs   163
15. The Harbor of Refuge   171
16. The Weather   184
17. The Hinterland   192
18. The Flora   199
19. The Fauna   206
20. The Indians   214
21. Archaeological and Artifactual Evidence   231
22. The Plate of Brass   242
23. The Departure   263
24. The "Portus Novae Albionis"   271
25. The Montanus Illustration   296
26. The Cermeño Visit   303
27. The Dudley Maps   316
28. The de Morena Story   331
29. An Overview of the Evidence   338

Part IV. Documents

Appendix

A. Excerpt from "The Famous Voyage," 1589, covering the California Sojourn   349
B. "The Course"   355
C. Comparison of Hakluyt's Three Accounts of the California Sojourn   361
D. Excerpt from *The World Encompassed* Covering the California Sojourn   364
E. Legends from Dudley's Charts of Northwestern America   381
F. Cermeño's Account of his California Visit   384

G.   Account of Pilot N. de Morena   387
H.   A Review of Hakluyt's Editorial Problems with
     "The Famous Voyage"   389
I . The Twenty Tenets of the California Historical Society's
     1974 Debate   396

Notes   401
Bibliography   431
Index   441

Illustrations

The Hondius Broadside map, entitled Vera Totius
    Expeditionis Nauticae (circa 1595)   endpapers
Sir Francis Drake, etching attributed to
    Jodocus Hondius   2
Queen Elizabeth I, portrait by Crispin de Passe   16
The *Golden Hind II*   18
Drake meeting the California Indians   26
The Montanus illustration   30
Map of the territory and villages of the Coast
    Miwok tribe   35
Sir Francis Drake, frontispiece of *The World
    Encompassed*   48
The crowning of Drake by the California Indians (1655)   57
The Father Crespi 1772 map of the San Francisco
    Bay region   59
George Davidson   71
Henry R. Wagner   72
V. Aubrey Neasham   75
Robert H. Power   76

Robert H. Power escorts Queen Elizabeth II through
    Drake 400 Exhibition, 1977   77
Chester W. Nimitz   79
Raymond Aker   81
Title page of the 1589 edition of Hakluyt's
    Principall Navigations   86
Excerpt from the Preface to the 1589 edition of
    Hakluyt's *Principall Navigations*   89
A part of the first page of "The Famous Voyage" (1589)   92
"The Course." Page 440 of Volume III of Hakluyt's
    1600 edition of *Principall Navigations*   94
Title page of *The World Encompassed* (1628)   97
Title page of Volume III of Hakluyt's 1600 edition of
    Principall Navigations   108
The Silver map of Drake's voyage   116
The French Drake map   118
The Dutch Drake map   120
The Hondius Broadside map of Drake's Voyage   122
Detail of Dudley's Carta Particolare, Chart XXXIII   127
The Molyneux map   131
The *Gulliver's Travels* map   132
Chart showing the "Spanish course" followed by Drake
    from Mexico to California   144
Title page of De Bry's 1599 *Americae Pars VIII*   154
The "Seven Sisters," white cliffs on the Sussex
    seacoast, England   164
The white cliffs of Drake's Bay, California   166
Drake's Beach   173
Bolinas Bay and Lagoon   178
Point Reyes   187
The Olema Valley   194
San Francisco Bay   196
Comparison of Marin County ground squirrel with
    barbarie conie   210
Sir Francis Drake, engraving by Paul de la Houve   216
Drake at Nova Albion   219
1567 Elizabethan sixpence found in Marin County   235
Photograph of the Shinn plate   244
X-ray of the Shinn plate   245
Site where Shinn said he found the plate   247
Walter Starr and wife at site where the plate was found   247

Aerial view of the southeast Farallon Island 264

The Portus Novae Albionis 272

A reconstruction of the Portus Novae Albionis
    at Drake's Estero 282

A comparison of the Portus plan with Drake's anchorage
    on Dudley's sub-map of the Carta prima Generale 283

A comparison of San Francisco Bay to the Portus plan 284

A drawing reconstructing Drake's Cove and presumed
    1579 encampment 286

A comparison of shorelines 298

Drake's Estero 308

The Carta prima Generale 318

Detail from the Carta prima Generale 319

Dudley's Carta Particolare, Chart XXXIII 321

Detail of the Carta Particolare 324

Unpublished Dudley Chart No. 85 325

Detail from the Carta prima Generale with inset
    superimposed 327

Prince Philip and Admiral Nimitz viewing the Shinn plate 342

The Prayer Book Cross 345

Preface

FOR NORTHERN CALIFORNIANS, 1979 will be a red-letter year, the quadricentennial of Sir Francis Drake's summer in the lost harbor of Nova Albion. It will commemorate the visit of a small English vessel to a port near San Francisco, bringing with it the plunder from many Spanish ships and settlements of South and Central America.

Drake's sojourn on the west coast of North America was undoubtedly one of the high points of his fabulous career. Those who wrote of the voyage gave interesting reports of his many exciting experiences on California shores; but they failed to include details which could have made it possible to identify with precision the harbor where he spent much of the summer of 1579. Hence the location of this historic port continues to be an unsolved mystery.

For more than fifty of the four hundred post-Drake years, I have been a fascinated observer of the impact of the great Elizabethan on the northern California scene. Through serendipity, a copy of John W. Robertson's *Francis Drake Along the Pacific Coast* came into my hands shortly after its publication in 1927; and the intense interest it aroused inspired me to become a collector of the literature on Drake's California visit. My bookshelves now contain almost everything of importance from the rare "The Famous Voyage" included in Richard Hakluyt's *Principall Navigations,* 1589, to the most recent publications on the subject, thus facilitating what is commonly referred to as research.

That research has culminated in this volume. It has been written for several reasons: No comprehensive review of the controversy over Drake's California anchorage has been published since Robertson's classic; and interest in the subject has reached a point where, in conjunction with the four hundredth anniversary of the visit, the public seems ready for an in-depth review of it from an objective and, at times, critical point of view. Moreover, the story of the personalities who have played leading roles in the anchorage controversy needs telling.

The most important reason, however, is the extensive development in the research and the discoveries by current Drake scholars. This book could not have been written in its present form

forty years ago when Robert F. Heizer had yet to publish the first of his authoritative treatises identifying Drake's natives as Coast Miwok Indians;

thirty years ago when the Drake Navigators Guild and Robert H. Power had not yet appeared on the scene to make known the results of their intensive research, and their respective findings and opinions on the anchorage site;

ten years ago when Raymond Aker's great monograph in support of his theory of a Drake's Estero anchorage had not yet appeared;

even five years ago when the landmark debate sponsored by the California Historical Society had yet to take place and its results to become available to all interested parties.

To these outstanding contributors to the literature and knowledge pertaining to Drake in California, who have given so willingly of their time, energy, and personal resources to bring this intriguing California historical mystery closer to solution, I express my appreciation.

Among those who have given me permission to borrow freely from their published materials, including contributions to the 1974 debate, are the California Historical Society, Robert H. Power Raymond Aker, and V. Aubrey Neasham. I am particularly indebted to Robert F. Heizer and Warren Howell, without whose assistance and encouragement this volume might never have been published, and to Max Knight who helped me so much in the final editing.

Kensington, California   WARREN L. HANNA

PART

THE CONTROVERSY

Sir Francis Drake, from the etching attributed to Jodocus Hondius.

1

The Great Drake Mystery

T HE CAREENING had been completed without mishap. Laboriously the barnacles and sea slime had been scraped from the hull's every plank. Each seam had been caulked, and the *Golden Hind,* seaworthy once more, rode quietly at anchor a safe distance from the shore. Her crew, skillful seamen and warriors on the briny deep, as well as competent ship repairmen in the harbor, now turned to their equally important duties as stevedores. Painstakingly, the sturdy chests laden with precious stones, gold bullion, ingots of silver, and other Spanish plunder were brought on board and stowed below deck. Scores of casks of fresh water, an even more important commodity, were placed in the bottom of the hold, along with a generous supply of firewood. Other available space was crammed with assorted provisions, paraphernalia, and armament. At last, the ship stood in perfect readiness, awaiting only the signal for departure.

The time was the twenty-first year of the reign of Her Most Gracious Majesty, Elizabeth I of England. In the years of our Lord, it was 1579. The place was a distant and lonely harbor on the "backe side of

America," as our Pacific Coast was then quaintly described. Commander of this gallant vessel and its unique company was Sir Francis, then only Captain Francis Drake, who had put nearly two years and fifteen thousand miles between himself and the English homeland, and who was now about to venture into the uncharted vastness of the Pacific on the last lap of a historic voyage around the world.

Summer was well along when the propitious moment arrived, and the *Golden Hind* resolutely headed seaward. On a nearby hill the lamentations of a band of friendly Indians intoned a sorrowful farewell. Gracefully, on the wings of a freshening breeze, the vessel skirted the headland that lay toward the sea and soon grew dim on the horizon. Behind him, as he sailed away, Drake left various articles and objects which no longer served his purposes; also, he left a mystery that was to deepen with the passing years. This unintended legacy to future generations was the riddle of the location of his "conuenient and fit harborough"[1] — the question of where Drake summered in 1579.

In California history, this is the great-grandfather of all questions. Unique, baffling, and highly absorbing, it presents an enigma which concerns the welfare of no one, yet challenges the imagination of everybody. Something of an index to its complexity may be derived from the fact that the search for an authentic answer continues, not only unabated, but actually at an increasing tempo. This does not mean, of course, that plausible solutions have never been proposed, but rather that none has yet gained universal acceptance.

Needless to say, answers of a general nature do not solve the problem. They have long been available. That some harbor on the west coast of North America and, more specifically, along the shores of California, provided a haven for Drake, has never been seriously questioned. Relatively recent developments have narrowed the area under consideration to the fifty miles just north of San Francisco and the Golden Gate — a substantial step in the right direction, but still far from a solution to the problem of the harbor's precise location.

The ultimate answer must point to a particular harbor, and prove beyond a reasonable doubt that it was Drake's anchorage. The purely circumstantial evidence — and none other is available — must be so effectively marshaled as to support only a single verdict. The various answers to date have tried to do that, but have only succeeded, so far as public opinion is concerned, in collectively achieving a hung jury. Being controversial, they are also inconclusive.

For four hundred years the probable location of Francis Drake's anchorage has been a subject of interest. Indeed, its consideration has given rise to a substantial body of literature reflecting the views and opinions of many would-be solvers of this mystery of history. All who have pondered the problem have necessarily had to start with the same set of premises, namely, the well-known factors of *who* paid the visit and *when* it took place. *How* the question arose, *what* efforts have been made to find a solution, *why* it has such a peculiar fascination and, above all, the bewildering evidence dealing with *where* the long-lost landfall lies, constitute a story which has never been told in its entirety.

Drake Comes to Nova Albion

Drake's role in northern California history is well established in most respects. Contemporary accounts are in agreement that he arrived on June 17, 1579, that he remained until July 23, and that he took possession of Nova Albion, as he called the country, in the name of England and good Queen Bess. Transposed into terms of the present Gregorian calendar, this sojourn of more than five weeks extended from June 27 through August 2 and inaugurated, as it were, the now delightful custom of summering on the cool seacoast of upper California.

The place of the great navigator's visit cannot be pinpointed with equal precision. The circumstances which brought him to California shores were such, both at the time and later, as to call for secrecy. They were also such, then and ever since, as to generate an intense curiosity of many people about his movements along the Pacific Coast of North America. Efforts to identify the particular harbor which sheltered the *Golden Hind* were initiated during Drake's lifetime and are still very much in progress.

Curiosity about Drake's California visit has been only a phase of the broader general interest in his world circumnavigation of 1577–1580. The beginnings of such interest date from September, 1580, when the *Golden Hind* returned to Plymouth harbor and notice of its arrival was rushed to Queen Elizabeth in London. From that metropolis, the tidings gradually spread by word of mouth until, at last, even the lowliest and most remote commoner knew that Drake had sailed around the world and had come home with a cargo of Spanish treasure. Within months, the story of the epic voyage had found its way to every continental capital.

The impact of this extraordinary news on the maritime world of the sixteenth century was enormous. In powerful Spain, already shocked by Drake's 1579 raids on her Pacific colonies and commerce, the voyage was viewed with revulsion and indignation. Elsewhere in Europe, it was regarded with a mixture of grudging admiration and uneasy perturbation. In England, though received in some quarters with considerable misgivings, it was generally hailed with joyful enthusiasm. Drake became the lion of London.[2]

The fabulous character of his globe-girdling exploit stimulated the public desire for details. Especially was there an eagerness for a personal report from or by the central figure of the great adventure. This widespread contemporary interest and corresponding hunger for information were strikingly reflected in a 1594 treatise by Thomas Blundeville, in which its author suggested:

> But if it might please Sir Francis to write a perfect Diarie of his whole voyage, shewing howe much he sayled in a day, and what watring places he found, and where hee touched, and how long he rested in any place, and what good Ports and Hauens he found, and what anchorage good or badde. . . . And finally what Moone doth make a full sea in euery port where he arriued, and what windes doe alter any tide or Current, and all other necessary accidents most meete for sea men to know. In thus doing the said Sir Frances I say should greatly profite his countrie men, and thereby deserue immortall fame, of all which things, I doubt not but that he hath already written, and will publish the same when he shall thinke most meete.[3]

This elaborate yet tactful plea for information failed to elicit the desired result. Although three brief reports from other sources finally made their appearance during the decade beginning with 1589,[4] there was nothing from Drake himself. The great navigator died in 1596 without having published any story of the voyage, nor has any personal account been posthumously printed or discovered. The lingering possibility that his original records of the voyage might eventually come to light somewhere in England has never materialized.

Interestingly, the long-cherished hope for a personal message from Drake was not entirely doomed to disappointment, because he did leave to posterity one document pertaining to his world voyage. However, he chose to leave this rare bit of Drake literature not in his native England but on the shores of far-away California. There it was that he caused a notice to be crudely inscribed upon a brass plate and nailed upon a "faire great poste," proclaiming the taking possession on behalf of England and Queen Elizabeth of Nova Albion[5] — a plate and proclamation which themselves have become a part of the great mystery.

Since the posting of that message in the summer of 1579, four centuries have come and gone. Yet it is not easy to realize that Drake's California advent actually antedated every English colony along the Atlantic seaboard; and that Portola's discovery of San Francisco Bay in 1769 stands approximately midway in time between Drake's visit and the present. To many, it may be a shock to learn that New England was originally on the shores of northern California. Yet the name Nova Albion is Latin for New England and it was a name found on maps of the California area for many decades after Drake's departure from the scene.

International Reverberations

A certain Drakean aura has lingered with strange persistence over the great buccaneer's entire Pacific theater of operations. No single voyage since the days of Columbus has produced a more profound or lasting impression. If Drake's circumnavigation continues to echo down the corridors of time and history long after many others have been forgotten, it will be because of the spectacular course of action he followed after passing through the Straits of Magellan into what was then called the South Seas.

Even before his arrival in California waters, Drake had acquired the status of public enemy number one with the Spaniards. His wholly unexpected depredations on their shipping and settlements along the western shores of South and Central America evoked torrents of anguished vituperation. His original squadron of five ships had been reduced by one mishap or another to a single vessel but, as Robert Greenhow tells us:

> Drake did not hesitate to proceed to the parts of the coast occupied by the Spaniards, whom he found unprepared to resist him, either on land or on sea. He accordingly plundered their towns and ships with little difficulty; and so deep and lasting was the impression produced by his achievements that, for more than a century afterwards, his name was

never mentioned in those countries without exciting feelings of horror and detestation.[6]

Spanish plans for reprisal were frustrated by Drake's disappearance into the North Pacific. Vigorous, though equally futile, protests were later lodged with her majesty's government by the Spanish ambassador to London.[7] Drake's conduct in the Pacific in 1579 undoubtedly contributed materially to the political tension that culminated in the abortive attempt of the Spanish Armada to invade England in 1588.[8] The situation in this regard has been summed up by Sir Winston Churchill as follows:

> This "Master Thief of the unknown world,"[9] as his Spanish contemporaries called Drake, became the terror of their ports and crews. His avowed object was to force England into open conflict with Spain, and his attacks on the Spanish treasure ships, his plundering of Spanish possessions on the western coast of the South American continent on his voyage around the world in 1577,[10] and raids upon Spanish harbors in Europe, all played their part in driving Spain to war.[11]

Drake's operations in Pacific waters again came into the international limelight during the first half of the nineteenth century, this time in connection with the Anglo-American dispute over possession of the "Oregon country." This controversial area, formerly claimed also by Spain and Russia, comprised the present states of Washington and Oregon, and the southerly portion of British Columbia. The claims of Great Britain and the United States were predicated upon the discoveries of their early explorers, and upon settlements within the region by their nationals.

Drake was the earliest, as well as the most illustrious, among those pioneers whose northwest Pacific discoveries were cited in support of the British contention.[12] His visit had antedated any by subjects of the United States or its predecessor colonies. However, on behalf of the American position it was pointed out that the extent of his penetration into northwest Pacific waters was a thoroughly controversial matter, having been placed by some of the early accounts at a point no farther north than the present California-Oregon border.[13] The fact that the dispute was ultimately resolved by fixing the international boundary at its present level, well above any latitude reputedly reached by Drake, suggests that his northerly progress, whatever its extent, was not a decisive factor.

Search Through the Centuries

During the final years of the sixteenth century interest in Drake's California anchorage was first manifested. Spanish consternation[14] over his attacks upon their South Seas shipping had been mingled with curiosity about where the "corsair"[15] had gone after being last seen off the west coast of Central America in April, 1579. Ultimately, a publication in London in 1589 by Richard Hakluyt entitled *The Principall Navigations,* containing an account[16] of his voyage, disclosed the fact that he had found a good harbor in latitude 38° on the California coast, a degree of latitude which runs fifteen miles to the north of present-day San Francisco. This news of Drake's Pacific Coast visit either inspired or increased a Spanish desire to locate a suitable harbor in that vicinity for the use of the "Manila galleons," which periodically sailed from the Philippines to Mexico.

At all events, the Spanish dispatched two expeditions to survey the harbor situation in northern California. One of these, in 1595, was under the command of Sebastian Rodriguez Cermeño;[17] the other, in 1602, was under Juan Sebastian Vizcaino.[18] Both were undertaken by royal order, after the viceroy of New Spain had succeeded in arousing the interest of Philip II.[19] It is almost certain that the English findings had come to Philip's attention and contributed to his willingness to authorize a search of the area visited by Drake for the purpose of locating a harbor such as that seadog had found.

Upon their returns to Mexico, both expedition commanders prepared reports that were silent on the subject of Drake.[20] Neither mentioned any order to search for the Englishman's anchorage, or the finding of any vestige of his California visit. Indeed, there was nothing in the wording of their accounts to suggest that the Drake discovery bore any relation, direct or indirect, to the Spanish search for a northern California harbor. Nevertheless, this seems to be one of those situations where actions speak more eloquently than words.

Both expeditions found their way, soon after details of Drake's voyage became public knowledge, to a harbor in the identical latitude reportedly visited by him. Now known as Drakes's Bay, this body of water lay just east of the protecting arm of Point Reyes. Though given differing names by the two expeditions, it was the only bay or harbor visited by both Cermeño and Vizcaino; it was also the setting where, to a greater or lesser degree, each came to grief.[21] To credit both visits to the same location entirely to coincidence requires a heavy dose of credulity, and it seems more reasonable to believe that both commanders knew what Drake was said to have found and were influenced by that information. As suggested by Robertson, in reference to the first of these expeditions;

> It is possible that the reason for believing that a good harbor could be found along this coast rested on the report of the "faire and goode baye" found by Drake near lat. 38°. It is certain that the Spaniards were informed that he had found a harbor suitable for careening and cleaning his vessel. The necessity for discovering this harbor for their own use probably induced them to send this surveying expedition.[22]

After the Vizcaino voyage, Spanish exploration of the area where Drake had found his anchorage was discontinued for more than a century and a half; yet the dream of a superb harbor in the vicinity of latitude 38° was never relinquished. In speaking of this "legend of the lost port," Robertson tells us:

> For one hundred and fifty years following the Vizcaino failure properly to locate the inner port of San Francisco there was a continuing belief among the Spaniards that somewhere near Point Reyes an inner harbor, great in extent, one suited to the necessities of their Philippine galleons, could be found.[23]

This persistent dream became a reality in 1769 when Portola, moving northward from San Diego by land, instead of by sea, stumbled onto the magnificence that is San Francisco Bay. Whether it had been visited earlier, and therefore discovered, by Drake is one of the collateral questions in determining where he summered in 1579.

Even before the nineteenth century, Anglo-Saxons were beginning to evince interest in a more precise location for the missing anchorage. Throughout California, this was a period of occupation and settlement of virgin territory. Among the many new inhabitants, especially in the areas traditionally associated with Drake, some became intrigued by the circumstances of his visit, and sought to ascertain its locale. Historians also began to compile a record of the state's background and development, and to discuss Drake's visit and the probable location of his Nova Albion harbor. Efforts in this direction were facilitated by the contemporaneous publication, in England, of a number of important early accounts of the circumnavigation.[24]

The upsurge of Drake interest has continued to reach new highs during the twentieth century, both in relation to the circumnavigation and to its California phases. In connection with efforts to solve the anchorage problem, armchair research has been supplemented by active physical search. Again, as in the sixteenth century, exploratory expeditions have been investigating likely areas in search of a harbor; this time, however, they have been ground crews nosing about for figurative footprints of the great freebooter. Powerful stimuli have been provided by the astounding population growth in the Golden State, by the finding of a brass plate[25] in Marin County by Beryle Shinn in 1936, and by the activities of the California Historical Society. Progress has been made, but the ultimate goal of precise and positive identification still remains just out of reach.

Pacific Pioneer

Drake did not "discover" northern California in the sense of being the first European to sight its shoreline. It is well established that Juan Rodriquez Cabrillo and Bartolomé Ferrelo, as leaders of an exploratory expedition sent out in 1542 by the Spanish governors of Mexico, had cruised along the coast to a point thought to be about one hundred and fifty miles north of the then undiscovered Golden Gate.[26] Records also show that Spanish galleons, which had begun in 1565 to ply between the Philippines and Mexico, customarily pursued a northerly course by which they approached the California mainland as much as two hundred miles above the Golden Gate, and then followed the coast southward to Acapulco.[27] But history discloses no actual landing, before 1579, by Spanish vessels at any point north of Ventura or the Channel Islands opposite present-day Santa Barbara.

Drake must therefore yield to the men of Spain the honor of having the first glimpse of northern California; yet he was the first traveler actually to set foot on the soil of this mecca of modern visitors. He was the first European to visit or explore any part of the California mainland north of Ventura, as well as the first Anglo-Saxon to pass through the Straits of Magellan and to visit the western shores of South and North America. Actually, he was the first sea captain to circumnavigate the globe in his own ship, because Magellan had died before the completion of his precedent-breaking voyage. Finally,

Drake was the first to hold Protestant services on the Pacific Coast if not, indeed, in the New World itself.

In view of such a series of exploits, it is not strange that the name of Drake is still one to conjure with in San Francisco. To its citizens, the Drake story is as familiar a tale as that of the Pilgrims at Plymouth Rock, and the *Golden Hind*[28] rates on a par with the *Mayflower*. The renown of its hero is represented in the San Francisco skyline by the Drake-Wiltshire and Sir Francis Drake hotels. Sir Francis Drake Boulevard is a prominent thoroughfare in more than one Marin County community. There is even a Sir Francis Drake Association which exists solely to perpetuate the memory of the navigator's California visit.

San Francisco is the *de facto* capital of Nova Albion. In its rich heritage, it combines the zeal of the Franciscan fathers with the zest of the swashbuckling seafarer, the prim virtues of the Victorian era with the fascinating vices of the old Barbary Coast. The more ancient origins of its saint-and-sinner background hark back, on the one hand, to St. Francis of Assisi as the city's patron saint and, on the other, to that eminent sinner and arch-adventurer, Sir Francis of England.

2

CHAPTER

The Circumnavigation

MONG THE many accomplishments of Drake's brilliant career, his 1577–1580 encirclement of the globe will no doubt be remembered the longest. His voyage brought him to, or near to, each of the seven continents and through the waters of the earth's major oceans, including the Antarctic. It took him further south and probably further north than any European had theretofore ventured in the Pacific. It inspired a whole series of great voyages of the Elizabethan age, and helped raise Britannia from a fourth-rate power to the ruler of the waves for the next three centuries.

Drake lived in an era when many of his countrymen were preoccupied with the idea of finding a northwest passage to the Orient. John Cabot and his son Sebastian had done much to promote the theory, and by 1575 the search for such a route had become almost an obsession. Shortly before Drake left on his voyage, a treatise on the subject had been published by Sir Humphrey Gilbert, and Martin Frobisher had already embarked upon the second of his three futile efforts to locate the Strait of Anian, as this imaginary passage was called. Its western entrance was believed by some to lie in a latitude somewhat below that of the present boundary between the United States and Canada.

Drake was fully aware of the efforts of his fellow mariners to locate such a seaway to Cathay, as Marco Polo called China. But Drake was a more practical man than Frobisher, Gilbert, or the Cabots, and accordingly made up his mind to head for the western shores of America by the one sure route of which he had knowledge. This was the southern, although not-too-well-explored, passage through the Straits of Magellan, discovered and first penetrated more than fifty years before by the man for whom they were named.

Setting up a Syndicate

The decision as to which route to follow had not been difficult, but the development of Drake's Pacific dream into a reality was a challenging project. Through a man named Thomas Doughty whom he had met in Ireland, Drake was put in contact with two prominent men at the Elizabethan court, Sir Francis Walsingham and Sir Christopher Hatton, and through them with others, including the Earl of Leicester and the queen herself.[1]

To finance the venture, a syndicate was put together, supported by contributions from a number of well-known people encouraged by the prospect of profit to be found in the Americas. Principal contributors included the earls of Lincoln and Leicester, Sir Francis Walsingham, Sir Christopher Hatton, Sir William and George Winter, and John Hawkins, the navy treasurer. Drake himself put in a thousand pounds, and it is said that Queen Elizabeth contributed a like amount.

Drake undoubtedly looked forward to transferring his sphere of activity from Atlantic to Pacific waters, where Spanish ships and settlements would be more vulnerable and richer prizes might be available. However, in recruiting personnel for the voyage, he merely let it be known that the destination was to be Alexandria; yet his elaborate preparations for the voyage belied the probability that they might be headed for Egypt. His selection of vessels, personnel, and equipment all suggested a more distant and lengthy project. He had secured a copy of Magellan's round-the-world chart[2] and he assembled a crew versed in many arts and skills essential to a long voyage, as well as a gun power that would have been superfluous except with Spanish encounters in mind.

The project undoubtedly had the approval of Queen Elizabeth; but Drake's claim that he possessed some sort of commission from her has not been authenticated by any reliable witness. Some historians have suggested that Drake had reached an understanding with the queen, secret from all or most of the other promoters, to make the voyage a raid on Spanish shipping and possessions. But the evidence does not bear out such a thesis, and it appears that Elizabeth neither initiated the venture nor knew its true purpose during the planning stage.[3]

Toward South America

The preparations were extensive. Drake's five vessels, the *Pelican* (later renamed *Golden Hind*), the *Elizabeth,* the *Marigold,* the *Swan,* and the *Christopher,* were assembled at Plymouth in the summer of 1577 for provisioning. Large supplies of biscuit, meal, beer, wine, pork, fish, beef, butter, cheese, rice, oatmeal, honey, sweet-oil, and salt were stocked. "Necessaries" included wood, coal, candles, wax, lanterns, platters, tankards, dishes, bowls, buckets, axes and spades, together with various carpenter's stores. Aqua vitae was the sole provision for the surgeons. Apparel included shoes, hats, and caps, as well as woolen and linen cloth.[4] Drake was known to have with him three books on navigation, as well as maps and charts.

After being driven back once by a great storm, the flotilla with 164 men aboard finally sailed out of Plymouth harbor on December 13, 1577. They headed for the Atlantic coast of Morocco, capturing Portuguese merchantmen en route and helping themselves to such of their provisions and goods as they saw fit. Their most important acquisition, however, was Nuño da Silva, a Portuguese pilot experienced in Brazilian waters where Drake was planning to go.[5] For the next fifteen months da Silva was to be an enforced passenger on Drake's flagship.

On April 1, 1578, Drake and his men sighted the coast of Brazil and continued south to Port St. Julian, a harbor on the South American coast, two hundred miles north of the entrance to the Straits of Magellan. They arrived there in June. It was mid-winter, bitterly cold, and the natives were hostile. It was here that Drake became aware that his

ELISABETH DEI GR. ANGL. FRAN. HIBER. ET VIRGINIA REGINA AVSPICATISSIMA.

POSVI DEVM ADIV-
TORE MEVM

Tantæ si vires, virtus mihi quanta Mariana est,
Littora iam pelagi dudum iuga nostra subißent:
Vnde etiam Oceani credor lectißima Nympha.
Quod si non animo fixum immotumque sederet
Ne cui me vinclo vellem sociare iugali,
Me sibi vel Nereus properaßet iungere sponsam.

Cris. de. Pas. scul. et ex.

The Crispin de Passe portrait of Queen Elizabeth I, 1598.

Number Two man, project contributor, and erstwhile friend, Thomas Doughty, had been fomenting mutiny among the crew. Drake empaneled a "jury" of forty men and tried Doughty for attempted subversion which, in Tudor eyes, was tantamount to treason. Doughty was found guilty and beheaded after receiving communion and having a final dinner with Drake.

The Straits of Magellan

At Port St. Julian two of Drake's five ships had become unseaworthy and were broken up for firewood. The contents and personnel were transferred to the remaining vessels after the latter had been cleaned and caulked. They headed for Cape Virgins, eastern entrance to the Straits of Magellan, and successfully threaded their way through in record time (sixteen days)[6] in spite of stopping to kill several hundred penguins for the larder. But hardly had they emerged into the South Pacific on September 6, 1578, when a powerful storm sprang up and blew ceaselessly for several weeks. It scattered the three ships and drove Drake's vessel which, in the meantime, he had renamed the *Golden Hind* (see page 49), six hundred miles southward. The *Marigold* was lost with all on board; the *Elizabeth* finally found her way back through the Straits and reached England on June 2, 1579.

An unintended result of the great storm was Drake's discovery that there was a route to the Pacific other than through the Straits of Magellan, namely, around the southern end of the continent (Cape Horn). He named what he believed to be the southernmost island below the tip of the continent *Elizabeth*, and set up there a stone engraved with the queen's name and the date. It has never been found.

Of the original company of 164, now an estimated 85 to 90 were left on the *Golden Hind*. But while on the Chilean coast in November, they ran into an ambush of more than a hundred natives and lost three men; a fourth was captured and slain on December 19. On December 6 they had reached Valparaiso, then a village of nine houses and a church. There they appropriated wine and provisions, as well as 25,000 pesos of gold that were in a vessel in the harbor.

English Sails on a Spanish Ocean

As the *Golden Hind* proceeded slowly north along the coasts of Chile and Peru, Drake began to earn the sobriquets that a stunned

The Golden Hind II. *Constructed in England in the early 1970s as an authentic replica of Drake's original vessel, it was sailed to California by Captain Adrian Small and a crew of eighteen, where it was berthed at San Francisco in 1975 for public viewing.*

Spanish world was soon to bestow upon him, such as the "corsair," the "dragon" (el Draque), and "master thief of the unknown world."[7] Seizing all vessels encountered, he confiscated such of their contents as suited his need or fancy, preference being given to gold and silver, of course. Occasionally, the "take" would include a crew member or passenger.

From the captain of a vessel captured on February 13, 1579, Drake learned that a Spanish ship carrying a large quantity of silver to Panama had left Callao, the port of Lima, only a few days ahead of the *Golden Hind*. Taking up the chase immediately, Drake on March 1 caught sight of and captured his quarry, the *Nuestra Señora de la Concepción*, nicknamed the *Cacafuego*.[8] Its treasure, in addition to twenty-six tons of silver, included thirteen chests of pieces of eight, eighty pounds (in weight) of gold, and miscellaneous jewels and plate.

On March 16, Drake arrived at the island of Caño in Costa Rica, where he found a secluded inlet in which he could clean and trim the

Golden Hind. Near that island, on the 20th, Drake's pinnace captured a Spanish frigate belonging to one Rodrigo Tello, with two "China pilots" aboard, named Alonzo Colchero and Martin Aguire. Both had their charts and sailing directions in readiness for a crossing to the Philippines. Drake seized their equipment and offered Colchero one thousand ducats to pilot him across the Pacific. Colchero refused, however, presumably because he would have been accused of collaboration with the enemy upon his return to New Spain, and also because it was already too late to head for the Philippines without encountering the dreaded typhoon season. Drake then took Tello's frigate with him (in the literature usually referred to as a "bark"), leaving its crew and Aguire on one of his pinnaces in an unequal enforced exchange of vessels.

On April 4, Drake captured a Spanish ship, the *Espirito Santo*, owned by Don Francisco de Zarate, its cargo including silk and porcelain bound for Acapulco. After taking what he wanted, including a young black woman, Drake let the ship go with its owner and crew, and sent Colchero with them.

Heading for the Northwest Passage

On April 13, 1579, Drake arrived at the port of Guatulco, south of Acapulco, in the state of Oaxaca, Mexico, his last port of call in settled Spanish America. His main purpose was to obtain water and provisions, but he also pillaged the town's warehouses and bodegas. There he left Nuño da Silva, the Portuguese pilot captured the preceding year, who was unfamiliar with trans-Pacific navigation. On April 16, Drake sailed out of Guatulco, using captured Spanish sailing directions to chart a favorable course toward the supposed Northwest Passage.

There is considerable uncertainty about the distances and directions sailed on this leg of the journey, as well as controversy as to the northernmost latitude reached. There seems to be no dispute about the fact that Drake encountered unfavorable weather conditions in the more northerly latitudes, forcing the abandonment of the quest for the Northwest Passage. On reaching the Oregon coast in stormy weather he anchored briefly, then headed south along the coast, searching carefully for a suitable harbor.

California and the Westward Journey

The accounts are in agreement that Drake sailed into a suitable harbor on June 17, 1579—a harbor where the *Golden Hind*, its crew and passengers remained for thirty-six days. They spent that time carefully making the ship seaworthy, replenishing their provisions and water, and entertaining the natives. By the time they completed their chores, the prevailing winds had changed so that it became feasible from a navigational standpoint to undertake their journey across the Pacific; and this they did. The story of their more than five weeks in their California harbor of refuge is what the great Drake mystery is all about. The details of that sojourn will be found in the next chapter.

The *Golden Hind* left its California anchorage on July 23 and headed for the Moluccas. Except for a brief stop at the Farallones, the ship and its company were out of sight of any land until September 30 when they came to an island where they encountered extremely hostile natives. From the latitude given of about 8° N, this may have been in the Palau group[9] of islands. They continued to the Philippines, sailed along the southwest coast of Mindanao, and headed for Ternate, which had been visited by the ships of Magellan sixty years before. Here they spent four or five days, taking on six tons of cloves and departing on November 6.

The *Golden Hind* was again in need of cleaning, and they found an uninhabited island where they spent twenty-six days, resting and putting their ship in final shape for the last leg of the long voyage home. On this island they left the black woman and two black men they had picked up along the coast of South America, and from here they sailed away on December 13, 1579.

A Brush with Death

In January, 1580, after following the east coast of Celebes for a considerable distance, the *Golden Hind* ran onto a shoal or reef. The wind drove the ship higher on the reef, and all on board were fearful that their time had come. They did nearly everything possible to lighten the ship, throwing overboard three tons of cloves, two of their large guns, meal, beans, and other provisions; in short, some of almost everything but their precious gold and silver.

As the situation grew more desperate, Parson Francis Fletcher preached a sermon, and administered holy communion to all members of the crew. Apparently he was indiscreet enough to suggest that their predicament was a divine judgment on their sins, notably that of Captain Drake in ordering the execution of Doughty.

Presently there was a miraculous change in the wind, and the ship slid easily off the reef. With danger no longer imminent, Drake vented his ire on the unfortunate Fletcher. He ordered him bound by one of his legs to the hatches in the forecastle, and after summoning the entire crew, said: "Francis Fletcher, I do here excommunicate thee out of the church of God and from all of the benefits and graces thereof, and I denounce thee to the devil and all his angels." As though that were not enough, he caused a sign to be bound around the parson's arm reading: "Francis Fletcher ye falsest knave that liveth."[10]

The journey continued toward Java without further incident, but with occasional stops for wood, water, and provisions. They arrived in Java on March 11. Drake went ashore on the 13th with some of the ship's company to visit the local potentates. A few days later, some of these chieftains came aboard ship and were regaled with food and musical entertainment. Food seemed to be plentiful there; the ship was stocked with a great quantity of provisions in anticipation of the long journey ahead.

The vessel had become heavily coated with barnacles and Drake availed himself of the opportunity to clean and wash its hull during the course of his visit in Java.

The Homeward Lap

After more than a fortnight in these pleasant surroundings, Drake set sail on March 26, 1580, on a west-southwest course for the Cape of Good Hope which he sighted on June 15. He did not land but continued along the west coast of Africa to Sierra Leone. There he spent two days taking on water and provisions. The company saw elephants and "oisters on trees of one kinde." Heading northwest for nearly 20 degrees of longitude and north to the 50th degree of latitude, they then followed a westerly course and arrived in Plymouth on Monday, September 26, 1580. Much to their surprise, they found that a day had been lost in the circumnavigation, since their records showed it to be Sunday.

Drake's first question upon his return concerned the health of the queen. When reassured in that regard, he sent a messenger to London to report his return, and remained on ship awaiting some word from Elizabeth. The queen conferred with her counselors to determine what position she should take with respect to the whole affair. In the meantime, Drake delivered a few samples of the gold and silver to an agent of the queen, who had it stored in Saltash Castle. Ultimately, Elizabeth found a way to reject the angry complaints of Bernardino de Mendoza, the Spanish ambassador, and had Drake's treasure, or much of it, transported from Plymouth and stored in the Tower of London.

Dividing the Spoils

The total value of Drake's loot will probably never be known. There is no record of the over-all amount of silver finally delivered to the Tower, nor of the disposition of the gold and jewels. It was said that members of the syndicate received a return of forty-seven pounds sterling for every one invested, and that 40,000 pesos (about 8,000 English pounds) were distributed among the crew. The Spanish merchants asserted that their losses had amounted to 950,000 pesos (332,000 English pounds). The queen received a substantial share, and Drake is known to have given away large amounts as presents to insure support among Council members.

The queen in turn gave an order in January, 1581, that 10,000 pounds sterling of the moneys lodged in the Tower be given to Drake as a reward for his voyage. With his newly acquired wealth he bought an estate in Devonshire called Buckland Abbey. At the order of the queen, he was knighted on April 4, 1581, on the deck of the *Golden Hind*, then docked at Deptford, where it remained on exhibition for more than eighty years. Drake enjoyed the queen's favor to a high degree, especially after presenting her with a diamond cross and a new crown made of Peruvian silver and emeralds. Other honors were soon heaped upon Sir Francis. In 1581 the city of Plymouth made him its mayor and in 1583 he became a member of Parliament.

Royal Censorship

Drake's return to England created an embarrassing situation for Queen Elizabeth and her advisors. There is no hard evidence that the queen had imposed a ban on the publication of any account of the voyage, but a few facts point in that direction. In 1582 a writer asserted that the queen had kept the official log of Drake's voyage so that it could not be published,[11] with a hint that she had been persuaded to do this from fear that some other nation might extract profit from it.[12]

In 1582 Richard Hakluyt published his *Divers Voyages* without mentioning the Drake circumnavigation,[13] although it was England's greatest voyage up to that time. One modern writer has suggested that the "only possible explanation is that this was omitted by order of Queen Elizabeth that she might not unduly antagonize the Spanish King, Philip II. The nations were nominally at peace and Philip was her brother-in-law."[14]

This explanation, however, was not altogether satisfactory, because the queen, in addition to accepting the greater part of the booty, had personally honored Drake in 1581 by visiting him on the *Golden Hind* at Deptford. In other words, it is remarkable that the prohibition against publication was allowed to stand for nearly a decade. All need for it was dissipated, of course, by the crushing defeat inflicted upon the Spanish Armada in 1588.

Significance of the Voyage

Drake became a great hero of the common people, although his ostentatious and arrogant manner did not endear him to the gentlemen of the Elizabethan court. The dramatic impact of his global exploits did much to stimulate the rise of England to her ultimate role as a great sea power, as well as to give hope to peoples elsewhere who had long suffered under the heel of Spanish oppression.

Drake was peculiarly a man for his own time, possessed of the special ability to arouse England to a sense of her destiny. The Elizabethan era produced half a dozen great seamen capable of duplicating his coup beyond the Americas, but no one else had his rare combination of qualities. Only he was gifted with the keenness of mind that enabled him to perceive the situation in the Pacific accurately, with a determination not to be deterred from his objectives, whether by threat of mutiny, by loss of the greater part of his fleet, or by the terrors of a vast and unfamiliar ocean, yet with a courtesy, restraint, and finesse in dealing with captives that often elicited even their reluctant admiration. Through his imagination, resourcefulness, superb leadership, and resolute courage he turned a potential disaster into a historic exploit.

3

CHAPTER

The California Sojourn

ORE THAN six months elapsed between the dates of
Drake's emergence into the South Pacific on December
6, 1578, and the arrival at his California anchorage on
June 17, 1579. During that interval he had accomplished the unusual
feat of spanning 100° of latitude, that is, from approximately 56° or
57° below the equator to 43°, 44°, or possibly as high as 48° above it.
Then, reversing direction, he sailed southward for several days along
the Oregon and California coasts, until, at last, he entered a "faire
and good Baye" and anchored in a "conuenient and fit harborough."
It was here, the principal accounts of the voyage agree, that the
Golden Hind was put in shape for the next leg of her journey and that
her captain and crew remained for thirty-six days.

During their stay, according to one of the contemporary accounts,
they were never comfortable: "notwithstanding it was in the height of
Summer, and so neere the Sunne; yet were we continually visited with
like nipping colds, as we had felt before."[1]

The account went on to state that the natives, although supposedly
inured to the climate, were shivering around and crowding together to
keep warm. Even the flora and fauna were adversely affected by the

raw weather. There was apparently a great deal of fog, with one of the accounts complaining that "neither could we at any time in whole fourteen days together, find the aire so clear as to be able to take the height of Sunne or starre."[2]

Indian Visitors

The day after the arrival of the *Golden Hind,* some of the natives, the "people of the countrey," put in an appearance. One of them left the shore in a "canow," stopping a reasonable distance from the ship to deliver a "long and tedious oration," using many gestures and signs. When this was finished, he returned to shore, but came back a second and a third time. On this last approach he brought with him gifts in the form of a neatly tied bundle of black feathers and a little basket

Drake meeting the California Indians. From The Annals of San Francisco *by Soule, Gihon and Nisbet, published in 1850.*

made of rushes and filled with an herb which the Indians called *Tobâh* or *Tabáh*.³ These he tossed into the ship's "boate," but would accept nothing in return except a hat, which he picked up from the water.

On June 21, after bringing the *Golden Hind* nearer to the shore, a part of the crew was landed to set up tents and to undertake the construction of "a fort for the defence of our selves and goods."⁴ Presumably only the *Golden Hind* was to be careened, but since Drake still had Rodrigo Tello's frigate with him, unloading procedures affected both ships. As for the *Golden Hind,* everything had to be transferred to the frigate or taken ashore, including armaments, provisions, personal effects, and the booty taken on the voyage.

When the local inhabitants became aware of what was going on, they came running, weapons in hand, hardly believing what they were seeing. It was apparent to Drake that they intended no harm and, by means of signs, he persuaded them to lay down their bows and arrows before coming nearer. As both men and women continued to arrive in great numbers, Drake offered them presents of shirts, "linnen cloth," and other items "to cover their nakednesse." In return, the Indians bestowed upon Drake himself, as well as his crew, a variety of gifts, including feathers, "cawles of networke, the quivers of their arrows, made of fawne-skins, and the very skins of beasts that their women wore upon their bodies."

Weeping and Wailing

When the natives had had their fill of mingling with and beholding the strange visitors, they joyfully returned to their houses. These were round excavations into the ground, with a conical roof of split lumber covered with earth to make them waterproof and warm. In most of them, the fireplace was in the center of the dwelling, and the single door served also as a chimney. The beds of the occupants were the hard ground strewn with rushes.

No sooner had the Indians returned to their village, which was situated three-quarters of a mile from Drake's encampment, than they began "a kind of most lamentable weeping ... the women especially, extending their voices in a most miserable and doleful manner of shreeking." All of this was plainly audible to Drake and his crew who still did not believe it wise to trust them too far, in the light of their previous experience with aborigines. So they entrenched themselves "with walls of stone" as a protection against "an alteration of their affections, or breach of peace if it should happen."

On June 23, a greater number of natives appeared on the hill above the camp, bringing the same kind of gifts as before. One of them, "with strange and violent gestures" delivered another "tedious oration." As the natives came down from the hill to visit with what they felt sure were gods, the women "as if they had been desperate, used unnaturall violence against themselves, crying and shreeking piteously, tearing their flesh with their nailes from their cheekes, in a monstrous manner, the blood streaming downe along their breasts." Holding their hands above their heads, they threw themselves furiously and repeatedly upon the ground, without regard to whether it consisted of "hard stones, hillocks, stocks of wood, or pricking bushes."

"This bloodie sacrifice" seemed to have an embarrassing effect on Drake and his men. They "fell to prayers," began singing psalms, and reading "certain chapters in the Bible." The Indians appeared to enjoy this turn of events. They sat attentively and took such pleasure in the psalm singing that whenever they visited the fort thereafter, they indicated their desire for more vocalizing.

A Visit from the Hioh

On June 26, as the news of the strangers became more widely disseminated, natives began to come from far and near. Among them was the king (*Hioh*) himself, "a man of goodly stature and comely personage, attended with his guard of about 100 tall and warlike men." The king was preceded by two messengers who indicated that he was on the way. One of them began, with some prompting from the other, an unintelligible proclamation lasting half an hour, the gist of which the Englishmen interpreted as a request that Drake give them "some token of his willingness to receive their chief." When it was supplied—whatever it was—they hastened back to their *Hioh* who then shortly appeared "with all his traine."

Preceding the king, however, was a large man bearing a scepter or royal mace about a yard and a half long, upon which hung two crowns made of knitwork and feathers, three "chaines of a marvellous length," and a "bagge of the herbe *Tobâh.*" The king wore a feather knitwork "caule" (cap) on his head and a coat made of the skins of small rodents referred to by the Elizabethans as "conies." His guards wore similar costumes, but some had their caules covered with a kind of down, which they obtained from a plant resembling lettuce. This was a decoration worn only by the attendants of the king.

Then came the common people, the men naked with their long hair gathered into a bunch behind, into which were stuck feather plumes. Through the front of their hair they had inserted single feathers like horns. Each had his face painted, some white, some black, some in other colors, and each had a present in his hand. They were followed by their women and children, each woman with a basket or two containing *Tobâh,* a root called *Petáh* (used for making meal or bread), broiled fish, and other gifts. The baskets were shaped like deep bowls, made of rushes so well woven that most of them would hold water. About the brims pearl shells were hung and, on some, two or three links of bone chains.

Uncertain of their attitude, Drake arranged his men for defense within his fortification. As the Indians came near, they stopped and the man with the scepter delivered a 30-minute harangue, followed by something like a common amen from the entire group. Then they came to the bottom of the hill and close to the fort, whereupon the scepter bearer went into a song and dance. Presently the king and all men were dancing and singing; the women danced silently.

A Coronation Ceremony

When Drake saw that the Indians intended no harm, they were permitted to enter the fortified compound. They did so, continuing their songs and dancing for a while. Then they made signs for Drake to be seated, followed by speeches apparently imploring him to "take the Province and kingdome into his hand, and become their king and patron." As described in "The Famous Voyage":

> In order to persuade us the better, the King and the rest, with one consent, and with great reverence, joyfully singing a song, did set the crowne upon his head, enriched his necke with all their chaines, honoring him by the name of *Hioh,* adding thereunto as it seemed, a signe of triumph: which thing our Generall thought not meete to reject, because he knew not what honour and profite it might be to our Countrey.[5]

"The Crowning of Drake by the California Indians" by Arnold Montanus (1671).

This was followed by another period of singing and dancing, after which the ceremonies ended. The Indians then circulated among the visitors, carefully examining them and offering presents to those that pleased their fancy, usually the younger ones. The women and even some of the old men accompanied these actions with shrieks and moans, weeping, and scratching their faces. The crew tried to stop this "madnesse," even to the extent of forcibly holding their hands; while some of those most adulated had to retreat to their tents to escape their more violent worshippers.

A Visit to the Interior

After that, few were the days when the natives did not come to visit, sometimes forgetting to bring food, so that Drake had to feed them with mussels and seal meat. They were people of a tractable, free, and loving nature. The men were swift of foot, and so strong that one of them could easily carry what two or three of Drake's men could hardly bear. Their only weapons were bows and arrows, which they used skillfully, although these weapons were not very effective. The men usually went naked; the women wore a loose garment of bulrushes hanging from their hips.

After the careening of the ship had been completed, Drake with members of his company made a journey "up into the land," to learn more about the way of life of the natives, and the "nature and commodities of the country." They found the interior to be far different from the shore, with several villages here and there. They saw thousands of "very large and fat Deere," and a multitude of "a strange kind of Conies." These were described as having small heads and bodies, with long, ratlike tails, feet like a mole, and pouches on either side of the chin for temporary storage of food. Their identification is part of the controversy about Drake's landing site.

Drake called the country Nova Albion[6] for two reasons: "one in respect to the white bankes and cliffes, which lie toward the sea; the other because it might have some affinities with our Country in name which sometime was so called." The accounts are in agreement that Drake caused an engraved plate to be placed on a post to give notice of his visit and having taken possession of the country, using the following language:

> At our departure hence our Generall set up a monument of our being there, as also of her majesty's right and title to the same, namely a plate[7] nailed upon a faire great poste, whereupon was ingraven her majesty's name, the day and yeere of our arrivall there, with the free giving up of the province and people into her Majesty's hands, together with her highnes picture and armes, in a piece of currant English money under the plate, where under was also written the name of our Generall.[8]

The principal contemporary accounts state: "The Spaniards had never had any dealing, or so much as set a foote in this country; the utmost of their discoveries reaching onely to many degrees Southward of this place." The source of this information, however, was not disclosed by either account.

On to the Moluccas

July 23, 1579, was the date of departure from Nova Albion[9] and, as the *Golden Hind* moved slowly out of the harbor and headed for the open sea, the natives ran to the hilltops to keep the objects of their adoration in sight as long as possible. Some of them lit fires on which, supposedly, sacrifices were offered.

The ship headed for a group of islands "not farre without this harborough," which they called the "Ilands of Saint James."[10] These were the Farallones, lying a few miles west of the Golden Gate and, likewise, a few miles southwest of Drake's Bay and Bolinas Bay. Arriving there on the 24th, they spent most of the day stocking up with a "great store of Seales and birds" which would "serue our turne for a while."

Incidentally, the departure was a solo performance. The Tello frigate which had followed doggedly in the wake of the *Hind* all the way from Caño in Costa Rica—for nearly three months and 1,500 leagues or more— faded into oblivion at this point, its fate unmentioned by the major accounts of the voyage. Only through the second deposition of John Drake[11] do we learn that it was here, at Nova Albion, that Drake "left the ship he had taken at Nicaragua"[12] [actually Costa Rica].

On July 25, the *Golden Hind,* heavily laden with provisions, water, and its precious cargo of gold and silver, pointed her prow southwestward and flew into the Pacific, away from the American continent and the Spanish turmoil to the south. And thus, with nothing in their "view but aire and sea," they continued their "course through the maine Ocean."

CHAPTER

The Kingdom of Nova Albion

I T WAS a "kingdome,"[1] according to Hakluyt's "The Famous Voyage," to which Drake gave the name Nova Albion[2] after he took possession of "this countrey" in "her Maiesties name," her majesty being Elizabeth I of England. Within its bounds was a certain "harborough" of a kind for which Drake had searched for days, and for which the world has since searched for centuries.

It would be interesting to know how much territory was embraced by Drake's "kingdome" of Nova Albion. Nowhere is this information supplied by any of the early accounts, nor do the contemporary maps clear up the question. The earlier maps[3] usually spread the name Nova Albion over the coastal area between Latitudes 48° and 52° N, whereas those appearing in 1595 and later[4] showed it, as a rule, between latitudes 38° and 42° N. Obviously, the mapmakers of the Drake era had no reliable information on the subject.

Drake himself probably had only a hazy idea of the extent of the territory that he called Nova Albion. However, since his territorial claim, at least so far as the language of the plate of brass was concerned, was limited to the "countrey" of his hospitable Indian hosts, it stands to reason that his concept of Nova Albion was coextensive with the ancestral homeland of the tribe whose king and people had, or so Drake purported to believe, so generously relinquished it to their visitors.

This is conjectural, although it rests upon reasonable inferences. Drake may have assumed that the tribe which he encountered was in control of a substantial area along the North Pacific.[5] Whatever his supposition in that regard, it was the "countrey" of the natives with whom he dealt to which, according to the contemporary accounts, he gave a special name. With this incontrovertible fact in mind, it then becomes relevant to determine the identity of the Indians which he met, and the extent of their "countrey" or "kingdome," if possible. Fortunately there is reliable evidence on this subject.

Scholars[6] have been able to identify the tribe encountered by Drake as the Coast Miwok Indians, who roamed the area from the Golden Gate to near the Russian River. The northern boundary of their homeland began at Duncan's Point, a few miles above Bodega Bay, ran eastward just above present-day Cotati and Glen Ellen, and thence southward to a junction with San Pablo Bay, a few miles west of Vallejo.[7] Thus it appears that this was the extent of their "kingdome," and that this was the region which Drake, although unaware of their boundaries, must have had in mind as Nova Albion. It included all of what is now Marin County, plus a southerly slice of Sonoma County, as delineated on the accompanying map.

Somewhere within this "kingdome" of the Coast Miwok Indians, if it is, in fact, the same as Nova Albion, lies the lost anchorage. In some snug harbor along the shores of Marin County, or possibly at Bodega Bay, partly in Sonoma County, Drake landed.[8] If it were true that Nova Albion, as rediscovered, had only a single harbor within its precincts, the answer to the anchorage riddle would be self-evident. No alternatives would require consideration, and no basis for controversy would exist.[9]

However, the situation is not that simple. In reference to the 38th parallel, which bisects the land of Nova Albion, a different set of circumstances prevails. For it so happens that within half a degree on either side of that line are to be found, not one or two, but eight bays

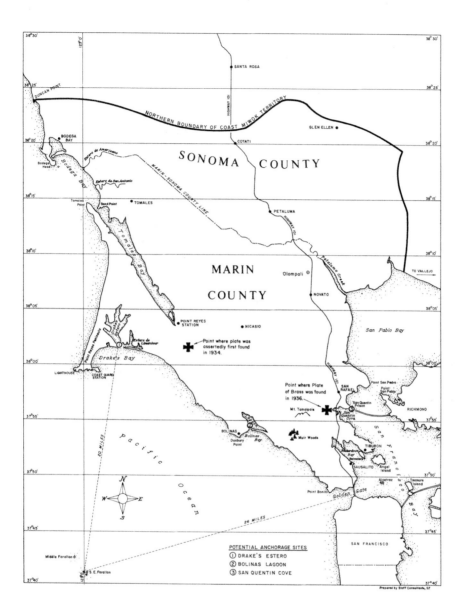

Map of the territory of the Coast Miwok tribe.

and an important estuary, not to mention a substantial portion of the world's greatest landlocked harbor. Several of these, although situated in some instances as far as twenty miles apart, are within five miles of the 38th parallel. Each of the latter forms a part of the shoreline of Marin County, and each falls within the boundaries of the "kingdome" which Drake assumed had been ceded to him by the natives.

Thus it is apparent that, for all practical purposes, Nova Albion was largely composed of what is today a single, small seacoast county draped across the 38th degree of latitude in northern California — the county of "Marvelous Marin."[10] In its peninsularity it is unusual, although not unique, among the counties of California. To this geographical circumstance, however, it owes the distinction of having the longest shoreline, in proportion to territorial expanse, among its sister counties. More than a hundred miles of it face the sea or bay. It is bounded on the east and southeast by the waters of San Pablo and San Francisco bays, on the south by the Golden Gate, and on the southwest and west by the Pacific Ocean.

The more important of the Marin-Sonoma shoreline indentations are the nine bodies of water previously referred to, five of them oceanward and four on the landlocked side of the peninsula. Set forth below, in the order in which Drake would have reached them, if sailing down the outer coast from a northerly direction, are brief descriptions of each.

The Oceanward Harbors

Bodega Bay, most northerly of the five oceanward harbors, extends partly into Sonoma County. The distance from its upper end to the Golden Gate is approximately forty miles as the seagull flies, or fifty miles as the schooner sails. From north to south, it measures about seven miles in length, with a width of less than two miles. It faces southwestward, the harbor opening lying between latitudes 38° 18' and 38° 14' N.

The bay derives its name from Juan Francisco de la Bodega y Quadra, by whom it was formally discovered on October 3, 1775, in the schooner *Sonora.*[11] Actually its waters had been visited much earlier by a small vessel of the Vizcaino expedition, the *Tres Reyes,* which passed unwittingly through its southerly end in the course of discovering nearby Tomales Bay in January, 1603.[12] Spanish efforts to establish a colony on Bodega Bay shores in 1793 were quickly abandoned,[13] but the Russians were more successful and occupied the bay from 1812 to 1841.[14] The first Yankee arrived in 1843,[15] soon after the area had reverted to Mexican control, and shortly thereafter was followed by other American settlers.

The entrance to the bay, between Tomales Point on the south and Bodega Head on the north, is approximately four and one-half miles in width. The only danger in the approaches is Bodega Rock, about one-third of a mile southeast of the Head.[16] At the lower end of the bay lies the entrance to Tomales Bay. At its upper (or Bodega) end, the distinguishing feature is a long sandspit which extends westward from the inner shore. North of this spit lies a shallow lagoon measuring between one and two miles in each direction, whereas south of it lies an anchorage with depths of twenty to fifty feet. It is reported that this anchorage, in the course of a storm, has accommodated as many as thirty or forty schooners and several steamers at one time.[17]

Use of the lagoon as an inner harbor began more than a century and a half ago, and in that capacity it has served successively the needs of Spaniards, Russians, Mexicans, and Americans. Situated on its eastern shore, and accessible now from the ocean only by means of a dredged channel, which penetrates the spit at its west end, stands the village of Bodega Bay. The lagoon was found by the Russians to be a convenient port during the summer, but a dangerous one at any other season.[18] Nevertheless, a large volume of coastal traffic moved through it before the coming of the railroad in the late seventies.[19]

Originally, the lagoon was of sufficient depth to serve the needs of this coastwise commerce without difficulty. However, the washing down of soil from the surrounding slopes, much accelerated by human settlement of the region, has combined with the blowing in of dune sand to reduce both the size and depth of this inner harbor.[20] Though still inhabited by a large fishing fleet capable of coping with the narrow channel and the shoal waters of the lagoon, the latter's days as a commercial port ended with the nineteenth century. In 1579, it would undoubtedly have been entirely serviceable for such a vessel as the *Golden Hind*.

Tomales Bay, lying just south of Bodega Bay and approachable only through the latter, is formed by an inlet of the Pacific Ocean which penetrates the coastal range to a depth of thirteen miles. Perfectly landlocked, this pencil-shaped bay averages about three-quarters of a mile in width, and runs in a generally north and south direction toward the center of the Point Reyes peninsula. Its entrance is situated forty-five miles north of San Francisco in latitude 38° 14' N.

When discovered in January, 1603, by the Spanish frigate, *Tres Reyes*, Tomales Bay was thought to be a large river and, accordingly, was named the Rio Grande de San Sebastian.[21] Juan Francisco de la Bodega saw it in 1775, at the time of his visit to the bay which bears his name. Believing it to be the Port of San Francisco, he anchored outside the entrance to await an opportunity to pass through, but presently realized his error.[22] In 1793, between September 4 and 11, Martinez y Zayas, commanding the *Mexicana,* a vessel of 45 tons, visited and carefully examined the bay.[23]

The entrance bar lies approximately one-third of a mile inside Tomales Point. Its depth in 1603 was reported to be forty-two feet.[24] By 1793, it was no more than fifteen feet;[25] by the final third of the nineteenth century it was reduced to ten or eleven feet,[26] and today it measures from seven to nine feet.[27] However, to any vessel able to cross the initial barrier, the bay itself is then navigable for a substantial part of its length. The entrance bar has always been dangerous, and there have been several casualties on this account, including the *Oxford* in 1858,[28] and the schooners *Anglo Saxon* and *Marin* at later dates.[29] Nevertheless, General Mariano Vallejo declared that it was in Tomales Bay that Drake had found his harbor of refuge.[30]

The area was settled by Americans about the time of the gold rush and, for the next quarter of a century, practically all of its traffic was waterborne. During the latter part of this era, regular steamer service was instituted between Tomales and San Francisco.[31] Preston's Point, on the east shore of Tomales Bay and some three miles south of the entrance, had a good wharf where schooners would call with frequency to unload merchandise and load products from nearby villages and farms.[32] The town of Tomales was linked with the bay by a three-mile-long estuary, and its embarcadero was a beehive of activity on shipping days during the 1860s.[33] The little paddlewheel steamer *Elk* was kept busy on the estuary, towing lighters piled high with grain, potatoes, and other produce to cargo ships anchored in the bay.[34]

An early end to this commerce was spelled by the coming of the narrow-gauge railroad[35] and the silting of the estuary and bay.[36] Tide waters receded year by year as winter rains washed tons of soil from the plowed hillsides. Frantic dredging of the estuary proved futile, and ships found it increasingly difficult to locate suitable anchorage in the bay itself.[37] Pasture grasses overgrew the estuary, and a county road — today a part of Highway Number 1 — was built along its former bank. Shipping dwindled and died, and the steamers and the schooners left the bay forever.

Tomales Bay is a product of the San Andreas Fault which was responsible for the San Francisco earthquake of 1906. Perhaps the greatest continental fault on the planet, the San Andreas has created a valley running from Bolinas Lagoon on the south to the long narrow finger of Tomales Bay on the north, into both of which waters of the ocean have found their way. This is the result of a massive lateral earth movement, known as the Great Rift, which has been in progress for eons. It has been responsible for displacements all along its course, the greatest of all having occurred in 1906 at the head of Tomales Bay where the area west of the rift was instantaneously jolted 20 feet to the north. As a result, roads, paths, fences, and rows of trees were crazily pulled out of line. It has been estimated that the Point Reyes Peninsula may have migrated northward as much as 65 feet since Drake's visit to northern California in 1579.

Drake's Bay, lying approximately midway between Bodega Bay and San Francisco, has borne its present name for more than a century. Before that it had been variously known. It is the same harbor which Sebastian Cermeño called Puerto (or Bahia) de San Francisco when he visited it in 1595.[38] It is the Puerto de los Reyes, or Puerto de Don Gaspar, of Sebastian Vizcaino who anchored there overnight eight years later.[39] It is the bay referred to by the early Spaniards as the "old San Francisco" after discovery of the present, or "new," San Francisco Bay.[40] It is the Jack's Harbor known to American sailing men in the days of the gold rush.[41]

Sitting precisely astride the 38th parallel, Drake's Bay comprises the water within the great arc formed by the southern shoreline of the Point Reyes Peninsula. It is walled off on the west by the towering headland of Point Reyes itself, a bold and distinctive promontory extending many miles to the west of the normal coastal contour. The lighthouse established at its southern tip in 1870[42] has made this land-mark even more familiar to mariners than in days of the Spanish Main. The bay, measured from east to west along the 38th parallel, is about nine miles wide; from north to south the distance is not more than three miles. White cliffs, beginning at its southwestern corner, con-tinue around to the east for several miles.[43]

The area adjacent to the bay has become a part of the Point Reyes National Seashore, having always been sparsely settled and devoid of cities, towns, or even villages. Along the shores are no piers, docks, wharves, or other structures, except at the Coast Guard Station sit-uated on the northern shore of the Point. Seldom do any but fishing craft frequent the bay today, nor has it ever been the scene of other important commercial activity.

The bay has been termed an "open roadstead"[44] and, generally speaking, this is true. It is certainly no landlocked body of water, yet it does have one area which is well protected against rough water and prevailing winds. This area is situated within the right angle formed by a rugged easterly projection from the tip of Point Reyes Head. It was within this angle that Vizcaino sought overnight shelter in 1603.[45] Bolanos, who visited the bay in both 1595 and 1603, referred to this "corner" as "a very good shelter and port."[46] Davidson described it as "a capital harbor," affording "a fairly large and admirable anchorage in the strong northwest winds of summer" and a "good but contracted anchorage" in the southeast storms of winter.[47] He further charac-terized it as easily entered and "so sheltered by the high lands which surround it on three sides, that many vessels may anchor there at one time in safety"; and recalled seeing sixteen vessels accepting its protec-tion "at one time under stress of weather" in 1872.[48]

Drake's Estero is really an arm of Drake's Bay, lying to the rear (north) of the latter. Like Tomales Bay and the inner harbor at Bodega, it is a landlocked tidal estuary, reached only by an entrance from the outer bay. Wings of it extend north of Point Reyes Head to within one mile of the ocean, and to within four miles of the nearest part of Tomales Bay.

There are actually several esteros lying immediately north of Drake's Bay, all reached from the latter by a common entrance. Origi-nally, all were called Estero de Limantour after the commander of the

Mexican vessel *Ayacheco,* which was lost at their entrance in 1841.[49] The U.S. Coast Survey gave the name of Drake's Estero to the westerly estuary in 1860,[50] leaving the original name to the others in the group. As early as 1603, Francisco de Bolanos wrote in reference to the three white cliffs on the northeast side of the outer bay: "In front of the one in the center there enters from the sea an estero with a good entrance without surf. Anyone who enters this will soon find friendly Indians and can easily find sweet water."[51]

The area surrounding these estuaries is grazing land, occupied only by a few dairy operators, their helpers, and their herds. It was the location in by-gone days, however, of many Indian villages, as evidenced by numerous shellmounds. Some of the latter have been excavated in the search for archaeological evidence of the visits of Drake and other early Europeans to this region.[52]

George Davidson said that the entrance to these esteros was narrow and usually marked by breakers on either hand.[53] He reported in 1889 that depth of the entrance bar varied from eight to thirteen feet, depending on the stage of the tide, and that small coasters could enter with the prevailing northwest wind.[54] As late as 1890, schooners were said to have visited the Estero on regular weekly schedules to pick up cargoes.[55]

Bolinas Bay, ten miles to the northwest of the Golden Gate, lies in a westward bend of the rugged Marin coastline. It is hemmed in on the seaward side by the treacherous Duxbury Reef, from which its shoreline extends east and finally south in a broad crescent to Rocky Point. Its east-west width is about four miles, and its north-south measurement hardly more than a mile. Davidson described it as a small summer anchorage with three to nine fathoms of water.[56]

Extending along its rear is a sandspit of substantial length and breadth, and behind the spit lies a shallow lagoon which stretches northward for nearly two miles. Much of the area adjacent to both lagoon and bay has become a part of the Golden Gate National Recreation Area. The only entrance from the sea to the lagoon is through a narrow channel which cuts off the town of Bolinas from the western end of the spit. Once the depth of water in this channel was ten feet at low tide, and small schooners passed through without difficulty at any time.[57] With the introduction of agriculture into the surrounding country, silting of the lagoon proceeded at an accelerated pace[58] until, by 1875 or earlier, even small vessels had to wait for high water before making an entrance or exit.[59]

In the days before the gold rush, magnificent stands of timber clothed the hills near Bolinas Bay. A forest of redwoods extended from about the middle of the eastern shore of the lagoon northward for several miles toward Olema. Other varieties of trees included Douglas fir, pine, oak and alder. Timbering operations began in 1849, and not long thereafter a large lighter wharf was built near the northeastern end of the lagoon. Here the lumber and cordwood were loaded onto lighters to be floated out to deeper water near the channel, there to be transferred to seagoing vessels for shipment to San Francisco. In the next thirty years, some fifteen million board feet of lumber and half a million cords of wood were thus moved.[60]

The Inner Bays

The "kingdome" of Nova Albion includes an additional series of bays, coves, and estuaries on the eastern side of Marin County. Some of these are small, such as Horseshoe Bay, just inside the Golden Gate, Hospital Cove on Angel Island, and Belvedere Cove, near the tip of the Tiburon peninsula. There are, however, in the shoreline facing San Pablo and San Francisco bays, four indentations of major importance.

Richardson's Bay is the first of these within the Golden Gate. Lying northwest of Sausalito and the southern end of Belvedere, it is about four miles long and its greatest width two miles. In 1889 Davidson reported only one fathom at low water a half-mile inside this bay,[61] and most of it, in fact, is exceedingly shallow. Its upper reaches are crossed by a large concrete bridge structure over which flows the eight-lane traffic of Highway 101.

The first white men to visit the waters of Richardson's Bay were members of the crew of the *San Carlos* which, under command of Don Juan Manuel de Ayala, had been the first Spanish vessel to find its way through the Golden Gate.[62] It was on the morning of August 6, 1775, that Ayala sent a launch in charge of a pilot to determine the possibilities of what is now Richardson's Bay as an anchorage. It was found to have sufficient depth of water, but a bottom of sticky mud, and the *San Carlos* therefore did not enter. The bay was then given the name of Ensenada del Carmelita (Bay of the Carmelite), a rock therein seeming to resemble a friar of the Carmelite order.[63] Near the bay entrance, on its west side, is a cove, which old Spanish charts called Ensenada del Consolación, and which Beechey in 1826 named Sausalito (Little Willow).[64] Here, in four to ten fathoms of water, was the one-time anchorage of foreign and American men of war; and here, also, was the rendezvous of the yacht fleet of San Francisco and of a part of the wheat fleet.[65]

San Quentin Bay lies between California Point on the Tiburon peninsula and Point San Quentin. Nameless on the charts of the United States Coast and Geodetic Survey, this inlet carries the run-off of Corte Madera Creek. It is only four miles south of the 38th parallel, and extends to within a few hundred yards of the hill where the Shinn plate (see Chapter 22) was found in 1936. The state penitentiary has occupied much of Point San Quentin for more than a century, and its grounds look across the bay toward the hills of Tiburon.

The channel of Corte Madera Creek wends its shallow way through the tidelands, keeping rather close to the San Quentin shore. The degree to which this small bay was navigable in the sixteenth century cannot now be determined with certainty. In view of the changes which nearly four hundred years can bring, and the amount of soil discharged for more than a century and a quarter by streams serving northern California's agricultural and mining areas, it is safe to say that much of San Quentin Cove has acquired bottom silts that make it much shallower than it was in 1579. By the same token, time and urban developments have brought material changes to its shoreline.

San Rafael Bay, next major indentation on Marin's eastern shoreline, lies within Point San Quentin on the south and Point San Pedro on the north. Into its three square miles debouch the waters of San Rafael Creek. A driver has an excellent view of this bay while en route from Richmond to San Rafael, both from the bay bridge and from the highway skirting the bay shore. This entire bay is characterized by great shallowness. A dredged channel, eight feet deep and one hundred feet wide, runs from the mouth of the creek out to deep water. As to the navigability status in days before the gold rush, the comments pertaining to San Quentin Bay are here equally applicable.

San Pablo Bay, or the westerly portion thereof, completes the Marin shoreline at its northeastern extremity. When San Francisco Bay was first visited by the *San Carlos* in August, 1775, Captain Ayala ordered a tour of exploration to be made.[66] It was in the course of carrying out this assignment that Don Juan de Canizares, first pilot, visited San Pablo Bay and named it Bahia Redondo (Round Bay).[67] It lies between San Pablo Strait and Carquinez Strait, and straddles the 38th parallel, twenty miles east of Drake's Bay. Several streams discharge their waters into its western shoreline, including Petaluma River, which forms the boundary between Marin and Sonoma counties, and the Napa River somewhat farther north. Near Carquinez Strait is Mare Island, for more than a century used by the United States as a naval repair base.

The Contenders

These are the principal bays of Nova Albion, but not all of them are candidates for having provided a berth for Drake's treasure ship. Yet claims have been advanced at one time or another on behalf of all except two of the nine bays or coves named, these two being Richardson's Bay and San Rafael Bay.

Bodega Bay, Tomales Bay, Davidson's site at Point Reyes, and the Petaluma River near San Pablo Bay, do not seem to be enjoying an active sponsorship at the present time. Thus, the controversy has narrowed to three real contenders: San Quentin Cove, Drake's Estero, and Bolinas Bay. Their contentions will be reviewed in Part III of this book.

5

CHAPTER

*The Elizabethan
Visitors*

DRAMATIC American history was created when Captain
General Francis Drake brought his expedition to northern
California and spent a good part of the summer of 1579 in
that mysterious region then usually designated on the maps as *Quivira,* and which Drake chose to call Albion or Nova Albion. It was an
English tour de force, brought off by English-speaking people acting
with apparent approval of the English queen.

No story of the historic visit of the *Golden Hind* to California
would be complete without a few words about the participants — the
colorful and extraordinary crew as well as the great freebooter himself.
A passing familiarity with the *dramatis personae* makes it possible more
readily to visualize the participants in this drama as they played their
roles on what was sometimes referred to as the "backside of America."

Who were these men who invaded the waters which theretofore
had been considered a Spanish lake — the American part of the Pacific?
Did the visitors to Nova Albion comprise all the same people who had
embarked in December, 1577, on what they believed was to be a short

trip to Alexandria, but which turned out to be a global circumnavigation? Were they, perhaps, the same fortunate few who survived the rigors and perils of a grueling voyage across the Pacific to return to England in 1580?

There are no fully satisfactory answers to such questions. As with everything else connected with Drake's great adventure, there is some available information, but never quite enough. After all, the voyage took place four hundred years ago, and under circumstances that could only be conducive to secrecy, rather than to publicity.

The Central Figure of the Circumnavigation

Francis Drake, of course, was the moving spirit of the great voyage. Without doubt, his were the ideas, opinions, and decisions that governed every phase of the project. The thought of such a venture beyond the Americas had been ever dominant in his mind since the day in 1573 when, upon climbing a tall tree on the Isthmus of Panama, he first beheld the Pacific Ocean and vowed that some day he would sail those waters.

Drake's rise to fame had been meteoric. Before reaching the age of forty, and despite the lack of a formal education, he had become wealthy, world-renowned, a friend of the queen of England, and an enemy thoroughly despised by the king of Spain. Though he probably never knew the exact date, Drake was born in 1542 or 1543[1] on a farm near Plymouth in Devonshire, England, the oldest of twelve children. His father's name was Edmund, and his Protestant beliefs made it neccessary, when the Prayer Book Rebellion broke out in 1549, to flee with his brood to a more tolerant location on the Medway (near Chatham Dockyard), England's main naval base. There the family lived in the hulk of an abandoned navy vessel, and the children grew up beside the sea.

In his early teens Francis became apprenticed to the old captain of a small sailing vessel. During the next few years he proved to be an apt student of navigation; in fact, he became so proficient that when the skipper died, he left the ship to his youthful apprentice. Francis kept it a while, then sold it and went into the service of his kinsman, John Hawkins, a wealthy shipowner of Plymouth.

Life on the Spanish Main

It was with Hawkins that Drake's life of adventure began. He soon rose to the command of one of his kinsman's vessels, which engaged in carrying slaves from Africa to the Caribbean. In 1568, several of Hawkins' ships were caught in a hurricane and forced to put in at San Juan de Uloa, a harbor near Vera Cruz, Mexico, where the Spanish governor promised that Hawkins' men might repair their vessels in safety. Three days later, however, they were attacked in force, and only the ships personally commanded by Hawkins and Drake made their escape. As a result of this duplicity and ensuing disaster, Drake acquired a life-long hatred for the king of Spain and a determination to seek revenge.

Soon the young Drake began organizing expeditions of his own, one of which, in 1572, culminated in a raid on the port of Nombre de Dios on the north coast of Panama. Although he succeeded in capturing the town in a brilliant amphibious operation, he was unable, because of a tropical storm and a serious leg wound, to carry away the tons of silver ingots he had found there. This failure, however, only whetted his desire for further action on what was then called the Spanish Main.

In the following year Drake returned to Panama and succeeded in ambushing a treasure-laden mule train on its way across the isthmus near Nombre de Dios. This time he was able to get his booty back to England, and it made him a wealthy man. Looking for further worlds to conquer, he now began to lay plans for the project that was to take him around the globe. The venture, as Drake conceived it, was ambitious, requiring the use of several ships and the careful selection of men and equipment.

Ships for the Circumnavigation

Quite a bit of information is available concerning the vessels with which Drake undertook his hazardous enterprise. It was a respectable naval force for the times, and consisted of the following:

The *Pelican,* 100 tons, eighteen guns. Captain-general: Francis Drake. Master: Thomas Cuttill.

Sir Francis Drake. An enlargement of the portrait which appeared as the frontispiece of The World Encompassed, *1628, by Sir Francis Drake, a nephew of northern California's first European visitor.*

The *Elizabeth*, 80 tons, sixteen guns. Captain: John Winter. Master: William Markham.

The *Marigold*, a bark, 30 tons, sixteen guns. Captain: John Thomas (later Edward Bright). Master: Nicholas Anthony.

The *Swan*, a fly-boat or store ship, 50 tons, five small guns. Captain: John Chester. Master: John Sorocold.

The *Christopher*, a pinnace of 15 tons, one gun, under the charge of

Thomas Moone, who had accompanied Drake on his expedition to the Spanish Main in 1572.

Of this imposing array of sea power, with its more than fifty guns, only the *Pelican* was to find its way to California, although not under that name. About the time Drake was ready to enter the Straits of Magellan and shortly after his execution of Thomas Doughty, he changed the name of *Pelican* to *Golden Hind* to honor one of his sponsors, Christopher Hatton, whose crest was a "hind trippant or," or golden hind. Presumably his motives in so doing were to allay any resentment on the part of Hatton at the execution of the latter's former private secretary, and to secure Hatton's support at court by emphasizing his patronage of the voyage. Though rather an obvious ploy, it was a shrewd one and proved to be successful.

The Vessels that Reached Nova Albion

History has not provided us with the dimensions of the *Golden Hind,* nee *Pelican*. However, estimates have placed its length at around 78 feet, its breadth at 22 feet, and its loaded draft at 13 feet. The ship was of the French pattern, according to Nuño da Silva, Drake's captive Portuguese pilot.[2] He described it as being well fitted out and finished with very good masts, tackle, and double sails. Though not new, it was stout, strong, and especially equipped with an ingenious underwater double sheathing designed to protect the hull against the ravages of the marine borer. With its 18 guns, ranging in probable weight from 1,000 to 2,000 pounds each, the vessel was really a private warship.

Although the *Golden Hind* was the only one of Drake's original fleet to reach Nova Albion, he brought with him to that port the vessel he had captured from Rodrigo Tello near the island of Caño off the coast of Costa Rica on March 20. This ship (name not given) was a bark of 15 tons, and its estimated measurements, based upon its weight, were 38 to 40 feet long, 10 feet wide, with a deep draft of about 5 feet.

This captive vessel was of the handy type called a *fregata* (frigate). It could carry fourteen persons, including several passengers, and was actually carrying six passengers when captured. To Drake, it was useful in a number of ways, not the least of which was to provide a convenient floating anchor point in connection with the careening of the *Golden Hind.*

Manning the Ships

It was an unusual company that Drake had assembled for his great venture into the Pacific. Since the fleet was virtually a floating arsenal, master gunners and an armourer were needed. The length of the voyage and type of territory to be covered made it necessary to carry coopers, caulkers, carpenters, mechanics, and a blacksmith (the *Golden Hind* carried a forge) for repairing and cleaning vessels in distant areas where shipyard facilities were not available. Cleaning and caulking were necessary every few months, and the *Golden Hind* was cleaned and graved at least six times in the course of the long voyage.

The number of "gentlemen and sailers" on the five original vessels was placed at 164 by most of the contemporary accounts. Besides Englishmen, they included a few Frenchmen, Flemings, Danes, Scotchmen, and Biscayans. In addition to being able seamen, many of them undoubtedly possessed second skills which would make them useful in connection with ship maintenance and repair. However, the company also included a doctor (possibly two), an apothecary, a shoemaker, and a tailor.

The inclusion of such specialized personnel is understandable in the light of Drake's wide experience in seafaring matters. But who, other than Sir Francis, would have graced his ship for such a lengthy voyage with a man of the cloth, or with a group of musicians for his listening pleasure (four of them on the *Golden Hind*)? There were even a number of young boys on board, at least three, according to observations made by one of Drake's prisoners. One of these lads, said to have been brought along as a page, was ordered to "dance in the English fashion" at a shipboard prayer service conducted by Drake and attended by Spanish prisoners.[3]

Other Nonmariner Personnel

Among those on board were several young gentlemen,[4] the number of whom is believed to have been twelve. Their motives in undertaking the voyage were various. Some had a financial interest in the venture; others may have desired to learn navigation or, perhaps, simply went along for pleasure or adventure. Like most of the gentlemen of the time, they were probably skilled in the use of the harquebus (a small-caliber long gun), thus adding to the fighting strength of the expedition.

The most prominent members of this group were Thomas Doughty and his half-brother, John. Thomas, originally a close friend of Drake as well as a promoter of, and investor in, the venture, was captain of the land soldiers. When found guilty of fomenting mutiny during the early part of the voyage, he was ordered by Drake to be executed. After the return to England, John Doughty undertook to prosecute Drake for the murder of his brother, but without success. Another member, said to have been a friend of the Doughtys, was Leonard Vicary whom Drake called a "crafty lawyer."

No complete list of these gentlemen has been preserved, but they included Lawrence Eliot, who was an amateur naturalist, and George Fortescue, who wrote an account of the voyage which has been lost. Others in this category were Gregory Cary, Gregory Raymond, Emanuell Wattkyns, Thomas Hord (or Hood), John Chester, and two men named Charles and Caube.

The personnel also included Drake's youngest brother, Thomas, and their youthful cousin John. Thomas survived Sir Francis and inherited most of his property. John subsequently served as commander of one of the vessels of an expedition under the leadership of Edward Fenton, an adventurer who sought to emulate Drake's success and left England for the Pacific in 1582. The expedition personnel also included a chaplain named Richard Madox and a number of men who had served on the *Golden Hind* in the 1577-1580 voyage. John's vessel, the *Francis*, was wrecked in the vicinity of Buenos Aires, and he was captured by the Spaniards and forced to give depositions in reference to both the Fenton and Drake voyages.

A prominent member of the entourage was Francis Fletcher, the parson who served as chaplain on the *Golden Hind*. His duties included the keeping of a record of the voyage, and he prepared an account of it after his return.[5] He achieved notoriety by incurring Drake's wrath during the latter part of the voyage.[6] Referred to in the accounts as doctors or surgeons, both Thomas Flood and Robert Winterhey met violent deaths at the hands of hostile South American Indians in the early part of the voyage.

Two men, undoubtedly merchants, were John Sorocold and John Audley,[7] a possible third being Edward Worrall. These men, acting in the capacity of supercargoes, probably had under their charge the goods to be used for trading purposes, and represented those of the adventurers who had supplied them. Both Audley and Sorocold returned to England in the *Elizabeth* with Captain John Winter, having been transferred to that vessel when their own ships were broken up at Port St. Julian in the summer of 1578.

Drake himself was an accomplished navigator, but much of the 1577–1580 voyage was to be through strange waters. No reference is made to the fact in any of the contemporary accounts, but it is probable that he had with him when he left England one or more pilots, either Portuguese, Spanish, or Italian.[8] One of these appears to have been N. de Morena who told authorities that he had succeeded in making his way overland to Mexico after having been left by Drake at Nova Albion some four years earlier.[9]

Blacks in Nova Albion

Among those who did not fall into any of the foregoing categories, but who did accompany Drake to California, were two male blacks and one female black, in addition to Diego, his black personal retainer. The latter had been with Drake since 1572 when the first raid on Panama was made. He spoke Spanish well, and upon occasion served as an interpreter.[10]

Drake was known to have a special affection for blacks, especially the Cimarrones, or Cimarons, with whom he had formed a friendly alliance during his months in Panama. One of his crew said that the Cimarrones "were the brothers of Captain Francis who loved them very dearly."[11] One of those brought with him to California had been taken near Paita off the South American coast (north of Lima) from a Spanish ship on February 20, 1579, and was said to have been a Cimarrone in Panama.[12]

The other male black was taken at Guatulco. When Drake's men invaded that port on April 13, 1579, they found the authorities engrossed in the trial of three blacks on a charge of conspiring to burn the town.[13] Since only one of them was taken to Nova Albion, it may be conjectured that he, too, was a Cimarrone.

The black woman was "a proper negro wench" (meaning a good-looking young black woman) named Maria,[14] who had been taken, as mentioned, from the *Espirito Santo*, when that ship was captured off the coast of Central America in April 1579.[15] Neither of the principal accounts of the voyage mentioned her capture by Drake, nor the fact of her presence on the *Golden Hind* or throughout the stay at Nova Albion.[16] One can only speculate as to the reason or reasons for adding her to his passenger list, particularly in view of the extremely cramped quarters on board the vessel and the problems of carrying adequate supplies of food and water for long periods at sea. Possibly, since she had been Don Francisco's personal plaything, Captain Francis may have felt that she could well provide similar comforts for himself or his men.

What Became of Maria?

Both accounts[17] in question do tell how, when the Indians came to Drake's encampment for his "coronation" on June 26, they went among their visitors, "taking a diligent viewe of every person," and of their frenzied excitement at being able to mingle with these extraordinary white strangers. The accounts do not say so but they must have been even more astonished and bewildered to find four faces that were black, rather than white, among them the one and only female of either color—a double minority, as it were.

There is one account of the voyage, however, that sheds some light on Maria's activities after joining the tour. As it described the situation, she had been "gotten with childe betwen the captaine and his men pirates" and by the time they reached Celebes in mid-November, 1579, she had become "very great."[18] It was here on December 13, on a small uninhabited island where the *Golden Hind* had stopped for wood, water, and repairs, that Drake left Maria and the two more recently captured male blacks, together with a supply of rice, seeds, and the means of making fire.[19]

In view of her pregnancy and the problem of adequate provisioning for the remaining nine months at sea, Drake evidently did not wish to carry food and water for three dispensable people, not to mention the impracticability of having an infant on board for several months. Moreover, due to her delicate condition, Maria's usefulness may have been largely impaired, if not terminated, by the time the *Golden Hind* had reached that part of the Pacific.

The chronology of Maria's pregnancy points to the probability that conception occurred during the stay at Nova Albion, nearly six months before the date of her abandonment on what Drake's men called "Crab Island" after the immense, very edible, king crabs which inhabited it. Drake himself named it the "Ile Francisca," after one of the blacks.[20] His action in leaving the three blacks on the island was both criticized and excused by his biographers. One[21] charged him with inhumanity for his seemingly heartless action, and another[22] defended him saying that "it must be remembered that he rescued these people from slavery and one of them from death, and was leaving them to a life which to them was perfect bliss." Given a choice, they may well have preferred such a fate to that of being left in the less comfortable northern California climate.

Be that as it may, the four blacks (counting the retainer Diego) comprised a substantial segment of the seventy to eighty-five people who spent much of June and July at Nova Albion. Maria was unquestionably the first of her race and sex ever to visit northern California; and although Drake was reportedly childless, no one can be certain that some of his descendants do not still populate a faraway island in the South Pacific.

Were Some of Drake's Men Left at Nova Albion?

There is evidence from Indian as well as contemporary European sources to indicate that a substantial number of Drake's crew never left California. When Munro-Fraser published his *History of Marin County* in 1880, he offered several reasons for believing that Francis Drake had landed in the bay that bears his name. Among them was "an old Indian legend[23] to the effect that Drake did land at this place, where some of his men deserted him, made their way into the country," and became "amalgamated with the aboriginals."[24] This "tradition among the people with whom he met while here"[25] is important because it provides a confirmation[26] from Indian sources of a story implicit in early European accounts of a substantial discrepancy between the number of men who came to Nova Albion with Drake in June, 1579, and the number who departed with him for the East Indies a few weeks later.

In the century following publication of the legend, it has been the subject of comment by several writers on Drake in California. George Davidson[27] was the first to mention it as evidence supporting his theory of a Drake's Bay anchorage. Other scholars, however, rejected it as beyond the bounds of probability. Among those regarding it as having little evidentiary value were John W. Robertson,[28] Henry R. Wagner,[29] and Robert F. Heizer.[30]

On the other hand, Wagner, despite his comment that such a story cannot represent "evidence of any value,"[31] mentioned the "likelihood" that some of Drake's men had deserted him at Nova Albion and stated "it seems certain that at least ten men had disappeared after the ship left Guatulco"[32] in Mexico and before reaching its next stop after leaving California. Raymond Aker, in his 1971 work dealing with Drake in California, wrote of the "extremely curious discrepancy in the number of persons comprising Drake's company when he was last seen on the coast of Mexico and when the company was again recorded in the East Indies."[33] He proceeded to discuss the question of "what happened to these 20 or so people."[34]

The Mystery of the Missing Men

The manpower discrepancy referred to is a subject that excites curiosity concerning its every aspect: the basis for believing that men were, in fact, left behind; the numbers of those that were left; the reasons for their leaving the expedition, or being left; and the evidence, beyond the legend itself, to support its interesting explanation of their ultimate fate.

The Spanish authorities took depositions from all of their citizens who had any contact with the dreaded Englishman in the course of his voyage along the west coast of the Americas. They did likewise with Drake's cousin John, following the latter's capture in Argentina in 1582; and also with Nuño da Silva, Drake's captive Portuguese pilot. One of the usual questions to those being thus queried concerned the number of men Drake had with him. The answers ranged from 71 or 72, representing an actual count made surreptitiously by a captive named Nicolas Jorje,[35] to 86 or 87 — estimates that may have included three boys among Drake's personnel and two captive blacks.[36]

Despite the fact that most of the erstwhile prisoners placed the number of Drake's men before leaving Guatulco at 80 or more, circumstances suggest that such estimates were high.[37] Jorje's figures were the most conservative as well as the only ones resulting from an actual count; therefore they have been taken as a basis for comparison with the numbers reported after leaving Nova Albion. Of the latter there were two reports, the first contained in a deposition by John Drake,[38] and giving the number as 60;[39] the second was from *The World Encompassed* and placed the number at 58. Comparing the latter figure with the earlier count of 71 or 72, there is still a discrepancy of 13 or 14 to be accounted for—exclusive of the black captives who were put ashore on an island in the East Indies.[40]

This startling information raises two pertinent questions: (1) What became of these people—a dozen or more—who came to California with Drake in June, 1579, but apparently did not leave with him when the *Golden Hind* departed for the Moluccas in July?[41] (2) Why did the various contemporary accounts neither explain nor mention this substantial discrepancy?

Reasons for the Discrepancy

The second of these two queries is one of the many which the contemporary accounts leave unanswered. One can only speculate that: (1) If those who failed to depart from Nova Albion on the *Golden Hind* were deserters, Drake would not have wanted that fact to be admitted or become known; (2) if left by some agreement, their position in Spanish America might have made them vulnerable to enemy attack if information as to their whereabouts were permitted to be published or to leak out.

The first question is a broader one, offering a greater latitude of imagination in suggesting a variety of answers. It seems rather clear that somewhere between one and two dozen people who came to Nova Albion did not leave with Drake for one reason or another. These reasons may have been among the following:

1. Desertion of malcontents among the crew. The possibility of dissension or mutiny was an ever-present hazard on these early voyages.[42] Magellan had to deal with the problem in the first circumnavigation. Drake had his difficulties, first with Doughty and later, by implication at least, with John Winter, captain of the *Elizabeth*. Even Cermeño had a threatened revolt on his hands from the time he first sighted the Pacific Coast in November, 1595.[43]

2. Voluntarily remaining behind for a variety of reasons, such as (a) lack of space on the *Golden Hind* (they needed two ships for the last leg of the journey to California); (b) unwillingness to risk the perils of the long Pacific voyage in such a frail and heavily laden ship; (c) having been bribed by Drake to remain for a time by leaving them the frigate with a substantial part of the silver or other valuable cargo; and even (d) seemingly hopeless illness.

The "Stay-Behinds"

It may be difficult, four hundred years later, to imagine any Drake crewman remaining of his own free will on that bleak and lonely coast or bay, no matter how friendly and worshipful the Indians may have seemed. On the other hand, it is not difficult to visualize the terror there may have been in some minds at the prospect of faring forth into the wilds of the unknown Pacific in such a frail and overcrowded vessel as the *Golden Hind,* without any assurance that the leaky condi-

The crowning of Francis Drake by the California Indians, from the etching by Gottfried, 1655.

tion that had developed while en route from Guatulco would not recur at a time and longitude where nothing could save them. Consequently, one can only speculate about the men's motivation or about the promises made in consideration of their remaining in Nova Albion.

There is, however, fairly dependable evidence to indicate that one member of the Drake party, pilot N. de Morena, stayed behind at his own request, pleading desperate illness, with the result that he was shortly able to stage a miraculous recovery and to make his way to Mexico on foot.[44] Others may have undertaken a similar course of action without managing to survive or, if able to reach civilization, without having their return made a matter of record, or they may have tried to sail the second ship back to some friendly harbor, but without success.

After his original publication of the Indian legend by Munro-Fraser, its next mention occurred a decade later when George Davidson, in his first treatise dealing with Drake in California,[45] included a paraphrased version of part of it as follows:

> Among the Nicasio Indians of the Nicasio Valley, which lies fifteen miles to the eastward of Drake's Bay, there is said to have been a tradition to the effect that Drake anchored in the Bay, and landed on these shores; that some of his crew deserted and lived among the Indians; and that he gave the natives some seeds for planting; and among other things some hard ship-biscuit which they innocently planted in the hope of similar bread growing there from.[46]

Such an abbreviated version suited Davidson's purposes since it not only placed the *Golden Hind* in Drake's Bay, but also enabled Davidson to argue against a San Francisco Bay anchorage on the ground that from such a location Drake would have had no contact with the Nicasio Indians.[47] However, from the source of Davidson's information comes the following more complete story:

> The Indians also state that some of Drake's men deserted him here, and making their way into the country, became amalgamated with the aboriginals to such an extent that all traces of them were lost, except possibly a few names which are to be found among the Indians. "Winnemucca," for instance, is a purely Celtic word, and the name "Nicasio," "Novato" and others are counterparts, with slight variations, of names and places on the island of Cyprus.[48]

Father Crespi's Amazing Discovery

Although the legend as a whole was given little credence by Wagner and Heizer, among others, its story about some of Drake's men remaining behind fits in rather well with another, more reliable report from the Crespi Expedition, which explored the San Francisco Bay Area in March, 1772. Wagner had found in Mexico a map of the Bay Area drawn from the diary and field notes of Father Crespi, on which map[49] was a legend which, in part, according to John Robertson, read as follows: "Around this bay the natives were found to be red-headed, bearded and fair complectioned. They were very good and friendly and they made gifts of fruit and food to the Spaniards.[50]

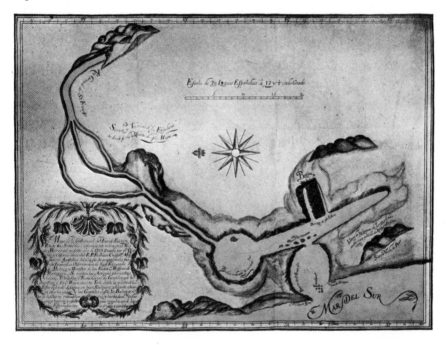

The Father Crespi 1772 map of the San Francisco Bay Region, with its legend telling of the "blond, fair complectioned and bearded" natives encountered.

Evaluating this information in his treatise on Drake, Robertson said:

The bearded, reddish-haired and fair-skinned (barbados, rubios y blancos) Indians that they found on this bay shore would be an excellent argument for those putting faith in Indian legends of the white Gods who visited them, had they been found in the bays near Point Reyes or in the port of Trinidad, even though 200 years and many Spanish sailors had intervened.[51]

Robertson appears to have been the only Drake scholar to print the Crespi map and information, as well as to add skeptical comment on its value in relation to the Nicasio legend. He discussed the legend in some depth, emphasizing what he felt were its inconsistencies concerning the subject of Drake's crew members. Unfortunately, Robertson made two mistakes in undertaking a discussion of this subject: (1) His translation of "rubios" as "red-haired" was erroneous; rather the word means "blond," and the phrase "rubios, blancos y barbados" means "blond, fair-skinned (or white) and bearded." (2) Instead of checking out what Munro-Fraser had said, Robertson merely repeated Davidson's inadequate synopsis of the legend,[52] and proceeded to base his own comments on these faulty premises.

Analysis of a Legend

Despite his mistranslation of the word "rubios," Robertson was aware of the fact that natives who were bearded and fair-skinned had been reliably reported as having been encountered around San Francisco Bay in 1772. Consequently, it would seem that he had been deserted by his usually logical mind when he undertook to rule out any possibility of a valid basis for the Nicasio legend. His reasoning on the subject was so palpably erroneous as to invite critical analysis; and his comments, along with the converse of the proposition in each case, are as follows:

1. The Indians, to whom he referred as "ignorant and unlettered troglodytes," could not have passed the name of Drake down through eight generations.[53]

Robertson overlooked the fact that the dozen or two English deserters (if such there were) were not necessarily "ignorant troglodytes," and that the legend would have been handed down by *them* and *their offspring* within the tribe. If there was one word they would have been sure to hand down from generation to generation, it would have been "Drake," and it would have become an important part of tribal lore. The reverse would have been true if, after Drake's departure, no adult Englishmen remained to perpetuate the name in future generations of the Coast Miwok tribe.

2. The Indians could not have differentiated between Drake's sailors and those of Cermeño, or other sailors who occasionally stopped at Bodega or Drake's Bay.[54]

No such differentiation would have been necessary. The hostility of the Indians encountered by Cermeño would have made amatory adventures unlikely and desertion unattractive. Even though Robertson may have overlooked these facts, he should have known that northern California was unvisited by Europeans during all the years between 1595 (Cermeño's departure) and 1750 when the fair-skinned adults seen in 1772 were probably born at the latest. His assumption that sailors stopped at Bodega or Drake's bays during that lengthy interval was erroneous.

3. There is no ethnological evidence of adventures with the "over-friendly and worshipping Indian women."[55]

On the contrary, such evidence was presented by Robertson himself in the form of the Crespi records. Moreover, the reference in those records to "the natives" encountered (rather than to "some of the natives" or to "an occasional native") suggests a substantial infusion of European blood into the tribe, such as might have been expected if a score of deserters had "become amalgamated with the aboriginals," rather than the result of a few amatory adventures that might have occurred during the relatively brief sojourns of either Drake or Cermeño.

4. If there had been any desertion from the English crew, Fletcher, "so verbose as to the minute incidents that happened between the sailors and the Indians, would have made some note of such an occurrence."[56]

On the contrary, Fletcher, verbose though he may have been about some things, was careful to avoid mention of anything that might tend to reflect unfavorably on the expedition. Such topics as Drake's black woman Maria, and amatory adventures of the crew, were taboo so far as the straitlaced parson was concerned. Drake himself would have regarded desertion as a defiance of his authority and have forbidden mention of the subject in any official account.

5. Mestizos, meaning persons of mixed European and American Indian ancestry, would have been met with, and association with white men would have been evident in many ways.[57]

Robertson seemingly shut his eyes to the fact that mestizos *were* encountered, these being the bearded, fair-skinned natives that, according to Crespi,[58] were kind to the Spaniards in 1772. Robertson was presumably unaware that other early visitors to northern California had reported contacts with blond Indians. The journal of Father Francisco Palou, under date of November 29, 1774, told of meeting (near what is now San Carlos) a group of "well formed Indians of tall stature, many of them fair and well bearded, as much so as any Spaniard."[59] Four days later, in the vicinity of the present San Bruno, the Palou party was visited by another group of twenty-four Indians "most of them bearded and some of them fair."[60]

Had he become familiar with all of these reports, as well as the *full* text of the legend itself, even Robertson might have conceded that the reports appear to provide rather convincing support for the legend in its reference to "amalgamation with the aboriginals."[61] The blond, bearded natives reported by Crespi and Palou were obviously mestizos. From the standpoint of physical appearance and numbers encountered, the evidence suggests a substantial infusion of European blood into the tribe several generations back. From a behavioral standpoint, the friendliness of the natives to their white visitors in the form of gifts of food and fruit and seeking out the Spaniards for purposes of visitation is also compatible with such a background.

Casualties and Survivors

Of the 164 people who left Plymouth with Drake in December, 1577—under the illusion that they were embarking on a voyage of relatively moderate duration and peril—scarcely more than 100 were ever to see England again.[62] The captain and crew of the *Marigold*, 29 in all, perished in a storm near the Straits of Magellan in September, 1578.[63] Seven others succumbed to enemy action, seven to hardships and privation, two to illness, and one to the executioner's ax. With another three who made it back to civilization on their own,[64] this accounts for a total of 49 who did not return to England with Drake or on the *Elizabeth* with Captain Winter.[65]

Assuming there were 71 or 72 on the *Golden Hind* in the spring of 1579 (reflecting a count made at that time),[66] these figures, added to the 49 enumerated above, would account for 120 or 121 of the original company of 164; and thus leave 43 or 44 as the number returning on the smaller *Elizabeth*. With all factors of the equation thus identified and evaluated, it only remains to combine the *Elizabeth's* contingent (43 or 44) with the numbers returning on the *Golden Hind* (58)[67] and those returning to civilization on their own or not at all (49), to realize from the resulting total of 150 or 151 that 13 or 14 of the original 164 are still unaccounted for. This confirms our earlier and simpler computation (71 or 72 minus 58),[68] based on the assumption that the figure of 58 reported by *The World Encompassed* may be taken as an accurate total.[69]

Why Leave Men at Nova Albion?

The consistency of the foregoing figures suggests the need for study of other pertinent evidence. It has not been generally realized that Drake had a problem of overcrowding on his tiny vessel—a problem that was to trouble him throughout much of his time in the Pacific. On five different occasions during that period he banished an individual or group from the *Golden Hind* to the relative insecurity of a smaller satellite vessel, or left them behind in an alien environment.[70] Not until he reached the Celebes area did he fully rid himself of the problem.[71]

The problem began in 1578 when two of Drake's five ships, having become unseaworthy, had to be broken up or abandoned and their crews redistributed among the other three ships. To the *Golden Hind,* as the largest of the three, the majority of this personnel was probably reassigned.[72] Although Drake himself was thus responsible for adding a substantial number of men to his already full crew, it is doubtful that he then appreciated the extent of the problem he had created for himself, or had any idea that within little more than a year he might be reducing the numbers of those on board by 20 persons or more.

The first indication that a problem existed, so far as the early accounts are concerned, was Drake's action, otherwise inexplicable, in ordering eight of his men into a small open boat "to waite upon the ship for all necessary uses."[73] Soon after this occurred in October, 1578, "foule weather suddenly arising" caused them to lose sight of the *Golden Hind,* and they were never reunited.[74] Despite this tragedy and the loss of other lives to enemy action along the Chilean coast, a substantial human overload continued, aggravated somewhat by the taking aboard of several captives and the acquisition of a heavy cargo of gold, silver, and other Spanish loot.

It was not, however, until Drake reached Central America that another opportunity to provide relief from the crowded conditions on the *Golden Hind* presented itself in the form of a captured Spanish ship of suitable size.[75] This was a small frigate engaged in coastwise trade and not designed for transocean use. Nevertheless, from the mere fact of his pressing such a ship into service for a 60-day voyage in the wake of the *Golden Hind,* it is obvious that Drake felt it necessary to reduce the number on board his vessel to a reasonable level forthwith — even if only on a temporary basis. So he manned the frigate with members of the *Hind*'s crew, and the two ships set off on the 4,000-mile voyage that was to bring them to California. Viewed realistically, Drake's action would have solved the overcrowding problem temporarily if the frigate miraculously survived the rigorous voyage, and permanently if it did not.

The Ultimate Solution?

The frigate, as we know, did reach California and went no further; but a variety of questions arise at this point. If the capacity of an additional ship was required for the shorter Mexico-to-California trip, how could the *Golden Hind* alone accommodate not only all the people in both vessels, but all the food, water, and supplies which the combined group would require for the long transpacific voyage? Was it mere coincidence that the frigate's carrying capacity (about 14) corresponded closely with the number of men unaccounted for after leaving Nova Albion? Could it have been that Drake, in manning the second vessel, preselected the members of his crew that could best be spared in the event it failed to survive or became separated? Or that such a selection would have served the same purpose if the frigate reached California, and a reduction of personnel then had to be made? If the frigate's crew, or others, were the ones who volunteered or were ordered to remain in California, were they influenced by promises from Drake of a special share of the treasure, and that he would later return to pick them up, together with possession of the small vessel for emergency use? Was Drake so ruthless that he would deliberately have abandoned a dozen or more of his crew to their fate halfway around the world — with or without promises?.

Authentic answers to such a series of questions are not available. However, there is evidence to suggest that Drake would not have hesitated to leave some of his crew at Nova Albion if he felt the success of the enterprise required it. In such a situation, he would have acted with no more compunction than he had shown in ordering eight men into an open boat on the ocean, knowing that they might be lost in the event of a storm (as indeed they were); with no more compassion than he had shown in putting his Portuguese pilot, Nuño da Silva, ashore in Mexico, knowing that it would probably mean his torture by the Spaniards,[76] or possible death; and with no more mercy than he was later to show in abandoning the three recently captured blacks, including pregnant Maria,[77] on a remote and waterless island in the East Indies.

So much for the legend of Nicasio, and the evidence tending to support it. The cited figures do not necessarily prove that there were a dozen or more Elizabethans who did not leave Nova Albion with Drake.[78] Nor do the reports of Crespi and Palou necessarily establish that England's first colony in the New World was actually on Pacific shores. The evidence, although persuasive, is only circumstantial. It can do no more than provide a plausible and fascinating basis for conjecture about how Drake may have solved a substantial part of his overcrowding problem, and what may have happened to those stay-behinds, if any, who did not find their way overland to Mexico, or sail away to a watery grave in the ship we know Drake abandoned at Nova Albion.

6

CHAPTER

The Anchorage Sleuths

T HE YEARS since 1579 have not brought a satisfying solution for the anchorage mystery, but they have seen the wilderness of Drake's day translated into the great community that is San Francisco and environs; and they have also seen the development of a wide interest among the citizenry in the Drake visit, as well as a controversy that is quite as fascinating as the mystery itself.

Succeeding generations of historians, amateur as well as professional, for more than 250 years have made strenuous efforts to provide solutions to the riddle. Theories supporting two or three entirely new anchorage sites have been put forward in the dozen or so years just past.[1]

For a zealous few, anchorage hunting has become a preoccupation of major proportions, requiring much time and money. Some of these interesting persons or groups, including such distinguished citizens as the late Admiral Chester Nimitz, have developed or espoused their own special theories, and press persuasive arguments in support of their solutions.

Over the years, claims have been advanced for several locations along the Pacific Coast, as well as a number of sites within San Francisco Bay. In respect to the former, the suggested harbors range from San Luis Obispo Bay on the south to Nehalem Bay in Oregon on the north, a distance of 750 miles.[2] But during the twentieth century the effective area of search has been narrowed to the Marin peninsula just north of the Golden Gate.

The Anchorage Controversy

For nearly 175 years following 1595, when Cermeño stopped briefly at Drake's Bay, no European set foot on northern California soil, and the anchorage mystery became dormant for the same period of time. However, as settlers came to the Golden Gate area, and more of them became aware of the early Drake visit, opinions about the probable location of his anchorage began to be voiced. As interest in the subject developed, so also did differences of opinion concerning the anchorage site. It was a subject that had to be covered by every author of a California history, and soon what had once been only a mystery became also an ongoing controversy.

Yet even the controversy itself is rather venerable, now going back the better part of two centuries. It may be said to date from 1792 when Captain George Vancouver visited San Francisco Bay in his ninety-foot sloop, the *Discovery*. In his *Voyage of Discovery*,[3] Vancouver stated that while "according to the Spaniards" the harbor now known as Drake's Bay was that in which Sir Francis anchored, he felt that it promised "little shelter or security," at least at the season (November) when Vancouver was there.

The source of Vancouver's information concerning Spanish beliefs was not disclosed. Bancroft, in his *History of California,* indicated that he was never able to find any evidence that this opinion had been the prevailing one.[4] However, in 1803 another English sea captain, James Burney, thought that Drake must have entered San Francisco Bay because the harbor behind Point Reyes would have offered inadequate protection against the weather.[5] When Alexander von Humboldt suggested in his 1811 *Political Essay On The Kingdom of New Spain* that Drake's landfall had been in Bodega Bay, Burney responded that

Humboldt didn't know what he was talking about. Since that time, few decades have passed without some fuel being added to the fire.

In any review of the scope of the controversy, California history may conveniently be divided into four eras: (1) Opinions from 1790 to 1849; (2) opinions from 1850 to 1888; (3) opinions from 1889 to 1936, when the Shinn plate was discovered; and (4) opinions since 1936.

The opinions expressed during the first two periods were largely bare conclusions without careful analysis. Those in the forty-seven years following 1889 included in-depth studies of the data, then available, by Davidson, Robertson, and Wagner. After discovery of the Shinn plate, the character of the controversy changed. Support for some of the site candidates was abandoned, a number of new suggestions for landfall sites appeared, and the competition between proponents has become intensified.

Opinions 1790–1849

This was roughly the period of Spanish occupation and an era of much uncertainty about the landfall site. In faraway London, a map of the Pacific by the cartographer Aaron Arrowsmith had placed it in San Francisco Bay.[6] Among writers who had visited northern California, opinions were rather evenly divided between San Francisco and Bodega bays. The former was the choice of Captain James Burney in 1803, as we have seen, and of Alexander Forbes in 1839. Bodega, as previously noted, was favored by Humboldt in 1811. Captain James Colnett with his ship, the *Argonaut*, visited a harbor in 1790 which he thought was Drake's Bay, and which was subsequently identified as Bodega Bay.[7] What the local Spaniards believed is, and apparently was, a matter of conjecture.[8]

The support for Drake's Bay during the Spanish era was rather negative. In addition to what Vancouver had to say, Captain Beechey, writing in 1832, opined that the harbor was too exposed to have been that in which "Sir Francis refitted his vessel." On the other hand, a French navigator, Eugene Duflot de Mofras, who visited California in 1842 reported that Drake had "discovered a port where he remained some time and which has since retained his name," namely Drake's Bay.[9]

Perhaps the earliest opinion by a historian was that of Padre Niel, writing about 1718. According to Bancroft, Niel in his *Apuntaciones,* at page 78, "declared his opinion that Drake's Bay was at the mouth of Carmelo River!"[10] This opinion had little significance, because Spanish knowledge of the California coast at that time was limited to information by Cabrillo, Cermeño, and Vizcaino, all before 1604.

Opinions 1850 – 1889

During this period of early California statehood, opinions were about equally divided betwen San Francisco and Drake's bays. Declaring in favor of the former were Franklin Tuthill in 1866, J. D. B. Stillman in 1866 and 1877, S. G. Drake in 1874,[11] Jules Verne (the French science-fiction novelist) in 1879, and Edward Everett Hale in 1884. Verne wrote that Drake "reached the 38° of north latitude, and landed on the shore of the Bay of San Francisco."[12] Stillman argued persuasively that Drake had entered San Francisco Bay on the grounds, largely, that Drake's Bay would not have provided sufficient protection for careening the *Golden Hind,* and that the strange kind of "conies" described by the Drake accounts did not live on the shores of Drake's Bay.

Drake's Bay nonetheless had its proponents, including Alexander S. Taylor in 1862, Edmund Randolph in 1867, Titus Fey Cronise in 1868,[13] and Theodore H. Hittell in 1885. Soule, Gihon and Nisbet, coauthors of a history of San Francisco published in 1850, opted for Drake's Bay, which they referred to as Jack's Harbor. They added, however, that "in popular estimation the bay which Drake entered is believed to be that of San Francisco."

Other historians were more uncertain. In his *Popular History of the United States,* published in 1876, William Cullen Bryant, the poet, reviewed earlier opinions and concluded that "the weight of Californian opinion at this time seems to be that Sir Francis Drake never entered the Golden Gate."[14] H. H. Bancroft devoted more than a dozen pages of the first volume of his *History of California* to a discussion of the claims of San Francisco, Drake's, and Bodega bays, finally concluding that San Francisco Bay could be ruled out. In 1884, he was willing to decide for Drake's Bay, but in 1886 found little to choose between Drake's and Bodega bays.

John W. Dwinelle, writing in 1878, made out a persuasive case for Bodega Bay, but General Vallejo, in an address delivered at the centennial celebration of the Mission Dolores, asserted positively that it was Tomales Bay.[15]

Opinions 1890–1936

The years 1889 and 1890 were memorable in the chronology of Drake in California. They were the years when the California Historical Society first provided a forum for the discussion of a controversy which even then had been smoldering for most of a century.[16] This the Society did by publishing in 1890 George Davidson's 58-page treatise (with maps) entitled *Identification of Sir Francis Drake's Anchorage on the Coast of California in the Year 1579,* which he had read before the Society on March 12, 1889. With the publication of this pamphlet and his pronouncement in favor of Drake's Bay, the tide of public opinion swung in that direction, and for many years thereafter it was almost an article of faith that Sir Francis had anchored in a cove behind the projecting shoulder of Point Reyes.

Davidson was acknowledged to have been one of the most eminent scientists of his day.[17] He was connected with the United States Coast Survey for several decades, and for a good part of that time was in charge of the Survey's work on the Pacific Coast. He probably knew more about the California coastline and sailing conditions than any man of his time. Consequently, his reputation was so substantial that his conclusions with respect to the Drake anchorage were accepted by most people as settling the question. He originally (1869) had believed that Drake entered San Francisco Bay, but subsequently changed his mind after a more thorough study of the evidence. He reinforced his 1889–1890 opinion with a second article in 1908 entitled *Francis Drake on the Northwest Coast of America in the year 1579,* published by the Geographical Society of the Pacific, of which he was then, at age 83, the president.

Supporting Davidson's conclusion during this period were James W. Dixon (1912–1914), C. Hart Merriam (1916), Alexander G. McAdie (1919), Charles E. Chapman (1921), and Alfred L. Kroeber, eminent ethnologist (1923). In 1908, Samuel A. Barrett, also an ethnologist, had published a detailed study of the ethnogeography of the Pomo and neighboring Indian tribes, supporting a conclusion that

George Davidson, nineteenth-century authority on Drake's California visit, and sponsor of the theory that his anchorage was on the north side of Point Reyes. (Circa 1900. From Charles B. Davenport's Bio-graphical Memoir of George Davidson, Washington, 1937.)

Drake's landing had taken place somewhere north of San Francisco Bay, possibly even north of Point Reyes.

Davidson Rejected

The years 1926 and 1927 produced two of the most scholarly and important books ever published on Drake in California. They were very different from each other, but neither was in accord with Davidson's Point Reyes opinion. John W. Robertson's *Francis Drake Along the Pacific Coast* included a comprehensive and critical review of earlier opinions about the bay Drake entered in 1579. In that part of it discussing "The Harbor of St. Francis," he pointed out the weaknesses in the arguments and opinions of nearly every commentator on the anchorage issue from Vancouver and Beechey to Chapman and Wagner, with particular emphasis on George Davidson's treatment of the subject. The author appeared to favor San Francisco Bay, although offering no convincing proof in support of such a belief.

Henry R. Wagner's comprehensive *Sir Francis Drake's Voyage Around the World* is the definitive text on that subject. Despite coverage of the entire circumnavigation, he still concentrated much attention on the question of the California anchorage. Wagner identified the native customs reported by *The World Encompassed* with those of the Yurok tribe of the Trinidad (California) area and the Coast Miwok at Bodega Bay. Since his opinion was reached before the identification by Robert F. Heizer of the Indians encountered by Drake as a Marin County tribe, it is no longer regarded as valid in respect to the Yurok.

The only other important documentation from this era was a report by an English historian, Miss E. G. R. Taylor who, in 1932, found in the British Museum an account by Richard Madox, a chaplain with the Fenton Expedition of 1582. It included two words and two phrases which members of the crew, who had also been with Drake, told him had been used by the Indians encountered near

Henry R. Wagner, author of Sir Francis Drake's Voyage Around the World *and outstanding authority on that subject. (Circa 1940. Courtesy California Historical Society.)*

Drake's Nova Albion encampment. These have been identified with the language of the Coast Miwok tribe, traditional occupants of the Marin County area.

Opinions after 1936

The publicity attending discovery of the Shinn plate in 1936 generated a great public interest in Drake's California visit, and brought about a proliferation of literature on the subject. Henry R. Wagner continued to insist that the site of the anchorage was at Trinidad Head,[18] a belief in which he was joined in 1953 by John W. Caughey, author of *California*. In a 1969 history, also entitled *California*, W. H. Hutchinson, speaking of Drake's landfall, said: "It appears safe, however, to accept it as the present Drake's Bay, north of San Francisco." Still another historian, Andrew F. Rolle, author of *California: A History*, published in 1969, elected to believe, as had H. H. Bancroft eighty-three years before, that the site was not in San Francisco Bay, but could have been in either Drake's or Bodega Bay. A similar uncertainty was shown by Lawrence Kinniard in *History of the Greater San Francisco Bay Region*, 1966, in which he had little to say about a possible San Francisco Bay anchorage and seemed to lean toward a Drake's Estero site.

Two other Drakophiles of recent vintage are Robert W. Pate of Carmichael and Richard Dobson of Rancho Cordova who, by 1967, had established to their own satisfaction that Drake's landing took place in a small inlet in San Luis Obispo Bay called Pirate's Cove.[19] Tom's Point, on the east shore of Tomales Bay, has been the choice of historian Robert Becker.[20] Donald Viles and Wayne Jensen are satisfied that Nehalem Bay on the north Oregon coast was the site of Drake's port of Nova Albion.[21]

The Ethnological Approach

Substantial contributions have been made to the search for Drake's landfall by Barrett and Kroeber, but the first to attack the anchorage problem in depth from a scientific standpoint was Robert F. Heizer of the University of California at Berkeley. His first published contribution was an article entitled "Francis Drake's California Anchorage in the Light of the Indian Language Spoken There" by himself and William W. Elmendorf, which appeared in 1942 in the *Pacific Historical Review*.

A more ambitious treatment of the subject was Heizer's treatise *Francis Drake and the California Indians, 1579,* published in 1947 by the University of California Press (*Publications in American Archaeology and Ethnology*).[22] His conclusion at that time was that "from a comparative analysis of the detailed descriptions of the native ceremonies, artifacts and language, I conclude that in the fullest authentic account, *The World Encompassed,* it is the Coast Miwok Indians that are referred to."

In 1974, Heizer published *Elizabethan California,*[23] dealing with the Drake anchorage controversy in a more general way as well as reviewing it from the ethnological standpoint. In this interesting treatise, he leaned toward San Francisco Bay, but concluded that "opinions have not and never will solve the question—only some kind of archaeological or documentary evidence to be discovered can solve the problem."

Opinion Favoring the Petaluma River

A novel and interesting theory has been propounded by Robert C. Thomas of San Francisco, a descendant of both Chief Marin and Chief Ynitia of the Coast Miwok tribe. In his as-yet-unpublished manuscript dealing with the California Indians, he presents a rather persuasive case for the proposition that Drake's anchorage was on the west bank of the Petaluma River near its outlet. He cites both cartographical and ethnological evidence, and relies upon the "Portus Novae Albionis" inset of the Hondius map, as discussed on p. 123 and in Chapter 24.

Proponents of Bolinas Bay

The most prominent supporter of Bolinas Lagoon as the Drake anchorage site is V. Aubrey Neasham, with encouragement and assistance from Thomas J. Barfield, San Francisco attorney and Bolinas historian. Neasham, professor emeritus of environmental resources at Sacramento State University, has been a professional historian since 1936 when he received his Ph.D. in history from the University of California at Berkeley. He has served as regional historian for the

V. Aubrey Neasham, distinguished historian and sponsor of the theory of a Drake landing at Bolinas Bay. (1975.)

National Park Service, president of Western Heritage, vice-president of the California Historical Society, and member of the Sir Francis Drake Commission.

Neasham's keen interest in the location of Drake's anchorage has led him on many field trips to Drake's, Bodega, and Tomales bays.[24] In 1948, while serving as Regional Historian for the National Park Service, he pronounced in favor of the Davidson site at Point Reyes. During the autumn of that year, he initiated exploratory excavations at the small beach where fisheries were situated, in the lee of the eastern shore of Point Reyes. With support from the California Historical Society and the University of California, a field crew uncovered a part of the original beach at that point and produced enough findings to make Neasham feel that there was at least a possibility of success if further excavation could be undertaken. This was not done.

In the early 1960s Neasham began to recognize the importance of the western shore of Bolinas Lagoon as a possible site for Drake's encampment. In 1962, he began investigation of various sites in that area; and with the assistance of Norman L. Wilson in 1962 and of Adan Treganza in 1965, archaeological tests were made at two sites without success. In 1973, with the assistance of William Pritchard, an archaeologist with the California Department of Parks and Resources, testing and excavating were begun at a third site and continued through much of 1974, again with disappointing results.

Neasham nevertheless continues to believe that Bolinas was the anchorage site, theorizing that the odd-shaped hole chiseled in the right lower corner of the Shinn plate to hold a sixpence must have been intended as a symbolic map of Drake's anchorage. He cites the applicability of such criteria as the "stinking fogs," the flora and fauna, the Indians, the "Portus Novae Albionis," and particularly the "Submap of the Carta prima Generale" published in the seventeenth century in Robert Dudley, *Arcano del Mare*.

Opinions Favoring San Quentin Cove

Before the twentieth century, the opinions favoring San Francisco Bay did not undertake to pinpoint the particular site within that vast harbor where the careening of the *Golden Hind* supposedly took place. This was a deficiency that Robert H. Power felt should be remedied

Robert H. Power, past president of the California Historical Society and principal champion of the San Francisco Bay anchorage theory. (1979. Bernard, San Francisco.)

when he entered the anchorage controversy in the early 1950s. He was apparently the first to perceive the strong case that could be made on behalf of San Quentin Cove.

Power became a Drake expert almost by accident. He grew up in Vacaville, California, where his family operated a roadside restaurant that has become the well-known and very successful Nut Tree, of which he is one of the owners. Little did Robert realize when, at age 11, he pasted a newspaper clipping about the finding of the plate of brass into his scrapbook, how Sir Francis Drake was to change his life. As a matter of fact, he had never been to Drake's Bay until 1952 and 1953 on family picnics.

Then, in February, 1954, he went to John Howell Books, well-known bookstore in San Francisco, and asked for a book on Drake. Warren Howell sold him a copy of Henry R. Wagner's classic *Sir Francis Drake's Voyage Around the World*. Thus young Power became

Robert H. Power escorts Queen Elizabeth II through the Drake 400 exhibition at Plymouth, England, on August 5, 1977. Designed to contribute to the celebration of the 400th anniversary of Drake's departure from England on his famous voyage, this exhibit featured the comprehensive collection of Drake material assembled over the years by Power. Two specially bound copies of the exhibit's catalogue, containing an introduction by Power, were presented to Queen Elizabeth and Prince Philip.

acquainted with the celebrated "Portus Novae Albionis" insert in the Hondius map, which almost every Drake aficionado uses to support his particular anchorage theory. After comparing it with a U.S. Geological Survey map of the eastern shores of Marin County, he decided that the two matched.

Thrilled by his discovery, he rushed down to the Academy of Sciences in San Francisco where the managing editor invited him to write an article for *Pacific Discovery.* He did, and it was published in the May-June, 1954, issue of the magazine. Since that time he has become one of the giants of the Drake controversy. He has been president of the Solano County Historical Society, president of the California Historical Society, a member of the California Heritage Preservation Commission and its chairman in 1970, and a member of the Sir Francis Drake Commission created by the legislature in 1973. He is the author of various articles seeking to prove that Drake spent the summer of 1579 at latitude 38° on Marin County shores but *within* San Francisco Bay. Power's contentions have had the support of Robert F. Heizer, as well as Walter A. Starr, Allen F. Chickering, and Francis P. Farquhar.[25]

In addition to relying upon the usual cartographic, ethnologic, and latitudinal evidence and the "Portus Novae Albionis" insert, Power points to the proximity of the Shinn plate discovery to San Quentin Cove, and to the evidence that a "good winde . . . sent" the *Golden Hind* into the Bay of Nova Albion, thereby matching today's conditions for entering the Golden Gate on a summer afternoon.

Proponents of Drake's Estero

In 1949 an organization known as the Drake Navigators Guild was formed for the express purpose of locating the site of the Drake encampment. Under the leadership of Adolph S. Oko, a former merchantship captain, this group of men, each an expert in at least one vital research area, decided to adopt the navigational approach to the problem.[26] Fleet Admiral Chester W. Nimitz, long the advisor and friend of the Guild, served as its honorary chairman.

Members of the Guild proceeded to institute what was perhaps the most intensive and comprehensive program of search and research ever carried out on the Drake anchorage. They began with a study of all available accounts, maps, and charts, and by establishing a set of

THE JAPANESE SURRENDER
U. S. S. MISSOURI
TOKYO BAY, 2 SEPTEMBER 1945

Chester W. Nimitz, Fleet Admiral, U.S. Navy, shown signing the Japanese Surrender on the deck of the battleship Missouri, *1945. For many years Nimitz was affiliated with the Drake Navigators Guild as their spokesman and honorary chairman. (The photograph was autographed to the author.)*

criteria to govern their activities. The rare materials in the fine Drake collection of Robert Marshall, a Point Reyes rancher and Guild member, proved to be of great assistance.

A study of the Hondius and Dudley maps was made by Guild member F. Richard Brace, electrical engineer and former lieutenant in the United States Navy. Documentary information was collected from scores of sources throughout the western world by Guild Member Robert W. Parkinson. Studies made by University of California anthropologists provided definite identification of the descriptions in early accounts as being of Coast Miwok Indian culture. Complementing these searches was a study of Elizabethan ships, navigation, and seamanship by Lieutenant Raymond Aker of the United States Naval Reserve, later to become president of the Guild, and to serve as a member of the Sir Francis Drake Commission.

With the aid of the data thus assembled, followed by a study of the course of the *Golden Hind* south along the California coast, they were led almost immediately to Drake's Bay. Among other persuasive factors were its white cliffs, its location squarely athwart the 38th parallel, and the fact that it had been Davidson's choice sixty years before. From that time on, they concentrated their search on the Point Reyes peninsula.

Enlisting the cooperation of William Hall and other Point Reyes ranchers, their field crews led by Matthew P. Dillingham, former Naval Reserve lieutenant, tramped scores of miles, took countless photographs, and studied winds, currents, tides, and storms. Months of work seemed to bring them no closer to an answer until suddenly, one series of photographs, taken from a bluff on the north side of a small harbor just within the entrance to Drake's Estero on November 23, 1952, disclosed a cove that seemed to fit the shape of the "Portus Novae Albionis" inset of the Hondius map, and to provide the very spot where Drake had found the answers to his water, wood, and careening problems.

An Indian village site was found three-quarters of a mile to windward up the Estero. At that location and at several others nearby, archaeological investigation disclosed iron spikes, Ming porcelain fragments, and other artifacts that could not be definitely linked to the *Golden Hind*. However, as one looks from the cove toward the bay, the white cliffs that lie "toward the sea" are plainly visible.

Presentation of Reports

The Guild felt that it had found the answer, and on June 14, 1956, Admiral Nimitz addressed the monthly meeting of the California Historical Society to announce the Drake Navigator Guild's findings. These findings, representing a compilation by Raymond Aker, Matthew P. Dillingham, and Robert W. Parkinson, were presented in manuscript form to the Society at that time, comprising 180 pages and entitled *Nova Albion Rediscovered*.

A subsequent report by Raymond Aker, Guild president, comprising 461 pages in manuscript form, together with many maps, charts, and illustrations, was presented to the Society in March, 1971. Its full title is *Report of Findings Relating to Identification of Sir Francis Drake's*

Raymond Aker, president of the Drake Navigators Guild, sponsor of a Drake's Estero anchorage, and author of a well-researched volume in support of that theory. (1979.)

Encampment at Point Reyes National Seashore. Its author states that it represents "an expansion of our original findings to include various additional new details and supplementary findings regarding the landing site and the voyage." Whatever the ultimate verdict concerning the correctness of the Guild conclusions, the document represents an impressive piece of scholarship as well as a gold mine of information about Drake's activities on the Pacific Coast.

A large part of the credit for the case presented over the years on behalf of Drake's Estero must be attributed to the Guild's perennial president, Raymond Aker, who feels that a working maritime or naval background is almost a prerequisite to a study of the anchorage problem. Aker himself has that background, not only as a graduate of the California Maritime Academy with a degree in navigation and seamanship, but also with eight years of service as a ship's officer, much of it in Pacific waters, including those visited by Drake. For many years he was an officer in the U.S. Naval Reserve, attaining the rank of lieutenant. Invaluable to his work on the anchorage problem has been his lifelong interest in maritime history, historical ship construction, and marine art.

In 1974 Samuel Eliot Morison, eminent historian and two-time winner of the Pulitzer Prize, published *The European Discovery of America: The Southern Voyages*. Chapter XXVIII is entitled "Drake In California, 1579," written after a visit to the Golden Gate area, a tour of Drake's Nova Albion country, and a review of the pertinent sources. The final paragraph of a section entitled "The Good Bay of Nova Albion" reads as follows:

> My conclusion, and that of my shipmates on our brief examination of the Marin County coast, is that Drake's Bay is correctly so named; that here he spent five weeks, repaired *Golden Hind,* sang psalms for the Indians, and marched up country. The white cliffs like those of Albion "on the side of the sea" (from the Estero) were for us the determining factors.[27]

II
PART

THE EVIDENCE

7

CHAPTER

"The Famous Voyage"

HE FIRST published account of the Drake circumnavigation, according to present knowledge, was the "The Famous Voyage" included in the 1589 edition of Richard Hakluyt's *Principall Navigations*. It comprised twelve large pages, two of which described the California phases of the adventure. The full title of the narrative was "The Famous Voyage of Sir Francis Drake into the South Sea, and therehence about the whole Globe of the Earth, begun in the yeere of our Lord, 1577."

The 1589 Hakluyt volume was an imposing work of more than 800 pages, with the even more imposing title *The Principall Navigations, Voiages and Discoveries of the English nation, made by Sea or ouer Land, to the most remote and farthest distant Quarters of the earth at any time within the compasse of these 1500 yeeres: Devided into three seuerall parts, according to the positions of the regions whereunto they were directed.* Its title page further informed the reader that it was "By Richard Hakluyt, Master of Arts, and student sometime of Christ-church in Oxford. Imprinted

THE PRINCIPALL
NAVIGATIONS,VOIA-
GES AND DISCOVERIES OF THE
Englifh nation,made by Sea or ouer Land,
to the moſt remote and fartheſt diſtant Quarters of
the earth at any time within the compaſſe
of theſe 1500.yeeres : Deuided into three
feuerall parts,according to the po-
ſitions of the Regions wherun-
to they were directed.

The firſt,conteining the perfonall trauels of the Englifh vnto *Iudæa,Syria,A-rabia*,the riuer *Euphrates, Babylon, Balſara,* the *Perſian* Gulfe, *Ormuz, Chaul, Goa,India*,and many Iſlands adioyning to the South parts of *Aſia :* toge-ther with the like vnto *Egypt,* the chiefeſt ports and places of *Africa* with-in and without the Streight of *Gibraltar,* and about the famous Promon-torie of *Buona Eſperanʒa.*

The fecond,comprehending the worthy difcoueries of the Englifh towards the North and Northeaſt by Sea,as of *Lapland, Scrikfinia, Corelia,* the Baie of *S.Nicholas,* the Iſles of *Colgoicue, Vaigats,* and *Noua Zembla* toward the great riuer *Ob,*with the mightie Empire of *Ruſſia,* the *Caſpian* Sea,*Georgia, Armenia,Media,Perſia,Boghar* in *Bactria,*& diuers kingdoms of *Tartaria.*

The third and laſt,including the Englifh valiant attempts in fearching al-moſt all the corners of the vaſte and new world of *America,* from 73.de-grees of Northerly latitude Southward,to *Meta Incognita,Newfoundland,* the maine of *Virginia,* the point of *Florida,*the Baie of *Mexico,* all the In-land of *Noua Hiſpania,* the coaſt of *Terra firma, Braſill,* the riuer of *Plate,*to the Streight of *Magellan :* and through it,and from it in the South Sea to *Chili, Peru,Xaliſco,* the Gulfe of *California, Noua Albion* vpon the backſide of *Canada,* further then euer any Chriſtian hitherto hath pierced.

Whereunto is added the laſt moſt renowmed Englifh Nauigation,
round about the whole Globe of the Earth.

By Richard Hakluyt Maſter of Artes, and Student fomtime
of Chriſt-church in Oxford.

Imprinted at London by GEORGE BISHOP
and RALPH NEWBERIE, Deputies to
CHRISTOPHER BARKER, Printer to the
Queenes moſt excellent Maieſtie,

1589.

Title page of the 1589 edition of Hakluyt's Principall Navigations Voiages and Discoveries.

at London by George Bishop and Ralph Newberie, Deputies to Christopher Baker, Printer to the Queenes most excellent Maiestie, 1589."

Richard Hakluyt (1552-1616), one of the foremost chroniclers of the Elizabethen era and a contemporary of Francis Drake, specialized in describing maritime exploits. His greatest works were published in the last two decades of the sixteenth century, the period when Drake was at the pinnacle of his career. Hakluyt's *Principall Navigations* has been considered a classic in the literature of discovery, and referred to as "the prose epic of the modern English nation."[1]

Compilation of "The Famous Voyage"

Nineteenth-century writers dealing with the literature of the circumnavigation have devoted much space to discussion of the identity of the author or compiler of "The Famous Voyage." Although the account itself carried no indication in that regard, authorship was frequently attributed to one Francis Pretty.[2] The reasons for such attribution are obscure, although one historian stated that Pretty had been "one of the crew on Drake's vessel,"[3] and another described him as "one of Drake's gentlemen-at-arms."[4] Pretty did sail around the world, but it was in 1586-1588 with Thomas Cavendish. There is no contemporary record of his having sailed with Drake, nor any other convincing data to connect him with the voyage of 1577-1580, either as a participant or as a narrator.[5]

Such evidence as there is points to the likelihood that Hakluyt himself was the compiler of "The Famous Voyage." A comparison of its text with other accounts indicates rather conclusively that it was not an original narrative but a compilation from three or four sources. In addition to the fact that Hakluyt would have been the logical person to undertake such a task, his own words suggest that he had, in fact, done so. In his preface to the 1589 edition he apologized "to the favourable Reader" for not including therein an account of Drake's world voyage "wherein I must confess to have taken more than ordinary paines, meaning to have inserted it in this work."

The earlier part of "The Famous Voyage" — dealing with the journey before the arrival in California — appears to have been based largely on material drawn from two manuscripts now reposing in the British Museum, one written by John Cooke, one by an unknown author (the "Anonymous Narrative").[6] In reference to the California sojourn, the original source material on which "The Famous Voyage" narrative was based has not survived—a misfortune that has complicated the anchorage mystery. On the other hand, Drake scholars have found it possible, with reasonable certainty, to identify the author as Drake's chaplain, Francis Fletcher. How this interesting determination has been made will be explained, to avoid repetition, in the next chapter.

Bibliographical Puzzle

Hakluyt's *Principall Navigations* has long been a collector's item because of its age and rarity. Its value and interest are enhanced, moreover, by other considerations. Historically, of course, it is important as the vehicle for the first known account of Drake's global circumnavigation. Bibliographically, it presents the novelty of a material variance between supposedly identical copies of the same edition, because some copies of the book contain "The Famous Voyage" and some do not. Even more puzzling is the fact that in the copies in which it does appear, it is without pagination or any means of locating it through table of contents or index.

Booksellers' catalogues, in their descriptions of the 1589 Hakluyt, usually refer to "The Famous Voyage" as the "rare Drake leaves," thereby conveying the impression that the latter are seldom found with the book. However, a provisional checklist of surviving copies of Hakluyt's 1589 edition was prepared in 1962 for the Hakluyt Society, an English association established early in the nineteenth century for the purpose of printing rare or unpublished accounts of early voyages and travels. This checklist shows that of a probable original printing of 1,000 copies, 113 are known to have survived throughout the world (59 of them in the United States).[7] Of these 113, all but 17 have the Drake leaves sewn in or, in one instance, pasted in.[8] Copies without the Drake leaves were thus the exception rather than the rule.

The copies that do not have the leaves are, to all discernible appearances, complete books. The pagination of each is without break in sequence and, with but one exception, there is nothing to indicate that the contents should in any way pertain to Drake's global voyage. This exception is found on the title page which, in its description of the

the two voyages made not long since to the Southwest, whereof I thinke the Spanyard hath had some knowledge, and felt some blowes: the one of Master Edward Fenton, and his consort Master Luke Warde: the other of Master Robert Withrington, and his hardie consort Master Christopher Lister as farre as 44. degrees of southerly latitude, set out at the direction and charge of the right honorable the Earle of Cumberland, both which in diuers respectes may yelde both profite and pleasure to the reader, being carefully perused.

For the conclusion of all, the memorable voyage of Master Thomas Candish into the South sea, and from thence about the globe of the earth doth satisfie mee, and I doubt not but will fully content thee: which as in time it is later then that of Sir Frauncis Drake, so in relation of the Philippinaes, Iapan, China, and the Isle of S. Helena it is more particular, and exact: and therfore the want of the first made by Sir Frauncis Drake will be the lesse: wherein I must confesse to haue taken more then ordinarie paines, meaning to haue inserted it in this worke: but being of late (contrary to my expectation) seriously delt withall, not to anticipate or preuent another mans paines and charge in drawing all the seruices of that worthie Knight into one volume, I haue yeelded vnto those my freindes which pressed me in the matter, referring the further knowledge of his proceedinges, to those intended discourses.

Now for the other part of my promise, I must craue thy further patience friendly reader, and some longer suspence from the worke it selfe, in acquainting thee with those vertuous gentlemen, and others which partly for their priuate affection to my selfe, but chiefly for their deuotion to the furtherance of this my trauaile, haue yelded me their seuerall good assistances: for I accompt him vnworthy of future fauours, that is not thankefull for former benefites. In respect of a generall incouragement in this laborious trauaile, it were grosse ingratitude in mee to forget, and wilfull maliciousnes not to confesse that man, whose onely name doth carrie with it sufficient estimation and loue, and that is Master Edward Dier, of whom I will speake thus much in few wordes, that both my selfe and my intentions herein by his friendly meanes haue bene made knowne to those, who in sundrie particulars haue much steeded me. More specially in my first part, Master Richard Staper Marchant of London, hath furnished me with diuers thinges touching the trade of Turkie, and other places in the East. Master William Burrowgh, Clarke of her Maiesties nauie, and Master Anthonie Ienkinson, both gentlemen of great experience, and obseruations in the north Regions, haue much pleasured me in the second part. In the third and last besides myne owne extreeme trauaile in the histories of the Spanyards, my cheefest light hath bene receiued from Sir Iohn Hawkins, Sir Walter Raleigh, and my kinseman Master Richard Hakluyt of the middle Temple.

And whereas in the course of this history often mention is made of many beastes, birds, fishes, serpents, plants, fruits, hearbes, rootes, apparell, armour, boates, and such other rare and strange curiosities, which wise men take great pleasure to reade of, but much more contentment to see: herein I my selfe to my singuler delight haue bene as it were rauished in beholding all the premisses gathered together with no small cost, and preserued with no litle diligence, in the excellent Cabinets of my very worshipfull and learned friends M. Richard Garthe, one of the Clearkes of the pettie Bags, and M. William Cope Gentleman Vssier to the right Honourable and most prudent Counseller (the Seneca of our common wealth,) the Lord Burleigh, high Treasourer of England.

Nowe, because peraduenture it would bee expected as necessarie, that the descriptions of so many parts of the world would farre more easily be conceiued of the Readers, by adding Geographicall, and Hydrographicall tables thereunto, thou art by the way to be admonished that I haue contented my selfe with inserting into the worke one of the best generall mappes of the world onely, vntill the comming out of a very large and most exact terrestriall Globe, collected and reformed according to the newest, secretest, and latest discoueries, both Spanish, Portugall, and English, composed by M. Emmerie Mollineux of Lambeth, a rare Gentleman in his profession, being therein for diuers yeeres, greatly supported by the purse and liberalitie of the worshipfull marchant M. William Sanderson.

This being the summe of those things which I thought good to admonish thee of (good Reader) it remaineth that thou take the profite and pleasure of the worke: which I wish to bee
as great to thee, as my paines and labour haue bene in bringing these
rawe fruits vnto this ripenesse, and in reducing these loose
papers into this order.   Farewell.

The excellent newe Globe of M. Mullineux.

Excerpt from the preface to the 1589 edition of Hakluyt's Principall Navigations, *which tells why he felt obliged to drop his original plan to print an account of Drake's world voyage.*

"three seuerall parts" into which the book was to be divided, speaks of "the English valiant attempt in searching almost all the corners of the vaste and new world of America ... to ... Noua Albion upon the backside of Canada, further than euer any Christian hitherto hath pierced." Since only Drake had then "pierced" to Nova Albion, this was a plain indication that the book would include a narrative of his great voyage. So far as the regular format was concerned, and those copies which did not include the Drake leaves, it proved to be an empty promise.

It is interesting to note that "The Famous Voyage" itself represents the only difference between the ninety-six known copies which contain it, and the seventeen which do not.[9] Upon a casual examination of any of the former, however, the Drake leaves are not readily found. One may search in vain for some reference to them or their subject matter in the table of contents, which Hakluyt called "The order of all the voyages comprised in this whole worke in generall." The same is true of the book's nine-page index, delightfully entitled "A Table Alphabeticall, containing a compendious extract of the principall names and matters comprised in the whole precedent worke: the numbers showing the names, where each particularitie is to be found." Only by thumbing carefully through the book itself does one finally come upon them, sandwiched between pages 643 and 644, but without page numbers of their own.

Rationale of the Insert

One other feature of "The Famous Voyage" not only invites, but requires, more than casual consideration, because it may have a bearing on the anchorage mystery, namely, the reason for the narrative's length, or lack of it. The fact that it comprises precisely twelve pages is no mere happenstance; rather it was a matter of careful design and laborious execution.

The six leaves of "The Famous Voyage" are printed on both sides to make a total of twelve unnumbered pages. The first three leaves are respectively marked Mmm 4, Mmm 5, and Mmm 6 (below the printed portion), with no corresponding indicia on the other three. The catchword "Instructions" appears at the bottom of the last page, all other printed material being the text of "The Famous Voyage" itself.

The first three of the six leaves immediately preceding the Drake material are marked Mmm, Mmm 2, and Mmm 3, whereas the other three carry no indicia. The next series, following the Drake sheets, begins with Nnn, Nnn 2, and Nnn 3 and continues with three un-numbered leaves, following a system of signatures used, not only throughout this volume, but rather generally in books of the sixteenth century. At the bottom of page 643 is the catchword "Instructions," matching the first word at the top of page 644, which, of course, represents the next page in those copies having no Drake leaves.

These various indications make it plain that the addition of the Drake material was in the nature of an afterthought, as well as a makeshift arrangement necessitated by the fact that the rest of the book was already paginated and printed. They indicate also that Hak-luyt was not content merely to have the leaves included at the end of the regular text, or at random, but was determined to have them inserted at one particular place in the book. They show, in fact, that the leaves were carefully designed to be inserted between pages 643 and 644, which is where they are found in most copies of the book.[10]

The number of leaves prepared by Hakluyt for this belated inser-tion happens to be the same as that used in the printing scheme of the book generally. The latter gives every indication of having been printed in sexto,[11] meaning that every original sheet of paper was printed and folded into a set of six leaves, or twelve pages. It is not surprising that such a pattern should have been duplicated, signatures and all, in the inserted leaves; for there is reason to believe that, for purposes of the latter, Hakluyt found the standard six-leaf setup advantageous, not only as a matter of printing convenience and ease of insertion, but also, perhaps, from the standpoint of binding limitations.

The Need for Condensation

How did it happen, then, that "The Famous Voyage" was of this most convenient length? Of what significance is the fact that it fills the entire six leaves to within two or three lines of the bottom of the final page? That these were matters of coincidence is possible, but not very probable in the light of all circumstances. Hakluyt had originally pre-pared his account of the Drake voyage for inclusion in the book

The famous voyage of Sir Francis Drake into the South Sea, and there hence about the whole Globe of the Earth,

begun in the yeere of our Lord, 1 5 7 7.

The 15. day of Nouember, in the yeere of our Lord, 1577. M. Francis Drake, with a fleete of fiue ſhips and barkes, and to the number of 164, men, Gentlemen and Sailers, departed Plimmouth, giuing out his pretended voyage for Alexandria: but the winde falling contrary, he was forced the next morning to put into Falmouth hauen in Cornewall, where ſuch and ſo terrible a tempeſt tooke vs, as few men haue ſeene the like, and was in deed ſo vehement, that all our ſhips were like to haue gone to wracke, but it pleaſed God to preſerue vs from that extremitie and vto afflict vs only for that preſent with theſe two particulars: The maſte of our Admiral which was the Pellican, was cut ouer boord for the ſafegard of the ſhip, and the Marpgold was driuen a ſhore, & ſomewhat bruiſed, for the repairing of which damages we returned againe to Plimmouth, and hauing recouered thoſe harmes, and brought the ſhips againe to good ſtate, we ſet forth the ſecond time from Plimmouth, and ſet ſaile the 13. day of December following.

The 25. day of the ſame moneth we fell with the Cape Cantine, vpon the coaſt of Barbarie, and coaſting along, the 27. day we found an Iſland called Magador, lying one mile diſtant from the maine, betweene which Iſland and the maine, we found a very good and ſafe harbour for our ſhips to ride in, as alſo very good entrance, and void of any danger. *The Iſle of Magador on the coaſt of Barbarie.*

On this Iſland our Generall erected a pinnaſe, whereof he brought out of England with him foure already framed. While theſe things were in doing, there came to the waters ſide ſome of the inhabiteunts of the countrey, ſhewyng foorth their flags of truce, which beyng ſeene of our Generall, he ſent his ſhips boate to the ſhore, to know what they would : they being willing to come aboord, our men left there one man of our companie for a pledge, and brought two of theirs aboord our ſhippe, which by ſignes ſhewed our Generall, that the next day they would bring ſome prouiſion, as Sheepe, Capons and Hennes and ſuch like, whereupon our Generall beſtowed amongſt them ſome linnen cloth and ſhoes, and a iaueling, which they very ioyfully receiued, and departed for that time.

The next morning they failed not to come agayne to the waters ſide, and our Generall againe ſetting out our boate, one of our men leaping ouer raſhly a ſhore, and offering friendly to imbrace them, they ſet violent hands on him, offering a dagger to his throte if hee had made any reſiſtance, and ſo laping him on a horſe, caried him away, ſo that a man cannot bee too circumſpect and warie of himſelfe among ſuch miſcreants.

Our pinnaſe beyng finiſhed, we departed from this place the thirtieth and laſt day of December, and coaſting along the ſhore, we did deſcrie, not contrary to our expectation, certaine Canters which were Spaniſh fiſhermen, to whom we gaue chaſe and tooke 3. of them, and proceeding further we met with 3. Caruels and tooke them alſo.

The 17. day of January we arriued at Cape Blanko, where we found a ſhip riding at anker, *Januarie.* within the Cape, and but two ſimple Mariners in her, which ſhip we tooke and caried her further into the harbour where we remained 4. dayes, and in that ſpace our Generall muſtered, and trayned his men on land in warlike maner, to make them fit for all occaſions.

In this place we tooke of the Fiſhermen ſuch neceſſaries as wee wanted, and they could yeld vs, and leauing here one of our litle barkes called the Benedict, wee tooke with vs one of theirs which they called Canters, being of the burden of 40. tunnes or thereabouts.

All theſe things being finiſhed, we departed this harbour the 22. of Januarie, carying along with vs one of the Portingall Caruels which was bound to the Iſlands of Cape de Verde for ſalt, whereof good ſtore is made in one of thoſe Iſlands.

The maſter or Pilot of that Caruell, did aduertiſe our Generall that vpon one of thoſe Iſlands *The Iſle of* called Mayo, there was great ſtore of dried Cabaritas, which a few inhabitaunts there dwelling, *Mayo.* did yeerely make readie for ſuch of the kings ſhips as did there touch, beyng bound for his countrey of Braſile or elſe where. We fell with this Iſland the ſeuen and twentieth of Januarie, but the inhabitants would in no caſe traffique with vs, beyng thereof forbidden by the kings Edict: yet the next day our Generall ſent to view the Iſland, and the likelihoods that might be there of prouiſion of victuals, about three ſcore & two men vnder the conduct & gouernment of M. Winter and maſter Doughtie, and marching towards the chiefe place of habitation in this Iſland (as by the Portingall wee were informed) hauing trauelled to the mountains the ſpace of three miles, and arriuing there ſomewhat before the day breake, wee arreſted out ſelues to ſee day

A part of the first page of "The Famous Voyage" from the 1589 edition of Hakluyt's Principall Navigations.

proper.[12] Since space limitations were not then a major consideration, length of the narrative would have been governed by factors of available material and importance of the subject. Neither of these would have warranted a mere twelve-page treatment of England's greatest voyage, and Hakluyt's original version was probably much more extensive. As a matter of fact, a comparison of "The Famous Voyage" with its sources shows a substantial degree of condensation,[13] and the original Hakluyt narrative, when the necessity arose, was undoubtedly reduced, in procrustean fashion, to the length most suitable for purposes of insertion.

Once the abbreviated narrative had been printed, it would then have been folded in the usual way and inserted in the proper place in the unbound quires. Presumably, this was done in the case of every book thereafter bound, barring intentional or accidental exceptions. The space between pages 643 and 644 was the ideal place for such an insertion, because it represented the end of a narrative, and because it was the logical spot, from a chronological standpoint, for inclusion of a report on the 1577-1580 voyage.

Undoubtedly Hakluyt had good reasons for omitting the account from some copies and for inserting it, in unpaged form, in others. If Hakluyt himself ever offered an explanation, no record of it remains. Drake scholars have often pondered this bibliographical mystery,[14] and their comments and conclusions, though not germane to the subject of this book, constitute a story of special interest.

The 1600 Hakluyt Edition

In 1599–1600 Hakluyt expanded his 1589 edition and republished it in three volumes with a total of more than 2,000 pages. Volume III was dated 1600 and contained 868 pages, exclusive of dedicatory epistle and table of contents. It dealt with voyages "to all parts of the Newfound world of America," and it is at pages 730–742 of this volume that Hakluyt repeated, with certain corrections, the original twelve-page version of "The Famous Voyage" from his 1589 edition. At pages 440–442, in a section of Volume III captioned "Certeine voyages made for the discouery of the gulfe of California, and of the sea-coast on the northwest or backside of America," he also printed an excerpt somewhat revised from the original longer account, dealing principally with the California visit, and bearing the following title:

The courſe which Sir *Francis Drake* held from the hauen of *Gua-* *tulco* in the South ſea on the backe ſide of *Nueua Eſpanna,* to the North-weſt of *California* as far as fourtie three degrees: and his returne back along the ſaid Coaſt to thirtie eight degrees: where finding a faire and goodly hauen, he landed, and ſtaying there many weekes, and diſcouering many excellent things in the ceun-trey and great ſhewe of rich minerall matter, and being offered the dominion of the countrey by the Lord of the ſame, hee tooke poſſeſſion thereof in the behalfe of her Maieſtie, and named it *Noua Albion.*

 Ee kept our courſe from the Iſle of Cano (which lyeth in eight degrees of Northerly latitude, and within two leagues of the maine of Nicaragua, where wee calked and trimmed our ſhip) along the Coaſt of Nueua Eſpan-na, vntill we came to the Hauen and Towne of Guatulco, which (as we were infozmed) had but ſeuenteene Spaniards dwelling in it, and we found it to ſtand in fifteene degrees and fiftie minutes.

Aſſoone as wee were entred this Hauen we landed, and went preſently to the towne, and to the Towne houſe, where we found a Iudge ſitting in iudgement, he being aſſociate with thzee other officers, vpon thzee Negroes that had conſpired the buining of the Towne: both which Iudges, and pziſoners we tooke, and bzought them a ſhippeboozd, and cauſed the chiefe Iudge to wzite his letter to the Towne, to command all the Towneſmen to auoid, that we might ſafely water there. Which being done, and they departed, wee ranſaked the Towne, and in one houſe we found a pot of the quantitie of a buſhell full of royals of plate, which we bzought to our ſhip.

And here one Thomas Moone one of our companie, took a Spaniſh gentleman as he was fly-ing out of the Towne, and ſearching him, he found a chaine of Gold about him, and other iewels, which we tooke and ſo let him goe.

The Poztugal Pilote ſet on land.   At this place our Generall among other Spaniards, ſet a ſhoze his Poztugall Pilote, which he tooke at the Iſland of Cape Verde, out of a ſhip of Saint Marie pozt of Poztugall, and hauing ſet them a ſhoze, we departed thence.

Our Generall at this place and time thinking himſelfe both in reſpect of his pziuate iniuries re-ceiued from the Spaniards, as alſo of their contempts and indignities offered to our Countrey and Pzince in generall, ſufficiently ſatiſfied, and reuenged : and ſuppoſing that her Maieſtie at his re-turne would reſt contented with this ſeruice, purpoſed to continue no longer vpon the Spaniſh coaſtes, but began to conſider and to conſult of the beſt way foz his Countrey.

He thought it not good to returne by the Streights, foz two ſpeciall cauſes : the one, leaſt the Spaniards ſhould there waite, and attend foz him in great number and ſtrength, whoſe handes he being left but one ſhip, could not poſſibly eſcape. The other cauſe was the dangerous ſituation of the mouth of the Streights of the South ſide, with continuall ſtozmes raining and bluſtring, as he found by experience, beſides the ſhoals and ſands vpon the coaſt, wherefoze he thought it not a good courſe to aduenture that way: he reſolued therefoze to auoide theſe hazards, to goe fozward to the Iſlands of the Malucos, and therehence to ſaile the courſe of the Poztugalcs by the Cape of Bona Sperança.

Vpon this reſolution, he began to thinke of his beſt way foz the Malucos, and finding himſelfe, where hee now was, becalmed, hee ſawe that of neceſſitie hee muſt bee enfozced to take a Spaniſh courſe, namely to ſaile ſomewhat Northerly to get a winde. Wee therefoze ſet ſaile, and ſayled 800 leagues at the leaſt foz a good winde, and thus much we ſayled from the 16 of Apzill after our olde ſtile till the thizd of June.

Sir Francis Drake ſayled on the backe ſide of America. to 43 degrees of Northerly latitude. 38 degrees.   The fift day of June being in foztie thzee degrees towardes the pole Arcticke, being ſpeedily come out of the extreame heate, wee found the ayze ſo colde, that our men being pinched with the ſame, complayned of the extremitie thereof, and the further we went, the moze the colde increaſed vpon vs, whereupon we thought it beſt foz that time to ſeeke land, and did ſo, finding it not moun-tainous, but low plaine land, ⁊ we dzew backe againe without landing, til we came within thirtie eight degrees towardes the line. In which height it pleaſed God to ſend vs into a faire and good Bay, with a good winde to enter the ſame.

In this Bay wee ankered the ſeuententh of June, and the people of the Countery, hauing their houſes cloſe by the waters ſide, ſhewed themſelues vnto vs, and ſent a pzeſent to our Generall.

When they came vnto vs, they greatly wondzed at the things which we bzought, but our Ge-nerall (accozding to his naturall and accuſtomed humanitie) curteouſly intreated them, and libe-rally

---

"The Course." Page 440 of Volume III of Hakluyt's 1600 edition of Principall Naviga-tions *represents the first of three pages devoted to a separate and considerably revised account of the California visit.*

The course which Sir *Francis Drake* held from the hauen of *Guatulco* in the South sea on the backe side of *Nueua Espanna,* to the Northwest of California as far as fourtie three degrees: and his returne back along said Coast to thirtie eight degrees: where finding a faire and goodly hauen, he landed, and staying there many weekes, and discouering many excellent things in the countrey and great shewe of rich minerall matter, and being offered the dominion of the countrey by the Lord of the same, hee took possession thereof in the behalfe of her Maiestie, and named it *Noua Albion.*

The excerpt which followed this title is usually referred to as "The Course."

For nearly four decades following its original publication, "The Famous Voyage" was the only reasonably complete account available. Consequently it was borrowed from extensively, both in England and on the Continent. In abridged form, it was translated into a Dutch text attached to a map supposedly engraved about 1595, and forming with the latter what is now referred to as the Hondius Broadside.[15]

A Latin version appeared in Theodore De Bry, *Americae Pars VIII,* Frankfurt 1599, and a very condensed German version in Part 6 of the works of Levinus Hulsius in 1603. A French translation was published in 1613 entitled *Le Voyage de L'Illustre Seigneur et Chevalier Francis Drach, Admiral d'Angleterre, alentour du monde.* To a substantial extent, also, it formed the basis for a part of a work in Latin by William Camden, 1615, which dealt with Drake's world voyage, including all the data concerning the California sojourn (see page 106). Samuel Purchas, in *Purchas, His Pilgrimes,* published in 1625, used the account practically without change, reprinting it from Hakluyt's 1600 edition.[16]

8

CHAPTER

The World Encompassed

THE MOST complete and detailed account of the circumnavigation, as well as of Drake's activity on the northwest coast of America, is the small 108-page book published in 1628, nearly half a century after his return to England, with the memorable title *The World Encompassed*.

The book's title page indicates that the work was "carefully collected out of the notes of Master Francis Fletcher, Preacher in this Imployment, and divers others his followers in the same"; and that it was "offered now at last to publique view, both for the honour of the actor, but especially for the stirring up of heroick spirits, to benefit their Countrie, and to eternize their names by like noble attempts." Most copies contained a portrait of Drake and a map of the world, but the latter showed neither the track of his voyage nor a reference to Nova Albion.

The World Encompassed was the second in a series of two books narrating the Drake achievements, both published by Sir Francis

THE WORLD
Encompaſſed

By
Sir FRANCIS DRAKE,

Being his next voyage to that to *Nombre*
de Dios formerly imprinted ;

Carefully collected out of the notes of Maſter
FRANCIS FLETCHER *Preacher in this im-*
ployment, and diuers others his followers in
the ſame :

Offered now at laſt to publique view, both for the honour ⊕
the actor, but eſpecially for the ſtirring vp of *heroick ſpirits,*
to benefit their Countrie, and eternize their names
by like noble attempts.

LONDON,
Printed for NICHOLAS BOVRNE
and are to be ſold at his ſhop at the
Royall Exchange. 1628.

Title page of The World Encompassed, *1628.*

Drake, the younger, Drake's nephew, son of Drake's youngest brother, Thomas, and heir to the Drake estate. The first of the two accounts is entitled *Sir Francis Drake Revived,* published in 1626 and relating the story of Drake's expedition to the Spanish Main in 1572–1573. Apparently it was written during Drake's lifetime, and even reviewed and checked by him. Its belated publication, thirty-five years after being written, probably inspired the younger Drake to put together and publish a similar account of the circumnavigation.

There has been considerable speculation about the identity of the author of *The World Encompassed.* This seems to have been rather unnecessary because the book itself attributes that honor to the younger Drake, and because, as the heir to the Drake estate, the nephew would logically have had possession of his uncle's records of the voyage, including any diaries and notes kept by others as well as by Fletcher. Not included, of course, were Drake's original log and other documents turned over to the queen and, unfortunately, never seen again. In any event, the nephew would have had access to everything dealing with the voyage published before 1628 including "The Famous Voyage." Even if he did not personally compile the account, it would have been prepared under his direction and subject to his approval.

Sources of the Account

It is well to keep in mind the incentives of the younger Drake in publishing *The World Encompassed.* As stated in his introduction to the book, he was trying to present "the whole history" of the voyage, that is, a complete account as contrasted with the abridged version that Hakluyt felt obliged to use. He claimed also to be presenting a true narrative, "with as great indifferency of affection as history doth require." Nevertheless, he was careful to exclude all material that might be unfavorable to Drake, such as is to be found in the "Anonymous Narrative,"[1] and in Fletcher's manuscript of the voyage preserved in the British Museum.[2]

The book's title page makes it clear that Fletcher's notes "in this Imployment" were the principal source of *The World Encompassed.* Particularly is this true of the California part of it, although that portion of Fletcher's narrative containing it was subsequently lost. However, the portion of his manuscript covering the first part of the voyage and describing the Indians of South America is still in existence (see note 2); and its language and style of writing are very similar to those appearing in *The World Encompassed* account of the California Indians.

In respect to the California visit, there is also a striking similarity between the text of *The World Encompassed* and that of "The Famous Voyage." Wagner has pointed out that "after leaving Guatulco to the time of leaving the Northwest coast, the *World Encompassed* account is practically the same, often in identical words and sentences, as that in the Famous Voyage."[3] Robertson commented: "These accounts are so confirmatory of each other as to paraphrase the events related, although the *World Encompassed* amplifies and minutely details matters only generally referred to by Hakluyt."[4]

Anyone who chooses to compare the accounts of the Nova Albion visit will find the account in *The World Encompassed* similar to that of "The Famous Voyage" not only in general content, but also in arrangement and style of expression. In view of the mentioned similarities to an earlier Fletcher manuscript on a related subject, and the fact that Drake scholars appear to recognize, without exception, the similarity of *The World Encompassed* account of the Nova Albion visit to that in "The Famous Voyage," the conclusion is inescapable that Fletcher was the primary source of both narratives.

Fletcher's Notes

Drake authorities, however, are not in agreement about the manner in which each account obtained and used its material. Wagner stated flatly that *The World Encompassed* was simply copied from "The Famous Voyage"[5] with the greater length being achieved by ample padding and "some additions of legitimate origin."[6] He has left the impression, moreover, that the expanded portion of the material may have been supplied by Fletcher after publication of the original account in "The Famous Voyage."[7] Unfortunately, Wagner cited no authority and offered no good reasons to support his theory.

As a matter of fact, the source material for both accounts of the Nova Albion visit may have been either Fletcher's original notes compiled in the course of the voyage or more likely in the form of a narrative prepared from them by Fletcher subsequently. The great similarity of the two narratives in style of expression and arrangement of material suggests the latter, as does the wealth of detail which they contain. A similar inference may be drawn from the fact that the two accounts do not contradict each other in any material way, although their respective references to latitudes and to the names given to the "countrey," that is, "Albion" versus "Nova Albion," were not identical.[8]

The primary differences in the accounts arose from the fact that the compiler of *The World Encompassed* was endeavoring to prepare and publish a complete and detailed report, his purpose being to take full advantage of the Fletcher notes or manuscript, as the case may have been. Therefore he made little or no effort to edit them or to put them in his own words, as Hakluyt had done in abridging the original material to fit the size of the insert he was obliged to use. The evidence suggests that in each instance the compiler drew his data directly from what was probably a manuscript by Fletcher based on his own original notes.

Did Fletcher Exaggerate?

Questions have been persistently raised in earlier years about the reliability of *The World Encompassed* account. Historian Bancroft characterized Fletcher "as a man not noted for his veracity,"[9] and added his impression of "the fundamental truth that Chaplain Fletcher was a liar."[10] In Robertson's opinion, "many facts related by Fletcher were exaggerated and ... his statements were untrustworthy."[11] Even Wagner called it "the most untrustworthy account of all," indicating that some of Fletcher's statements concerning the Nova Albion weather were exaggerated.[12]

With the passage of time, however, the interpretations placed on the contemporary accounts have undergone modification. Some Drake scholars still place their primary reliance in "The Famous Voyage,"[13] but there is no longer a tendency to accuse Fletcher of gross exaggeration, or to question the trustworthiness and value of *The World Encompassed* account of the Drake visit to California. One of the leading experts on the subject has recently commented that Fletcher's descriptions were valid and could well have reflected conditions actually encountered on the northwest coast in June and July, 1579, giving reasons for his conclusion.[14] Even Wagner, however, had been willing to concede that Fletcher's seemingly bizarre comments about the frigid weather at Nova Albion could be explained on the basis of the much colder climate known to have prevailed on the California coast in the latter part of the sixteenth century.[15]

Later Editions

As might have been expected, the original publication of *The World Encompassed* was followed by later editions, one of which appeared as part of a small book entitled *Sir F. Drake's Voyages,* published in London in 1653. It comprised more than 250 pages, and consisted of three parts. The first of them was a reprint of *Sir Francis Drake Revived,* originally published by Drake's nephew in 1626, followed by a reprint of the original *The World Encompassed,* and concluded with a sixty-page narrative entitled *A Summarie and True Discourse of Sir Francis Drakes West-Indian Voyage.*[16] *The World Encompassed* section represented a page-by-page and word-for-word duplication of the original 1628 text, save and except for minor changes in spelling, punctuation, and paragraphing. Frontispiece of the volume is an excellent 5″ by 5½″ engraving of Sir Francis.

The Hakluyt Society reprinted the text of *The World Encompassed* in 1854 under the title *The World Encompassed by Sir Francis Drake.* It was edited by W. S. W. Vaux, and contained several appendixes pertaining to the 1577–1580 voyage. These included various extracts from Hakluyt's 1600 edition, among which were "The course of Sir Francis Drake to California and Nova Albion," as shown at pages 440–442 of Volume III of that edition, and the text of "The Famous Voyage" itself, but omitting that part of it pertaining to the California sojourn with the idea of eliminating duplication. Also included, as Appendix III, was a "short abstract of the present voyage, in handwriting of the time." The abstract itself bore the title "A discourse of Sir Francis Drakes iorney and exploytes after he had past y[e] Straytes of Megellan into Mare de Sur, and throughe the rest of his voyadge afterward till hee arived in England. 1580 anno." This is the same account later referred to by Wagner as the "Anonymous Narrative."

With the Hakluyt edition of 1854 was a 17″ by 21″ copy of the famous Hondius map entitled "Vera Totius Expeditionis Nauticae" (see Chapter 10). It lacked the "Portus Novae Albionis" inset that had appeared in the Hondius map; but it did show the tracks of Drake and Cavendish around the world and the legend "Nova Albion" between latitudes 38° and 43°.

A de luxe edition of *The World Encompassed* was published in 1926 by the Argonaut Press of London, edited by N. M. Penzer, with a valuable "Appreciation of Drake's Achievement" by Sir Richard Carnac Temple. It did not show the Hondius map, but it did have a facsimile of a map that has come to be known as the French Drake Map.[17] For the text of that part of *The World Encompassed* pertaining to the California visit, see Appendix D.

9

CHAPTER

Other Early
Accounts

PART FROM the principal accounts set forth in Chapters 7 and 8, a few other contemporary reports discuss Drake's California sojourn or data pertinent thereto. Most of these are fragmentary. Only three of them represent eye-witness accounts of the Nova Albion scene, and even these add little to the information contained in the principal accounts. Nevertheless, for the sake of completeness, the pertinent portions of these less important narratives are presented in this chapter.

Among the earliest of these accounts were the declarations given by John Drake, a cousin of Sir Francis, who had accompanied the latter on the 1577–1580 voyage. While serving with the Fenton Expedition of 1582, the ship he commanded was wrecked and he was captured in Argentina by the Spaniards. While he was a prisoner in that area, he gave the first of two depositions covering his voyages, on March 24, 1584. So far as relevant to the 1579 visit to California, it was as follows:

He does not know what day they left Guatulco, only that it was in April. They sailed out at sea always to the northwest and north-north-west the whole of April and May until the middle of June, from Guatulco, which lies in 15 degrees north, until they reached 48 degrees north. On their voyage they met with great storms. All the sky was dark and full of mist. On the voyage they saw five or six islands in 46 and 48 degrees. Captain Francis gave the land that is situated in 48 degrees the name of New England. They were there a month and a half, taking in water and wood and repairing their ship.[1]

The Second Declaration

John Drake was subsequently taken to Lima, Peru, where, on January 8, 1587, he was again examined about the events of 1579. On this occasion, his narrative in reference to the California sojourn[2] was lengthier and more explicit, the portion of it having to do with that part of the voyage being as follows:

> Then they left [Guatulco] and sailed, always on a wind, in a north-west and north-north-westerly direction, for a thousand leagues until they reached forty-four degrees when the wind changed and he went to the Californias where he discovered land in forty-eight deg. There he landed and built huts and remained for a month and a half, caulking his vessel. The victuals they found were mussels and sea-lions. During that time many Indians came there and when they saw Englishmen they wept and scratched their faces with their nails until they drew blood, as though this were an act of homage or adoration. By signs Captain Francis told them not to do that, for the Englishmen were not God. These people were peaceful and did no harm to the English, but gave them no food. They are of the colour of the Indians here [Peru] and are comely. They carry bows and arrows and go naked. The climate is temperate, more cold than hot. To all appearance it is a very good country. Here he caulked his large ship and left the ship he had taken in Nicaragua. He departed, leaving the Indians, to all appearance, sad. From here he went alone with the said ship, taking the route to the Moluccas.

Portions of John Drake's first deposition were printed, although with some errors, in the second volume of Antonio de Herrera's *Historia General del Mundo,* published in 1606.[3]

The Anonymous Narrative

Preserved in the British Museum is the "Anonymous Narrative,"[4] apparently written shortly after completion of the circumnavigation, from information supplied by some one who had made the voyage. Its full text has been printed as an appendix to the Hakluyt Society's 1854 edition of *The World Encompassed by Francis Drake,* Vaux, ed., under the title "A discourse of Sir Francis Drakes iorney and exploytes after he had passed ye Straytes of Megellan." Because the identity of its author is unknown, Wagner referred to the document as the "Anonymous Narrative," and that title has been used here. It is the most picturesque account that has survived, and covers events that have been discreetly censored from the principal accounts, particularly with respect to the black woman Maria.[5] Its tale of the California visit,[6] however, is brief:

> Here [Guatulco] drake watered his ship & departed sayling northwardes till he came to .48. gr. of the septentrionall Latitud still finding a very lardge sea trending toward the north but being afraid to spend long time in seeking for the straite hee turned back againe still keeping along the cost as nere land as hee might, vntill hee came to .44. gr. and then hee found a harborow for his ship where he grounded his ship to trim her, & heere came downe vnto them many of ye contrey people while they were graving of their ship and had conference with them by synes, in this place drake set vp a greate post and nayled thereon a vj^d, which the contreye people woorshipped as if it had been god also he nayled vppon this post a plate of lead and scratched theron the Queenes name, and when they had graved & watred theire ship in the latter ende of August they set sayle and bent their course S.S.W. and had not the sight of land againe till ye latter end of november

Stow and Blundeville

A brief account of the circumnavigation had been included in a 1592 history entitled *Chronicles* by John Stow,[7] a contemporary of Drake. After Stow's death, the *Chronicles* were continued by Edmund Howes, from the 1615 edition of which the following account of the California visit has been excerpted:

The golden Hinde (or Pelicane I thinke) held on her course to Chily, Lima, Coquimbo, Arica, Panama, & so all along the backe side of America to the lineward, and passed the line the first day of March, and the 16. of March being on land at the Ile of Canoes, hee passed foorth northward till he came to the latitude of forty seauen, thinking to have come that way home; but being constrained by fogs and cold windes to forsake his purpose, came backeward to the lineward the tenth of June 1579,[8] and stayed in the latitude of thirty eight to graue and trim his ship, untill the fiue and twenty of July, and from thence setting his course Southwest.

In 1594, Thomas Blundeville published *M. Blundeville, His Exercises, containing sixe Treatises.*[9] In one of these treatises, he undertook to describe the Drake circumnavigation as he had perceived its route on the Molyneaux Globe, which had been published in 1592. He succeeded in being more confusing than enlightening, his comment on the California segment of the voyage being as follows:

> From thence he sayled stil Northernly to the Cape Mondecino, which is in the land called Quivira, and sayled still Northward vnto a certaine Bay in the West part of Quivira, which he named Noua Albion (that is to say) new Englande hauing in North Latitude 46. degrees, and from this Bay Sir Frances himselfe (as I haue heard) was of good will to haue sailed still more Northward, hoping to find passage through the narrow sea Anian, but his Mariners finding the coast of Noua Albion to be very cold, had no good will to sayle any further Northward, wherefore Sir Frances was faine to come backe again Southward to Mondecino, which (as hath beene said before) is distant from the foresaide Bay of Noua Albion 140. leagues.

A Twice-Translated Account

William Camden was an English historian who in 1615 published the first volume of *Annales Rerum Anglicarum, et Hibernicarum, regnante Elizabetha, ad Annum Salutis M.D. LXXXIX.* In 1624 a translation from the Latin to French was issued in London, from which a writer named Abraham Darcie made the first English version, which he published in 1625. The source of Camden's information was undoubtedly "The Famous Voyage." From Darcie's translation is taken the following excerpt dealing with the California sojourn:

Drake then tooke his way toward the North, at the latitude of 42. Degrees, to discouer in that part if there were any straight, by which he might find a neerer way to returne; But discerning nothing but darke and thicke cloudes, extremity of cold and open Cliffes couered thicke with snow, hee landed at the 38. Degree, and hauing found a commodious Rode, remained there a certaine time. The inhabitants of that Countrie were naked, merry, lusty, jumping, leaping and dancing perpetually, sacrificing, and showing by signe and words, that they would elect Francis Drake for their King: neither could it be coniectured that euer the Spaniard had bin there, or so farre in that Countrie: Drake named that very countrey, being fat and good, full of Deeres and Conies, the new Albion; Causing a great Poste to be there erected, vpon which there was ingrauen an Inscription, which shewed the yeere of our Lord, the name of Queene ELIZABETH, and their landing there, and vnderneath a piece of silver of Queene ELIZABETH'S Coine was nailed to the said Poste.[10]

Purchas Duplicates "The Famous Voyage"

In 1625, Samuel Purchas published *Purchas, His Pilgrimes,* the second volume of which bore the title "A Description Of All The Circum-navigations Of The Globe." Chapter III was entitled "The Second Circum-Navigation of the Earth: Or the renowned Voyage of Sir Francis Drake, the first Generall which euer sayled about the whole Globe, begun in the yeare of our Lord, 1577, heretofore published by M. R. Hackluyt, and now reviewed and corrected."

Purchas made corrections, primarily in the earlier part of the account discussing the trial and execution of Thomas Doughty. The narrative dealing with Nova Albion was a word-for-word duplication of the Hakluyt version of "The Famous Voyage" as it appeared on pages 737—738 of the third and last volume of Hakluyt's 1600 edition.

Account by a Naval Historian

William Monson, a contemporary of Drake, was one of the most distinguished naval officers of his time.[11] Around 1640, near the end of his long life, he put some of his information and opinions into manuscript form. Eventually, in 1704, these were published in London as a part of Awnsham Churchill's *Collection of Voyages* under the title of

THE

THIRD AND LAST

VOLVME OF THE VOY-
AGES, NAVIGATIONS, TRAF-

fiques, and Difcoueries of the *Englifh Nation*, and in
fome few places, where they haue not been, of ftrangers, performed within and before the time of thefe hundred yeeres, to all
parts of the *Newfound* world of *America,* or the *Weft Indies,* from 73.
degrees of Northerly to 57.of Southerly latitude:

As namely to *Engronland, Meta Incognita, Eftotiland,*
*Tierra de Labrador,Newfoundland,*vp *The grand bay,* the gulfe of *S.Lau-*
*rence,*and the Riuer of *Canada* to *Hochelaga* and *Saguenay,*along the coaft of *Aram-*
*bec,*to the fhores and maines of *Virginia* and *Florida,*and on the Weft or backfide of them
both, to the rich and pleafant countries of *Nueua Bifcaya,Cibola,Tiguex,Cicuic,*
*Quiuira,*to the 15.prouinces of the kingdome of *New Mexico,*to the
bottome of the gulfe of *California,*and vp the
Riuer of *Buena Guia:*

And likewife to all the yles both fmall and great lying before the
cape of *Florida,The bay* of *Mexico,*and*Tierra firma,*to the coafts and Inlands
of *Newe Spaine, Tierra firma ,*and *Guiana,* vp the mighty Riuers of *Orenoque,*
Deffekebe, and *Marannon,*to euery part of the coaft of *Brafil ,* to the Riuer of *Plate ,*
through the Streights of *Magellan* forward and backward,and to the
South of the faid Streights as farre as 57.degrees:

And from thence on the backfide of *America,* along the coaftes,harbours,
and capes of *Chili,Peru,Nicaragua,Nueua Efpanna,Nueua Galicia,Culiacan,*
*California,Noua Albion,*and more Northerly as farre as 43.degrees:

Together with the two renowmed, and profperous voyages of Sir *Francis Drake*
and M.*Thomas Candifh* round about the circumference of the whole earth, and
diuers other voyages intended and fet forth for that courfe.

Collected by RICHARD HAKLVYT *Preacher, and fometimes*
ftudent of Chrift-Church in Oxford.

¶ Imprinted at London by *George Bifhop,Ralfe*
*Newberie,*and ROBERT BARKER.
ANNO DOM. 1600.

Title page of Volume III of Hakluyt's 1600 edition of Principall Navigations.

"Sir William Monson's Naval Tracts." This material included a brief account of Drake's voyage around the world, for which his sources, upon analysis, turned out to be "The Famous Voyage" and *The World Encompassed*. His reference to the California interlude was one of extreme brevity, as follows:

> From the 16th of April till the 5th of June, he sail'd without seeing Land, and arriv'd in 48 Degrees, thinking to find a passage into our Seas, which Land he nam'd Albion; the People were courteous, and took his Men for Gods; they live in great extremity of Cold and Want; Here they trim'd their Ship, and departed the 25th of July, 1579, standing his Course for the Molucco's.

The Madox Diary

Another early account dealing with the California phase of the Drake epic has been discovered in the British Museum. This was the diary of a Drake contemporary, which an English historian, E. G. R. Taylor, found in 1932 and made known to the world in an article entitled "Francis Drake and the Pacific: Two Fragments." It was published in the *Pacific Historical Review*, San Francisco. The diarist, Richard Madox, did not accompany Drake on his world voyage; rather he was a chaplain aboard Edward Fenton's ship in 1582. But his diary disclosed information gained from conversations with members of the Fenton crew who had accompanied Drake on the circumnavigation. So far as relevant to the California sojourn, the Madox account is as follows:

> In ships land wh is ye back syde of Labradore and as Mr. Haul [Christopher Hall] supposeth nye thereunto Syr Frances Drake graved and bremd his ship at 48 degrees to ye north. Ye people ar for feature color apparel diet and holo speach lyke to those of Labradore and is thowght kingles for they crowned Syr Frances Drake. Their language is thus.
>
> | *Cheepe* | bread |
> | *Huchee kecharoh* | sit downe |
> | *Nocharo mu* | tuch me not |
> | *Hioghe* | a king |
>
> Ther song when they worship god is thus — one dauncing first wh his handes up, and al ye rest after lyke ye prest and people Hodeli oh heigh oh heigh oh hodali oh Yt is thowght yt they of Labradore [do] worship ye son and ye moon but [whether they] do of Caliphurnia I kno not.

This hearsay information, belatedly discovered 350 years after its receipt and recording, has proved to be valuable in identification of the anchorage site, because the quoted vocabulary has been assigned conclusively to the Coast Miwok language.[12] Thus we have another clue tieing the Drake visit to Marin County.

Accounts Accompanying Contemporary Maps

The celebrated Hondius Broadside Map, entitled "Vera Totius Expeditionis Nauticae" has been described elsewhere herein.[13] It was reputedly published in 1595 in Amsterdam where Jodocus Hondius had established a map-publishing business at about that time. With the map was a Dutch text which, upon translation of the Nova Albion portion, was an almost verbatim copy of "The Famous Voyage." Such minor differences as there were have no bearing on the site of Drake's California landfall; hence no purpose would be served by setting them forth.

In 1646 or 1647, Robert Dudley published an atlas of charts entitled *Arcano del Mare* in Italy. His various maps of the northern California coast reflect some special knowledge of Drake's movements in that area, as discussed later.[14] On two of his maps were legends in Italian pertaining to the Nova Albion visit.[15]

Latin and German Texts

An account of the circumnavigation was included in a series of voyages entitled *Grande et Petits Voyages,* published in Frankfurt, Germany between 1590 and 1634 by Theodore De Bry and his successors. De Bry was a Flemish engraver who lived at various times in the Netherlands, Germany, and England. In London he became acquainted with Hakluyt and did some engraving of New World pictures at the latter's request.

His illustrated *Voyages* comprised 57 volumes in a complete set. In the America series, there were 13 parts in Latin and 14 in German. *Americae Pars VIII* was published in 1599 in both Latin and German, having been prepared by De Bry before his death in 1598, but actually published the following year by his widow and sons. It was elaborately illustrated.

From translations of the German and Latin texts in those volumes, it is apparent that De Bry, like Hondius, used a word-for-word version of "The Famous Voyage," at least so far as the material pertaining to the California visit was concerned. This was to be expected because of his contacts with Hakluyt and the fact that no other narrative as complete as the "The Famous Voyage" was available before 1598.[16]

The De Bry narratives describing the Drake visit to California are among the earliest of such accounts, and therefore may be regarded as primary source materials. However, since their texts are identical with similar portions of the 1589 edition of the "The Famous Voyage," apart from minor variances attributable to the effects of translation back and forth between English, German, Latin, and back into English again, there is no point in setting forth the final versions here.

Important Spanish Accounts

In the present century much of the valuable information long buried in Mexican and Spanish archives has become available. One of the most interesting of such stories is that of a pilot named N. de Morena, originally reported in 1626 by Father Salmeron and ultimately translated and published in *The Land of Sunshine* in 1900.[17]

Another important Spanish narrative, dating from the sixteenth century, reposes in the Royal Archives at Seville. This is the account by Captain Sebastian Rodriguez Cermeño of his visit to Drake's Bay in 1595. A translation by Henry R. Wagner was published in the *California Historical Society Quarterly* for April, 1924.[18]

In contrast to the English "cover-up," Spanish authorities were very thorough in their accumulation and preservation of information concerning the Drake voyage. Sworn statements were taken from almost everyone who came into their custody after having contact with the "corsair." Most were from their own citizens, of course, who had been taken captive in Spanish American towns or ships. In the case of Nuño da Silva, the Portuguese pilot captured by Drake in the Atlantic, a number of statements were taken, the first at Guatulco shortly after he had been put ashore there by Drake. Later declarations or "confessions" were made in Mexico City on May 20 and again on May 23, 1579. In addition, Silva's log book was confiscated. Fortunately, all these documents have been preserved in the National Archives at Mexico City.

Although these Spanish narratives have great value to any study of the circumnavigation as a whole, their inclusion here would serve no purpose because none of the declarants had any knowledge of the California visit. Drake took no captives after leaving Mexico. Of those captured in Spanish America, only the three blacks (Maria and the two males) accompanied him to California and there are, unfortunately, no records of their comments.

Some of the useful information (from the Nova Albion standpoint) in these so-called minor accounts did not become available to Drake scholars until the twentieth century, and then only by reason of the diligent research of two women. Zelia Nuttall's *New Light On Drake* did not make the John Drake declarations available until 1914 and E. G. R. Taylor's discovery of the Richard Madox diary was not published until 1932.

10

CHAPTER

Contemporary Maps and Charts

THE DISCOVERY and exploration of the New World gave an extraordinary impetus to mapmaking. The unfolding of the outlines of this great new hemisphere occupied more than three centuries. During this period, the horizon of cartographical knowledge was expanded with the return of every expedition to America, and the mapmakers vied with each other in recording and collating the resulting flood of geographical data. Much of it was inaccurate, and cartographers were frequently issuing sets of maps[1] that were at variance, not only with those published by rivals, but with other maps in their own sets.

Through the prodigious research of Henry R. Wagner, we know that more than 850 different maps or sets of maps dealing with the northwest coast of America were issued before 1800.[2] Of these, 235 appeared in the seventy years between Drake's return to England in 1580 and the year 1650, and Drake scholars have considered hopefully that within this vast storehouse of material might be found valuable clues to the location of the missing California anchorage or, perhaps, the answer itself. Hence, this evidence has been carefully examined.

The maps of the first ten years after the conclusion of the great voyage of the *Golden Hind* are singularly devoid of information concerning its geographical impact, probably because of the tense political and economic rivalry between Spain and England. Spanish vessels had been plying the Pacific for nearly half a century before Drake invaded that part of their domain, yet their navigational charts remained jealously guarded secrets. Conceivably, a reciprocal attitude on the part of the English may have hampered the efforts of mapmakers to picture the Drake voyage and its results.

Early English Maps

The first bits of cartographic information on the 1577–1580 voyage seem to have been from English sources. Two references to the Pacific Coast phase of the circumnavigation appeared on maps of the 1580–1590 era. Interestingly enough, each of these maps accompanied a volume edited by Hakluyt. His *Divers Voyages,* published in 1582, included a map by Michael Lok,[3] which carried a somewhat cryptic notation to the effect that the northwest coast of America had been visited by the English in 1580. Hakluyt's 1587 edition of *Peter Martyr's Decades* included the so-called Peter Martyr Map,[4] which carried a legend on the Pacific northwest coast reading: "Nova Albion discovered by the English in 1580". Aside from these partly erroneous references,[5] no other dated map of that decade alluded to the subject, and none showed the name of Drake himself.

It was not until 1592 that any map of known date provided more specific information about the Drake circumnavigation. This was the celebrated Molyneux Globe,[6] first of all English-made globe-maps, which showed NOVA ALBION at latitude 50° on the northwest coast, with the name *F Dracus* just below it in smaller letters. Also outlined were the routes of both the Drake and Cavendish voyages. That of Drake, marked *Sir Fr. Drack,* was depicted as running up the coast to approximately 48°, then back to the vicinity of 42° before turning westward. These same indications, except for the mention of Drake on the coast itself, were duplicated in the John Blagrave Map of 1596,[7] which was presumably intended to accompany his book entitled *Astrolabium Uranicum Generale,* also published in 1596.[8]

These few early maps represent the principal English contribution to the cartography of the Drake voyage. It is true that subsequent maps showed the name Nova Albion,[9] others showed a port bearing Drake's name on the coast of northern California,[10] and in at least one instance both appeared on the same map.[11] In general, however, the English maps of seventeenth-century provenance added little, if anything, to our knowledge of the whereabouts of Drake's California harbor of refuge.

To the mapmakers of Holland, France, and Italy must go the greater credit for colorful and interesting portrayals of the "famous voyage" in its various aspects. Their masterpieces were, in many instances, undated but some of them probably preceded 1600, and perhaps even 1590. Noteworthy, on the other hand, are a few which did not appear until the seventeenth century was near the midway point. Those of sufficient importance from the standpoint of the California anchorage problem are discussed below.

Special Drake Maps

The Silver Map of the World[12] was one of the earliest[13] maps, and undoubtedly the most unusual, to deal with Drake's voyage. It was in the form of a silver medallion, presumably cast or struck in Holland[14] during the lifetime of Sir Francis to commemorate his feat of global circumnavigation. It was the probable pattern and prototype of later, but more conventional cartographical efforts to tell the same story.[15] Such is the medallion's rarity that only nine specimens are known to exist.[16] There may never have been more.

From a structural standpoint, the medallions have been superbly executed, whether by sixteenth- or twentieth-century standards.[17] Each medallion is identical with the others, thereby pointing to the probability that they were stamped from a common die, rather than individually engraved.[18] Each is a thin, circular disk, slightly less than three inches in diameter and not exceeding one thirty-second of an inch in thickness.[19] The only variance, except for differences attributable to wear and tear, is in thickness and weight, the latter varying from as little as 260 to as much as 424 grains troy.[20]

From a cartographical standpoint, the Silver Map is an exquisitely wrought *mappemonde,* or world map, designed to reflect the known

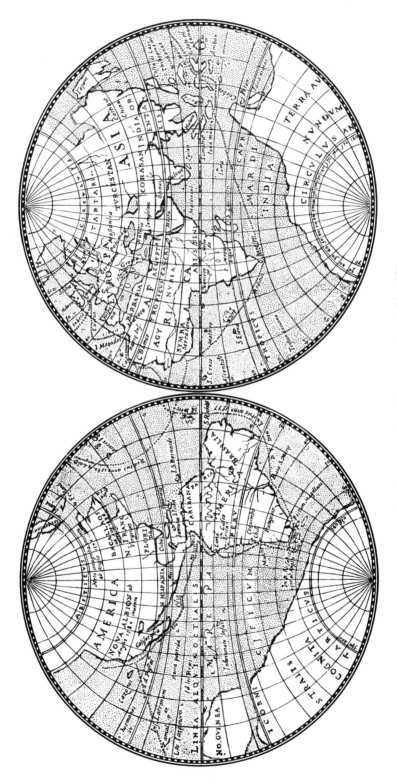

The Silver map of Drake's voyage, circa 1581–1585.

facts or prevailing ideas of the geography of the late sixteenth century. On the face is the Western Hemisphere and, on the reverse, the Eastern, with a dotted line running across both to indicate Drake's sailing track. The wealth of geographical detail includes the usual lines of latitude and longitude, the Equator, the Tropics of Cancer and Capricorn, the Arctic and Antarctic Circles, as well as the various continents and oceans. Eight symbols, legends, or inscriptions appear, in addition to 67 geographical names in the Eastern Hemisphere and 43 in the Western.[21] Detectable by the eye of the expert are a few errors in reference to dates, geography, and the course followed by Drake.[22]

Authorities have speculated whether the Silver Map was struck at the order of Queen Elizabeth to commemorate the first English circumnavigation,[23] whether it was created at the request of Drake himself,[24] or whether it was prepared at the instance of some chronicler, such as Hakluyt, or of some engraver, such as Hondius, in token of appreciation for information or assistance received.[25] There has been similar conjecture as to the identity of the person who engraved the die from which the medallions were stamped,[26] as well as to the date when they came into being. None of these questions has been conclusively answered. It appears, however, that the die could hardly have been engraved earlier than the latter part of 1584, because the name "Virginea" on its face was not known in England until Sir Walter Raleigh returned from America in September of that year.[27]

With reference to Drake's California visit, the Silver Map is not too helpful. Near latitude 50° on the northwest Pacific Coast is found the legend "NOVA ALBION ab Anglie 1580 inuenta" (New Albion discovered by the English in 1580). This duplicates the error found in the Michael Lok and Peter Martyr maps. Drake's name, while not shown in this area, appears elsewhere as an identification of the sailing track. That route is shown proceeding up the Pacific coast to approximately 48° before turning back to a point several degrees southward, from which it makes a right angle westward across the Pacific.

The French Drake Map[28] is an indication that contemporary interest in the 1577–1580 odyssey was not confined to English borders. Exceptionally rare, most of the known copies have been found in early seventeenth-century editions of the French translation of Hakluyt's "The Famous Voyage."[29] The date and place of publication are unknown. The engraver was Nicola van Sijpe of whom nothing whatsoever has been learned.[30]

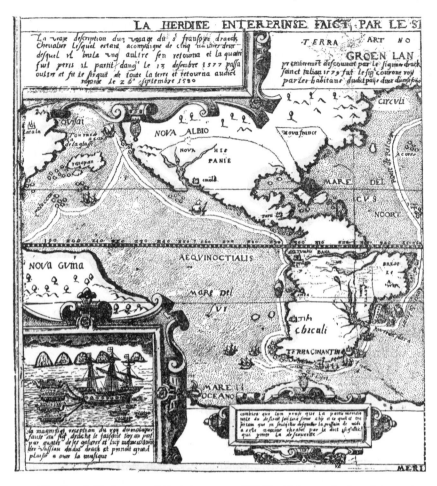

The French Drake map of Drake's voyage, 1581(?). This reproduction of the western half of the map is surrounded by a border, the lower half of which carries two illustrations similar to those on the Hondius Broadside. The upper half bears a legend which takes the place occupied by the "Portus Novae Albionis" on the Hondius Broadside.

The map is a double hemisphere production and measures 17 7/16 by 9 7/16 inches.[31] It is in French, except for a few place names in Spanish.[32] At each of the lower corners is an inset, that at the left showing the *Golden Hind* at Ternate in the Moluccas, while that at the right shows the ship aground on a reef near Celebes. In the lower central part is a portrait of Drake, including a notation of his age as forty-two. Below the portrait is an inscription "Carte veuee´ et corige par le dict siegneur drack" (map seen and corrected by Drake). Boundary lines for Nova Albio, Nova Hispanie, and Nova France are shown on the North American continent.[33] What appear to be coats of arms, presumably those of Queen Elizabeth, are placed on Nova Albio and below South America at points where Drake is credited with the discovery of new territory.[34]

The map is very similar in many respects to two other contemporary maps, the Hondius Broadside and the Dutch Drake Map. The legend in the upper left-hand corner of the French Drake Map contains a part of the information which also appears in the title of the Hondius Broadside. The insets in the two lower corners are almost identical with those of the Hondius Broadside and those of the Dutch Drake Map, and are similarly placed. The portrait of Drake is similar, but not identical, to that appearing on the Dutch Drake Map.

The date of the map has been the subject of controversy among Drake authorities. In 1927 the British Museum published a monograph on the French Drake Map by F. P. Sprent, superintendent of its Map Room.[35] He argued that its general appearance, the portrait, the watermark, and the absence of any allusion to the Cavendish circumnavigation of 1586–1588 all point to a date not later than 1585, possibly as early as 1581.[36] Wagner, on the other hand, thinks a 1641 date more likely.[37] He takes issue with the Sprent contentions in respect to the map's appearance and watermark, and points out that all but two of the known copies have been found in 1641 editions of the French version of Drake's voyage.[38]

Similar differences of opinion have arisen in respect to the statement on the map that it was seen and corrected by Drake. Zelia Nuttall accepted this assertion without reservation and speculated that it must have been Drake himself who "set the crowned arms of Elizabeth over Nova Albion, intentionally placing them higher north than his place of landing."[39] Later Drake scholars have been unimpressed by the map's reference to its correction by Drake himself, concluding that such an event was highly improbable, and that the legend may have been "inserted by an unscrupulous publisher in order to make the map sell."[40] Some support for the latter view is added, perhaps, by the numerous inaccuracies and careless errors which are disclosed by a close examination of the map.[41]

The map does show NOVA ALBIO on the Pacific northwest coast, as previously mentioned, along with what is supposedly the

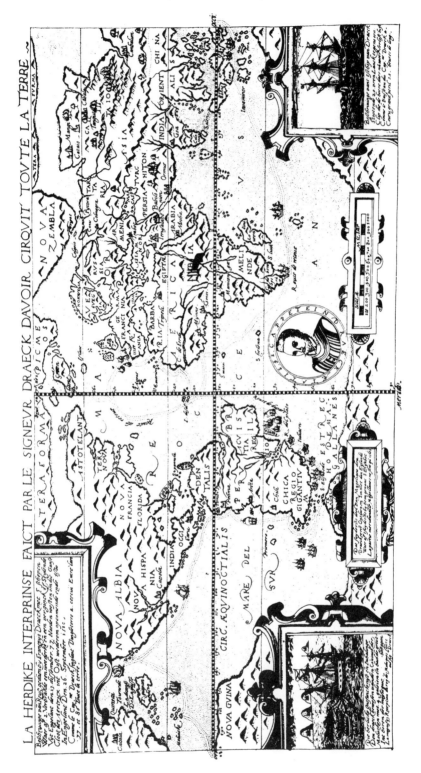

The Dutch Drake map of Drake's voyage (date unknown).

Elizabethan coat of arms. It shows the route of the Drake voyage running to approximately 48° N, to the left of which, above Japan, is the legend: "Tournede la acanst delaglasse" (Turned back because of the ice). It then retraces itself southward a few degrees to a point on the coast near a group of islands, from which it turns westward, as on other maps showing the Drake sailing track in the North Pacific.

The Dutch Drake Map[42] provides further evidence of the interest aroused on the continent by Drake's globe-girdling exploit. It is even rarer than the French Drake Map and only two copies of it are known, one in the Huntington Library and one in the New York Public Library.[43] The map's date and place of publication are unknown, as well as the identity of its engraver.

In most respects, this map is a counterpart of the French Drake Map.[44] It is in two hemispheres, measures 17 5/8 by 9 9/16 inches, and is in Dutch, except for the French title and the three inscriptions obviously borrowed from the French Map: *route de retour, route de duparte,* and the inscription above Japan. The Dutch legends are similar in content to those on the Hondius Broadside. The insets at the lower corners are similar to those appearing in the same locations on the French Drake Map and Hondius Broadside. The Drake portrait is very similar to that on the French Drake Map, but with the age listed in the rim of the portrait's oval border. It omits most of the errors and inaccuracies of the French Drake Map,[45] as well as the Elizabethan coat of arms, and the inscription that the map had been seen and corrected by Drake.

The age of the map offers an interesting subject for debate. Authorities are inclined to believe it a later production than the French Drake Map because its title and inscriptions are apparently copied therefrom, and it omits most of the French Map's mistakes.[46] Curiously, however, the only two known copies are bound into editions of a book on Drake's 1585 voyage to the West Indies, one being a Latin version published in 1588, the other a German edition published in 1589.[47] This is puzzling, because the map obviously bears no relation to the subject matter of the text.[48] If, however, the maps were in fact issued with the books in which they are now found, then it would appear that the Dutch Drake Map, as well as the French Drake Map, antedated 1590, and that both were predecessors of the Hondius Broadside itself.

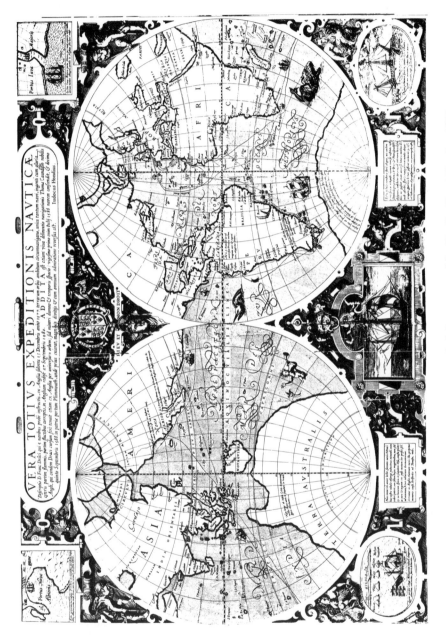

The world map of Drake's voyage which forms a part of the Hondius Broadside, circa 1595.

From the standpoint of the quest for Drake's California anchorage, the Dutch Drake Map supplies no information not already shown by the Silver Map and the French Drake Map. It shows NOVA ALBIA in large letters in the general area of the Pacific Northwest, and uses three dotted lines, instead of one, to indicate the Drake sailing track.

In depicting the route through the North Pacific, however, an interesting variation appears between the two copies of the Dutch Drake Map. One merely duplicates the pattern of the French Drake Map, but the other extends the route from its most northerly point sharply westward to a point near the Asiatic coast above Japan.[49] In the latter copy, the second line of the legend about turning back on account of the ice is slightly different.[50]

The probable explanation of this is that in making the original copy from the French Drake Map, the latter was faithfully duplicated, and the result was used in the earlier edition of 1588. Before more copies were run off for the 1589 edition, the engraver noted that the sailing track, at its northerly point, failed to reach the spot on the map where, according to the legend, it was necessary to turn back on account of ice. Thinking, no doubt, that this was an error, he made what he assumed to be a correction, and in extending the sailing track to the westerly edge of the legend, had to revise the middle line of the legend itself. In replacing this middle line, the slight change in the legend was a probable inadvertence.

The Hondius Maps

The Hondius Broadside is the most famous of all contemporary maps bearing on Drake's activities on the Pacific coast.[51] It is extremely rare, and the reproduction here is taken from the British Museum copy.[52] Not reproduced, however, is the printed text attached to both sides and to the bottom of the original, thereby increasing its dimensions to approximately 37 by 25 inches and causing it to be referred to as a "broadside". It is not known whether map and text were published at the same time, or had any connection with each other beyond their subject matter, since they have obviously been pasted together.[53]

The text is in Dutch and describes the voyages of Drake and Cavendish around the world. That pertaining to the Drake circumnavigation is, with minor variations, an abridged version of "The

Famous Voyage" as it appeared in Hakluyt's 1589 edition.[54] Embraced within the text material are portraits of Drake and Cavendish. On the lower part of the Drake portrait[55] is a small map of the world in twin hemispheres, as well as a ship probably intended to represent the *Golden Hind*.[56]

The map has no place of imprint and is undated. It is reputed to have been issued in 1595, but confirmation on this score is lacking.[57] However, it must have been published after 1588 for it shows the route of the Cavendish circumnavigation completed in that year. On the other hand, it undoubtedly was issued before 1599, in which year a small copy of it appeared in De Bry's *Americae Pars VIII*. The text seems also to antedate 1599, because it does not reflect the revisions made by Hakluyt in his 1598–1600 edition.[58]

The engraver of this noted map was Josse de Hondt, the Elder, better known by his Latinized name of Jodocus Hondius. Born in 1567, he served his apprenticeship as an engraver in Antwerp. He lived in London for several years (*circa* 1585–1593) and, upon his return to the continent, settled in Amsterdam. After his death in 1611, the map-making business was carried on by his sons, Jodocus and Henricus.[59] Material for the map was undoubtedly collected during the years in London, but there is no conclusive evidence whether its publication took place in London or Amsterdam.[60] Despite the Dutch text attached to the map, the names and legends on the latter are in Latin, the only exception being at the eastern end of the Straits of Magellan where there appears, in English, the name "The fortunate cape." The several legends on the map deal with events of the Drake voyage.

Shown on the map by means of dotted lines are the routes followed by Drake and Cavendish in circumnavigating the world. Opposite Nova Albion is an asterisk on the path of the Drake route at about the latitude of 42° N. A corresponding asterisk on the coast precedes a legend stating that it was at this point on June 5 that Drake turned back to the south on account of the cold weather. The dotted line nevertheless continues beyond the asterisk to approximately 48° and then retraces itself to 38° where there is an indentation in the coastline presumably intended to indicate the California anchorage.[61] The route then turns sharply across the Pacific.

The map contains five insets. At the middle of the lower border is a likeness of the *Golden Hind,* which Hondius himself may have seen at

Deptford, near London, where she was preserved for many years.[62] At each of the map's four corners is a view depicting some outstanding episode in the course of the Drake circumnavigation. At the upper left is pictured a ship in a harbor inscribed "Portus Novae Albionis" (of which more in Chapter 24) and at the upper right is a scene near the stopping place in Java. At the lower left is shown the reception given to the *Golden Hind* by the Sultan of Ternate. At the lower right is a representation of the vessel when aground on a reef near Celebes.[63]

Other Hondius maps of North America or the world were published by Hondius, the Elder, or by his successors during the seventeenth century. According to Wagner,[64] a total of thirty-four were produced between 1600 and 1650, many of which were undoubtedly revised issues of earlier editions. The earliest of such productions was the Hondius Globe of 1600,[65] one of which is now in the Huntington Library at San Marino, California.[66] This globe erroneously placed Cape Mendocino, ever a prominent feature of California coastal geography, at latitude 50°, rather than at 40°. It showed Nova Albion at latitude 42°, accompanied by a legend reciting that Drake encountered frigid weather in that latitude and was obliged to reverse his course. No harbor with any Drake connotation was indicated.

The pattern thus established was followed by most later Hondius maps. The world map of 1611, for example, is believed to have been republished, probably with some corrections, in 1618 and 1627.[67] Unfortunately, all copies of the two later issues have disappeared, including a 1627 map formerly owned by Captain Gustav Niebaum of San Francisco,[68] but apparently destroyed in the San Francisco fire of 1906.[69] Copies of the portion of this map referable to the California coast have survived, however, and show the same information relative to the Drake visitation as on the 1600 Hondius Globe.[70]

The Hondius Map of 1629[71] seems to have been the first to deviate from the Hondius firm's traditional pattern of the California area. It reflected the idea, then gaining considerable currency in cartographical circles, that California was an island.[72] It also broke with previous Hondius tradition in two respects: The name "Nova Albion" was omitted, and a "Pº [Porto] Sir Francisco Draco" was shown at latitude 38° N.

The Maps of Dudley

Robert Dudley was a mapmaker whose career, bridging the six-teenth and seventeenth centuries, is described in Chapter 27.[73] Three of his cartographical works have a bearing on the site of Drake's California anchorage, two of them published in 1646 or 1647 as a part of an atlas entitled *Arcano del Mare*,[74] and the third an unpublished map discovered in a library in Munich, Germany.

One of the two published maps, known as the "Carta Partico-lare,"[75] is in four sections, the most northerly of which shows the northwest Pacific coast from just below latitude 38° to above 50°. The engraving was by Antonio Francesco Lucini, but the maps were the work of Dudley. The most northerly section of this map (Chart XXXIII) is the one with a bearing on Drake's anchorage, and it con-tains a number of legends in Italian.

Among the legends of Drake interest is one just under the 40th parallel stating that Nova Albion was discovered in 1579. Near 44° of latitude are two legends, one at the coastline itself, saying that Drake discovered the coast in 1579 and found the cold insupportable in June. The principal legend was placed between 41° and 42°. It was to the effect that many maps put Cape Mendocino in 50° and Cape Fortune in 60°, which is a great error because Drake and the Spanish pilots found Mendocino in 40° and, although the ordinary maps show the length of California as 1,200 leagues, it is only a little more than 600, according to Drake and other pilots. In that portion of Dudley's text describing this chart, he had a lengthy note about Nova Albion.[76]

A little north of the 38th parallel is shown the "Po^to di Nuoua Albion," with a river or estero opening into it from the northeast. Within the port, and just outside its entrance, are numbers evidently intended to represent the depth of the water in fathoms. These depths range from 3 fathoms near the mouth of the river, 4 fathoms on the easterly side of the harbor, and 6 fathoms at the entrance, to a maximum of 8 fathoms just outside the entrance. An anchor is situated at the northerly part of the harbor, but west of the entering river, presumably to indicate a point of anchorage.

The "Carta prima Generale"[77] was also a part of Dudley's *Arcano del Mare,* and outlined the California and Pacific Coast from 27° to 42½°.[78] It was based, to some extent, on the discoveries of Sebastian Vizcaino, Spanish explorer who charted a portion of the California

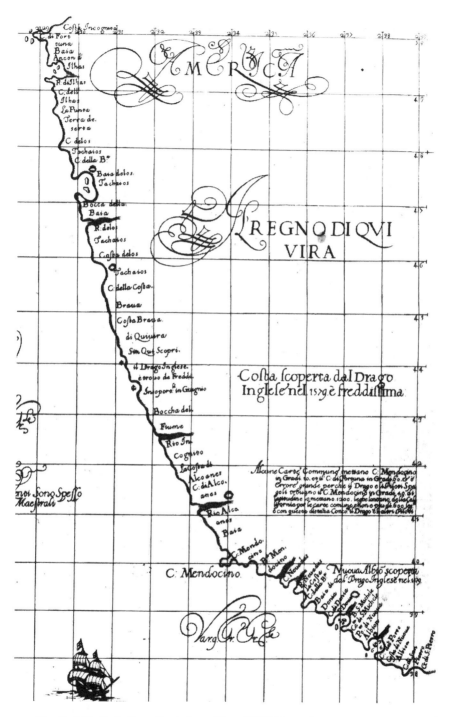

Detail of Dudley's Carta Particolare, Chart XXXIII, 1647.
(See page 321 for complete map.)

coast during his voyage of 1602–1603.[79] Shown on this chart are several items of Drake significance. In latitude 42°, the country is designated "Nuoua Albione." Just above it is a legend that "some [mapmakers] locate Cape Mendocino in 41° of latitude and that the coast is cold." Just below latitude 38° is shown a small harbor bearing the name "P⁰ dell nuoua Albion" with the additional notation that it was discovered by "Drake, the Englishman." No soundings appear in the harbor, but it is embellished with a small anchor, the customary indication that it had at some time served as an anchorage.

The one manuscript chart of special interest[80] is known as Chart No. 85. It is the northerly one of a series of three charts extending from above Cape Mendocino to below latitude 38°, and is assertedly the basis of the material used by Dudley in constructing his "Carta Particolare."[81] Just north of 38° is a bay entitled "B: di noua Albion." Just below the name is a further inscription "Il Por.⁰ boniss.ᵐ⁰," meaning "the best of harbors." Above the name is a legend stating that Nova Albion was discovered by General Drake, the Englishman, in 1579 (the "7" having been corrected from an originally shown "8.") As in most of his charts, Dudley included on No. 85 a rather extensive legend.[82]

Accompanying Chart No. 85 were Chart Nos. 84 and 83 (not reproduced here). Chart No. 84 represents a continuation of No. 85, but displays no significant information in relation to Drake.[83] Chart No. 83 is in two parts.[84] In latitude 46° is shown the port of Quivira, followed by this legend:

> Discovered by Drake, the Englishman, in 1582, who found it so cold in the month of June that it was necessary to return to latitude 38½° to which he gave the name New Albion. The other port which was insupportably cold was in 43 degrees. [The "3" in "43" had plainly been changed from a "2" by putting a tail on the bottom of the latter].

Despite the information in the legend about a port of New Albion at 38½°, none was shown.[85] A "P de Sardina" does appear at approximately 38°. No other items of Drake interest appear on this or any other Dudley manuscript chart.

Maps from Early Books on America

The *De Bry Map*[86] is from *Americae Pars VIII* by Theodore De Bry, published in 1599 at Frankfurt-am-Main. In the form of a copper engraving, it adorns the title page of that rare volume containing, among other accounts of the New World, a condensed Latin version of "The Famous Voyage." Shown also on the map are a portrait of Drake and a picture of the *Golden Hind*.

The De Bry Map is interesting for several reasons. First, it is clearly a copy, on a much reduced scale, of the Hondius Broadside Map. Secondly, it represents one of the few dated maps which depict the route of Drake's circumnavigation. Thirdly, because it is such a copy and is dated, it supplies evidence which helps to identify the appropriate publication date of its prototype.

Wagner has pointed out that the De Bry Map differs from the Hondius Broadside Map in only one particular. It omits that portion of the dotted line which, in the latter map, represents Drake's sailing track above latitude 42°. Wagner suggests that this may have been an intentional omission, possibly to make the map correspond in that respect to the accompanying text which, being an abridged version of the 1589 Hakluyt account, mentioned no latitude more northerly than 42°.[87]

The *Ogilby Map*[88] appeared in a volume entitled *America, being the latest, and most Accurate Description of the New World* by "John Ogilby, Esq. His Majesty's Cosmographer, Geographick Printer, and Master of the Revels in the Kingdom of Ireland."[89] Published in London in 1671, the text of this massive tome is in English and contains a three-page dissertation on California, based on the Hakluyt and *The World Encompassed* accounts of the Drake voyage, as well as a very brief description of the voyage itself. Neither made any reference to the latitude of the California anchorage.

The map itself showed the western hemisphere with Latin names and inscriptions.[90] It was engraved by F. Lamb and dedicated to Lord Ashley.[91] It measured 24 by 19 inches, and was placed between the Table of Contents and the first page of the text. Conforming to then current beliefs, it depicted California as an island terminating in latitude 43°.[92] Near its northerly end, at approximately latitude 40°, appeared the name "Nova Albion". In latitude 38° was shown a small harbor marked "P S^r F Drake". No explanatory legends were included.

Maps of Literary Note

In the study of cartographical material pertaining to Drake's California visit, two maps of unique interest have been encountered. Neither adds anything of importance to the search for the missing anchorage, but both are noteworthy because they impart something of a literary flavor to the task of geographical research.

The Twelfth Night Map is mentioned by Shakespeare in Act III, Scene 2, of his play by that name. Near the end of Scene 2, one of his characters is made to say: "He does smile his face into more lines than are in the new map, with the augmentation of the Indies."

The map in question is believed to be the Molyneux Map of 1600,[93] and a glance at it, as reproduced here, will convey the exact impression intended by Shakespeare. Quaritch in 1875 had originally advanced the idea that the *Twelfth Night* reference was to a globe map constructed by Emery Molyneux between 1589 and 1592, the first of its kind to be made in England.[94] In 1878, however, C. H. Coote, in an article entitled *Shakespeare's New Map in "Twelfth Night,"* applied Quaritch's theory to the Molyneux Map of 1600; and this view was subsequently reasserted in the Hakluyt Society's 1880 edition of *Davis' Voyages.*[95] The map has gained further literary reputation through Henry Hallam's allusion to it in his *Literature of Europe* as the "best map of the sixteenth century."[96]

The Molyneux Map of 1600 shows no indication of Drake's California visit, other than the name NOVA ALBION along the coast at about 48° of latitude. The more complete data shown by the Molyneux Globe of 1589–1592 and on the 1596 copy by Blagrave have been outlined earlier.[97]

The Gulliver's Travels Map appeared in the original edition of Jonathan Swift's celebrated book. For its discovery in connection with Drake's visit to California, we are indebted to John W. Robertson, who offered these interesting comments:

> I have found another map of this coast, more curious than authentic. It is an item properly included in our *Californiana,* although as far as I know, never before published or catalogued. It was used by Swift to localize *Brobdingnag* and can be found in the original edition of *Gulliver's Travels,* published in 1726. Necessarily this map was of English deriva-

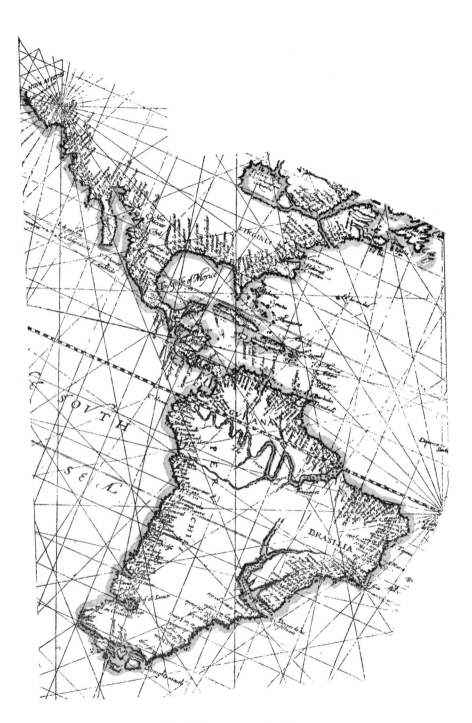

The Molyneux map of 1600.

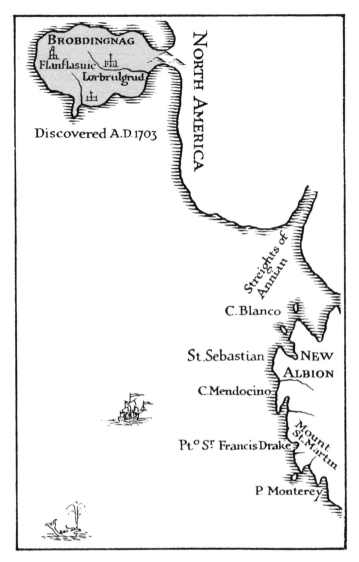

The Gulliver's Travels *map from Jonathan Swift's book by that name, 1735.*

tion, otherwise it would not have contained "Nova Albion" as a country nor would it have designated 'P°. S. Francis Drake.'

That Alaska was chosen as the land of the Giants may account for such magnified imaginings having their origin in this country of mystery and legend. The possibilities of finding its hyperborean inhabitants and its other *lusus naturae* have been no more wonderful than the actualities of its auriferous tundra and its golden sands.[98]

As Robertson indicates, Swift merely adopted a Pacific Coast locale as a setting for his imaginary tale of the Brobdingnagians.
Nevertheless, he followed the custom of contemporary mapmakers in
placing Nova Albion somewhat above Cape Mendocino, and "P^{to} S^{r}.
Francis Drake" somewhat below it.

III
PART

THE DEBATE

11
CHAPTER

*A Format for
Review and Analysis*

T HE DEBATE about Drake's anchorage location has been in progress for nearly two centuries. Navigational experts were the first to offer their comments and theories on the subject. Later, historians began to wrestle with the problem. In more recent times, ethnologists and archaeologists have spread their views on the record. The controversy reached such proportions that the California Historical Society sponsored research directed toward a solution of the riddle, and interested laymen have been intensely probing the subject. Public meetings have been held to permit the airing of views by proponents of rival anchorage locations.

The mystery surrounding Drake's California anchorage has a great appeal to scholars and laymen alike. Its background is a blend of land and sea, of the old world and the new, of the twentieth century and the sixteenth. Its characters move from the shores of old England to those of Nova Albion, from the busy bustle of the port of Plymouth to the loneliness of a never-before-visited Pacific harbor, from the high intrigues of the British court to the primitive rites of the California Indians. It dates back to the days when geographers dreamed of a northwest passage from Atlantic to Pacific, when explorers eagerly searched for a shorter route to the Spice Islands of the Orient, when treasure-laden galleons sailed the Spanish Main, and the life of an English freebooter was adventurous, albeit seldom long.

The Drake mystery, with the Pacific rim of North America as its backdrop, is centered in what was once the fabled land of Quivira and is today the Golden Gate country of northern California. Its plot involved the second world circumnavigation at its midway point, where crude headquarters had been established so that the loins of the *Golden Hind* might be girded for the final lap of the arduous journey. Its central character was the greatest adventurer, explorer, and freebooter of his time, a naval hero whose skill and daring were later to play an important role in the vanquishing of the mighty Spanish Armada, thereby saving his homeland from invasion and possible conquest.

An Approach to the Mystery

From a structural standpoint, the Drake anchorage puzzle has most of the characteristics common to every conventional tale of mystery. Its "clues" are just as numerous and fully as confusing. Its cast of characters — red, white and black[1] — is quite as colorful. Its pattern of suspense conforms to the usual standard in presenting a problem of proof, the necessity for sifting and weighing evidence, and a bewildering series of alternatives from which an answer may be selected.

The Drake enigma is, of course, unique, and its differences from the conventional pattern of mystery stories are threefold: (1) Its actors were men of flesh and blood, and its action was not a matter of imagination; (2) the underlying data can be found in any work on California history, although the century-old version in Bancroft, the original classic,[2] is still unexcelled; and (3) the reader is not limited to the presented facts, because in addition to examining the available evidence and forming his own conclusions, he has the opportunity of personally joining in the search for new evidence and of perhaps turning up a clue of his own.

As set forth in earlier chapters, our sources of information concerning Drake's activities on California shores have been threefold. They consist of (1) the contemporary accounts, containing a wealth of descriptive data about Nova Albion, but a tantalizingly limited amount of material about the harbor itself; (2) the maps and charts of the late sixteenth and early seventeenth centuries, many of them elaborate, but all of post-hoc origin and from sources of unknown authenticity; and (3) other circumstantial evidence, which has been found or may yet be found in northern California.

These sources supply the highlights of a mystery that had its origin in the earliest episode of northern California history, and in the thrilling deeds of men who dared the unknown, who lived dangerously amid the perils of sea, savages and Spanish foes, who brought a glittering fortune to California shores, and who took it away with them. In combination, they spell out the story, as we presently know it, of how the first Englishmen came to California, and also provide the only available clues to where they spent the summer of 1579.

Men with a Mission

It is amazing that there can still be available, after four hundred years, as much information as has survived to this date. No less amazing is the vigor and intensity with which advocates of the various harbors support their theories of the anchorage location. From the beginning of the controversy, the subject was never free from the heat of partisanship. In recent years, it has been aptly characterized as "this remarkably persistent, always complex, and often contentious debate."[3]

Twenty years ago, the flavor of the controversy was not lost upon Margaret Trumbull, a feature writer for one of the San Francisco dailies. In an article bemoaning her inability to attend a Historical Society meeting commemorating the 380th anniversary of Drake's arrival in California — which sounded like an innocent, if specialized, subject for an evening's gathering of people mainly interested in California history — she said:

> But having been exposed for years to the amazingly dedicated and sincere people who are firmly convinced that there is absolutely *no* mystery about *where* Sir Francis Drake landed in America ("Don't be ridiculous, of course he landed in Drake's Bay") and then meeting an equally dedicated and sincere man who also *knows* Drake landed in another place ("It's so obvious he sailed through the Golden Gate"), I've

come to the conclusion that the Hatfields and the McCoys weren't even really feuding.

Robert H. Power was the young man scheduled to speak last night at the Historical Society. And it is Power's unshakable belief that Drake and his *Golden Hind* entered the Golden Gate. Power's opposition just as sturdily affirms that Drake sailed into an inlet of Drake's Bay under Point Reyes. And there are still others who say his first landing in America was in Bolinas Lagoon or Bodega Bay.

As for me, I'm strictly neutral and uninformed. But fascinated with the fact that Power who, by the way, is a partner in the famous Nut Tree restaurant, has devoted every spare hour in the last five years to research on this subject, has absorbed an entire library of books on the life and times of Drake and his colleague, Queen Elizabeth.

Undoubtedly those who disagree with him have exactly the same fervor. And this, of course, is what makes life and horse racing. But the very thought that anything so far away and long, long ago can reach out and obsess anyone in this mobile day and age I find most impressive.

Power's explanation for choosing this particular chapter and personality in history is: "I always loved history from the sixth grade on, particularly historical mysteries. This was one. And since Drake so deeply affected American lives, I set out to try and solve."

As I say, I deeply regret I wasn't present at the Historical Society's meeting last night to hear both sides of the Drake landing question. I have a hunch that the get-together must have been explosive, exciting and provocative.[4]

In the twenty years since the foregoing words were written, there has been no abatement in the fervor of the advocates for the principal candidates for the honor of being recognized as Drake's California anchorage. Shining through every publication in which, from time to time, they air their views, is the singlemindedness with which they present their contentions and reject those of any who dare to disagree.

A Plan to Analyze the Clues

The details of how this mystery was unwittingly concocted, and of how its solution has been sought with diligence and persistence, will be unfolded in the chapters ahead. The clues to the riddle are so numerous that one would think it difficult, with their aid, to avoid arriving at a solution.

Taking the important clues — twenty in all — as a starting point, the California Historical Society conceived the idea of inviting proponents of three leading landfall locations to enter into a written debate designed to demonstrate how, if at all, the evidence associated with each clue could support the respective theories of the three debaters. The fall 1974 issue of the *California Historical Quarterly* was given over to this debate which, with its introduction, exhibits, bibliography, and explanatory notes, comprised nearly one hundred pages.

Each of the twenty clues was summarized in a sentence or two followed by a request for each debater's opinion on the subject and his explanation of how the available evidence served to support his choice of landing site. These topics or discussion subjects were given the name "Tenet"[5] as a kind of shorthand term in reference to the clues constituting the subject of debate. The hope was, of course, that from this concentrated presentation of views, some clarification might result, or consensus of opinion.

The chosen debaters were the Drake Navigators Guild for the Drake's Estero site, Professor V. Aubrey Neasham on behalf of Bolinas Lagoon, and Robert H. Power in support of San Quentin Cove. Necessarily limitations had to be put on the amount of space which the debaters could use for argument and rebuttal on each of the twenty tenets. This made it impossible for the debaters to present their arguments and counter-arguments in depth; nevertheless, they were able to set forth the substances of their positions on each tenet, and to point out, not always dispassionately, what they believed to be the weaknesses of their fellow debaters' contentions.

The Historical Society felt that from this structure of information and opinion, evidence and counterevidence, the Drake controversy could be understood by the general reader newly introduced to this historic subject and reevaluated by the scholar already acquainted with its nuances and complexities. For the purposes of this book, the structure of tenets and comment has provided a convenient framework on which to hang the pros and cons of each clue, as well as the relevant comments of earlier scholars, and conclusions from a disinterested point of view.

12

CHAPTER

The Approach

Tenet 1: Reaching the coast of what is now called South-ern Oregon early in June, 1579, Drake searched for the Northwest Passage. Not finding it, he sailed south some 300 miles to about 38° latitude where he stopped to repair the Golden Hinde. What relevance does the search for the Northwest Passage have to the landing-site controversy?

ANY STUDY of the clues pertaining to the location of Drake's California anchorage should logically begin with a review of his Mexico-to-California voyage, the story of which has been briefly told in Chapter 3.[1] Without such a review, there can be no full appreciation of the voyage's significance as a potential landing site clue, or of the inquiry by Tenet 1 concerning relevance of the search for the Northwest Passage. That search, incidentally, was made *before* Drake reached the Oregon coast, rather than after, as implied by the tenet's second sentence.

Even before leaving Guatulco, the small port south of Acapulco, Drake realized that his problem had now become one of getting safely back to Britain with his ship, its crew, and its treasure. There were three possible return routes. The first was by the way they had come, through the Straits of Magellan. The second was by way of the

Molucca islands in the East Indies, and then around the Cape of Good Hope. The third was over the top of North America, then referred to as the Northwest Passage or the Strait of Anian.

The original plans for the voyage had not contemplated a return by either of the latter two routes; in fact, no consideration had been given to the possibility of Drake even crossing the equator into the North Pacific. However, his decision at this juncture was undoubtedly largely influenced by the capture of the Rodrigo Tello frigate and its two pilots experienced for the route to the Philippines, Alonso Colchero and Martin Aguire.[2] From their navigation charts and sailing directions based upon the experience of the Manila galleons in the North Pacific, Drake probably obtained his first definite information concerning the seasonal winds and unique currents of that area, and was able to formulate his plans for the homeward journey with more certainty than theretofore.

The return route through the Straits of Magellan was ruled out for two reasons. First, he anticipated that the Spaniards would be waiting for him there "in great number and strength," as indeed they were. Second, the severe storms in that area constituted an extreme hazard.

The transpacific return route by way of the East Indies also had its drawbacks, one of which was its great length. The other was the fact that the captured sailing instructions prescribed the end of March as the official deadline for departure of Manila galleons from Acapulco if the dread typhoon season in the Philippines was to be avoided, and it was already too late to meet that deadline. Moreover, the *Golden Hind* had sprung a leak, making it necessary to find better repair facilities than were available at the Island of Caño, not to mention the need to lay in the ample supplies of wood, water, and provisions needed for a Pacific crossing or other long journey.

With these two alternatives ruled out for the time being, at least, Drake began to consider seriously the possibilities of a shorter route to home base, one which British cosmographers felt must exist. This was a waterway above what is now Canada which, if it existed and were navigable, would have provided a relatively safe and expeditious route between the Atlantic and Pacific oceans. As far back as 1564, a cartographer named Ortelius had produced a map of the world picturing the western approach to this so-called Northwest Passage as somewhere

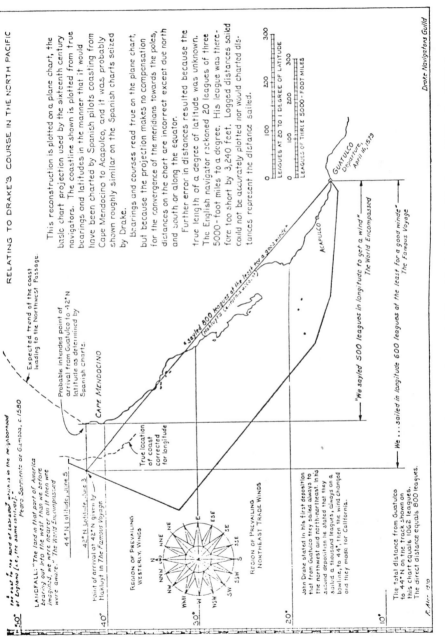

Chart by Raymond Aker showing the "Spanish course" followed by Drake from Mexico to California. (1974.)

between 45° and 48° N,[3] making it likely that it could be found, if at all, by coasting the shores of northwest America to the vicinity of 48°. Undoubtedly this was a map with which Drake was familiar.

The legendary Northwest Passage was a geographical phantasy to which even Drake had paid lip service. As he left England, interest in finding the eastern entrance to this mythical shortcut to the Orient was at its height, although no one had really given serious thought to a search for the western approach. But with his routes to the south and west temporarily unavailable, and his crew anxious to complete their already over-long journey, Drake began to think seriously of his one remaining alternative. When he talked it over with his staff, they unanimously agreed with his suggestion to try the polar route,[4] realizing at the same time that it would be necessary to make a stop somewhere along the line for repairs and reprovisioning.

Upon studying the charts and sailing directions which he had captured, Drake began to obtain an understanding of the unusual sailing conditions north of the equator. The strong winds and oceanic currents at that time of year would make it very difficult to simply hug the North American coast up to 48° N or wherever the Northwest Passage had its beginning. Rather he would have to follow what one of the contemporary accounts referred to as a "Spanish course."[5] Such a route, for Drake's purposes, would involve sailing several hundred miles due west or northwest from Mexico, then north a substantial distance to reach the eastbound sea lanes used by the galleons. Since Guatulco was approximately 2,000 miles south and 1,500 miles east of latitude 42° N, for which Drake, under his Spanish navigation plan, was heading, it was roundabout and lengthy, but nevertheless much less difficult as well as less time-consuming than the coastal route.

This leg of the journey was unusual in several respects, including the fact that few other vessels may have had occasion to sail that particular course in succeeding centuries. The status as a treasure-laden vessel made such a route rather extraordinary, as well as the fact that Drake's was a two-ship operation. Day in and day out for some 60 days and more than 3,500 miles, Rodrigo Tello's frigate, manned by members of Drake's crew, followed tenaciously in the wake of the *Hind* without losing contact—something of a feat of seamanship, if one considers the contrary winds and dense fogs encountered.

What Happened to the Search

The 3,500-mile voyage from southern Mexico to latitude 42° in the North Pacific was apparently accomplished without incident in the forty-nine days beginning April 16 and ending June 3, 1579. From that point, Drake headed their course still further north or possibly northeast (the accounts are unclear) with a view to making contact with the coast. During the night of June 3, however, the weather suddenly worsened. Despite the inclemency and bitter cold, the same course was held until somewhere between latitudes 43° and 44° N when the discomfort became so great that further northward progress was abandoned. About this same time Drake and his men found themselves unexpectedly close to land with the foul weather continuing. As a result, on June 5 they put into what *The World Encompassed* has referred to as a "bad bay." They did not land here, nor is there any record of the length of time during which their anchorage continued. However, it was at this point of the voyage that any hope of locating the Northwest Passage appears to have been abandoned.

Southward Along the Coast

The location of this "bad bay" has never been identified with certainty, except that it was on the Oregon coast. Davidson believed it to have been Chetco Cove, just above the California line, at latitude 42° 03' N.[6] On the other hand, the Drake Navigators Guild was convinced that the probable location was a cove on the south side of Point Arago, in latitude 43° 18' N (just south of Coos Bay).[7]

Although the length of layover at this cove was not reported, the early accounts did say that strong winds "commanded us to the Southward whether we would or no." The next several days were spent in sailing down the coast by day, and probably tieing up well off shore at night so as not to miss any suitable harbor in the darkness or early morning fog. Actually, the adverse weather conditions which had been encountered conferred a favor on Drake by forcing him to turn south when he did. Had the weather permitted him to continue his search for the Northwest Passage, he would probably have wound up in Puget Sound, and have spent days, possibly weeks, exploring that spacious body of water for its supposed outlet to the fabled

Northwest Passage with resulting disappointment and frustration. According to *The World Encompassed,* Drake ultimately concluded "that either there is no passage at all through these northern coasts (which is most likely) or if there be, that yet it is unnavigable." Time has proved him right.

South of Cape Mendocino

At all events, Drake continued southward, searching the coast diligently for some five degrees of latitude or more (at least 350 miles) for a suitable location for the purposes which he had in mind.[8] In all the stretch of coast from the vicinity of Coos Bay, Oregon, to that of central California, he found no protected harbor that he felt would have served his needs.

How much Drake was able to see as he cruised along, two miles or so off shore, is uncertain. From this distance, Bodega Bay would have appeared as only a minor break in a long, low plateau, while the inner waterways offered by its lagoon, or by Tomales Bay, would have been screened from view by their headlands. Visibility would have been seriously impaired whenever, as apparently was often the case, low fogs hung over the shore. The difficulty in perceiving either Bodega Lagoon or Tomales Bay from a coasting position is borne out by the fact that neither Cermeño nor Vizcaino left any record of them in exploring that area.[9]

Point Reyes is the most distinctive landmark along the northern California coast, projecting nearly ten nautical miles into the sea from the general trend of the shore. It is visible in good weather for approximately 25 miles, and ships following the coast closely have to change course to starboard to clear its massive bulk. What Drake did at this juncture has a crucial bearing on any identification of the anchorage site.

Point Reyes is situated precisely on the 38th parallel. The principal accounts say that Drake coasted the shore all the way to 38°, and we know that he saw enough of Drake's Bay to have become fully aware of the white cliffs that rim its shores. If his southward movement halted at that point, and his reading of the latitude was accurate, then it would appear that his landfall took place in Drake's Bay or Estero. If, on the other hand, his reading of 38° represented a "sea latitude,"[10] and his readings of such latitudes are known to have been 20 to 30 minutes too high,[11] then his 38° could have embraced the slightly lower 37° 49′ latitude of the Golden Gate; and the bay he entered at that latitude would have been San Francisco Bay. One can only conjecture whether the 38° was a "sea latitude" or not.

Differing Views of Men of the Sea

It was no coincidence that most of the early opinions concerning the Drake landing site were expressed by English sea captains visiting the Pacific Coast on voyages of exploration. These included Vancouver, Burney, and Beechey, each of whom was interested in the sailing route to San Francisco Bay, each took note of the ancient visit of their illustrious predecessor to the same waters, and each, like Drake, came from the north. Since each had followed, figuratively speaking, in Drake's footsteps, each had viewed Drake's Bay from what might be termed the navigational approach, that is, through the eyes of a mariner appraising it from the standpoint of Drake's needs and purposes. However, none of the three sea captains of more than a century and a half ago felt that Drake would have anchored in the bay that today bears his name.

In the latter part of the nineteenth century, another extraordinary man of the sea became a life-long student of the Drake visit to California. This was George Davidson, author of the *Coast Pilot,* the man who, as earlier indicated,[12] may have known more about the California coastline, its tides, currents, and weather, than anyone before him. Despite his original belief that Sir Francis would not have chosen Drake's Bay as an anchorage, it was his final conclusion that the *Golden Hind* had been careened, not in the Estero, but in a small cove on the north side of Point Reyes itself.

With the twentieth century, as previously noted,[13] came another marine-minded group, with a membership which included, among others, such sea lovers as Admiral Chester Nimitz and former sea captain Adolph Oko. This small dedicated band of anchorage seekers, the Drake Navigators Guild, has probably devoted more time and effort to the Drake enigma than all of their predecessors and contemporaries put together.

Despite the similarity of their backgrounds, the three groups referred to arrived at three different answers. The original sea captains unanimously voted against Drake's Bay as a feasible anchorage. Davidson opted for a cove in the outer part of Drake's Bay, but held that the Estero would not have been adequate. The Guild, premising its conclusions, like the others, to an important degree on navigational considerations, found the Estero to be the answer, not Davidson's cove in the outer bay.

Latest of the seagoing notables to register an opinion was Admiral Samuel Eliot Morison, distinguished American historian. He not only placed his stamp of approval on the Estero site, but firmly rejected the idea that Drake could ever have seen the Golden Gate.[14] It was his view that in approaching it from the north and clinging to the coast before sighting the Farallones, as Drake might have done, it would not have been possible to see the Golden Gate three miles away.

The Northwest Passage as an Anchorage Clue

Returning to Tenet 1 of the 1974 debate and its question concerning the relevance of Drake's search for the Northwest Passage, the debaters do not agree. Power stated flatly that there was no relevance. A contrary view was expressed by the Guild and Neasham; they felt that the search for the Northwest Passage was of primary importance in the identification of the California anchorage but offered no explanation of how Drake's abandonment of the search for the passage affected his ultimate selection of an anchorage.

Instead, they turned the discussion to the California scene, suggesting that if Drake had entered the Golden Gate, he would have seen waterways "leading an indefinite distance inland, possibly the sought-for passage to the Atlantic." The Guild commented that if Drake had come into San Francisco Bay, the impressions and exploration would have been documented, and the discovery would not have remained a secret for long.

These departures from the original purport of Tenet 1 caused Power to comment that his fellow debaters had changed this into a new tenet more appropriately entitled "Why Drake didn't discover the Golden Gate" and had then proceeded to make unfounded speculations. He asserted that the discovery of San Francisco Bay did not remain a secret because one Thomas Talbot, Keeper of the Records in the Tower of London, apparently provided Drake documents containing a world map and the "Portus Novae Albionis" to an associate, Jodocus Hondius; that Hondius later used the Portus Plan as an inset in his Broadside map, on which he also depicted an inlet "extending some 150 miles northeast into the land with its mouth in 38° latitude."

Summary

As Power pointed out, the Guild-Neasham comments have no relevance to the question of Drake's search for the Northwest Passage. Both conceded that Drake had made an effort, abortive though it was, to find the Northwest Passage, a circumstance which was implicit in the question posed by the tenet, and with respect to which their subsequent comments, though interesting and provocative, were beside the point. Clearly the brief search for the Northwest Passage had no relevance to the landing-site controversy.

Nevertheless, the Guild-Neasham speculative comment as to what Drake might have done in further search for the Northwest Passage within the confines of San Francisco Bay, had he ever entered that body of water, and the ideas generated by the resulting exchange of contentions are most interesting, particularly Power's allusion to a 150-mile inlet shown on the Hondius Broadside.

A closer examination of that map makes it apparent that such an inlet *is* shown at latitude 38°, extending to and beyond 38° 30' in a northeasterly direction. If one were to speculate as to a possible exploration of its "farthermost reaches using the small bark that he had with him," as the Guild suggested would have been started at once, this may, in fact, have been done, possibly during the three or four days between June 17 and 21, 1579. There is nothing in the accounts to indicate that such an exploration was not undertaken; but if not, on the other hand, how did Hondius get the information that enabled him to depict an inlet in that location and of that length? Moreover, it is conceivable that the visit of Drake and his company to the hinterland was made, in part at least, on board the bark, if his anchorage site was within San Francisco Bay.

On the other hand, there is a touch of hyperbole in the Power statement that "the discovery of San Francisco Bay did not remain a secret," apparently on no basis other than the wholly speculative statement that confidential information had been given to Hondius by a friend. If it did not remain a secret, this will come as news to a great many California historians who have long been under a contrary impression. But the additional suggestion by Power that Talbot apparently provided a world map to Hondius, although equally speculative, does offer a basis for still further comment as follows:

1. The "world map" assertedly furnished to Hondius, or to which he was given access, could have been a copy of the French Drake Map or the Silver Map.[15]

2. Both of these extremely early maps, the former dating back in the estimation of experts to 1581, undoubtedly formed the basis for Hondius' Broadside, the Silver Map because of important similarities to the Broadside indicating that Hondius used it as a model, and the French Drake Map because of his obvious borrowing of its two lower insets.[16]

3. Assuming that Hondius did obtain his information in part from the French Drake Map, or from such original sources as the Drake or Fletcher records, of what significance is the fact that his Broadside pictures the bay of Nova Albion as extending from 38° inland and northward to 38° 30' and beyond?[17]

13

CHAPTER

The Latitudes

Tenet 2: Several early accounts of the Drake voyage report conflicting latitude designations for Drake's landing site. How are these to be reconciled with the proposed landing site?

IN UNDERTAKING to pinpoint the location of Drake's California anchorage, the reports of the early accounts with respect to its latitude are among the most important clues. The contemporary narratives usually mentioned a latitude for Nova Albion, but they varied widely, from 48° on the north, which would be near the island of Vancouver, to 38° in central California. Even the figures of the two primary accounts, based on reports prepared by, or from information furnished by, members of the crew of the *Golden Hind*, were not in agreement with each other.[1]

"The Famous Voyage," in describing Drake's approach to his California landfall, reported that when we "came within 38. degrees towards the line ... it pleased God to send us into a faire and good Baye, with a good winde to enter the same." The essential information on the same subject in *The World Encompassed* was as follows: "From the height of 48 deg., in which we now were, to 38, we found the land by coasting alongst it, to be but low and reasonable plain.... In 38 deg. 30 min. we fell with a convenient and fit harborough, and June 17 came to anchor therein."

Since a degree of latitude is equal to approximately 70 miles, and there are 60 minutes in each degree of latitude, one latitudinal minute amounts to slightly more than a mile and 30 minutes to approximately 35 miles. So, although the discrepancy between the two accounts, 38° versus 38° 30', is only 30 minutes, or half a degree, roughly equal to 35 miles, it has become controversial because within that area of 35 miles lie the several harbors referred to earlier. A decisive determination between these two latitudes may never be possible, yet it is worthwhile to review the language of the accounts, as well as other evidence, to see whether anything has been overlooked, or the two latitudes can be reconciled with each other.

Preliminary Considerations

In evaluating the information contained in these accounts, some assumptions will be made: (1) That the latitudes given were not intended to refer to the same location, that is, the place where Drake entered the bay and the place where he repaired his ship (although this in itself is controversial and will be discussed later);[2] (2) that the two accounts had a common source, as established in Chapter 8;[3] and (3) that it is therefore reasonable to believe that differences in the latitudes given by the two accounts are attributable to the treatment of Fletcher's original journal or material by their respective compilers.

Based upon such assumptions, two questions appear pertinent: (1) Can the Nova Albion latitudes set forth in the two narratives be reasonably reconciled with each other? (2) Which compilation, in the light of all circumstances, is the more reliable and persuasive?

Also entitled to preliminary note is the fact that *The World Encompassed* appears to have used the Fletcher journal essentially *in toto* to present as detailed a narrative of the California visit as possible.[4] *The World Encompassed* contains dates and details that could not have been recalled fifty, or even five, years later, thereby suggesting the probability that it reflected rather accurately the events of the voyage as they were recorded day by day by Fletcher in his journal. *The World Encompassed* has been found to be reasonably error-free, so far as the

AMERICÆ PARS VIII.
Continens

PRIMO, DESCRIPTIONEM
TRIVM ITINERVM NOBILISSIMI
ET FORTISSIMI EQVITIS FRANCISCI DRAKEN,
QVI PERAGRATO PRIMVM VNIVERSO TERRARVM ORBE,
poſtea cum nobiliſſimo Equite IOHANNE HAVCKENS, ad expugnandum ciuitatem PANAMA, in Indiam nauigauit, vbi vitam
ſuam ambo finierunt.

SICVNDO, *iter nobiliſſimi Equitis* THOMÆ CANDISCH, *qui duorum ferè annorum ſpacio, 13000. Anglicana miliaria in mari confecit, vbi deſcribuntur quoque omnia quæ in hoc itinere ipſi acciderunt & viſa ſunt.*

TERTIO, *duo itinera, nobiliſſimi & fortiſſimi Domini* GVALTHERI RALEGH *Equitis & deſignati gubernatoris Regij in Anglia præſidij, nec non fortiſſimi Capitanei* LAVRENTII KEYMS.

QVIBVS ITINERIBVS DESCRIBITVR AVRIFERVM ET PÓ-
tentiſſimum Regnum GVIANA, ad Septentrionem fluminis ORENOQVE, aliàs ORE-
LIANA dicti, ſitum, cum metropoli eius MANOA & MACVIEGVARAI,
aliisq́; finitimis regionibus & fluuiis, mercibus item præſtantiſſimis,
& mercatura, quæ in regno hoc exercetur.

PRIMO QVIDEM ANGLICANA LINGVA PARTIM AB EQVITIBVS IPSIS, PAR-
*tim ab aliis, qui hiſce itineribus interfuerunt, ſparſim conſignata: Iam verè in vnum Corpus
redacta, & in Latinum Sermonem conuerſa, auctore*

M. GOTARDO ARTVS DANTISCANO.

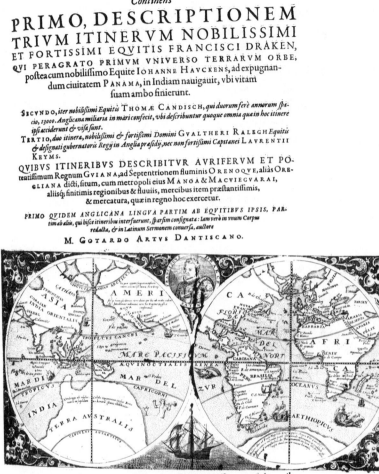

Figuris & imaginibus artificiosè illuſtrata & in lucem emiſſa, opera & ſumptibus
THEODORICI de BRY P. M. relictæ Viduæ & filiorum.
ANNO M. D. XCIX.

Title page of De Bry's 1599 Americae Pars III.

California sojourn is concerned. Apart from the elimination of material unfavorable to Sir Francis (none of it pertaining to Nova Albion), it has been found to be a substantially accurate, as well as the only unabridged, report of the entire circumnavigation.

Hakluyt, on the other hand, had many problems. He operated under the handicap of having to prepare an abridged version of the voyage and to publish it surreptitiously. He was also error-prone, and

"The Famous Voyage," particularly the 1589 version, was loaded with mistakes of commission, omission, and inadvertence. So many were his errors that a separare chapter would be required to tell their story alone, if that subject were to be adequately treated.[5] However, his eminence as a chronicler of maritime affairs has been such that his infallibility has been taken for granted. His tomes on adventures of the sea have been generally accepted as accurate and reliable although, if "The Famous Voyage" is typical, the opposite is true. This, of course, is an important factor to be considered when weighing the differences in latitudes reported by the two principal contemporary accounts.

Other Factors to be Considered

In addition to the actual or apparent inconsistencies of the accounts themselves, and particularly the known unreliability of "The Famous Voyage," we may not be dealing with precise latitudes, but rather with those which Drake was able to obtain with the instruments at his disposal and under varying conditions. As for Nova Albion, the reported latitudes were almost certainly those listed in the official diary or notes of Francis Fletcher (a journal, rather than a log), possibly rounded out to even degrees, or major fractions thereof. So we have a double factor of potential variance, and consequently no assurance that the discrepancy in latitudes can be resolved by any present means of analysis.

Getting back to our specific problem, the principal accounts provide us with seemingly simple alternatives: The rather fundamental 38° of "The Famous Voyage" or the somewhat less familiar 38° 30′ of *The World Encompassed*.[6] Actually both accounts mentioned the latitude of 38°, from which it appears that this was the southernmost point reached in the run down the coast, before the eventual departure in July. *The World Encompassed* did not contradict this statement, but did say that after coasting along the land from 48° to 38°, Drake dropped anchor at latitude 38° 30′, leaving the inference that the coast was left behind at 38° although the "convenient and fit harborough" was not reached until 38° 30′.

What of the conflict between "The Famous Voyage" latitude of 38° and the 38½° of *The World Encompassed*? Despite Hakluyt's anxiety to correct all his various errors, he did not succeed in doing so. In his blundering efforts with the 1600 edition, he only managed to rectify some of the errors that had been called to his attention. As to the finer points not picked up by others nor originally perceived by himself, no changes were made. Could it be that one of the latter was his failure to grasp the significance of Fletcher's original statement that while Drake sailed south along the coast to latitude 38°, he came to anchor in a "convenient and fit harborough" at latitude 38° 30'? If so, and he had corrected the oversight in his 1600 edition, a source of much confusion and apparent conflict that was to baffle students of the Drake anchorage mystery for generations to come might have been avoided.

Possibility of Reconciliation

A reconstruction of Drake's movements with a view to achieving a reconciliation of the accounts in reference to the latitudes which they mention, suggests that their compilers, between them, were intending to say something like the following: "With the help of a good wind it pleased God to send us into a fair and good Bay at latitude 38°, after which we continued to latitude 38° 30' where we fell with and anchored in a convenient and fit harborough."

This proposed reconciliation of the accounts in reference to the California latitudes does no violence to the language of either. There is nothing in it inconsistent with the information contained in "The Famous Voyage." Both accounts say that the ship was *anchored* on the 17th, but neither says *when it entered* the bay or *how long* it took after entering to reach the anchorage site. "The Famous Voyage" did say that anchorage took place in the bay, but this does not rule out a protected cove or small haven within the bay, nor preclude one which might require sailing for several minutes of latitude to reach after entering the bay. All of such apparent discrepancies can well find explanation in Hakluyt's need for condensation, as witness his glaring omission of key information as to the arrival date at the anchorage site.[7]

Such a proposed reconciliation necessarily becomes feasible only if the latitude at which entry into the bay is contemplated is adjusted to reflect the known factor of Drake errors in reports of other latitudes (averaging 16 minutes),[8] for example, to reduce the 38° figure to approximately 37° 44', which is roughly equivalent to the latitude of the

Golden Gate entrance to San Francisco Bay. If the bay entered was the San Francisco Bay, it follows that the movement thereafter to, or toward, the anchorage site at 38° 30' must have been within the bay.

The foregoing hypothesis represents one of three alternatives, the other two being to assume that Drake simply backtracked along the coast, or to do as Hakluyt did and simply disregard the report of a further movement to 38° 30'. Assuming a northward trek by one route or another, consideration would again have to be given to adjustment for the factor of latitudinal error.

Responses by Debate Participants

When Tenet 2 asked how the conflicting latitude designations of the early accounts were to be reconciled with the proposed landing site, it meant, of course, with the site proposed by each answering participant. The question was not really covered by any of the answers, apparently because the word "reconciled" was disregarded. Apart from a bare mention of latitudes 48° and 44°, and an equally desultory reference to the 38° 30' of *The World Encompassed,* the responses were limited to a discussion of latitude 38°, and each participant contented himself with asserting that the evidence pointed to 38° as the correct latitude.

The Guild stated that ". . . study of the various latitudes shows that relaxation of secrecy surrounding Drake's voyage reduced the published latitude to 38°. Point Reyes lies at 38° 00' N and the Drake's Estero encampment at 38° 02' N." Neasham disposed of the subject with the comment that "Most authorities today accept 38°, essentially as given in Hakluyt's account," adding: "The only plausible anchorage for Drake within this range would be Bolinas Bay, which lies at about 37° 54'. Bolinas Lagoon, its inner harbor, is about 37° 55'."

Power put it this way:

> The first published account of Drake's landing in Nova Albion . . . states that the 'faire and good Baye' was in 38°. This has proven to be the correct latitude. . . . For Dr. Neasham to make the statement, "The only plausible anchorage for Drake within this range [i.e., south of 38°] would be Bolinas Bay, which lies at about 37° 54'," is deceptive. San Francisco Bay in the exact same range is *prima facie* a plausible anchorage.

The Case for Latitude 38°

This imaginary line runs squarely through the heart of Marin County from east to west. Marin County has enjoyed a special status in California history, with a tradition antedating even such early Spanish visitors as Cermeño and Vizcaino, to both of whom it was inhospitable. It teems with small harbors, having three situated within six latitudinal minutes, that is, one-tenth of a degree, of the 38th parallel on the county's Pacific side, and another two within the same distance on the bay side.

The number of small harbors is a geographical feature in which the Marin citizenry take considerable pride. Along with Mount Tamalpais and Muir Woods, the Marin inhabitants tend to regard the harbors as one of the county's great natural resources and to look askance at anyone having the temerity to question latitude 38° in relation to Drake. If invited to do so, they would probably present the case for latitude 38°, stated succinctly, as follows:[9]

1. Hakluyt was the most celebrated chronicler of voyages of the Elizabethan era, and "The Famous Voyage" was not only the first but the most significant account of the circumnavigation. Working from contemporary sources, he reported the latitude of the California anchorage to have been 38°.

2. His report was soon followed by other accounts giving the same latitude, such as Stow's *Chronicles Of England* (1592),[10] Blundeville (1594), Camden (1615), and Dudley (1646-1647), each showing some indication of having been based upon first-hand sources. The Stow account may have even preceded that of Hakluyt, because it is not clear whether the inserts comprising "The Famous Voyage" appeared in any copies of Hakluyt's volume before 1593 or 1594.

3. There are several reasons for believing latitude 38° to have been correct. Drake was proficient in the determining of latitudes and his observation, presumably made on land, was therefore likely to have been accurate. Nova Albion was the departure point for the long transpacific leg of the journey, hence accuracy was of vital importance. And finally, according to Raymond Aker: "The status of this latitude is almost conclusively resolved in favor of 38°, however, by the evident fact that Hakluyt who had access to the same source as the compiler of the *World Encompassed*, . . . rejected '38 deg. 30.' in favor of '38. degrees towards the line'."[11]

Rebuttal

1. The reporting by later chroniclers of the same latitude as Hakluyt is of questionable significance. There is persuasive evidence that "The Famous Voyage" was indeed the first published account of the circumnavigation, since it has been found in all but a few copies of Hakluyt's 1589 edition.[12] This means that it served as a fountainhead of information for later mapmakers and chroniclers whose reporting of a similar latitude represented a borrowing rather than a confirmation.

2. Since the sources of "The Famous Voyage" and *The World Encompassed* were the same, so far as the California visit was concerned, it is obvious that Hakluyt omitted a substantial part of Fletcher's story on Nova Albion because of Hakluyt's problem in having to condense his material to fit into the twelve pages he had available for the entire account. Whether he "rejected" the omitted portions or simply edited out the material that *he* happened to consider nonessential may be regarded as a matter of semantics.

Hakluyt had a genius for making mistakes, some of them important, in his editing of unfamiliar material, and his handling of latitudes was no exception. The question is to what extent did Fletcher's mention of a second latitude, that is, 38° 30′, after stating that Drake had coasted Northwest Pacific shores all the way to 38°, confuse Hakluyt. If he deleted the 38° 30′ in an attempt to clarify the matter—for himself, at least—such confusion is understandable. Historians and anchorage seekers alike have usually had their minds so firmly focused on the concept of a small coastal bay that they have found it impossible to comprehend the possibility of Drake's having to travel another several minutes in latitude after entering the "faire and good Baye."

3. The accuracy of the Nova Albion readings of latitude is suspect. No one knows with certainty who took the readings or where either was taken, and any ideas on the subject can only be conjectural. Indeed, the well-known differences between actual latitudes and those taken at Nova Albion would seem to be indispensable factors in arriving at any resolution of the latitude controversy.

The Case for Latitude 38° 30′

1. *The World Encompassed* (as well as "The Famous Voyage") relied on Fletcher for its story of Nova Albion. There are good reasons for

believing that it used the Fletcher account substantially verbatim, including, of course, its report of the two Nova Albion latitudes. While Hakluyt had the same account before him, he was not averse to taking liberties with it to suit his own purposes.[13] Of these, the most impelling was his necessity for abridgment, but other factors included his penchant for recasting some of Fletcher's statements in his own words and his tendency to edit out data which he considered confusing or nonessential. Since his ensuing record of known omissions and errors is what may be expected from this type of editorial treatment of an unfamiliar manuscript,[14] there is every probability that Hakluyt simply deleted the reference to latitude 38° 30′ without realizing what he had done.

2. As the only uncondensed account of the voyage, *The World Encompassed* is more explicit in every way. It is the only narrative that speaks of a "harborough," of winding up at 38° 30′ after coasting southward to 38°, of the details of time spent in survey after first arriving, and of more than one Nova Albion latitude. Since it is the only account that mentions both 38° and 38° 30′, it is conceivable that each had a separate significance, and that both may be capable of coordination or reconciliation.

3. Latitude 38° 30′ had early cartographic confirmation. The Hondius Broadside plainly shows 38° as the latitude of the point of entry into the Bay of Nova Albion, with the latter then extending inward and northward to 38° 30′ and beyond, evidently based on information obtained from original sources and subsequently confirmed by *The World Encompassed* latitudes for bay and anchorage. The French Drake map appears to show the Nova Albion latitude at approximately 38½°.[15] This map, possibly dating back to 1581,[16] before the imposition of a ban on the publication of accurate information, could have provided the very first indication of the anchorage latitude, either by publication or cartography, thus antedating "The Famous Voyage" by several years.

4. The known inaccuracy of Drake's latitudes is a factor to be considered, because they were ordinarily a few minutes too high,[17] particularly when taken under unfavorable conditions. The anchorage solutions based on 38° are predicated on the assumption that Drake's latitudes were entirely accurate.

5. Importance must be attached to the fact that the two principal accounts really do not contradict each other in any material respect

and, assuming the previously mentioned latitudinal adjustments, are capable of being read together. In a mystery which has thus far proved to be solution proof, and with the paucity of available clues of fully dependable character, no scrap of evidence, however obscure or unpromising, should be disregarded. *The World Encompassed* clue, on careful analysis, may have more to offer than meets the casual eye.

Rebuttal

1. Since *The World Encompassed* differs from other sources in giving Drake's port a latitude of "38 deg. 30 min.", somewhere in one of the collections of notes at the compiler's disposal, he probably found a description of Nova Albion prefaced with this latitude and, since it was contemporary, accepted it at face value.[18] However, "The Famous Voyage" was the original and is still the accepted authority for 38° as the latitude for Nova Albion. The repeated and uncontradicted statements of a similar figure by other early accounts suggest that the 38½° latitude is incorrect.

2. *The World Encompassed* was not published until forty years after "The Famous Voyage," and its compiler could have had no personal knowledge of the many details which it purported to present. Hakluyt, on the other hand, probably had opportunities to secure first-hand information from both Drake and Fletcher. *The World Encompassed* is of greater length, but this does not assure its accuracy in every particular.

3. The discrepancy in the latitude of Drake's port can be accounted for by the probability that the 38° 30' of *The World Encompassed* was taken at sea, that is, by dead-reckoning, since Drake's sea latitudes have been found to be invariably too high by 20 to 30 minutes.[19] The observation for Nova Albion was probably made on land, and therefore any error in the reading of 38° would have been minimal.

4. In referring to a map of California by Henry Briggs published by Purchas in 1625 and showing a port by the name of Sir Francisco Draco, Wagner commented: "There can hardly be any doubt that the appearance on this map of a Port Sir Francis Drake in 38½° convinced the compiler of the *World Encompassed* that the 38° in which it had been located in the *Famous Voyage* was an error and thus brought about the interpolation of the new figure in that book."[20]

Summary

An analysis of the contentions advanced in support of each latitude makes it clear that there is no conclusive evidence to provide support for either position. Nevertheless, the theories and arguments advanced have been set forth as confidently and positively as though they were established facts. Such phrases as "most significant account," "almost conclusively resolved," "primary source of information," "evidently based on information," and "can hardly be any doubt" are all words of wishful thinking and expressions designed to bolster a particular point of view.

Returning, however, to the comments of the debaters themselves, they contain no hint of any conflicting latitudes that might require reconciliation. This is one of the few tenets of the 1974 debate on which there is virtually no disagreement. As the Guild has said: "Latitude 38° limits the area of search for the landing site to a small distance north or south but does not pinpoint the site."

Since the debaters are satisfied that 38° was the correct latitude, the express request of Tenet 2 for a reconciliation of latitudes given by the principal accounts has been disregarded. Whether it was a matter of oversight or simply felt not to be necessary was not made to appear. No one would suggest that it was in any way influenced by the fact that latitude 38° constitutes an integral factor in the anchorage theory of each of the participants. Whatever the reason, the evidence of the narrative which offers more information than any other on the subject of anchorage latitudes has been quietly relegated to limbo.

14

CHAPTER

The White Cliffs

Tenet 3: Drake discovered "white bancks and cliffes, which lie toward the sea" rimming what is today called Drake's Bay on the south (sic) side of Point Reyes. They reminded him of old England (Albion) and inspired the name Nova Albion. What course did Drake follow after sighting the remarkable coastal formation?

THERE IS one clue to the anchorage puzzle which remains as visible and durable as in the days of Drake—the white cliffs of Drake's Bay. Presumably, these were the same white cliffs referred to in virtually identical language by "The Famous Voyage" and *The World Encompassed*. Both accounts spoke of "the white banks and cliffs, which lie toward the sea," and indicated that they were one of the reasons why Drake gave the country the name of Nova Albion.

Along the western and northern shores of Drake's Bay are narrow beaches, backed by rolling lands rising to two and three hundred feet. The ridges of these rolling lands lie transversely to the sea. Weatherbeaten and seaworn, these ridges present a series of white cliffs which commence at the southwesternmost angle of the harbor and sweep for six miles to the east-southeast. They attain elevations of up to three hundred feet, and were particularly referred to by Cabrera Bueno as landmarks for the Estero Limantour.

By those who are convinced that the rocky features thus described by the principal contemporary accounts were those situated at Drake's Bay, the latter are regarded as a benchmark,[1] so to speak, in connection with Drake's visit to California for a number of reasons: (1) They represent a spectacular, enduring, and unmistakable landmark indicating that he came at least this far south, if no farther; (2) they must have seemed a good omen to Drake, providing a sentimental reminder of the homeland; and (3) their deep impression on Drake played a part in his naming this newly found region New England, after Albion, the Latin name for England, presumably because of their remarkable resemblance to the celebrated white cliffs of Dover.

The *"Seven Sisters," white cliffs on the Sussex seacoast of England. (From* Pacific Discovery, *March-April, 1958, p. 14.)*

Differing Views on the Subject

As with most anchorage clues, the opinions of Drake scholars about the white cliffs differ. Henry R. Wagner, for example, questioned whether the white banks and cliffs thus referred to were indeed those in the bay in which Drake anchored. Wagner believed that since there were many white cliffs along the coastline, as well as very conspicuous white sand dunes, it was the general white aspect of the shoreline, resembling that of the English Channel, which brought to

THE WHITE CLIFFS

Drake's mind the name of Nova Albion, and not any white cliffs at the particular anchorage site. In other words, Nova Albion was not the particular spot where Drake repaired his ship, but an expanse of country covering perhaps five or six degrees of latitude. When Wagner listed the factors that might serve to identify the harbor in which the *Golden Hind* was repaired, he did not include the white cliffs as a significant factor.

John W. Robertson, a contemporary of Wagner, listed five conditions which the true anchorage must satisfy, one of which was that "the coast must be marked by white cliffs bearing some resemblance to the white cliffs of Dover that gave to England the name 'Albion'." He went on to say that white cliffs are a marked feature of the California coast, that they are found at Bodega Bay, as well as at the approach to the Bay of San Francisco. Moreover, nothing, he felt, in either "The Famous Voyage" or *The World Encompassed* can be so construed as to make it a necessary conclusion that the Drake harbor was marked by white cliffs; that "the white cliffs" is merely an identification of that coastline "which lies toward the sea," in other words, a part of the ocean shore which marks and characterizes the country that Drake called Nova Albion.

A third Drake expert, Raymond Aker, agrees that the principal accounts attribute the name Nova Albion, in part at least, to the white banks and cliffs which lie toward the sea, but also believes that these features may bear no direct relationship to the landing site. Yet he believes that to inspire the name, they must have been relatively close by, as well as to have some likeness to the cliffs bordering the English channel. The California coast has no white cliffs that show prominently from the sea, and those at Drake's Bay are not significant to ships passing offshore. Aker directs attention to the fact that some orientation may exist in the words "which lie toward the sea." In summarizing the case for Drake's Estero, Aker argues that white cliffs do, indeed, lie toward the sea from the Estero; and that the white cliffs at Drake's Bay — reminiscent of home — offered a persuasive reason for conferring the name Nova Albion on the area visited.

Poorly Framed Query

Tenet 3 referred to the white cliffs of what is today Drake's Bay, and asked the debaters to indicate the course followed by Drake after

The white cliffs of Drake's Bay, California. (From Pacific Discovery, *March-April, 1958, p. 15.)*

sighting them. Unfortunately, this was not a query designed to elicit meaningful answers. To begin with, the question was based on an assumption, not agreed to by either Wagner or Robertson, that the white cliffs referred to were those which rim Drake's Bay. It mistakenly referred to Drake's Bay as being on the *south* side of Point Reyes; and, finally, it was pointless in asking about the course followed by Drake after sighting the cliffs which it assumed were those at Drake's Bay.

In other words, the question posed to the participants was simply, assuming that Drake had come this far, where did he go after seeing the white cliffs of Drake's Bay. The question really represents the crux of the whole landfall controversy. In a sense, the search for the anchorage begins at this point and there, also, is where the Drake Navigators Guild thinks it ended.

Views of Proponents of the Coastal Bays

As the Guild sees it, when the white cliffs were sighted, the *Golden Hind* had inadvertently entered the mouth of Drake's Bay, "sent in, as it were, by godsend."[2] At this point, Drake had diligently searched along 350 miles of coast, and was in urgent need of a suitable harbor. Why pass by this bay and estuary without examination when nothing better was in sight? Actually the Estero was visible from outside the bay, and could have been seen at a distance of more than six miles from a height equivalent to that of a lookout's post in the *Golden Hind's* tops.

To one searching for a harbor and source of fresh water, the Estero to the north could not have failed to attract attention. With a change of course and a single tack with the prevailing westerly wind, Drake's ship would have brought him to the mouth of the Estero. His ship's tender would soon have found the entering channel, and a flood tide near high water would have allowed the ship to kedge to an inner anchorage on the day of arrival at the site.

According to the Guild, there are no breakers at the Estero entrance, and Davidson stated in the nineteenth century that "coasters can enter with the prevailing northwest wind." Francisco de Bolanos, who visited the bay with Cermeño in 1595 and with Vizcaino in 1603, wrote: "An *estero* enters with a very good mouth without breakers." The Guild believes that the Estero would have been a pleasant surprise to Drake, and he would not have looked further.

As visualized by Neasham, Drake probably rounded Point Reyes and then would have followed generally an eastsoutheast course in the direction of what is now Bolinas Bay. He would have had a good view of Drake's Bay and its two possible careening sites on the lee side of Point Reyes and at the Estero entrance. He may even have altered his course somewhat to look at them. Apparently neither spot fitted his requirements. Going on to the indentation marked by Bolinas Bay, which was visible, he anchored some distance offshore. He did not enter the inner harbor on the day of arrival, June 17. His ship lay four days in the outer harbor, while his small boats searched carefully for the place he sought.

The Case for San Francisco Bay

As Power viewed the situation, Drake was sailing under a cloud of discouragement on June 17, 1579. He had failed to find the Northwest Passage, his ship leaked, water and provisions were in short supply and, in more than 400 miles of exploration, the coast had not yielded a suitable anchorage.

But, as Power explained, signs of good fortune came in rapid succession on June 17. When Drake's two ships rounded Point Reyes and sailed eastward across Drake's Bay to engage the coast again, the white cliffs amazingly like those of England became visible, but insignificant from the sea was the entrance to Drake's Estero. The coast continued to hold past Bolinas and Mount Tamalpais. Then the Golden Gate came into view, and a wind peculiar to the Golden Gate (Power calls it the unique bernoulli[3] wind) "sent" the expedition into that waterway. The captured frigate served as a pilot for hidden dangers, so Drake was able to progress with safety into San Francisco Bay. The bernoulli wind's principal force turns northward, and thus the *Golden Hind* probably sailed into Raccoon Strait, where it came to anchor in the lee of Angel Island.

In rebuttal to the position of the Guild, Power contended that its statement that Drake "had inadvertently entered the mouth of Drake's Bay" is erroneous, because to the Elizabethans Drake's Bay was a part of the ocean and had no definable "mouth." In rebuttal to the statement that the Estero to the north "could not have failed to attract attention," Power cited Davidson's 1887 statement that Drake "could not have detected the entrance [to Drake's Estero] from his vessel." There is a conflict between the Guild's statement that the *Golden Hind* was kedged into an inner anchorage and Hakluyt's account which said the anchorage was entered with a "good wind." In rebuttal to the position of Neasham, Power had the following to say: "Bolinas Bay is even more a part of the ocean than Drake's Bay. It, too, has no mouth to enter; it is neither fit, convenient, fair, nor a good 'Baye harborough'."

Unhelpful Responses

The debaters were obliged by the language of Tenet 3 to assume that the white cliffs at Drake's Bay were those referred to by the contemporary accounts, although there is no certainty that such was the case. There are other cliffs of a whitish hue[4] on the coastal side of California,[5] including Lime Rock near the north portal of the Golden Gate.[6] On the other hand, two facts link the cliffs with the naming of the Nova Albion area: (1) The remarkable resemblance of those at Drake's Bay in size and configuration to the chalky cliffs, known as the Seven Sisters, which overlook the channel at Dover; and (2) their location virtually on the 38th parallel.

How often Drake may have seen the cliffs was not reported. Perhaps they were visible on clear days from the anchorage site; perhaps he saw them only once, as he passed through Drake's Bay waters heading for his "convenient and fit harborough." Whatever may have been the case, the cliffs made a deep impression on Drake because the accounts agree that they were one of the principal factors in his selection of a name for "this country."

From an objective point of view, the answers to Tenet 3 could only describe a more or less direct movement from the vicinity of the cliffs to whatever site each participant happened to espouse. No new or helpful purpose could have been expected to be served by such a request, nor was any useful information elicited thereby.

Summary

Despite the negative implications in the views of Wagner and Robertson, and the negative results so far as responses to Tenet 3 are concerned, it is possible that the white cliffs do provide a clue. As suggested by Aker, the cryptic words "which lie toward the sea" may denote some orientation. They represent a rather unusual wording which suggests not only a common source, but also one for which (or for whom) the language in question had a special significance.

What the intended meaning of this ambiguous phrase may have been will always remain the author's secret. Power has concluded that the "white banks and cliffs" are unquestionably those at Point Reyes, and that the textual association of the cliffs is "toward the sea," in other words, "not in the port itself."[7] He adds: "Admittedly, an anchorage at Drake's Estero would meet these criteria since it would lie just north of the white cliffs. On the other hand, in no sense does this disqualify San Francisco Bay as a moorage site, for no one can dispute the fact that the white cliffs do indeed lie 'toward the sea' from San Francisco Bay."

Power has also reasoned that the phrase "toward the sea" disqualifies at least one previously proposed anchorage site, to wit, that within the sheltering arm of Point Reyes espoused by Davidson.

Power based this conclusion on the fact that at the Point Reyes site, the white cliffs would have been east of and fully visible from the anchorage. This geographical fact has contributed to the opinion of the Guild that the only possible anchorage at Drake's Bay was north, that is, behind the white cliffs in Drake's Bay.

Taken at face value, the ambiguous phrase may have been describing features of the coastline generally, cliffs that merely face toward the Pacific somewhere in the general area referred to as Nova Albion, since they were a part of the inspiration for its name. This is a reasonable interpretation of its significance, but would, of course, divest it of any value as a clue to the landing site, and thus entitle no one of the debate participants to points in the anchorage contest.

Conceivably, however, Fletcher's mysterious phrase may have had a more subtle significance. It did not speak of cliffs which *face* the sea, but of cliffs which "*lie toward* the sea." The word "face" could be one of location, whereas "lie," coupled with "toward," tends to be one of direction. From this repeated use of the word "lie" may well be inferred an intent to identify the location of the cliffs, not only with relation to the sea, but also with relation to the anchorage itself.

If intended to convey such an orientation, the phrase, as Power has indicated, would fit the Estero perfectly. Also, as he has asserted, although less plausibly, no one can deny that the cliffs do "lie toward the sea" from San Francisco Bay. They can hardly be said, however, to lie between Bolinas, Bodega, or Tomales bays and the sea, and the same is true of the anchorage in the lee of Point Reyes which was Davidson's choice. The weight to be attributed to such an interpretation, as well as its application to the competing harbors, can only be a matter for individual conjecture.

CHAPTER

The Harbor of
Refuge

*Tenet 4: Identify the "faire and good Baye" mentioned in
Richard Hakluyt's accounts and the "conuenient and fit
harborough" described in* The World Encompassed.

URING THE circumnavigation Drake found it desirable to
make periodic stops to recondition his ship and rest his crew.
The sojourn at Nova Albion was one of the lengthiest and
most important of such breaks in the tedium of the long voyage.
Hakluyt regarded it as of such interest and significance that he gave it a
separate and special write-up in his 1600 edition.

Even before leaving Mexico, Drake's plans had included a rest and
reconditioning stop on the northwest coast, with the idea that it would
also serve as the jumping-off place for the first long leg of the homeward journey. He had a good idea of the kind of location needed, but
only a vague notion of where he would find it. Dogged by unfortunate weather and slowed by a heavily laden and leaky ship, he was in
desperate need of that "conuenient and fit harborough". How urgent
the need finally became may be judged by the fact that although he left
Mexico with a 50-day supply of water, he did not reach Nova Albion
until 62 days later.

None of the accounts tells us what the characteristics of a "fit harborough" may have been in the peculiar circumstances in which Drake found himself in the summer of 1579. However, they were not limited to a mere need for good careenage and resupply facilities. The great freebooter had created his own set of additional requirements by the enmity engendered in Spanish America and the special part of the world in which he chose to seek refuge. Hence the requisite characteristics would have included the following:

1. A sheltered harbor suitable for the careening and repair of a leaky vessel, together with a safe means of access into the harbor with sufficient depth to accommodate the draft of the ship in its loaded condition.

2. A location with adequate supplies of food, water, and firewood close by, or within a reasonable distance.

3. A location suitable for construction of a fort of sorts, including natural materials for that purpose nearby.

4. A location that would be reasonably secure from Spanish discovery and attack while the ship is in a vulnerable position.

5. A location that would also be free from attack or other interference by natives of the area.

"Baye" or "harborough"?

Tenet 4 is the first of a series (4 to 7 inclusive) dealing with the features which Drake might have considered essential in the harbor he sought on the northwest coast, together with a debate comparison on how well each of the three proposed anchorage sites supplied these features. Underlying the whole matter of harbor suitability, however, has been the perplexing question of whether the *Golden Hind* anchored in a "Baye," as stated by "The Famous Voyage," or in a "harborough," as reported by *The World Encompassed*. It is to this issue that Tenet 4 has been directed.

It was Power's position that the "Baye" and the "harborough" were one and the same body of water. He asserted that there was no significance to the editorial choice of these terms since they were, to all intents and purposes, synonymous. The Guild and Neasham espoused the contrary view, suggesting that it would seem manifest that Drake put into some kind of an inner waterway from the use by various

Drake's Beach. (Philip Hyde.)

accounts of the terms "harborow" ("Anonymous Narrative"), "harborough"(*The World Encompassed*), "Il porto bonissimo" (Dudley), and "Portus" (Hondius).[1] They pointed to Drake's Bay and Estero, and to Bolinas Bay and Lagoon in support of this position.

The Guild argued that Drake's Bay meets the criteria of Hakluyt's "faire and good Baye," "faire" meaning attractive and impressive, and "good" in the nautical sense of having no navigational dangers while providing good shelter and holding ground with reasonable depths for anchoring. For Drake's purposes, "conuenient and fit" would have referred to an inner cove suitable for careening, ready access to the sea, adjacency to the beach, a freshwater spring, and a site from which surveillance of the outer bay could have been maintained. According to the Guild, the Estero had been used as a harbor well into the 1920s by small vessels.

The Guild contended further that in Drake's day a bay was open to the sea, whereas a harbor was protected by natural or man-made features, citing Sir Henry Mainwaring's *Seamen's Dictionary* published in 1623. In England, even today, waterways with a constricted entrance, such as San Francisco Bay, are called harbors. In Spanish accounts, such a waterway is referred to as *estero* or *puerto,* never *bahia* (bay). Accordingly, had Drake's entry been into San Francisco Bay, his first impression would not have called to mind the word "bay."

Power, however, in a rejoinder to the Guild's persuasive argument, said: "I know as fact that 'bay' and 'harbor' were synonymous in Elizabethan times. Hakluyt in the 'Catalogue' to his 1600 edition, says there is 'a very good *harbour*' in Nova Albion, but in the text he states it was a 'faire and good Bay.'[2] There is no higher authority than Hakluyt on this issue."

Power then issued a special challenge to the position of the Guild on this point, saying:

> The Guild is forfeit on this crucial Tenet. The Guild reluctantly admits the implication that the "Baye" and "harborough" in the two written accounts are "one and the same" body of water. Unable to match the evidence concerning the "Baye/harborough" to one body of water at Point Reyes, they improperly introduce a Dudley chart of questionable validity to contradict the written accounts. They can make some of the evidence match Drake's Bay and some Drake's Estero, but neither match both the "Baye" and the "harborough" in the written accounts.

A Question of Semantics

Did the compilers of "The Famous Voyage" and *The World Encompassed,* when they wrote about anchoring in a "faire and good

Baye" and in a "conuenient and fit harborough," have in mind one and the same thing? In other words, did these compilers (or Fletcher alone if he were the original common source) simply use synonymous phrases to describe the same body of water, that is, the Drake anchorage? So far as our problem is concerned, the circumstance that in one account the "Baye" was entered in latitude 38°, while in the other the latitude of the "harborough" was 38½°, raises the question of whether the differential represented an inadvertence or was intended to convey two separate concepts.

The importance of such a difference is emphasized by consulting an authoritative lexicon for the meaning of the words "bay," "harbor," and "port," as to the last of which the phrase "Portus Novae Albionis" (not used in the accounts) obviously applied. According to *Webster's Third International Unabridged Dictionary*, the primary definitions of these three words in their maritime use are as follows:

BAY: An inlet of the sea or other body of water usually smaller than a gulf, but of the same general character; a large tract of water around which the land forms a curve.

HARBOR: A part of a body of water partially or almost totally enclosed so that ships or boats entering it may be protected when they are moored: haven, port.

PORT: A place where ships may ride secure from storms: harbor, haven.

Assuming that the foregoing terminology had the same significance in the sixteenth century as today, the source of "The Famous Voyage" was describing a different event when he wrote of entry into a "Baye" than was he, or his fellow-compiler, in describing entry into a "harborough." The adjectival phrases "faire and good" and "conuenient and fit" both convey favorable connotations; yet here, too, a not entirely identical significance may have been intended. "Faire and good" could mean "fine," "excellent," or "favorable" in a general way; while in using the phrase "conuenient and fit" the writer undoubtedly had in mind such specific attributes as ready accessibility, suitability for intended use, that is, for purposes of careening the ship and of obtaining wood, water, and supplies. Thus the adjectives, as well as the nouns, point to the happening of different events.

A Review of the Rebuttal

The position taken by Power in his rebuttal is somewhat difficult to follow. First, the Guild did not admit that "Baye" and "harborough" were one and the same body of water, and they reiterated their position in this respect in their rebuttal. Second, the Guild made no reference to a Dudley chart in support of their position (the only reference to Dudley was by Neasham). Third, the evidence presented by the Guild very clearly matched both the "Baye" and the "harborough" of the early accounts, assuming, of course, that the Estero was usable as a careening basin in 1579. Fourth, the Power position that "Baye" and "harborough" are identical in meaning is weak. The dictionaries of today make obvious the fact that a bay is a body of water open to the sea while a harbor or port is one protected from the sea; and the same distinction existed in Elizabethan times, according to definitions in a contemporary lexicon discussing such matters.[3] Hakluyt's status as an authority on such subjects is questionable. Although he had no peer as a maritime historian, he was not infallible when it came to getting his facts straight. Nevertheless, that he was not totally confused by the seeming contradictions in his source material may be inferred from the facts that his only mention of a "faire and good Baye" was to indicate that it had been entered with the aid of a "good winde," but when he came to speak (in the table of contents of his 1600 edition) about the place where Drake had "graued his shippe," he was careful to describe it as "a very good harbour."

"Baye" versus "harborough"

Viewed from a disinterested point of view, the result of the debate on Tenet 4 is not favorable to the contentions advanced by Power. His position that "Baye" and "harborough" are synonymous is not persuasive when all the evidence is considered, and the same is true of his appeal to Hakluyt. Nowhere in the text of "The Famous Voyage" did Hakluyt say that Drake had "graued his shippe" in the "Baye," but merely that he entered it.

Incidentally, the Power argument would seem to have been largely beside the point. A synonymous construction of the terms "Baye" and "harborough" is not in any way essential to the position of San Quentin Cove as a landing-site contender, nor would a contrary interpretation of those terms in any way detract from the strength of its position. Assuming that Drake did in fact penetrate the Golden Gate, he could have succeeded thereafter in finding within its spacious inner bay, and along the shores of Marin County, a protected inlet or cove that was indeed a small harbor. It now serves that purpose for the ferryboats that daily ply between San Francisco and Larkspur, with their terminal in plain sight of the spot where Beryle Shinn said he picked up the controversial plate.

Tenet 5: The World Encompassed *reported that Drake's ship, "hauing received a leake at sea," needed to be brought to shore and unloaded for repair. Discuss the suitability of the proposed landing-site for careening and graving.*

A principal key to the selection of a potential landing-site would necessarily have been its suitability for the purpose of graving and refitting a leaky and heavily barnacled ship. The conditions at the Island of Caño had not been such as to permit a thorough overhaul, and Drake knew that it was imperative that he locate a harbor where that kind of attention was possible. Careening, which means keeling over a lightened ship in shallow water, was the only procedure by which the leak could have been repaired, and by which the hull could be given the kind of cleaning and retallowing needed for a Pacific crossing.

Which of the three anchorage candidates would have been most suitable for these purposes? Each debater asserted that his chosen site would have provided the right kind of conditions needed for a complete overhaul of the *Golden Hind*. The Guild claimed this sort of suitability for the Estero in the sixteenth century, while Power told how the old cove *Bahia de las Calaveras* at Point San Quentin on San Francisco Bay had been "used in historic times to careen whaling ships," and therefore would have been *prima facie* a suitable careenage and graving cove for Drake's vessel.

Power, however, contested the suitability of the other two sites for careenage purposes. In reference to Bolinas Lagoon, he agreed with the Guild's contention that it would not have provided an adequate site because early charts showed only "a small backwater slough not likely to have had sufficient water even in Drake's time."[4] Power also contended that the suitability of the Estero for careenage purposes was purely theoretical, saying: "The Guild has created a geographic myth that they named 'Drake's Cove' in order to provide an anchorage suitable for careenage in the Point Reyes area. Today this so-called 'cove' is filled with rock, sand and drift, and part of it has been there long enough that Coast Miwok Indians encamped on it."

Bolinas Bay and Lagoon. (Aero Photographers, Inc.)

The Question of Accessibility

Accessibility proved to be another hotly contested point. Neasham asserted that the *Golden Hind* would have had no difficulty in entering Bolinas Lagoon in 1579 because then it was open. Lumbering operations began in 1849, and sedimentation proceeded thereafter. According to the U.S. Geological Survey, when vessels first started using the port, schooners drawing ten feet of water could pass over the bar with ease at any tidal stage, but by 1880 the same vessel could hardly pass at the highest stage.

The Guild cited U.S. Coast Survey figures for 1859 showing only two feet of water at the mouth of Bolinas Lagoon, just as today, and an allowance of five to six feet for high tide would not have permitted the *Golden Hind* to enter the lagoon, much less find sufficient depth of water nearby for careenage purposes. With this evaluation, Power was in accord.

Power had already established that there was no depth or accessibility problem at the San Quentin Cove site because Drake's requirements, so far as can be known today, would have been similar to those of the captains of whaling vessels that were careened there *circa* 1850. There was no disagreement by the Guild or by Neasham.

The Guild asserted that the bar to the Estero, according to Davidson, had a depth at low tide of 8 feet, and of 12.8 to 15 feet at high tide, with a depth of only 13 feet being adequate for the *Golden Hind* when heavily loaded. Power took exception to the foregoing contention, pointing out that Davidson had said that the channel had only 13 feet of water on the bar at the highest tide, and that "Drake would not have hazarded his vessel in entering such a doubtful anchorage."

Neasham took the position that all three proposed anchorage sites would have been adequate for Drake's purposes in every respect, but he found little agreement among his fellow debaters. There was also a lack of agreement in reference to the Estero, except that the challenge came only from Power. Objectively viewed, it is apparent that San Quentin Cove had the better of the argument on Tenet 5, emerging unscathed on all counts.

> *Tenet 6: Conscious that his crew would need to supplement their meager supplies with food and water from the land while the* Golden Hind *was undergoing repair, Drake chose to camp at a site at which such supplies were readily accessible. Discuss the suitability of the proposed site for watering and victualling.*

Drake's arrival at Nova Albion was more than eighteen months after his departure from Plymouth, and his original stock of comestibles had long since given out. He had to live off what he was able to find as he went along, from the ships and towns he robbed. But along the North Pacific coast there were no towns or ships on which to prey, and the problem of food increased enormously, particularly because it would be necessary before leaving California to lay in provisions sufficient to last whatever number of months it might take to complete the next leg of the homeward journey. Water was likewise a critical need, being a cogent consideration in any choice of an anchorage.

The contemporary accounts provide little information on this subject. *The World Encompassed* mentioned the use of such edibles as "Muscles, Seales and such like," while near the water. Doubtless there were available plenty of fish and shellfish, and the Indians may have supplied bread made from the root *Petáh* or, possibly, supplies of the root itself. Inland from the anchorage site, meat was available from elk, deer, and "conies."

This was not, however, a controversial point, so far as the debaters were concerned, in responding to the request by Tenet 6 for discussion of their respective anchorage sites for purposes of "watering and victualling." It was conceded by the participants that all three sites would have satisfied the requirements for Drake's anchorage so far as food and water were concerned. Fresh water from springs and streams was no problem, and the men of the *Golden Hind* had access to the same kind of food supplies as the natives of the area. Accordingly, no participant gained any advantage from the discussion of this tenet.

> *Tenet 7: According to* The World Encompassed, *Drake's men constructed a fort "for the defence of our selues and goods" while they repaired his ship. Discuss the suitability of the anchorage site for location of a fort and how the fort was constructed.*

Drake's paramount need for the purposes of careening and repairing his ship was a place with a friendly native population, or none at all. Indeed, it was essential to the success of the expedition that a harbor be found where his men could overhaul the *Golden Hind* secure in the knowledge that they would not be ambushed or massacred. Neither the early accounts nor later commentators pay attention to this factor, but it could have been one of the concerns uppermost in Drake's mind as he searched for a suitable harbor.

Fresh in memory must have been the disastrous experiences with native peoples earlier in the voyage. As told in a previous chapter,[5] it was at Port St. Julian, on the eastern shore of lower South America

(Argentina), that Drake and four of his men went ashore to establish friendly relations with the Patagonian Indians of the area. The encounter turned unexpectedly into a hostile action with fatal results for two of the party. This was in June, 1578.

This unhappy incident was repeated a few months later at the island of Mocha off the coast of southern Chile. When Drake and several of his men came ashore to obtain water, after a friendly reception the preceding day, they were ambushed by the treacherous natives. Before Drake's men could regain the safety of their ship, three had been killed and the rest wounded, including Drake himself.

The delays in debarking (June 17–21) at Nova Albion may, to some extent, have been due to a need to assess the possibilities in this regard. The natives had behaved in a friendly manner for the first several days, but vivid memories must have passed through the minds of Drake and his men as the California Indians came surging over the hill above their encampment on June 26, 1579, a thousand strong, with no assurance that there might not be a repetition of the South American treachery at a time when retreat was impossible. For all Drake and his men knew, this was to be Armageddon, with life and death hanging in the balance.

Fortunately for all concerned, the natives proved to be amicable, if not particularly helpful. Had the situation been otherwise, the story of Nova Albion might have been different; indeed, the world might have wondered whatever became of Francis Drake and his crew.

Safety from Spanish Reprisal

By the time Drake had completed his depredations on the Pacific side of America, he was the most wanted man in New Spain. An issue that he could hardly afford to disregard, it would seem, was that of safety from Spanish pursuit and attack. His vessel, as he well knew, was a hunted ship, and the great value of the cargo which it carried now made it imperative that he take no unnecessary risks. He could assume that few Spanish ships were familiar with the California coast, but he could have no doubt that even the inner lagoons or esteros of the shallow coastal bays could readily be looked into by passing ships.

Did his apparent lack of concern provide a clue to the type of site which he selected? On this point only two Drake experts have commented. Power said: "There is no inference that Drake was concerned with pursuing Spaniards. San Francisco Bay would have provided insurance against discovery by pursuit."

The danger from this source has also been minimized by Heizer, who felt that Sir Francis had every reason to believe that the Spanish either would not follow him or, if they did, were not likely to find him.[6] However, while the early accounts give no hint that Drake anticipated pursuit and discovery while refitting his ship, this may have been due in part to his being in a well-hidden spot where a passing ship would have been unable to see him.

Suitability of Sites

A response to the request of Tenet 7 for discussion of sites for construction of a fort required a review of the contemporary accounts for relevant comments. "The Famous Voyage" spoke of the Indians coming in large numbers "towards our bulwarks and tents" and of how "our Generall gathered his men together, and marched within his fenced place, making against their approaching, a very warlike shewe." *The World Encompassed* told of how Drake's first move in landing on June 21 was to "build tents and make a fort for the defence of ourselues and goods"; of how their fort had been built at the bottom of a hill; and of how they "intrenched ourselues with walls of stone" in case of a sudden show of hostility by the Indians. Plainly a site that could be put into a posture of defense was a matter of at least some concern.

Apart from the foregoing comments, the debate participants had no hard facts on which to base their responses. They were obliged to assume that Drake's "fort" or "fenced place" fronted on a hill for maximum protection from its crest, that it consisted of walls of earth or sand erected through trenching, and that these walls were faced with rocks from on or near the site. The only clue to its shape would have been the square or rectangular enclosure pictured by the "Portus Novae Albionis" insert on the Hondius map. Apparently the one important need for construction of such a fort was an ample quantity of rocks, and each debater asserted that his particular site had a plentiful supply.

Power, in addition, insisted that the earth at Point San Quentin would have been more suitable for a firm entrenchment than the soft sand at the Estero. The Guild countered with the assertion that walls of stone would not have been needed at Point San Quentin because the earth from a trench around the fort's perimeter would have been sufficient for the walls.

A review from a disinterested point of view of the responses to Tenet 7 makes it evident that the discussion provided no advantage to any of the debate participants. Indeed, a similar conclusion may be reached with respect to the subject of the suitability of the various sites for the purpose of Drake's need for a harbor when all four tenets are considered as a whole. The edge, if any, would seem to favor the Power position.

16

CHAPTER

The Weather

Tenet 8: Accounts of the voyage report that Drake's men experienced severe and uncomfortable weather on the west coast of North America. What do the accounts' descriptions of weather and climate contribute to the identification of Drake's anchorage?

FOR A century and a third, at least, Drake scholars have made the weather at Drake's California anchorage a subject of discussion. Some have regarded it as controversial; others have treated it as a significant clue to the identification of the anchorage.

The World Encompassed contained nearly a thousand words describing, explaining, and complaining about the cold, the fog, and the winds at Nova Albion. On the other hand, the subject was not mentioned in "The Famous Voyage," no doubt because Hakluyt felt that Fletcher's wordy essay on the subject, in view of the former's need for condensation, could readily be dispensed with. Only two or three other early sources made passing mention of the fact that it was "cold"' at Drake's California landfall.

For the full text of *The World Encompassed*'s vivid and lengthy discussion of the Nova Albion weather see Appendix D. In the course of Fletcher's dissertation on the subject, which commenced with the date of arrival, he insisted that for the full period of their stay they were "continually visited with like nipping colds as we had felt before," with the result that were it not that they had their "necessarie labors" to perform, they would have preferred to stay in bed. Indeed, he asserted, they were unable "at any time, in whole fourteen days together, to find the air so clear as to be able to take the height of Sunne or starre."

Opinions of Early Scholars

One of the earliest discussions of the Nova Albion weather appeared in the *History of Oregon and California,* published in 1845.[1] In that volume its author, Robert C. Greenhow, commented in a matter-of-fact way that Drake had reached that part of the Pacific, near the American coasts, where the winds blow constantly and violently during the summer, from the north and the northwest, generally accompanied by thick fogs that obscure the heavens for days and even weeks at a time.

In the *Dictionary of National Biography,* published in London in 1885–1891, the author of an article on the life of Drake was critical of Greenhow's description of the weather at Nova Albion[2] as excessively cold and foggy, calling it "more than an exaggeration." Indeed, he went so far as to say that it represented "a positive and evidently willful falsehood, credulously inserted by the original compiler of the 'World Encompassed.'"

Davidson, in his 1890 treatise on Drake in California,[3] was able to provide specific information on the summer weather in the Drake's Bay area. He referred to the fact that from July 2, 1859, fog hung over the Point Reyes promontory for thirty-nine consecutive days and nights. For the first nine days, the sun was invisible, and for the next thirty days, although it became visible at midday, fog continued to hang densely over the water.

A study of the records of the weather station at Point Reyes Head was made in April, 1902, by Professor Alexander G. McAdie,[4] then the forecast official and Director of the U.S. Weather Bureau at San Francisco. His study embraced a period of five years, and was limited to the same five summer weeks corresponding to those spent by Drake at his California anchorage. His observations showed a mean daytime temperature of 52.5 degrees Fahrenheit, with only five days when the thermometer exceeded 60 degrees. During that period there were 97 days of fog, 3 of rain, and 81 clear, often with strong winds from the north and northwest, just as *The World Encompassed* had reported.[5]

Comments of Later Scholars

Charles E. Chapman, well-known California historian, considered Fletcher's comments about the cold weather on the California coast and offered an explanation for them. He thought that summer fogs along the northern coast "do indeed seem cold to me who is not acclimated; many a man from the east of the United States will shiver through his first summer but rarely afterward."[6] He felt that the chill encountered by Drake and his men might have seemed worse because they had "for a long time been in the tropics."

Maurice G. Holmes, an authority on maritime matters in the Pacific area of the Drake era, cited the Chapman comments in Holmes' treatise *New Spain to the Californias by Sea,* saying: "Chapman rather airily pooh-poohed the cold weather Drake reported. . . . The writer is inclined to believe that Drake's account of the cold he encountered was based more upon fact than fancy."[7] Holmes cited the fact that when Vizcaino was at Monterey on New Year's Day in 1603, he found the well from which they were drawing water had frozen over to a depth of more than eight inches.

John W. Robertson, in commenting on the weather reportedly encountered by Drake at Nova Albion, was impressed by the statistical data cited by Davidson and McAdie, remarking that between them they had produced "meteorological tables demonstrating that this [Fletcher's] account accurately describes the climate found at Drake's Bay." He added that this seemed to be Davidson's most convincing argument in favor of a Point Reyes anchorage site, because no San Franciscan would "acknowledge that such a description could be rightfully applied to the Bay of San Francisco."[8]

Robert H. Power, writing in a 1973 *California Historical Quarterly* article[9] about the fortnight of limited visibility at the California an-

Point Reyes, its granite cliffs pounded ceaselessly by the surging sea.

chorage mentioned by *The World Encompassed,* conceded that such an extended period of limited visibility in July is typical of the coast and not of the Bay area, but insisted that prolonged spells of overcast are not unknown in the Bay area. Weather-station records for San Francisco have shown a period of fifteen consecutive days of morning overcast as recently as the summer of 1962.

Power also directed attention to the fact that the "fourteen dayes" without benefit of "sunne or starre" coincides precisely with the fourteen days' voyage (June 3-17) through miserable weather from Oregon to the Port of Nova Albion, and suggested that it is not impossible to conceive that this particular stretch of bad weather may have occurred during the time the party was sailing down the coast.

The Little Ice Age

Henry R. Wagner referred to the cold weather and snow mentioned in some of the early accounts, and especially in *The World Encompassed*. He was inclined to dismiss them as "no doubt largely some of the exaggerations so common in that book." Nevertheless, he felt that there may have been some foundation for the stories, because "very considerable evidence is to be found in accounts of other Sixteenth Century voyages to those regions that the weather there was much colder than it is at the present time and that the rainfall was much heavier."[10]

Robert C. Thomas asserted that central and northern California were in the depths of a relatively unknown "Little Ice Age" during the Drake era, the coldest part of which occurred not more than a century after the arrival of Columbus in the New World. He stated: "Modern authorities tell us that there was a four-century interval, from about 1400 to 1800 A.D., when the entire northern hemisphere went through the Little Ice Age, meaning that temperatures were low enough . . . to produce a climate much colder than in present times."[11]

Science has provided confirmation of the kind of weather that prevailed through much of Europe and North America in Drake's time. As James L. Dyson said in his *World of Ice*: "Late in the 16th and early in the 17th centuries the climate became cooler.[12] . . . In the present century alone winter temperatures at various points in the United States and Europe have risen on an average of 3 to 10 degrees."[13]

Comments by Debate Participants

Tenet 8 of the 1974 debate inquired "What do the accounts' descriptions of weather and climate contribute to the identification of Drake's anchorage?"

The Guild emphasized the similarity of Drake's Bay weather to that described by *The World Encompassed*, remarking that "Point Reyes is noted for its fog; this fog is well known for its cold penetrating quality." A feature of that locale is the prevailing northwest wind that sweeps across the peninsula and funnels down Drake's Estero as a north wind. *The World Encompassed* mentioned both winds as "constant" at Drake's port.

In his book dealing with the Drake visit, Raymond Aker, president of the Guild, commented that to a sixteenth-century European, the Nova Albion weather must have seemed truly unusual. He added that a world map shows that the areas of the world in latitude 38° to which Europeans are accustomed, such as Greece, Italy, Spain, and Portugal, are warm in the summer; even the highest latitudes reached by Drake in the Pacific were no higher than those of Tuscany and Rome.[14]

Aker went on to contrast the lack of greenness at Point Reyes with similar coastal areas in England in the summer months, saying: "The Point Reyes Peninsula, however, is not only dry in summer, but the wind and fog blowing across the open downs in the spring and summer contrive to produce a thin and stunted ground cover in all exposed areas, a feature notably true in the vicinity of the cove."

Comments on Behalf of Bolinas and San Quentin Cove

Neasham, in reference to Fletcher's vivid description of weather conditions at Drake's encampment, felt that such conditions are rather typical of the coastal region north of San Francisco Bay, including Bolinas Bay. During the summer months, particularly, northwest winds, cool weather, and fogs are predominant there. He added that "modern weather data verify the fact that on occasion from June to September the sun is not seen for several days at a time, even for periods exceeding the fourteen days mentioned in *The World Encompassed*," while, on the other hand, "at Point San Quentin during the summer months, fog usually burns off by noon."

Power referred to the "long reflective essay" of *The World Encompassed* on the unfavorable climate of Nova Albion; but particularly to its statement that after the *Golden Hind* left the Farallones on July 25, the "cold not only continued but increased . . . the wind blowing still . . . from the Northwest." He felt that this observation suggested that there had been a respite from the northwest wind and the extreme coastal climate such as would have been the case if Drake had anchored in San Francisco Bay. In his opinion, the Fletcher weather accounts shed little light on the anchorage site except for the significant statement that the stinking fog was much greater in the higher latitudes, that is, along the Oregon coast, than in the lower latitudes, that is, in the vicinity of the Bay of Nova Albion. Power's statement in response to Tenet 8 included the following:

Drake's Bay by government records has more fog than the Oregon coast, and only San Francisco Bay would have "so much" less of those "thick mists and most stinking fogges." . . . In any event, this Tenet is "sixes and sevens" as several quotations in the accounts favor San Francisco Bay and several favor a coast anchorage.

Summary

If there is a summer climate on the California coast that matches *The World Encompassed* description of Nova Albion weather, it undoubtedly has to be that of the Drake's Bay area. Anyone who has visited that part of the Point Reyes Peninsula in June or July is likely to agree that there was little exaggeration by the author of *The World Encompassed*.

Official records by such competent authorities as George Davidson and Alexander McAdie provide tangible support for such a conclusion. In speaking of *The World Encompassed* comments in relation to the Drake's Bay climate, McAdie stated:

> The description fits the facts. . . . It is plain that the fog and wind conditions are remarkable and in accord with the experience of Drake's party. . . . How well that description (speaking of Davidson's record of 39 consecutive days and nights of fog over Point Reyes) tallies with the narrative where it says "neither could we at any time in the whole fourteene dayes together, find the aire so cleare as to be able to take the height of Sunne or starre."[15]

Bolinas, as a coastal bay, seems to share much the same weather pattern as Point Reyes, although somewhat less rigorous. Point San Quentin, on the other hand, is on the inner, protected side of the Marin peninsula, within two or three miles of Greenbrae and San Rafael, where summer temperatures range up to 90 degrees and protracted periods of fog or overcast are rare.

Nowhere in his responses to the question posed by Tenet 8 does Power assert that the summer climate at Point San Quentin tallies with or resembles that described in *The World Encompassed*. As best we are able to analyze his position, he appears to contend that (1) most of Fletcher's discussion of the weather is directed at that encountered on the Oregon coast and is too vague to be of much value in the search for the Bay of Nova Albion; (2) the only light Fletcher really sheds on the weather at the anchorage site is to suggest that the Oregon coast has more fog than San Francisco Bay, and therefore that the anchorage site must have been within the latter; and (3) the increasing cold after leaving the Farallones suggests that there had been a respite from the winds and cold "such as would have been the case if they had anchored in San Francisco Bay."

Power also suggests that the score on Tenet 8 is "sixes and sevens." *The World Encompassed* made it clear, however, that whatever the conditions may have been off the Oregon coast, the weather at the Drake anchorage was so frigid that even the natives suffered, that the vegetation was severely affected, and that the "thicke mists and most stinking fogges" were such that they could not "at any time [between June 17 and July 23, 1579] in whole fourteene dayes together, find the aire so cleare as to be able to take the height of Sunne or starre."

From a disinterested point of view, accordingly, there is little doubt that the summer weather of the Point Reyes Peninsula tallies closely with that belabored by Fletcher in the account in question, and that the evidence with respect to this tenet favors the Drake's Estero position.

17

CHAPTER

The Hinterland

Tenet 9: Discuss the comparative observation from The World Encompassed *that when Drake and his men "made a journy up into the land . . . to be the better acquainted with the nature and the commodities of the country . . . the inland we found to be farre different from the shoare . . .*[11]

TOWARD THE end of his stay at the California anchorage site Drake made a "journy up into the land" with "his gentlemen and many of his company." This excursion took place after "our necessary businesses were well dispatched," meaning only after the *Golden Hind* had been made fully seaworthy again, and after the tedious task of reloading the ship with everything previously transferred to the Tello frigate, as well as most of the shoreside encampment, had been completed. Only then would Drake have felt secure in undertaking a sightseeing trip, and only after posting a heavy guard on the ship and encampment.

The purposes of the journey, according to *The World Encompassed,* were to see "the manner of their dwelling," meaning the living quarters of the natives, as well as to become "better acquainted with the nature and commodities of the country." They found the houses of the Indians to be similar to those observed near the anchorage site, that is, "low vaulted, round" structures, "digged round within the earth" and covered with "clefts of wood" joined close together at the top. In the course of their journey they saw several villages.[1]

Both of the principal contemporary accounts of the visit to California made mention of the excursion "up into the country," and *The World Encompassed* also had something to say about the abundance of wildlife observed by the Elizabethans (of which more in Chapter 19).[2] However, the most significant comment was that of *The World Encompassed* to the effect that they found the inland "to be farre different from the shoare, a goodly country, and fruitful soyle, stored with many blessings fit for the use of man."

The accounts do not tell us how long the journey was in either distance or time of travel. The probabilities are that it was not a lengthy one, not only because sailors are not noted for being enthusiastic hikers, but also because of a lack of equipment for camping away from their shoreside quarters. This means that although they got far enough away from tidewater to see a number of villages, their trek was probably limited to a one-day hike, or two days at most.

Little attention has been paid to this inland visit by students of the anchorage question, obviously because of the slenderness of the clue which it provides. Really the only basis for an inference of any kind is to be found in *The World Encompassed* comment to the effect that they found the inland "to be farre different than the shoare." The problem is how such differences are to be gauged. So far as the debate participants are concerned, each had in mind such an inland area, the Guild thinking primarily of Olema Valley beyond Inverness Ridge, Neasham of the Olema Valley and possibly Nicasio, and Power of the Novato area.

The Case for Drake's Estero

The Guild directed attention to the comments in *The World Encompassed* about how bitter a place the shore was where Drake camped, both in aspect and climate. For four consecutive paragraphs, beginning with the arrival, the account's author reviled the weather and surroundings at the landing place. He said, for example, "how vnhandsome and deformed appeared the face of the earth itselfe" and deplored "the generall squalidnesse and barrennesse of the countrie," all by way of describing the area immediately surrounding the anchorage site.

These words and phrases, according to the Guild, are peculiarly applicable to the Drake's Bay area today. The Point Reyes peninsula is swept from one side to the other by cold wind and fog—hence its

The Olema Valley, looking toward Point Reyes. (Aero Photographers, Inc.)

barren, treeless, inhospitable aspect. On the other hand, because the Inverness Ridge cuts off wind and fog, the Olema Valley on the inland side has a totally different climate and aspect. This was equally true in the sixteenth century, according to the report by Cermeño who visited the north end of the valley at the fresh-water marsh in 1595. There he found three Indian villages, and reported that "the country appeared to him to be well adapted to sow and reap any kind of seed, as it looked like the country of Castile and was of good character."

The Guild asserted that the words "farre different" used to characterize, the interior, as compared with the anchorage site on the seashore, were of greater significance when applied to Drake's Estero versus the Olema Valley than would have been the case with either Bolinas Lagoon or San Quentin Cove and the inland areas near them.

The Case for Bolinas

In 1579 the country north and inland from Bolinas Lagoon was different from the shore, according to Neasham. To reach this well-wooded area, *The World Encompassed* indicated that Drake went up into the land, or north. Leaving the comparatively barren west shore of the lagoon, on which the predominant plant life was a few native oaks and willows, and which is now marked by many eucalyptus, pine, cedars, and other trees as well, the Englishmen probably went as far as Olema and possibly to Nicasio, where the main Miwok Indian villages were situated.

As Drake went northerly up the Olema Valley, the land became more and more wooded, with evidence, according to Neasham, of oak, pine, buckeye, laurel, and redwood, among other varieties. Eastward, several miles away across Bolinas Lagoon on Bolinas Ridge, was seen much foliage. Treelined gullies running east and west from the top of the ridge between barren hills came down to the east shore of the lagoon. East and south of Bolinas Ridge was Mount Tamalpais, the slopes of which were heavily wooded. This feature, mostly hidden by or blended with Bolinas Ridge, could not be seen easily from Drake's fort. Bolinas Point to the west and south was largely barren, covered by dry grass.

In Neasham's opinion, there is a marked difference between the shore of Drake's presumed encampment at Bolinas Lagoon and the country inland up the Olema Valley, a difference that is also applicable to Drake's Estero and a journey across Inverness Ridge to the vicinity of Olema. Such a marked difference will not be found between Point San Quentin, although somewhat barren, and the fruitful soil of the Novato area.

The Case for Point San Quentin

The various differences between the presumed Drake anchorage near Point San Quentin and the Novato area, twelve miles to the north, are self-evident, according to Power. Reports of the inland journey did not mention a weather differential, but did speak of the numerous Indian villages seen during the journey,[2] and of the fact that Drake's party found the inland "a goodly country, and fruitful soyle."

In the nineteenth century Novato Valley was a productive apple orchard.

Power took issue with the Guild's implication that the Olema Valley is a "goodly country, and fruitful," saying that in reality it is a small 250-acre flood plain bounded on the west by low-rift hills with little, if any, "fruitful soil." He denied that the main Miwok villages were situated at Nicasio, as Neasham had stated, and said that they "were not in Olema or Nicasio, but from San Rafael north to Olompali."

The Guild disputed the Power statements, asserting that Novato was not likely to be "farre different" from the land around San Quentin and San Rafael, or any more fertile, or so greatly different in climate as to be *far* different. From a San Quentin site, Drake would have had two small craft with which to explore the bay long before he went inland, and could have seen the nature of the land for miles around, including the Novato area, from his boats.

San Francisco Bay, looking northward from the Golden Gate, showing Richardson's Bay, tip of Angel Island, San Quentin Cove and Point. (Aero Photographers, Inc.)

THE HINTERLAND

Neasham took strong exception to the Power comments about Olema Valley, saying:

> That the Olema Valley occupies only 250 acres of a flood plain would raise the eyebrows of more than one rancher who, in some instances, can claim the ownership of much larger areas in what historically has been known as the Olema Valley. Rather large Miwok villages were located at Olema, Nicasio, San Rafael, Olompali, and other sites.

Summary

Tenet 9 of the 1974 debate requested discussion of *The World Encompassed* comment that "the inland we found to be farre different from the shoare," obviously seeking its significance from the standpoint of the landing-site location. But the request offered little for the debaters to get their teeth into. It presented them with a rather vague travel situation, asking them to show, as best they could, the extent to which their respective anchorage sites might have fitted into it.

As everyone knows, seashore conditions invariably differ from those of an interior area in general climate, day-to-day weather, and other ways. Apparently, in Drake's case, the only respect in which the inland areas did not differ from the proposed anchorage sites was in the type of native houses. Apart from that, the visitors found a greater number of villages, more plentiful wildlife, what appeared to be more fruitful soil, and presumably, although the subject was not mentioned by the accounts, an entirely different climate.

Power contended that as between Point San Quentin and Novato, all these differences would have been found, not excluding that last mentioned. The Guild asserted, in effect, that the biggest differences of all would have been between the barren aspect of the Estero site and the fruitful character of the interior, and especially between the raw, biting coastal weather and the pleasant climate of the Olema Valley. A similar position, although with less vigor, was taken in respect to Bolinas Bay by Neasham.

An interesting element was introduced by the Guild's comment that Drake, if his landfall was in San Francisco Bay, would have had two small crafts at his disposal with which to explore the bay long before he went inland; and that he could have seen the nature of the land for miles around, even including the present Napa and Novato areas, from one of his boats. This gives rise to the further thought that his inland visit may have been to an area which could have been reached partly, and possibly entirely, by small boat. In other words, it could have been a journey up into the land by water, rather than on foot, an inconceivable thought in connection with coastal bays other than Tomales.

Viewing the result of the discussion from an objective point of view, the evidence tends to favor the Drake's Estero position, on the ground that if the interior was found to be "farre different," rather than merely "different," it was because of the greater contrast between all conditions at the Estero site and whatever part of the hinterland Drake and his party visited.

18

The Flora

Tenet 10: Botanical observations in The World Encompassed *include mention of the Indians' decorative use of
"a certaine downe, which groweth vp in the countrey
vpon an herbe, much like our lectuce which exceeds any
other downe in the world for finesse [fineness]," and a description of the landscape which showed "trees without
leaves, and the ground without greennes." Correlate these
observations with the flora of the proposed landing site.*

TO WHAT extent do the flora with which Drake came in
contact during his Nova Albion sojourn provide subtle clues
to the location of the anchorage? At least one Drake scholar
is convinced that some species of plant life, assertedly identifiable with
flora mentioned in one of the contemporary accounts, are to be found
only in a locale related to his choice of landing site. For an anchorage
sleuth, no clue is too tenuous or obscure.

The World Encompassed account of the California sojourn made
reference to more than half a dozen types of plant life, two or three of
which were also mentioned by "The Famous Voyage." Most of these
botanical observations were merely incidental to the description of
events or climatic conditions; however, in connection with the visit of
the Indian king on June 26, 1579, the author went into considerable
descriptive detail concerning an herb "like our lectuce."

Members of the king's guard, so the account reported, wore "cawles . . . covered over with a certaine downe, which groweth vp in the countrey vpon an herbe much like our lectuce, which exceeds any other downe in the world for finenesse, and beeing layed upon their cawles, by no winds can be removed." The account went on to say that not only was this herb so highly esteemed that its down could only be lawfully worn by persons "about the king," but its seeds were used only in "sacrifice to their gods."

The author was obviously impressed by the herb as well as its down, but one can only wonder how much of his information was factual in view of the communication gap between natives and visitors. By what means could he have learned that the source of the down was an herb, that it grew up in the country, that its seeds were used only for sacrificial purposes, and that the wearing of its down was restricted to those connected with royalty? On what basis, moreover, was he able to state that the down exceeded any other in the world for fineness! One is forced to conclude that much of the story is due to a fertile imagination, although it may contain enough facts to make possible an identification of the herb or plant.

Identification by the Guild

Despite the rather specific description of this plant, debate participants totally disagreed on its identity. According to the Guild, the herb in question compares with *Rafinesquia californica,* a native species closely related to English wild lettuce, which grows in the Olema valley and bears a soft down. This plant was singled out by the Guild because it is the only native plant physically similar to English wild lettuce, because it has fine, soft down, collectible seeds, and white sap, and because it matures during the season of Drake's visit. Most important is the down's pinnate structure that gives it a unique tenaciousness suitable to the statement that, being laid upon "cawles, . . . by no winds can [it] be removed."

According to Power, however, *Rafinesquia californica* is a plant which Richard Brown, research biologist for the Point Reyes National Seashore, had never noticed growing anywhere in the Point Reyes-Olema region. Power added that the Guild had failed to demonstrate how this "short down similar in size to lettuce down" could be used to decorate Indian headdresses, or that it is "finer than any other to the touch or the eye."

According to *The World Encompassed,* this herb "groweth up in the countrey," rather than near the anchorage site where the Indians happened to be seen wearing its down; so with a statement by Neasham that he had seen *Rafinesquia californica* growing "at the suggested Drake fort site at Bolinas Lagoon in September, 1973," a note of further botanical confusion was added to the controversy.

The American Milkweed

According to Power, the lettuce-like herb was the American milkweed, a popular plant in the age of exploration, for which the botanical name is *Asclepias mexicana.* This is a plant that grows in Marin County only in the valleys north of San Rafael, according to *Marin Flora,* by John Thomas Howell (page 219). Milkweed down has a ¾ inch staple that can readily be used for headpiece decoration. This down is easily collected and has a resilient character like silken goose down, yet its structure is finer than either silk or down. The similarity between it and the *Rafinesquia* is the free-flowing *lactus* (milk) in the stem; the dissimilarity is the finer usable down produced by the American milkweed.

Despite irrelevance to the question propounded, Neasham stated twice that he had personally observed *Asclepias mexicana* growing at the proposed fort site at Bolinas Lagoon in September, 1973. To which Power responded that Neasham's identification was incorrect, because it "does not grow, nor has ever been known to grow, west of Bolinas Ridge."

"Trees Without Leaves"

A similar lack of agreement is encountered in relation to *The World Encompassed* reference to "trees without leaves." This was a phenomenon, however, that did *not* occur "up in the countrey," but at the anchorage site itself. The phrase is contained in that part of *The World Encompassed* that complains about the frigid weather upon arrival, and reads: "Besides, how unhandsome and deformed appeared the face of the earth itselfe! shewing trees without leaves, and the ground without greennes in these moneths of June and July."

Comment by the Guild was that "trees without leaves" compare with the blue blossom (*Ceanothus thyrsiflorus*), a large evergreen shrub that grows to the size and shape of a small tree and often carries whole, apparently dead, leafless branches on a living tree. These are found at Drake's Cove and in the Drake's Bay area. "Trees without leaves" were seen in June and July near the encampment, not on the inland journey.

With respect to the Guild identification of "trees without leaves," Neasham observed merely that "'Ceanothus,' with partial dead branches, does not fully meet the descriptive criteria." He suggested, instead, that the trees in question were probably buckeyes. The Guild offered no comment on this suggestion, but Power stated that the "trees without leaves" are identifiable as the buckeye tree. This is the first tree to enter its autumn season, beginning in early July in the warm and dry parts of the San Francisco Bay area. In Marin County the maximum early season of the buckeye tree occurs in the Novato area. There the summer heat and absence of fog yellows and dries the leaves that are then blown from the twigs by the afternoon breezes, literally creating "trees without leaves" by the end of July.

Despite the foregoing, Power asserted that Neasham's identification of the "trees without leaves" seen in June, 1579, was erroneous because "he holds to the 'country' being Bolinas to Nicasio, while the buckeye's autumn does not occur in that area until after Drake had left California."

"Ground Without Greennes"

This phenomenon, as reported by *The World Encompassed,* was compared by the Guild to the dry ground, dead grass, and small-plant life typical of the Drake's Bay area in summer. Neasham commented that in July, dry ground, dead grass, and small plants are to be found variously in Marin County, including Drake's Bay, Bolinas Bay, and San Francisco Bay. Power offered no comment on this point, apparently having no disagreement with the Guild-Neasham statements.

The Guild, however, made the general observation that comparison of the flora and plant products with descriptions in the accounts "are no more significant in identifying a landing site at San Quentin than in Bolinas Lagoon, or Drake's Bay. They are of interest and importance to the site, but each site has the necessary counterparts." With this statement, Power took issue, saying that every proposed anchorage does not have "comparison of flora and plant products." In support of this comment, he cited his previously mentioned contention of Neasham's incorrect identification of the American milkweed at Bolinas, and the asserted error of the latter in respect to leafless trees in that area in July.

Other Flora

A review of other types of plant life mentioned in the accounts sheds no additional light on the location of Drake's anchorage, but they are at least worth mention in passing for the sake of completeness. They include "bulrushes," "stocks of wood," "pricking bushes," the root called *Petáh,* and the substance or substances referred to as *Tabáh* and *Tobâh.*

"Bulrushes" were mentioned in both *The World Encompassed* and "The Famous Voyage" as the source of an article of clothing which, after being combed in the manner of hemp, the women wove into skirts which they wore hanging loosely from their hips to provide a "covering of that which nature teaches should be hidden." Both accounts say also that within the Indian dwellings, their beds were the hard ground "onely with rushes strewed upon it." These are believed to be the cattails commonly found in Marin County marshes, but known in England as "bulrushes."

The "stocks of wood" against which the Indian women threw themselves on approaching the Drake camp were low stubs of small trees or stout bushes. In the Point Reyes area, these could have been the Blue Blossom or the Coyote Bush, and similar types of stunted or broken trees and bushes would undoubtedly have served a similar purpose elsewhere in Marin County. The same is true of the "pricking bushes" against which the native women also dashed themselves as a form of sacrifice near Drake's stockade. These bushes would have been members of the rose family or of other varieties of bush native to the Marin peninsula.

"Petáh" was a root, one of several found in Marin County, going by such common names as Indian Potato, Squaw Potato, Breadroot, and Yampa. They could be eaten raw, ground into flour, made into bread, or could be boiled or prepared in the manner of other vegetables. They resembled tiny sweet potatoes, growing up to three inches long and three-fourths of an inch thick. They had a sweet, nutty flavor and were extensively used by the Indians.

Controversial Herbs

The meaning of the terms *Tabáh* and *Tobâh* has never been satisfactorily determined. According to *The World Encompassed,* Tabáh was an herb which the Indians gave to the English, sometimes in baskets, and at other times in bags. It was not food, and since it was usually presented with feathers, it may have had some sacrificial or ceremonial significance. "Tabâh" and "Tobâh" were apparently not the same substance, because both were referred to in relating the events of a single day, June 26, 1579. Although the spelling was similar, different diacritical marks were used. Moreover, Tabáh was always delivered by a male emissary, whereas Tobâh, on one occasion, at least, was carried by women. Some differentiation may also be inferred from the fact that Tabáh was referred to each time as an herb.

The authorities are in conflict as to whether either term had reference to tobacco. John P. Harrington identified the material referred to by Fletcher as tobacco,[1] without stating his reasons for doing so. Heizer[2] and Wagner[3] doubted that the herb was tobacco; and both Kroeber[4] and Heizer felt that Tobâh was a name applied to the herb by the English narrator, since there are no such words as "Tobâh" or "Tabáh" in the Coast Miwok language.[5] Yet, as Aker has pointed out, Fletcher would appear to have been carefully recording sounds he heard, rather than offering a corruption of the word "tobacco," in view of the frequent rendering of other Indian words and his consistent use of diacritical marks.[6]

Even the accounts are inconsistent on the matter. At the place where *The World Encompassed* tells of the natives visiting a second time and bringing "feathers and bagges of Tobâh for presents,[7] or rather indeed for sacrifices," Hakluyt in "The Famous Voyage" substituted "brought with them feathers and bags of tobacco for presents." As Wagner says, this was probably Hakluyt's idea of what it was,[8] but if so, there is nothing in the accounts to support such an editorial change in Fletcher's narrative. Moreover, Fletcher and Drake's nephew referred to the substance or substances repeatedly in *The World Encompassed* as "Tabáh" and "Tobâh," and they knew tobacco and its name very well.[9] If the English had seen it smoked, they would have commented on it.[10] Further speculation would seem to serve no purpose.

Summary

Tenet 10 requested that some of the botanical observations in *The World Encompassed* be correlated with the flora of the proposed landing site. As with almost every phase of the Drake visit to California, the subjects of this tenet have proved to be controversial — teapot tempests unequaled even by the furor over "conies" in a later chapter.[11] With respect to the two principal topics on which discussion was requested, to wit, the herb similar to lettuce and the trees without leaves, no consensus was reached. Moreover, in some cases answers referred to plant life at the anchorage site, although the question asked about conditions "up in the countrey."

The three debaters have given their answers, each purporting to identify the flora that he believes supports his particular choice of landing site. No one who is not a trained botanist could possibly sort out the correct from the incorrect answers, if indeed, such a thing were possible on the basis of the data available. The laymen might choose to accept the Guild's rationale in respect to the "lectuce" issue, and to accept Power's analysis of the "buckeye" situation; but without more study, plus expert advice of a disinterested character, any attempt to resolve even these minor phases of the larger over-all controversy, on the basis of what has been developed by the participants, interesting as it was and is, would be foolhardy.

From a nonpartisan standpoint, the opinions expressed in the course of the debate over Tenet 10, taken as a whole, offer no satisfactory basis for a conclusion, or even speculation, on the identification of the anchorage site.

19

CHAPTER

The Fauna

Tenet 11: Identify the fauna described in the Drake sources, especially The World Encompassed*'s observation: "we sawe . . . a multitude of a strange kind of Conies . . ."*

THE CONTEMPORARY accounts provided little information on the wildlife which the Elizabethans found at or near the anchorage itself. Whether the latter was a coastal harbor or a bay inlet, its faunal inhabitants would have been comprised of the usual type of marine life and shore birds that even today are found about much of the Marin County perimeter. These would have included sea lions and seals, and to secure an ample supply of either or both would have taken no more than a day or two with the small boat.

Fish were plentiful at each of the three projected anchorage sites. *The World Encompassed* described how Drake's men watched admiringly as the Indians caught fish in shallow waters with their bare hands. There were California sardines, sometimes called pilchards (the term used in *The World Encompassed*), as well, possibly, as "broyled herring" that the Indians could have brought from Tomales Bay.

There were such shore birds as cormorants and the California murre, the eggs of which undoubtedly constituted a welcome addition to the diet of Drake and his men. *The World Encompassed* made much of the fact that after the first eggs were laid in the nest, the "poore birds and foules" would not dare, because of the chilly weather, leave it until the offspring had been hatched and become able to look after themselves. But since most of these creatures would have been found in plentiful numbers at any of the three harbors under consideration, they do not provide useful clues to anchorage identification.

Fauna of the Inland Area

Rather it was the members of the animal kingdom seen by Drake and his cohorts on their visit to the interior of the Nova Albion area that interested the visitors the most, and which, if they were not the subject of controversy, could furnish significant clues for the location of their anchorage.

According to *The World Encompassed,* they saw a herd of "very large and fat Deere" numbering in the thousands. In addition, they saw a "multitude of a strange kind of Conies, by far exceeding them in number." These conies seemed to fascinate Fletcher, for he went into some detail in describing them:

> Their heads and bodies, in which they resemble other Conies, are but small; his tayle, like the tayle of a Rat, exceedingly long; and his feet like the pawes of a Want or moale; under his chinne, on either side, he hath a bagge, into which he gathereth his meate, when he hath filled his belly abroade, that he may with it, either feed his young, or feede himselfe when he lists not to travaile from his burrough; the people eat their bodies, and make great account of their skinnes, for their kings holidaies coate was made of them.

The trek was also reported by "The Famous Voyage" in somewhat condensed form, although obviously by the same author. It changed the gender of the conies from masculine to feminine, and likened their heads to "the heads of ours," meaning conies of England. It introduced two new elements: One was the word "warren" used to describe the innumerable burrows of conies extending over the "whole countrey." The other was a reference to "Barbarie" Connies (sic),[1] to provide a means of comparing body size.

Squirrels or Gophers?

One of the most controversial issues in the dispute over the anchorage site is the identification of the conies so carefully described by the early accounts. Were they ground squirrels or pocket gophers?

One of the first to pay serious attention to this phase of the Drake anchorage mystery was a California writer of the 1860s and 1870s, J. D. B. Stillman. In *Seeking the Golden Fleece,* he discussed the subject at some length, taking the position that the ground squirrel is the only animal in the state conforming to any manner to the description of the cony.[2]

Stillman stated flatly that there was not one ground squirrel to be found in the County of Marin. Where found, it lives in vast communities; but it does not inhabit the cold, foggy regions of the coast, nor San Francisco County. It is found in Sonoma, and in the warm valleys north of Petaluma. In 1824, Johann Friedrich Eschscholtz, a German naturalist, spent several months in California making collections of the natural history of the coast, from Bodega Bay to the Bay of San Francisco.[3] He found no ground squirrels in the area covered. Wherever they have once colonized, they make such extensive burrowings that ages will not suffice to obliterate them from ground that has not been tilled.

The zoological name for the California ground squirrel is *Citellus beecheyi beecheyi* (Stillman had referred to it as *Shermophilus Beecheyi"*). It is 9 to 11 inches long, and has a tail 7 to 9 inches in length "with hairs." A bold rover, he gathers great stores of wheat in his burrow after filling his belly abroad. He is easily captured and "if he was as much valued as an article of food by whites as he was by the Indians in Drake's time, could be made to supply no inconsiderable amount of animal food to our entire population."[4]

The California gopher, according to Stillman, is 11 inches long; it has a tail 2½ inches in length covered with closely pressed hairs. This gopher is the only other rodent in the state that is numerous. It is solitary, subterranean, and is rarely seen above ground. It never goes abroad for its food; it is discovered only by its ravages to roots, and by small parcels of earth which it throws out where it breaks the surface of the ground at night. In short, its habits are those of the mole, wherever found. It can be caught only by the use of traps peculiarly constructed and planted in their underground runways, or by poison. A whole tribe of Indians, according to Stillman, could not capture enough to make a coat of their skins in a lifetime. Although those suffering most from the ravages of these rodents are farmers, few have ever seen the species, unless they have killed one in one of the ways mentioned.

Other early students of the Drake controversy have not treated the "cony" situation in the same depth as did Stillman. Nevertheless, it was the subject of a comment a century and a half ago when Captain Beechey, in writing of the natural history of the region interior to San Francisco, described some of the rodents that infested the country.[5]

John W. Robertson commented on the special stress laid by Stillman on his ground-squirrel theory as proving that Drake landed neither at Drake's Bay nor at Bodega, and upon his insistence that no other animal than a ground squirrel could have been intended by the descriptions given in the early accounts. He suggested that it is "generally assumed by naturalists that this ground squirrel bears the closest resemblance to the animals described by these narratives."[6]

Henry Wagner devoted little space to the subject, but propounded a rather novel theory. He felt that the description fits no known California mammal but seems to be that of two or more different ones badly mixed. Nevertheless he concluded that because ground squirrels answer a part of the description, are extremely numerous, and are much more in evidence than gophers for some little distance in the interior beyond the redwood belt, it is probable that ground squirrels were the conies.[7]

Conclusions of Debate Participants

Although Tenet 11 invited discussion of all fauna described in Drake sources, the debate never got much beyond the subjects of the conies and the "very large and fat Deere" referred to in the accounts. The latter were undoubtedly elk. The Guild was satisfied that they were Roosevelt elk,[8] which ranged over much of California and were known to have been numerous in Marin County in days before the gold rush. Neasham expressed no opinion on the subject.

According to Power, the animals in question were tule elk, which are associated with marshlands where tules grow. In Marin County the only area of this kind is along the San Pablo Bay shore north of San Rafael and into the area of Novato. The latter was also a region inhabited by ground squirrels.

The identity of the conies was a subject on which members of the Guild had made intensive studies, as the result of which they were satisfied that the rodents referred to by the contemporary accounts

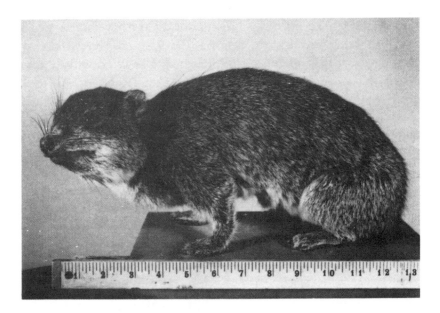

Comparison of Marin County ground squirrel (below) with barbarie conie (above). (Courtesy Robert H. Power.)

were members of a species called the Botta pocket gopher "whose burrowings create an apparent warren throughout the Point Reyes peninsula and inland. Identifying features are a rat-like tail, mole-like forepaws, and external, fur-lined pouches under the chin on each side corresponding to the 'bagge' mentioned in the accounts."

Neasham rejected the conclusion of the Guild, asserting that the pocket gopher, although having a tail somewhat similar in texture to that of a rat, has a shorter tail, not usually exceeding two inches. This cannot be considered as long, like that of a rat.

Power took a similar position, contending that the conies of Nova Albion are not the Botta pocket gopher for several reasons. The gopher is a shy, nocturnal rodent living most of its life underground and seldom seen abroad. Because of this fact, and his short, stubby tail, it is unlikely that it was the animal which the Elizabethans watched gathering his food.

According to Power, the ground squirrel is associated with warm, open grassland hills studded with oaks. The only area that fits this description in Marin County is along the San Pablo Bay shore north of San Rafael into Novato, corresponding to the range of the tule elk. Neasham agreed that the conies seen by Drake during his journey "up into the countrey" were probably ground squirrels, because of their location, number, and long tails. He added that they are to be seen on Bolinas Ridge today.

Rebuttal by the Guild

The Guild registered strong disagreement with the Power-Neesham identification of the conies as ground squirrels. The squirrel, the Guild said, was no stranger to the English. Squirrels were a familiar sight at home, and if the ground squirrel was what they saw, they would have compared it and its parts with a squirrel, not with a cony, rat, and mole. What they saw was an animal that they referred to as strange, and they compared its parts to animals with which they were familiar.

The Guild felt that the key point in identifying the cony is the reference to the "bagge" under the chin on each side. This is characteristic of the pocket gopher, which has fur-lined pouches on either side of its chin, extending to its shoulders, an unusual feature. Squirrels carry food in their cheeks. Furthermore, the gopher has the paws of a mole and the naked tail of a rat.

The Guild felt that it was not necessary to see these animals in number. *The World Encompassed* infers thousands, but "Hakluyt's account makes it evident that what was seen were the burrows of the gopher, which are abundant in the Drake's Bay area: 'We found the whole Country to be a warren of a strange kind of Conies.'"

Power's rebuttal to the Guild asserted that the Guild's contention in reference to a "bagge under the chin on each side" is not a key point. Zoologists report that the ground squirrel of Marin has especially well developed cheek pouches which often seem to be bulging with the contents of those pouches. Since "bagge" and "pouch" are synonyms, "under the chin" vs. "bulging cheeks" is hardly a key issue. Power added that Neasham's comments were so "unspecific" that "it isn't worth the space in this limited-word debate to respond to his weasel-worded statement."

To this comment, Neasham's sole and pithy rejoinder was: "Ground squirrels!"

Summary

In dealing with the issues presented by Tenet 11, the participants found themselves in rather serious controversy. The difference of opinion regarding the elk has already been mentioned. In reference to the identity of the conies, the debaters seemed to be in a three-way disagreement.

The Guild is convinced that the Marin County conies of the sixteenth century were our twentieth-century Botta pocket gopher, and they cite good reasons for their belief. Power is equally convinced that Marin's ground squirrels were the conies of the Drake visit, and he pleads his case persuasively. Nevertheless, he also finds it possible to disagree with Neasham, despite the latter's rejection of the Botta pocket gopher theory and having opted for ground squirrels. Although not entirely clear, the reason for this would appear to be that Neasham repeatedly reported seeing ground squirrels in the southwestern part of the county, on Bolinas Ridge, whereas Power's theory is based upon the supposed fact that habitation by the species is limited to the Novato, or northeastern, part of Marin County.[9] At all events, he dissociated himself from Neasham's support.

It appears that two important factors must be taken into consideration in weighing the evidence. One of these is the locale where the animals were seen by Drake; the other is the characteristics of the creatures themselves. As to the first, it was not until the party "travailed up into the Countrey" that they saw a multitude of conies. From this it is reasonable to infer that these rodents were of a species found in large numbers only in warm, sunny areas. Eschscholtz surveyed only the cold, foggy coastal area, so it is not surprising that he found no conies. Stillman's assertion that ground squirrels do not inhabit Marin County is borne out by Power, except for the northeastern section of the county "along the San Pablo Bay shore north of San Rafael into the area of Novato." This is a warm, sunny area.

The second factor is the characteristics of the conies: (1) length of tail; and (2) food-carrying pouches. On the basis of Stillman's description of the 2½-inch length, it is apparent that the tail of the gopher is neither "exceeding long" nor of "great length," as described in the accounts. While only the gopher has "external, fur-lined pouches under the chin on each side corresponding to the 'bagge' mentioned by the accounts," the ground squirrel is also equipped with "especially well-developed cheek pouches" for carrying surplus food.

Taking all these factors into consideration, the ground squirrel's habits, appearance, and living area would seem most nearly to resemble those of the animals described in the narratives. From a disinterested point of view, particularly in the light of the data, the weight of the evidence tends to favor the Power position in respect to this tenet.

20

CHAPTER

The Indians

Tenet 12: What is the significance of Drake's contact with and observations of the people of Nova Albion, description of whom comprises a large portion of the narratives of Drake's visit?

THE VISIT of the Elizabethans to Nova Albion was a signal event for all concerned. A unique relationship developed between hosts and visitors. From the native standpoint, the visit must have provided an unforgettable interlude in the otherwise dull existence of these primitive folk. From Drake's point of view, the California Indians represented an extremely fortuitous development as well as a significant highlight in his historic year in the Pacific. From the standpoint of our twentieth-century anchorage sleuths, the natives supplied a prominent, but not decisive, clue to the location of the lost harbor.

For nearly 350 years the identity of the tribe encountered by Drake remained a mystery. Its members had carried on a peaceful existence in Stone Age communities, innocent of agriculture, pastoralism, or metal. Their dwellings were circular huts dug out of the earth topped by a timber roof sealed with mud, with the only ventilation being through a single door. Their staple diet was a meal derived from the pulping of acorns. The men, apart from the chief and his retinue, wore no clothing whatever; the women partly covered themselves with crude garments fashioned from skins and bulrushes.

The peaceful pattern of their culture reflected their environment—a land of abundance. Food was no problem, since the waters were full of fish and marine mammals, and the sands were thick with clams to be dug at low tide. Elk and small game were plentiful in the hills. The Indians were able to make their acorns palatable through the development of techniques for removing the tannicacid content, and they had dry granaries for storing them. Their skills included the making of elaborately woven watertight baskets, and circular boats constructed of bulrushes.

Fletcher observed them to be "a people of a tractable, free and loving nature, without guile or treachery." He described their men as "strong of body" as well as "exceeding swift in running" and skilled in the spearing of fish in shallow waters. Concerning the women, he described them as "very obedient to their husbands, and exceedingly ready in all services; yet of themselves offering to do nothing without the consents or being called of the men."

Who Were the Indians Encountered by Drake?

Not until the twentieth century was any real effort undertaken to ascertain, on a scientific basis, the identity of the natives visited by Sir Francis in 1579. In 1908 S. A. Barrett published his work on Pomo ethnogeography in which he reproduced the California data on the voyage of Drake and made a brief evaluation.[1] After making a linguistic check with the word *Hioh* and directing attention to the feather-decorated baskets as Pomo-like, he concluded that the facts pointed to tenability of the belief that Drake's landing was somewhere north of San Francisco Bay. He felt that it might even have been north of Point Reyes, although Pomo tribesmen of the southern and southwestern dialectic area may have journeyed down to Drake's Bay bringing their ornamental baskets with them.

In his monumental *Handbook of the Indians of California,* originally published in 1923, Professor A. L. Kroeber of the University of California offered one of the first attempts by an anthropologist of stature to arrive at an identification of Drake's anchorage on the basis of information supplied by the principal contemporary accounts.[2]

Le vray portraict du Cappitaine Draeck, lequel a circuit toute la terre, en trois années, moins deux mois, et 17. iours. il partit du Royaulme D'Angleterre, le 13. de Decembre 1577. et fist son retour audict Royaulme, le 26: iour de Sept. 1580.

Paul^{ts} de la Houue excud.

Sir Francis Drake, from the engraved portrait by Paul de la Houve.

Kroeber made a comparison of the manner of life, habits, dress, customs, and habitations described in the accounts with those of various tribes in central and northern California. He felt that the evidence with respect to language was too scant to be conclusive, but that it was at least favorable to the interpretation of Drake's friends having been Coast Miwok. In his estimation, "the root called Petah referred to the *Brodiaea* and other lily bulbs consumed in quantities by all Californians." He added that "the word [Petah] stands for 'potato,' as 'Tobah' does for 'tobacco.' It is to be noted that the narrative [presumably "The Famous Voyage"] does not specify who called the plants thus."

On the basis of the ethnological evidence, he concluded that Drake had "summered on some piece of the coast not many miles north of San Francisco, and probably in the lagoon to which his name now attaches"; further, that the recent native culture in this stretch existed in substantially the same form more than three hundred years ago, making it reasonable "to believe that the Indians with whom the great explorer mingled were the direct ancestors of the Coast Miwok."

The most prominent scholar in the ethnological approach to the Drake landing site mystery has been Robert F. Heizer.[3] His studies of the ethnographic evidence dealing with the relationship between the Indians and Drake have led him to the conclusion that such evidence indicates strongly, indeed almost conclusively, that Drake landed in territory occupied by Coast Miwok Indians. He based this conclusion largely on the fact that all the unquestionably native words mentioned in the sources (Hioh, Gnaah, Huchee kecharo, Nocharo mu, Cheepe) are of Coast Miwok derivation. His original opinion was that the Indians referred to by *The World Encompassed* were of the Coast Miwok tribe and that Drake probably landed in what is now known as Drake's Bay.

Update and Re-valuation

When Heizer published *Elizabethan California* in 1974, he reviewed his earlier studies of the Drake anchorage problem and undertook to bring matters up to date on that subject from a general point of view as well as in reference to its ethnological aspects.[4] In this treatise he reviewed the various opinions published in the preceding twenty-five years, as well as some unpublished ones. In reference to the subject of

Coast Miwok Indian culture, he stated that not enough additional information had accumulated since his early publications (the last in 1947) to require a new analysis. He did, however, direct attention to the publication in 1969 of a narrative by Father Vicente de Santamaria, priest on board the *San Carlos* at the time of its entry into San Francisco Bay in 1775, and the possibilities raised by it as to the identity of the tribe (possibly Costanoan) occupying Marin County's eastern and southern shores in pre-mission times.[5]

Nevertheless, Heizer reevaluated his 1947 opinion, largely on the basis of new arguments since that date, and strictly on the assumption that the Shinn plate could in some way be authenticated. His revised opinion was that Drake had probably landed in San Francisco Bay; but he warned that "opinions have not and never will solve the question—only some kind of documentary or archaeological evidence to be discovered can solve the problem."[6]

Seeking the Significance of Drake's Contacts

Tenet 12 of the 1974 debate referred to the fact that Drake's contacts with the Nova Albion natives had comprised a large part of the contemporary narratives of the California visit, and asked for comments on the significance of Drake's contacts with the Indians.

As indicated by the tenet, the Indians did provide the major part of the discussion on Drake's visit in both principal early accounts. In "The Famous Voyage," two-thirds of the paragraphs dealing with Nova Albion discussed the natives. In *The World Encompassed,* the fraction amounted to three-fourths. The text of each has been set forth in full in the appendixes.

The request of Tenet 12 was for the "significance" of Drake's contacts with the Indians, without further indication of the context in which the evaluation was desired. Presumably, what the framers of the tenet had in mind was to elicit discussion of the clues, if any, provided by the natives about the anchorage site—a purpose consistent with that of questions propounded by other tenets. The ambiguity of Tenet 12 was reflected in the discussion which ensued, at least one of the participants having construed it to refer to the significance of Drake's contacts with the Indians in a much broader sense than that of a mere anchorage clue. As it happened, this served to add interest to the

V.

FRANCISCVS DRACO CVM
IN LOCVM QVENDAM VENIS-
set, à Rege istius regionis conuenitur.

 Vm Franciscus Draco aliquando ad locum quendam in America venisset, vidit in littó-
re quædam incolarum tuguria,quæ ex rotundis paludibus vel arboribus potius compacta,
& in formam pyramidis fastigiatá,ab externa parte terra vndique oppleta erant.Cumǭ,
ea ingressus esset, inuenit homines in circumferentia, confusè in stramine dormientes,
nullo vel ætatis vel sexus seruato discrimine, qui in medio domus ingentem ignem ex-
truxerant. Hi homines Anglis multa exhibebant beneficia,cumǭ, de eorum aduentu Rex
audiisset,venit eò cum 12000 viris, satis splendidè magnificeǭ.Ac omnes quidem sub-
diti sui nudi incedebant,ipse vero solus cuniculorum pellibus vestitus erat. Eum caduceator præcedebat,sce-
ptrum & regalia regni gestans. Hunc cum DRACO vidisset,instructa statim acie, aduentum eius expecta-
uit,sed ipse pacifice veniens,prolixa eum oratione per caduceatorem allocutus est,finitaque oratione imposuit
ei duas coronas de sceptro siue caduceo dependentes,& tres catenulas ex ossibus artificiosè factas à collo eius su-
spendit,quibus ipsi se & totum suum regnum imperiumǭ subiicere voluit. Interea mulieres etiam non paucæ
accedebant,quæ præ lætitia,maxillas & faciem, ad sanguinem vsque lacerárant, incedebant ipsæ quoque nudæ;
nisi quod femorali ex scirpis facto,pudenda aliquo modo circumdederant,& ab humeris pellem ceruinam de-
pendentem habebant.

b 2̂

Drake at Nova Albion, from Theodore De Bry's 1599 Americae Pars VIII.

debate on a topic otherwise somewhat lacking in definitive anchorage clues.

Views of the Participants

Some geographical relationships are established by references to Indians in the accounts. At Drake's Bay many former Indian village sites dating back to the sixteenth century have been found. For example, *The World Encompassed* mentioned one group of natives who watched Drake set up camp, then returned to their houses "neere about 3 quarters of an English mile distant" where they began a kind of weeping and crying out audible to the English at their camp. Today on the west bank of the Estero and north of the cove, there are the remains of a corresponding sixteenth-century habitation, about 1,300 yards from the presumed Drake camp site. Audible range between habitation and camp site is facilitated by the latter being downwind.

Also, the accounts refer to the Indians as coming *down* to the camp from the nearby hill. At Drake's Cove, the only convenient approach to the camp is from the surrounding hills. This was also the route followed by the large delegation that arrived on June 26, 1579.

Neasham asserted that the descriptions of Indians by the early accounts would apply to the lagoon area where he believes Drake built his fort. The remains of several Indian middens are to be found there near the water's edge. About three-quarters of a mile away, on McCormick Creek, is a rather large site. Up in the land, in the Olema and Nicasio areas, were the main Indian villages.

Power indicated that the fact that Drake met and dealt with the Indians in the summer of 1579 is the crux of why the location of Drake's landing is important. He explained:

> The contact with the Indians by Drake in Nova Albion resulted in the first incorporation of a non-European people as subjects of the English Crown. This was the effective founding of the overseas British Empire and the beginning of the Anglo-American experience. Francis Drake's success in Nova Albion, and especially with the Indians who surrendered their sovereignty and offered their power and faith to Britain, gave to that nation a sense of destiny that North America was a vast fifth region of the world where people were crying out to be subjects of the English Crown.

The grand dream for an overseas British Empire in North America which developed after Drake returned from Nova Albion in 1580 and before Sir Humphrey Gilbert departed for Newfoundland in 1583 was a reasonable concept if the setting for Drake's experience was within the great harbor of San Francisco Bay, but one of some foolishment if the setting was in an insignificant coastal inlet.

Rebuttals

The Guild commented that "Mr. Power's political interpretation of Drake's contact with the Coast Miwok Indians has nothing to do with identification of the landing site." Neasham pointed out that all three potential anchorage areas were inhabited by Coast Miwok Indians who had sites near the water's edge; that all three have middens about three-quarters of a mile away from suggested Drake fort sites; and that near each were hills over which the Indians could have approached.

With respect to the statement that "the grand dream for an overseas British Empire in North America was one of some foolishment if the setting was in an insignificant coastal bay," Neasham asserted that it was "invalid" because Drake, on the contrary, would have sought a hidden spot for his anchorage, the more insignificant the better. Moreover, Nova Albion was a vast area, running as high as latitude 48° N, as many maps showed, hence its claiming was not dependent solely on Coast Miwok Indians or on the setting of the spot where he built his fort, careened the *Golden Hind,* and nailed the plate of brass. In response to which Power, having the last word, insisted that "the political history that flowed from Drake's experiences with the Coast Miwok Indians is what gives substance to this debate."

Evaluation of Evidence

The natives encountered by Drake at Nova Albion did indeed provide a major clue to the anchorage site, although not a complete solution. Ethnologists have been able to establish that the Indians described by "The Famous Voyage" and *The World Encompassed* were members of the Coast Miwok tribe; and further that the area occupied by this tribe was substantially coextensive with the Marin County of today. Consequently, all three of our proposed sites were inhabited by

Coast Miwok tribesmen, but this information does not provide evidence favoring one site over another. Even the fact, as mentioned in *The World Encompassed,* that there was an Indian village within three quarters of a mile from Drake's camp is not helpful because, as Neasham has pointed out, an Indian village existed at about that distance from each of the proposed sites.

But even with these potential sources of controversy thus disposed of, debaters cited two additional points. One was Power's contention that, although the "generalized conditions surrounding the Indians may be applied to all three sites," there was one important distinction: the greater number of Indians living in the San Francisco Bay watershed, and not in the coastal area. He reasoned, therefore, that it would seem more likely that the large visitation of Indians to Drake's campsite came from these greater centers of Miwok population. The rebuttal to this contention was that the nine-day period between Drake's arrival and the visitation on the twenty-sixth would have given ample time for word to be gotten to the Indians of the San Francisco Bay watershed, and for a delegation from that area to reach Drake's Bay or Bolinas Bay.

The Coast Miwok and the British Empire

The second and more important contention, from Power's standpoint, was the impact of the location of the anchorage on political history. With this there was disagreement by the other participants, the Guild declaring flatly that Power's political interpretation of Drake's contact with the Coast Miwok Indians had nothing to do with the identification of his California landfall. Neasham described the whole concept as invalid, namely, the concept that Drake must have been in San Francisco Bay to insure a "sense of destiny" in the founding of the British overseas empire.

It is clear that for a period of five weeks, four hundred years ago, northern California was claimed and occupied as a possession of the English Crown, then personified by Queen Elizabeth I, and that this occupation, however brief, was never challenged. For thirty-six days, between June 17 and July 23, 1579, Nova Albion could be said to have been a part of Elizabethan England.

Drake, however, was not content to rest his claim on behalf of England upon his discovery, occupation, and brief but unchallenged possession of that part of northern California. Rather he chose to rest it upon the alleged surrender by its original owners, the Coast Miwok, of their sovereignty and offer of their power and faith to Britain. Power has construed the actions of the Indians as "the effective founding of the overseas British Empire."

Unofficial Ambassador

Speaking of the British Empire that was, Power has done no little to advance its renown. He has made several trips to England, and is perhaps as well known in the Drake circles of Plymouth and London as in those of San Francisco and Marin County. He would appear to have drawn British-American ties closer by recognition in the mother country of his part in acclaiming Drake not merely as England's earliest visitor to California, but as the discoverer of San Francisco Bay.

When the English people celebrated the 400th anniversary of Drake's circumnavigation in 1977, Power acted as ambassador without portfolio from America. In his roles as prominent Drake scholar and president of the California Historical Society, he was among those invited to participate in the quatercentenary ceremonies and exhibitions, and brought his entire collection of Drakiana (some two-hundred items, mostly rare early publications) to the British Library and Museum, where they were on display for several weeks. Power had the honor of escorting Queen Elizabeth and Prince Philip through his part of the exhibit and explaining its significance, and no doubt propounding his theory of the location of Drake's lost California harbor.

Undaunted, however, by the Power prestige, his friendly rivals have been unimpressed by his contention that by reason of Drake's asserted discovery of San Francisco Bay, California was really the birthplace of the British overseas empire. They find his theory of a connection between that empire and whether the Drake anchorage was on the coastal or bay side of Marin County difficult for the average mind to follow.

Significance of the Ceremony of June 26, 1579

For a full four centuries the myth of "the free giving up" by the California Indians "of the province and people into her Majesties hands" has been perpetuated. It originated with Drake himself, if one can rely upon the language of the plate of brass as set forth in Hakluyt's 1589 account. Since that time it has been frequently repeated, although not without challenge by historians and Drake scholars. James Burney, in his *Chronological History of the Discoveries in the South Seas or Pacific Ocean,* published in 1803, was the first to turn an analytical eye on this subject.[7] In writing of the ceremony in which the natives honored Drake, Burney commented that "these honors paid to a stranger have more than a shade of resemblance to the custom found among many Indian nations of exchanging names with those whose alliance or friendship they desire. The compliments and ceremonies of the native chief were differently understood, and it was imagined that he had invested Drake with the insignia of royalty," and that the natives "with 'true meaning and intent,' had resigned to him their right and title in the whole land, and made themselves and their posterity his vassals." Burney continued to make his skepticism evident at considerable length.

Not long after the Burney visit, Alexander Forbes, an early writer on California history, commented on the subject in a similar vein, saying: "Sir Francis Drake mistook the common head dress . . . worn around the head, somewhat in the manner of a crown, as the emblem of royalty, and considered the gift made of this to him, by one of the chiefs, as the abdication of the sovereignty of the country in favor of Queen Elizabeth!"[8] (The exclamation point was that of the author.)

Comments of Other Scholars

Davidson gave the subject a brief, but caustic, treatment, saying:

> To those who know the character of the natives the solemnity of crowning Drake is painfully absurd. . . . Drake set up a monument or post with an inscription to prove his having been there; and he declared the natives had surrendered themselves and the whole land, and had become his vassals. . . . Yet could neither party understand a word of the other! See Burney's criticisms thereon.[9]

In full agreement with the foregoing were Wagner's comments:

> Fletcher's childlike credulity and love of the marvelous and extraordinary no doubt induced him to read into some very simple actions of these Indians a meaning totally contrary to that intended by them. According to him Drake accepted the crown and the chains placed around his neck as a sign that the Indians were conferring the sovereignty of the country on him, and he assures us that Drake took these into his hand in the name and to the use of her most excellent Majesty. Nothing can be more certain, of course, that the Indians had no such idea.

He continued at length along the same vein.[10]

The foregoing, however, was not Wagner's only comment on the subject. He had occasion to discuss the views expressed by Sir Travers Twiss in *The Oregon Question Examined*,[11] published in London in 1846, as the principal argument supporting the British claim to the Oregon territory. In that connection, Wagner stated: "Dr. Twiss was still foolish enough to think that the taking possession by Drake had been made with the consent of the natives, a ridiculous pretension that could only have originated from a lack of even the most rudimentary knowledge of the Pacific Coast Indians."

In a recent book dealing with the circumnavigation, its author, in speaking of the ceremony of June 26, 1579, concluded that Drake and his companions could only understand it in terms of English royal ceremonial, and added: "What was probably happening was that the English leader was being made an honorary chief of the tribe. That was not how Fletcher chose to interpret it."[12]

Forceful and impressive as these statements by perceptive individuals have been, they do not appear to have fully accomplished their intended purpose of debunking the venerable myth of surrender by the Indians of their sovereignty to the English Crown. Even today, in the face of the circumstances under which the events of June 26, 1579, took place, knowledgeable people are still accepting Drake's unrealistic and self-serving explanation of what the Indians had in mind at face value, and treating it as the inception of Britain's overseas empire. It would appear, however, that most modern Drake scholars follow the Burney-Davidson-Wagner line of thought on this subject, concurred in by the Guild and Neasham, and reject the Power concept and reasoning.

Francis Drake and the Coast Miwok

From the standpoint of those who disagree with the Power concept, the Indians of Nova Albion had no intention or awareness of surrendering their "sovereignty" or offering their "power and faith to Britain," and the idea that they "were crying out to be subjects of the English Crown" is totally unrelated to reality. The Coast Miwok had never heard of England, and in their primitive minds would have been unable to understand where that small country was, much less the nature of its aims and objectives. They regarded their visitors as gods, according to *The World Encompassed*,[13] and therefore not as Englishmen or even as human beings, but rather as deities from another world, to be honored and worshipped as such.

As for the contact with the Indians being "the first incorporation of a non-European people as subjects of the English Crown," this can only be regarded as a figment. Knowing that the natives regarded Drake and his men as gods, how could he have believed that they were surrendering their sovereignty to the English Crown! As *The World Encompassed* indicated, Drake accepted the homage and obeisance of the Indians because he was afraid not to ". . . both for that he would not give them any cause of mistrust or disliking of him (that being the only place, wherein at this present, we were of necessitie inforced to seeke reliefe of many things), and chiefly for that he knew not to what good end God had brought this to pass."

In other words, Drake was in a position where the last thing he wanted to do was to antagonize the entire native population. He perceived that he had nothing to lose by going along with a gag, and might have something to gain, to wit, a continued freedom from hostility on the part of the Indians.

The supposition of the English that the natives regarded them as gods was, of course, no more than a surmise. After all, it was the Indians who planned and staged the great ceremony of June 26, 1579, who gathered by the hundreds from many miles around, and who, of course, were the only ones who knew precisely what they were doing and why. It is safe to say, however, that they did not congregate to demonstrate their desire to become "subjects of the English Crown," or to offer "their power and faith to Britain." What they did know, if the supposition set forth in *The World Encompassed* be credited, was that they had been favored with an unexpected visitation by the gods, who had suddenly appeared in their floating abode from whence the natives knew not.

Drake, the Opportunist

Beyond that point, the thoughts and actions of all concerned provide only an interesting basis for conjecture. For example, the extremely religious Drake must have felt rather silly being honored as their chief god by a horde of pagan natives; and therefore not to appear too ridiculous in the eyes of his crew, who had only a slight idea of what was going on, he probably decided that the better part of discretion, not to mention valor, would be to accept whatever it was the Indians had to offer, but to do so in the name of the queen. At least, it is interesting to speculate that he may have explained it that way to the crew afterward, just in case any of them started to call him "king," rather than Captain Drake.

Actually, since there was a complete language barrier with the natives, there would have been no possible way for Drake to know the true meaning of the rite the Indians performed. It may have been a form of mass worship, an intertribal type of welcome, such as making him an honorary chief, or a ceremony of purely religious or ritualistic significance. The circumstances contraindicate any political intent or purpose.

Whatever the fact, it is certain that Drake, ever the shrewd opportunist, perceived a means by which he could take advantage of this unexpected turn of events upon his return to England, that is, by claiming the acquisition of new territory for the English Crown with the consent of its inhabitants. Indeed, this may have been what went through his mind when one of the reasons given by *The World Encompassed* for his participation in the ceremony was that "he knew not to what good God had brought this to pass."

"Sense of Destiny"

While we are dealing with this phase of the contacts between Drake and the Indians, the question arises what evidence there was to support a statement that Drake's "success in Nova Albion" (using "success" to mean anchorage in such a body of water as San Francisco Bay, rather than in a coastal harbor) gave Britain a "sense of destiny."[14]

Granting the probability that Drake's circumnavigation and general activities while en route may have made a contribution to a "grand dream for an overseas British Empire" and possibly to a "sense of destiny" on the part of the English nation, as stated by Power, nevertheless there is not a scintilla of evidence to support the contention that such a "grand dream" and "sense of destiny" were a reasonable concept only if Drake's anchorage had been in San Francisco Bay. On the contrary, such an assertion is illogical, from a disinterested standpoint, for three reasons: (1) Where Drake spent his time in the summer of 1579 represented what is today called "classified" information. The rigid censorship imposed soon after Drake's return kept the English people from learning anything of importance about his activities in North America, let alone whether the harbor visited was magnificent or miniscule; (2) even today we have no convincing evidence that the anchorage was in San Francisco Bay; and (3) even if the English people had full knowledge on the subject, it is inconceivable that their development of a "sense of destiny" depended upon whether Drake's California setting was San Francisco Bay or an "insignificant coastal inlet."

The Reverse of the Coin

If, by some miracle, there were to be discovered the equivalent of a Dead Sea Scroll left by the Indians who participated in the events of June 26, 1579, it might serve to dissipate the confusion as to the meaning of the elaborate ceremony of that date.[15] Obviously, this will not occur but, in lieu thereof, it is interesting to read a reconstruction from the Coast Miwok standpoint of what may have taken place on that fateful day in early California history.[16]

This reconstruction by Dr. Robert C. Thomas, a Coast Miwok descendant, suggests that on June 21, 1579, the members of the tribe at Olompali received word of the arrival of a spirit ship (the *Golden Hind*). This alarming news caused distress and hysteria among the natives who nevertheless laid plans for, and staged, a confrontation with the mysterious strangers—a ceremony that was a combination of bravado and propitiation, since they were uncertain whether they might all be facing their day of doom. The author summarized the result by saying: "When the feared death or disaster failed to descend upon them, they understood that these strange aliens were not malignant spirits, and the later legend reported only that a party of alien men had once visited Olom-kocha (homeland of a sub-tribe of the Coast Miwok)."[17] The author expressed his belief that Drake had "purposely misinterpreted the June 26th ceremonies as a surrender of the native 'kingdom' to the English in order to establish English claim to the land and its gold."[18]

Summary

Throughout the voyage, the role played by the native people encountered by Drake was a prominent one. Those in South America were uniformly hostile and accounted for the death of several crew members. Those in North America were friendly, and their behavior was indispensable to the purpose and success of the visit. Consequently, the attention they were given by the contemporary narratives was such that they are among the important clues to the location of the Nova Albion anchorage.

In this context, the California Indians really must be considered from three points of view. The most valuable clue is that of language, that is, the words which have enabled modern ethnologists to identify the tribe encountered and thus to narrow the location of the Drake visit to Marin County shores. The second lies in the fact that *The World Encompassed* placed a native village within three quarters of a mile from the Drake fort, a clue that has proved to be of little help because the finding of middens indicates that such a village was located within that approximate distance of each of the three sites.

The third clue, if we can call it such, was the ceremony staged by the Coast Miwok at the anchorage site on June 26, 1579. It was this rite that furnished the basis for the contention that the "grand dream for an overseas British Empire . . . would have been one of some foolishment if the setting [for Drake's experience] was in an insignificant coastal inlet" — a novel concept, but one which clearly represents speculation on a rather grandiose scale. While it serves to belittle the coastal harbors, it is neither probative nor persuasive on the issue of the landing-site location. From the standpoint of a disinterested observer of the anchorage scene, the response to Tenet 12 provides no logical basis for pinpointing Drake's landfall.

21

CHAPTER

Archaeological and Artifactual Evidence

Tenet 13: Discuss the significance of archaeological evidence related to Drake's landing.

WHEN DRAKE and his associates sailed away from Nova Albion and its presumably grieving populace, inevitably they left tangible reminders of their visit. Having in mind their encampment of some eighty people for a period of several weeks, it would have been difficult for them not to leave various traces of their presence. Some of these would have been portable artifacts — things that they brought with them, but elected not to carry away. Others would have been in the nature of rearrangement or change in the area occupied, such as the fort or compound which they constructed for living space as well as for temporary storage of their equipment and treasure.

The contemporary accounts afford us information about some of these artifacts, large and small. The most specific, of course, are the statements of both "The Famous Voyage" and *The World Encompassed* concerning the plate, the post on which it was mounted, and the sixpence left with it. However, both accounts also mentioned the "necessarie things to cover their nakednesse," which Drake bestowed on the natives; and *The World Encompassed* made a brief reference to the "walls of stone" about their encampment. But only John Drake, in his second deposition to the Spaniards in South America, mentioned the largest artifact of all, Rodrigo Tello's frigate, which had been "taken from Nicaragua" on March 20, 1579, and was left at Nova Albion.[1]

Search for Artifacts

For more than 350 years after Drake's departure from California, there was no record of the finding of any relic or artifact having a possible connection with the 1579 visit. Nor had there been any effort, organized or otherwise, to search for articles of this kind. However, the appearance of the Shinn plate in 1936 not only created a greater interest in the Drake controversy, but also had a stimulating effect on archaeological investigations in Marin County. The earliest of such investigations began with the Indian middens at Drake's Bay in 1940. The program was initiated by the Department of Anthropology of the University of California under the direction of Professor Robert F. Heizer, director of the University of California *Archaeological Survey,* and continued later under Professors R.K. Beardsley and Clement W. Meighan.[2]

Intermittently over a period of twelve years, this exploration of Indian midden sites was carried on with the hope of identifying sixteenth-century materials brought to the area by European visitors. During that period, a considerable quantity of material was excavated, including fragments of Chinese porcelain, iron spikes and rods, and fragments of oriental stoneware. Most of these were considered to have come from the wreck of Cermeño's *San Agustin* in 1595. None could be definitely linked to Drake, although, in the course of his buccaneering activities along South and Central America, he is known to have appropriated a certain amount of earthenware of Asian origin.

After 1952, excavations continued from time to time at various Drake's Bay Indian sites, of which thirteen were found in all. Some of these had been located through surveys conducted by members of the Drake Navigators Guild, who also assisted occasionally in digging. In the years immediately preceding 1959, work on the middens on

Limantour Spit was carried on by Professor Adan E. Treganza, of San Francisco State College, for the University of California; and again in 1964–1966 for the National Park Service. In 1961–1962, a field archaeology class headed by Edward von der Porten, a Santa Rosa teacher, did considerable work under the auspices of the Community Service Program of the Santa Rosa Junior College.[3]

As a result of these excavations during more than a quarter of a century in the Drake's Bay area, some 800 artifacts of sixteenth-century origin have been turned up, of which more than 650 were porcelain sherds. Most of these have been identified as of Chinese origin, probably from the Wan-li era (1573–1610). The Guild members concede that most of this material must be attributed to the Cermeño visit, but they contend that it is not possible completely to rule out the possibility that some of it was of Drake origin. Disinterested archaeologists, however, have found no conclusive evidence of Drake at the bay which bears his name, nor at Bolinas Bay. Heizer said:

> Attempts by archaeologists to discover some undoubted sixteenth century material which could have been only left by Drake in Indian village sites, at Drake's Bay or in San Quentin Cove within San Francisco Bay have been carried on for years, and not a single item has been found . . . . There is no point in summarizing work done since 1940 at Drake's Bay by various archaeologists, or in the vicinity of San Quentin since the discovery of the brass plate for the reason that all such rummaging in Indian sites has produced nothing that can be referred to Drake.[4]

Looking for the Fort

In addition to the investigation of Indian sites for possible artifacts relating to Drake, much time and effort has also been expended by proponents of the coastal bays searching for remains of the fort itself. Nothing of this sort has been possible at the San Quentin site because of the enormous changes brought about by urbanization of the area.

In 1952 the Guild came upon what it believed was the site of Drake's fort, an area just inside the Estero which assertedly had been a sheltered inlet or cove in 1579. The group then made plans to uncover, if possible, the stone walls believed to have been a part of the fort.

Photographs were taken from the nearby hills, as well as from the air, in the hope that some indication of the structure's outlines might be detected. After the area had been gone over with a mine-detector without result, test pits were dug to intercept traces of stone walls, but little of interest was uncovered. The searchers were hoping to find, also, bits of pitch, tallow, coal, and charcoal; but that which they found was in such small quantities that it could not be related to the sixteenth century. Although extensive digging continued until 1961, by which time nearly a mile of trenching had been completed, no artifact had been found clearly relating Drake with the cove; and it was realized that better proof, if any there were to be, would have to await a major archaeological effort.

The same result was reached at Bolinas Lagoon, where further archaeological activity was discontinued after 1974. At that time California Department of Parks and Recreation archaeologist William E. Pritchard, who was in charge of it, conceded that the investigation had disclosed nothing that would specifically link the site with Drake or any other explorer of the sixteenth or seventeenth century. Nevertheless, Neasham has continued to explore other sites in the Lagoon area in the hope of finding artifacts related to Drake.

Elizabethan Sixpence

Both "The Famous Voyage" and *The World Encompassed* stated that when Drake left his plate of brass on the shores of Nova Albion, it was "together with her highnes picture and armes, in a peece of sixe pence of current English money." However, when the Shinn plate was produced in 1936, the coin was missing and people have been expecting it to turn up almost any day. Heizer, in speaking of Marin County finds that may have been left there by Drake, has made skeptical reference to "the unconfirmed reports of English silver sixpences, no doubt always with a pre-1579 date, found on the beaches of Point Reyes."[5]

Ironically, that comment made in early 1974 was followed in the latter part of the same year by announcement of the finding of just such a coin, an Elizabethan sixpence, minted in 1567.[6] Its finder was Charles Slaymaker, a young archaeologist and University of California Extension Division lecturer. According to Robert H. Power, chairman of the California Heritage Preservation Commission, this is

1567 Elizabethan sixpence found in Marin County in 1974.

the first Elizabethan coin ever found in North America and its discovery at Olompali has made that location "the oldest Anglo-Indian contact site" on the continent.

Slaymaker had been digging at Rancho Olompali, site of an ancient Coast Miwok village, since 1972, and he lived on the site. He stated that he found the coin on June 14, 1974, while hand-troweling the ground over a Miwok ceremonial dance floor. The coin was two to three feet into the debris covering the floor. Also found in the same location were two glass beads of the type used by Europeans for trading with Indians. On June 27, 1974, Slaymaker presented the coin to the Bancroft Library, where the Shinn plate also reposes. It was later authenticated by chemical tests and by sending it to England to make certain of the date of minting.

Heizer's reference to "unconfirmed reports of English sixpences" found in Marin County brings to mind an article by Harold Gilliam entitled "Drake's Missing Coin?" which appeared in *This World,* a supplement to the *San Francisco Chronicle* of May 31, 1964. The occasion for the article was a report which Gilliam had just received of a 1573 sixpence, pictures of both sides of which were published with the article. Its finding was described as follows: "According to evidence that cannot be completely confirmed, the coin was discovered at some unknown point in Marin County between about 1900 and 1915 by a San Franciscan now deceased."

Gilliam went on to speculate that the coin would more likely have been found on the bay side of Marin County, because before 1915 a lack of transportation facilities to the Point Reyes region would have made visiting the area difficult. He also indicated that the 1573 coin came to light after publication by the *Chronicle* of an earlier Gilliam article, which reported the finding of another English sixpence dated 1593, also in Marin County, and brought to the attention of Walter Heil, director emeritus of the De Young Museum.

These reports lend force to Heizer's skeptical reference, because it appears that there is now a record of the finding during the twentieth century of three sixteenth-century sixpences, all discovered in Marin County, two of them bearing dates before that of the Drake visit. For two of them, also, no information about the precise locale of discovery was available, and none was discovered under circumstances entitling it to be considered as archaeologically authenticated.

Anchor Found at Drake's Bay

One of the more interesting artifacts supposedly left in Nova Albion in 1579 was a large anchor of ancient design which, in the latter part of the nineteenth century, was accidentally retrieved near Point Reyes and was said to have borne Drake's name.

According to the story, as it was pieced together by attorney Hart H. North[7] of San Francisco in the 1920s, Captain Charles E. Raynor, of Seattle, was master of the sealing schooner *Allie I. Algar* in 1887. In February of that year, after refitting his vessel in San Francisco harbor and heading out for a sealing voyage, he was overtaken by a severe storm. He put into Drake's Bay where he anchored in the lee of the point known as Chimney Rock, this being just off the old road that ran to the small beach on the north side of Point Reyes.

When the weather abated some five days later, he attempted to raise his anchors, but found that one of them was snagged. Raising it with great difficulty, he found the anchor chain had wrapped itself around the fluke of a very old, much rusted, and unusual appearing anchor. He estimated its weight at 1,200 pounds, and lashed it on the forward deck of his vessel.

When members of the crew found time, they chipped off the heavy coat of rust with which it was covered and Raynor, to his amazement, thought he was able to make out the name D R A K E cut into the iron in ancient lettering. On the opposite side was other lettering which he was unable to decipher. He proceeded on his voyage, but put in at Port Townsend on the way to the Bering Sea and left the anchor on the old Katz wharf where, to his knowledge, it remained for many years. He passed away in 1927 or 1928.

When North, a member of the California Historical Society, learned of the anchor in 1925, he notified the History Department of the University of California by letter but received no response. He then began to take steps to gain some word of the anchor's whereabouts through people in Port Townsend, and by offering a reward for finding it, but without result. After discovery of the Shinn plate and a conversation with Allen Chickering, president of the California Historical Society, he again tried to follow up the matter.

Although Captain Raynor was dead, North succeeded in locating others who had been with him in 1887. One of these was Captain A. J. Bozarth, who had served as a sailor on the *Allie I. Algar,* and another was A. C. Simons, of Chico, who had been employed on the ship as a hunter. From both of these men he obtained affidavits attesting in detail to the finding of the old anchor and to the wording on it, although the letters *D* and *E* were not very plain.

With his interest in Drake renewed by word of the Shinn plate's discovery in 1937, North visited the Point Reyes area where the *Allie I. Algar* had been anchored, and made a careful inspection of the area, taking photographs as well as notes of what he saw. He felt that the site tallied rather closely with that described in *The World Encompassed,* and accordingly prepared and sent to the Historical Society an article entitled "Another Chapter on Drake's Anchorage," together with photographs, copies of the pertinent affidavits, and a sketch of the anchor based on its description by Captain Bozarth. The publication committee of the Historical Society returned the material to North with the comment that it was "most interesting," and a suggestion that, if possible, additional documentation be obtained.

The story of the anchor ended at that point. No one has seen the anchor at close range for at least ninety years; and even those who examined it originally could not be positive that the name they saw was DRAKE. So another potential Drake relic has vanished, probably now resting at the bottom of the bay at Port Townsend; and, as with the plate itself, we can only speculate as to its authenticity and relevance to the site of Drake's landing.

Mortar and Halberd

Ancient relics discovered in the Marin County area are always of special archaeological interest because of the possibility, even though remote, of a Drake connection. One such artifact is a blackened brass mortar that was donated to St. Francis Episcopal Church in Novato in 1950 by Katherine Ebright, now deceased.[8] It is of a type said to have been made in Nuremberg not later than 1604. This one looks like a mug with two handles, and is 5½ inches high and 4 inches in diameter at its base, with the numerals 1 5 7 0 crudely chiseled on its side. Similar mortars were in common use in Europe in the sixteenth century by doctors and chemists.

This particular object's history is unknown, but it seems to have been buried a long time in adobe-like soil. According to an unsubstantiated legend, it was found during a church picnic at Drake's Bay. There is no proof, however, to indicate that it was not brought to Marin County long after Drake's visit to that area.

Another ancient artifact came to light near Tiburon in the spring of 1955, when a Petaluma man named Bernie Roth, aged 27, picked up what has been identified as a Javanese halberd tip probably dating back to the sixteenth century.[9] He turned it over to Alan E. Treganza, who had been engaged in excavating Indian sites in the vicinity of the San Quentin Cove. Treganza felt that the ornamental spear tip (20 inches long) could have been brought to California by Drake, but probably wasn't; at least there was nothing to relate it to Drake.

Comments by Debaters

Tenet 13 focused attention on the possibility that archaeological or artifactual findings in the Marin County area might provide clues to the anchorage location. The Guild stated that of the more than 800 artifacts of sixteenth-century European origin found in Drake's Bay sites since 1940, most were fragments of Chinese porcelain and most were probably from the Cermeño wreck. However, since it is known that Drake had four chests of porcelains when he came to California, the Guild felt there was a possibility that some fragments might be from this source. Similarly, with goods and materials common to both and a short intervening time span, the Guild felt the bulk of artifacts cannot positively be attributed to either source.

Thirteen habitation sites at Drake's Bay have been dated to the sixteenth century. According to the Guild, one of these, MRD 235, corresponds to that described as being near three-quarters of a mile from Drake's camp. Six unusual items of European origin were found there at the same level as porcelain sherds: a small copper cone, a shred of dark wool cloth, a peach pit, a clinker, fragments of tar, and an iron item resembling a compass needle with a pivot-like projection near the center. These were said to be different from artifacts found on Limantour Spit where Cermeño camped.

After the Guild's discovery of the Estero site, which it called Drake's Cove, the Guild undertook a search for traces of Drake's fort, and exploratory digs continued there until 1961. More than ninety pits and trenches were dug. Before the work ended, it seemed apparent to the Guild that Drake's fort had been on the beach outside the excavation area and long since destroyed by the sea and erosion of the shore. Accordingly, the net result of this work was an outlining of "Drake's Cove." Trenching revealed what was "probably" the inner bank of his careening basin. On this there was a layer of uniformly large stones, lying over sand and gravel, that may have washed in from remains of the fort.[10] The Guild believes that further excavation is required.

At Bolinas Bay, archaeological investigations were conducted in the summers of 1973 and 1974 to determine whether a prospective site on the tidal flats of the interior lagoon could be identified with the foundations of Drake's encampment of 1579. It had been believed that a "fish pond" constructed in 1872 possibly overlay an earlier structure of the size and shape that could have served Drake as a fort. Pritchard, after extensive excavation at the site, concluded that it disclosed no evidence related to Drake. Excavations in the area are still continuing.

Power asserted that the only archaeological artifact ever discovered in California which has been identified as Elizabethan is Shinn's plate of brass. It was Power's position that this find established the Marin shore of San Francisco Bay as the only Drake archaeological discovery zone in California.

Many sixteenth-century artifacts from the wreck of the goods-laden *San Agustin* in Drake's Bay in 1595 have been unearthed at Indian village sites in the Point Reyes area. The fact that these artifacts apparently were not dispersed beyond Point Reyes is evidence, according to Power, that the Indians did not trade or transport European artifacts *circa* 1595. This fact suggests that the Indians would not have transported the plate of brass or other Elizabethan artifacts any great distance from the place where they were left by the English and, therefore, that the Elizabethan archaeological zone is limited to the San Francisco Bay shore of Marin County.

What Became of Tello's Frigate?

There was no discussion of the subject by the debate participants, but we know that Drake brought two vessels with him to Nova Albion, departing with only the *Golden Hind*. As stated earlier, this second ship was Rodrigo Tello's frigate,[11] which had followed the bigger vessel throughout the long journey into the North Pacific. Drake undoubtedly needed its capacity, such as it was, to get his heavily loaded, leaky ship to a point where it could be fully graved and repaired.

There is no information concerning the fate of the frigate after the departure of the *Golden Hind*. From a conjectural standpoint, there are several possibilities: (1) It could have been burned or broken up for firewood;[12] (2) it could have been left intact in the harbor; or (3) it could have been sailed away by crew members who deserted or elected not to depart with Drake. If it never left Nova Albion, its remains would provide almost certain evidence of Drake's visit from an archaeological standpoint. However, no hint of its fate has ever been heard and, at this late date, there is no reason to expect that any part of the vessel will ever be found.

Summary

It would appear that this tenet has generated more discussion over fewer findings than any of the other nineteen. To put it bluntly, there have been no findings whatever that can definitely be connected with Drake. Suspicion has been cast upon the authenticity of the Shinn plate (see next chapter), and the Elizabethan sixpence unearthed at Olompali in 1974 was only one of three allegedly found in Marin County during the past few decades. There is no way that it can be proved Drake-related, and skeptics find it as easy to disbelieve that the 1567 sixpence was brought to Marin County in 1579 as that the Shinn plate is genuine.

Without having any definite archaeological finds to support their respective claims, our three debaters have used their respective allotments of space to describe their efforts — in some cases considerable — to uncover something, in fact almost anything, that might add a bit of plausibility to their various contentions. The story of their efforts is interesting, but the answer to Tenet 13 is clear: There is no archaeological or artifactual evidence that can positively be related to Drake's visit. Consequently, this chapter throws no additional light on the elusive mystery of the anchorage site.

22

CHAPTER

The Plate of Brass

*Tenet 14: Before Drake left the bay in which he had an-
chored, according to* The World Encompassed, *he
"caused to be set up a monument of our being there . . .
namely a plate of brasse." This plate was discovered in
1936 by Beryle Shinn on a hill overlooking San Francisco
Bay. After the discovery was announced, William Caldeira claimed to have previously discovered this same plate
near Drake's Bay in 1933 and to have discarded it near
the Greenbrae hillside where Shinn found it. What is the
significance of the plate to the landing site controversy?*

T HE MONUMENT set up by Drake during his sojourn at
Nova Albion has been described in an earlier chapter.[1] That
such a monument was left in Nova Albion upon Drake's
departure is well documented by the contemporary accounts. The
resemblance between the versions of this incident appearing in "The
Famous Voyage" and *The World Encompassed*[2] is striking, making it
obvious that both were derived from the same source. Both accounts,
as well as that appearing in the "Anonymous Narrative,"[3] used the
words "post," "nailed," and "plate." However, *The World Encompassed*
described it as a "plate of brasse," the "Anonymous Narrative" as a
"plate of lead," while "The Famous Voyage" did not state the kind of
metal.

Despite the similarity between the versions of this incident contained in the two principal contemporary accounts, there were certain differences in wording. Considerable ado was made over these differences by Herbert E. Bolton, professor of American History and director of the Bancroft Library, University of California, in his speech announcing the finding of the plate.[4] The only difference that seems worthy of mention at this time is with respect to the sixpence. According to "The Famous Voyage," it was "under the plate," whereas *The World Encompassed* stated that it was held "by a hole made of purpose through the plate."

The Shinn Plate

For years Professor Bolton had been telling his history classes at the University of California at Berkeley to "keep an eye out" for Drake's "plate of brasse" and the silver sixpence bearing the image of Queen Elizabeth. Yet he was thrilled as well as surprised when a young man telephoned him in February, 1937, to seek his opinion about a metal plate he had picked up the preceding summer in Marin County — a plate whose identity Bolton sensed even before seeing it, from the area of discovery and the general description given over the phone. Even upon superficial examination, he felt that it was indeed the plate which had been left on California soil 358 years before.

The plate's finder was Beryle Shinn, a department-store clerk, aged 26, of Oakland, and his story, later put into writing, was as follows:

> In the summer of 1936 I was traveling south on Highway 101 from San Rafael and when coming down the ridge approaching Greenbrae one of my tires was punctured. Veering to the side of the road I stopped my car. On the ridge was a likely picnic spot. I climbed under a barbed wire fence and climbed to the top of the ridge. There an extensive view presented itself. To the east was Point San Quentin and upper San Francisco Bay, bounded on the southwest by the Tiburon peninsula. Below was the tidal estuary of Corte Madera Creek. Approaching an outcrop of rock near the top of the ridge, I picked up rocks and rolled them down the hill. As I pulled a rock from the soil, I saw the edge of a metal plate which was partly covered by the rock. When I pulled the plate free from the ground, I noticed that it was about the size to repair the frame of my automobile.

So when I returned to my car I took it along and tossed it in. Several months later I thought of repairing the frame. While handling the plate, I noticed that it seemed to have some inscription on it. I scrubbed it with a brush and noted a date, 1579, near the top of the plate. This interested me, so I showed it to a few of my friends, but none could make out what it was until one, a college student, deciphered the word Drake and suggested that the metal plate be shown to Dr. Herbert E. Bolton of the University of California. This was done and Dr. Bolton discovered that it was Sir Francis Drake's Plate of Brass.

Shinn was asked if he thought anyone could have deciphered the letters or figures on the plate before he scrubbed it with the brush, and replied that he was sure that they could not have done so. On February 28, 1937, Bolton and Allen L. Chickering, president of the California Historical Society, went with Shinn to Marin County where he led them to the spot on the ridge where he said he had found the plate. Within a few days, photographs of the place of discovery and views from the location were taken by Walter A. Starr and Francis P. Farquhar of San Francisco, interested members of the California Historical Society.

Photograph of the Shinn plate of brass found in Marin County in 1936. (Courtesy Bancroft Library.)

THE PLATE OF BRASS

X-ray of the Shinn plate. (Courtesy Bancroft Library.)

The plate was of solid brass, about five inches wide by eight inches long, and an eighth of an inch thick. At its top and bottom, equidistant from each end, were notches half an inch square, presumably to permit its being nailed to the "firme poste." Incised on its surface, apparently with a small chisel, was the inscription which Bolton called "California's choicest archaeological treasure." It read as follows:

BEE IT KNOWNE UNTO ALL MEN BY THESE PRESENTS
JUNE 17, 1579
BY THE GRACE OF GOD AND IN THE NAME OF HERR
MAIESTY QUEEN ELIZABETH OF ENGLAND AND HERR
SUCCESSORS FOREVER I TAKE POSSESSION OF THIS
KINGDOME WHOSE KING AND PEOPLE FREELY RESIGNE
THEIR RIGHT AND TITLE IN THE
WHOLE LAND UNTO HERR
MAIESTIES KEEPEING NOW NAMED BY ME AN TO BEE
KNOWNE UNTO ALL MEN AS NOVA ALBION
G. FRANCIS DRAKE

(Hole for Sil-
ver Sixpence)

Once personally satisfied that he was dealing with the genuine article, Bolton began to wonder how this archaeological relic could be acquired and preserved for all time. For advice, he turned to Chickering who, beside being a friend and alumnus of the University, was an attorney. Negotiations with the finder of the plate were begun and successfully concluded, after a group of San Franciscans, all members of the California Historical Society, joined him in furnishing the necessary funds. On behalf of the Historical Society and themselves, these seventeen public-spirited gentlemen made a gift of the plate to the University of California where it is now prominently displayed in the Bancroft Library. Names of the donors were: Wallace M. Alexander, James B. Black, Charles R. Blyth, Everett J. Brown, Allen L. Chickering, Allen L. Chickering, Jr., Sherman Chickering, Sidney M. Ehrman, Edward L. Eyre, Harry H. Fair, Donald Y. Lamont, James K. Moffitt, Henry D. Nichols, Jack Okell, Stuart L. Rawlings, Rudolph Schilling, and Walter A. Starr. Their deed of gift not only included the plate itself, but also funds for its care and preservation.

As for Beryle Shinn, the somewhat dazed but delighted producer of the plate, he too acquired a new home. With the proceeds of the sale of the plate in the amount of $3,500, he was able to buy a modest residence, and get married.

The Caldeira Plate

Soon after the meeting of the California Historical Society on April 6, 1937, at which Bolton announced the finding of Drake's plate of brass, William Caldeira, a chauffeur employed in Piedmont, came forward and stated that he had found the same plate in 1933. He said that he had found it on the Laguna Ranch, a property bordering on Drake's Bay and owned by Leland S. Murphy. On the day he assertedly found it, he had driven his employer at that time, Leon Bocqueraz, vice-chairman of the Bank of America, to the Laguna Ranch to hunt.

While Bocqueraz was engaged in hunting, Caldeira passed the time in walking around; and while doing so, he saw and picked up a metal plate in the "Y" between two intersecting roads near the Laguna Ranch house, at a point about 1½ miles interior from Drake's Bay. He assertedly washed it in a creek, after which he was able to make out the

Site where Shinn said he found the plate in 1936. (Photograph 1937 by Walter Starr.)

Walter Starr and his wife near the spot where the plate was said to have been found. (Photograph by Starr in 1937.)

letters D R A K E and a signature at the foot of the plate but could not make out any other words. He thought it was foreign writing of some kind.

Later that day he showed it to his employer. Bocqueraz was tired and declined to examine it. Caldeira kept it in a pocket of the car for several weeks and then, according to his story, threw it out of the automobile on the right hand side of the road from San Quentin to Kentfield in the first meadow after leaving the intersection of the San Francisco-San Rafael road (now Highway 101) with the San Quentin-Kentfield road. On being shown the Shinn plate later, he stated that he was sure it was the same one he had picked up, because he remembered the hole in it and the letters D R A K E. He did not remember the notches at its top and bottom.

After the Caldeira story was told to the California Historical Society, it seemed for a time to eclipse Shinn's discovery because the impression got around that the spot where Caldeira threw out the piece of metal was at almost the same location where Shinn found the plate. However, it was presently realized that the airline distance from the place in the valley where Caldeira said he had discarded his metal plate to where Shinn found his on top of a ridge was between half a mile and a mile and a half, depending upon the meadow from which measurement was made. From the point where Bocqueraz said it had been discarded, the distance would have been about two miles.

Is the Plate Genuine?

For many decades before Shinn made his discovery, historians have been quoting the contemporary accounts in reference to Drake leaving a possession plate, and the fact that it had never come to light was mentioned by various writers. It was said that "if ever there was an open invitation to some literate and skillful forger to create a hoax, it is the century-long reminder that Drake 'engraved' and left the plate of brass with its legend."[5]

It was not too surprising, accordingly, that almost from the day of the plate's discovery, there were expressions of sincere doubt as to the plate's authenticity. To deal with such doubts from a metallurgical standpoint, Dr. Robert G. Sproul, president of the University of California, appointed a committee consisting of Professors Herbert E. Bolton, J. M. Cline, and Joel E. Hildebrand, together with Allen L. Chickering, to determine upon and have made such tests as to the authenticity of the plate as in its judgment seemed proper.

The committee agreed that any tests of the plate should not be made by anyone connected with the University of California, but rather that the matter should be submitted only to an impartial expert of the highest quality. After much study, it was decided to refer it to Professor Colin G. Fink, head of the Division of Electro-Chemistry, Columbia University, since the committee felt him to be the best qualified man in the United States to make the investigation. Assisting him was his associate, Dr. E. P. Polushkin, consulting metallurgical engineer. They enlisted the services of George E. Harrison of Massachusetts Institute of Technology, a recognized expert in the field of spectroscopy.

Fink and Polushkin retained the plate for more than seven months. During that period they obtained information from several sources, including a report on the climate and temperatures of the region in which the plate was found or in which it might have been set up, by Professor John Leighly of the University of California, a report on the geology of these regions by Dr. O. P. Jenkins, chief geologist of the California State Mining Bureau, and samples of soil from the place where Shinn assertedly found the plate, the place where Caldeira supposedly found it, and from the site of a monument of Drake now standing at Point Reyes.

Metallurgical Findings

Fink and Polushkin went into a variety of factors, such as the shape and dimensions of the plate, the engraved letters, the indentations of the front surface, the back surface, the material from the plate, the microstructure of the plate's metal, and, finally, the chemical composition of the patina. They summarized their findings as follows:

1. There is no doubt whatsoever that the dark coating on the surface of the plate is a natural patina formed slowly over a period of many years.
2. Numerous surface defects and imperfections usually associated with old brass were found on the plate.
3. Particles of mineralized plant tissue were firmly embedded in the surface of the plate. This is likewise a very positive proof of the age of the plate.
4. Cross sections of the brass plate showed (a) an excessive amount of impurities, and (b) chemical inhomogeneity, as well as (c) variation in grain size. All three of these characteristics indicate a brass of old origin.

5. Among the impurities found in the brass of the plate there is magnesium, which is present far in excess of the amount occurring in modern brass.

6. There are numerous indications that the plate was not made by rolling but was made by hammering, as was the common practice in Drake's time.

Their conclusion, on the basis of these findings, as well as upon other data outlined in their report, was that the plate examined was the genuine Drake Plate referred to in *The World Encompassed*.[6]

Doubts In Other Areas

In the meantime, even before the Fink–Polushkin tests were under way, other questions were being raised about the plate's authenticity, because the latter, in itself, contains no evidence that establishes with certainty that it is a genuine Drake artifact.

One of the earliest to raise the question of authenticity was Captain R. B. Haselden, former curator of the Huntington Library, and an expert in Elizabethan literature. In an article appearing in the *California Historical Society Quarterly* for the fall of 1937,[7] he stated that fraudulent metal tablets have frequently turned up in Europe, and are not uncommon even in California. He suggested that points to be covered for the purposes of authentication should include the type of metal, the kind of lettering used, the position of the date, the orthography, and the extent and effect of erosion, weathering, and deposits. He felt that the fact of the plate's tallying to an astonishing extent with the language of *The World Encompassed* did not preclude fraud but, on the contrary, was in itself enough to give rise to suspicion. To some extent, his points were rebutted by a response prepared by Chickering and published in the same issue of the *California Historical Society Quarterly*.[8]

Undoubtedly the best article in support of the plate's authenticity was written by Joseph W. Ellison, professor of history at Oregon State College.[9] It appeared in the *Saturday Evening Post* for April 3, 1943, pointing out that the plate was either a priceless treasure or a brassy fake, and suggesting that Beryle Shinn was the first alchemist able to convert brass into gold.

Ellison was at considerable pains to mention the plate's defects: the crudity of its workmanship, the haste and carelessness with which the inscription had apparently been executed, the unorthodox spelling and use of letters, the position of the date on the plate, the use of an arrival date rather than that of acceptance of the "kingdome," and various unexplained and inconsistent findings in the Fink report. He apparently had access to a number of hitherto unpublished communications between Haselden and various other experts,[10] including British Museum authorities, each giving their reasons for believing the plate to have been of doubtful authenticity. Nevertheless, he concluded that the evidence in favor of the plate's genuineness, though not absolutely conclusive, was "quite convincing."

Opinions on the Significance of the Plate

Following publication of the Ellison article, open discussion of the plate's authenticity subsided almost entirely for the next three decades. Even the triangular debate of 1974 raised no question of genuineness, with Tenet 14 simply reciting the asserted actions of Shinn and Caldeira in respect to the plate, and then inquiring about the plate's significance to the landing site controversy.

Although the subject of authenticity did not enter the discussion, and none of the participants expressed any doubt about the finding of the plate by Shinn, there was a lively disagreement as to the role played by Caldeira. The two proponents of coastal anchorage sites were satisfied that he was telling the truth about finding a plate near Drake's Bay, while the lone advocate of the San Quentin Cove site referred to him as "an untruthful fabricator of evidence."

The Guild felt that the plate was not significant to an identification of Drake's landing place, since it was a portable artifact not found *in situ*. They defended the integrity of Caldeira, pointing out that his word had been accepted by Attorney Allen L. Chickering, president of the California Historical Society, who had interviewed him on the subject; also by Caldeira's employer, Leon Bocqueraz, an official of the Bank of America, who said he would "take his word absolutely."[11]

Dr. Neasham felt that Caldeira was believable since the Indians could have carried the plate from place to place subsequent to 1579, and had added:

> In any event, its original placement was at or near Drake's fort. If the fort was at Bolinas Lagoon, then necessarily the plate was erected in that vicinity; . . . and some one earlier than Caldeira may have found it either

at Drake's Bay or Bolinas Bay, only to divest himself of it at the Laguna Ranch ... [where Caldeira found it, after which it] was carried to its final site near Greenbrae by someone unknown, after it had been discarded by Caldeira.

In other words, Neasham suggested the possibility of at least three movements of the plate: From Bolinas to Laguna Ranch by unknown persons; from Laguna Ranch to Greenbrae by Caldeira; and from Greenbrae to the site of the Shinn discovery, again by unknown persons.

Power commented that there is an old adage in archaeology that the further one speculates an artifact traveled, the less chance he has of being correct, since most artifacts fall to earth near where they are used by man. He felt there was only a remote chance that Indians would have carried this relic from a coastal anchorage and have "discarded it on a hill overlooking Point San Quentin which is the location of Drake's fort in the San Francisco Bay—*Portus Novae Albionis* comparison."

In response to the Guild's assertion that "Mr. Power's contention that William Caldeira was lying when he claimed original discovery of the plate at Drake's Bay is irresponsible," he responded: "Irresponsible! The irresponsibility in this Tenet lays with the Guild and Dr. Neasham in believing Caldeira's 1937 statements and that Bocqueraz, in a 1955 interview on file at the Bancroft Library added credence to Caldeira's claims."

Priceless Treasure or Brassy Fake?

Since the language of Tenet 14 did not ask specifically for comment on authenticity of the plate found by Shinn, the subject was not referred to by any of the participants except for mention by the Guild that lack of authenticity, in view of the Fink-Polushkin findings, was only a "remote possibility." None of the comments made reference to Wagner's opinion that the plate was "not authentic," or to any of the earlier attacks on its genuineness.

Necessarily, of course, unless it can be established that the plate is genuine, it matters not where it was found, or from whence it was carried. In other words, authenticity of this key artifact is virtually a condition precedent to any meaningful response to Tenet 14 and its request for a statement on the "significance of the plate to the landing site controversy."

As heretofore indicated, the full text of the debate was published in the *California Historical Quarterly* for the Fall of 1974. Only a few weeks later, the second volume of Admiral Samuel Eliot Morison's *The European Discovery of America* was published, its final chapters containing a vigorous attack on the authenticity of the plate that was to startle the unsuspecting students of Drake in California.

The Plate Branded as a Hoax

Morison's second volume devoted forty-five pages to the Drake circumnavigation, eighteen of which were under the heading "The Good Bay of Nova Albion," and three of the latter under the subheading of "The Plate of Brass—Or Was It Lead?" The author had come into possession of copies of the extensive correspondence carried on between Captain Haselden and others soon after the plate's discovery, but never made known to the general public. After reemphasizing all of the unfavorable points mentioned by Haselden, Morison asserted that the conclusions reached by the various experts, including British Museum authorities, made Fink's metallurgical findings questionable, and he gave his own conclusion as follows:

> In my opinion, the Plate is a hoax perpetrated by some collegiate joker who knew little about Drake except what he had heard from Dr. Bolton and read in one of the modern editions of the *World Encompassed*. He naturally chose that text to be blown up for the inscription, tried to give it a "quaint" look by odd lettering and spelling, then dropped it at a place where it was likely to be picked up. "Drake's Plate of Brass" is as successful a hoax as the Piltdown Man or the Kensington Rune Stone.[12]

Morison's views coincided with those of Wagner, whose opinion with respect to authenticity had been set forth in a posthumous booklet published in 1970, entitled *Drake on the Pacific Coast*. Relying on his own metallurgical background, Wagner asserted that sixteenth-century brass was made in Germany, but not in England, and that the brass in this plate might not have been older than sixty to seventy years. He was of the opinion that the plate was not authentic, and asserted that there is no record of any plate being set up within two hundred years of Drake's plate which was not made of lead.[13] The latter was cheap and easily inscribed, whereas brass was extremely expensive and hard to inscribe.

Plans for a New Examination

Even before Morison's book was issued, the Bancroft Library, custodian of the plate, had decided to embark upon further investigations. This decision was made in part because a new director, wholly unassociated with the subject but aware of its controversial nature, thought that a fresh inquiry was warranted; and in part because, with the appointment of a Sir Francis Drake Commission by the governor of California and the advent of the quadricentennial of Drake's landing, interest in the plate was bound to grow.[14] Moreover, new techniques of scientific analysis had been discovered during the approximately forty years since the earlier tests were made. Accordingly, representatives of the Library met with Heizer to formulate plans for further investigation of the plate.

After initial inquiries had been made, various types of study were projected. These included not only physical and chemical tests but also scrutiny directed at historical aspects of the plate. The latter investigations were addressed entirely to matters of text and orthography, not dependent on metallurgical or other scientific analyses. These tests and studies continued for two years, their results being made public in the summer of 1977. In July of that year, a comprehensive report prepared by Dr. James D. Hart, director of the Bancroft Library, was issued.

Opinions and Conclusions

The report opened with a review of the discovery of the plate and of the uncertainties which had led to the Fink-Polushkin report of 1938. It summarized the metallurgical criticisms by Professor Earle R. Caley of Princeton University, as well as the learned comments of such other experts as Captain R. B. Haselden of the Huntington Library, Dr. Vincent T. Harlow of Oxford University, and Dr. Robin Flower of the British Museum, all skeptical about the plate's authenticity.

In connection with the current studies, the lettering on the plate was a subject of prime interest. Opinions were obtained from Professor Thomas G. Barnes of the Department of History of the University of California at Berkeley, as well as from two experts of the Folger

Shakespeare Library, Giles E. Dawson and Laetitia Yeandle, authors of *Elizabethan Handwriting, 1500–1600* (1966). They raised many questions concerning the wording and lettering on the plate, and Professor Barnes additionally had misgivings over "the crudeness of the engraving."[15] He gave several reasons why he thought the plate a forgery, including the spelling, the terminology, and the quality of engraving. Also summarized by the 1977 report were the current comments of such experts as O. B. Hardison, Jr., director of the Folger Shakespeare Library, Professor Wayne Shumaker of the Department of English at the University of California at Berkeley, Professor Alan Nelson of the same department, Professor Wayne L. Fry, Department of Paleontology, University of California at Berkeley, Professor Philip W. Rundel, Department of Biology, University of California at Irvine, and noted bibliographer R. B. McKerrow.[16]

However, these opinions concerning the inscription were surface matters that could help to determine authenticity only if the brass were found to be of sixteenth-century origin. Consequently, metallurgical tests were concurrently pursued. These investigations were assigned to the Research Laboratory for Archaeology at Oxford University, to the Chemistry Division of the Lawrence Berkeley Laboratory under Drs. Helen V. Michel and Frank Asaro, and to Dr. Cyril Stanley Smith, professor emeritus of the Massachusetts Institute of Technology, outstanding authority on the history of metallurgy. Extensive tests were done by these scientists.

Testing Against Ancient Brasses

For comparison, Oxford employed eighteen brass instruments in twenty-three separate analyses and four memorial brasses in five analyses, the examples being mostly English and from a time span beginning in 1540 and ending in 1720. It was found that the plate's lead and tin contents were unusually low for Elizabethan brass and its zinc content unusually high. Because of these differences, R. E. M. Hedges of the laboratory pointed out that "the analytical evidence cannot be used to support the contention that the brass is of the Elizabethan period." He went on to say that "on the whole I agree with [Caley's] critique of Fink's report," but cautioned that "while the results of the analysis are consistent and clear, I do not think they can provide *unequivocal proof* of the authenticity or of the forgery of the Plate."[17]

After making a careful microscopic examination of the plate, Smith found himself in disagreement with Fink's conclusion that the plate had been made by hammering rather than rolling. He was also impressed by the close agreement between the results of the analyses conducted by the Oxford University Laboratory and those by Lawrence Berkeley. He stated that "Both the high zinc content . . . as well as the low general impurity content are consistent with a piece of modern 'common high brass' and are at least improbable for a XVI-century calamine product."

These and other findings led Smith to state: "I now incline to the belief that it is a product of the present century." While he was of the opinion that evidence from the viewpoint of a materials scientist is not in itself sufficient to form a historical conclusion, he nevertheless, on the basis of his scientific examination, finally declared: "All of the features that I have noted make me incline to the opinion that the plate is a modern forgery."[18]

The Lawrence Laboratory Conclusion

Various other tests proposed by Smith were undertaken by the Lawrence Laboratory, including gamma-ray absorption to measure variations in plate thickness, and X-ray diffraction studies and sound-velocity measurements to determine grain orientation. These, as well as a radiograph, confirmed the absence of internal discontinuities in the plate. Special analyses of metallic material extracted from the plate were also helpful in reaching a determination.

The formal report of the Lawrence Berkeley Laboratory, entitled *Chemical Study of the Plate of Brass,* was issued on July 27, 1977. It was numbered LBL-6338, and comprised forty-six pages. Its conclusions were summarized as follows:

> The low level of lead and iron in the Plate of Brass indicates it was made from zinc metal which had probably been produced by the retort process and possibly redistilled. This indicates a date of the XIX or XX century although a late XVIII century date might be possible. The low level of antimony, arsenic, nickel, cobalt, silver, and gold in the Plate of Brass indicates it was made from high purity copper which would not have been generally available until about the middle of the XIX century although an XVIII century date is possible. The high degree of chemical

uniformity of the Plate of Brass, better than 0.45% from the zinc to copper ratio, and the small variations in thickness in the areas away from the edges, 0.001 inch, are consistent with XX century rolled brass. The average measured thickness of the Plate of Brass away from the edges, 0.129 ± 0.002 inches, is consistent with the specifications for No. 8 gage brass of the American Wire Gage standard used in the 1930's. The Plate of Brass therefore was made in the XVIII to the XX centuries. The most probable period is the late XIX and early XX centuries.[19]

The Bancroft Library Report

Issued concurrently with the report of the Lawrence Berkeley Laboratory was the report by Hart, entitled *The Plate of Brass Reexamined, 1977.* As stated in the report, "it is presented to provide the best information now available about the Plate, made with the recognition that this will probably not be accepted everywhere as the definitive or conclusive word on the subject."[20]

The reports in question made headlines when released to the press on July 28, 1977. The opening paragraphs of the San Francisco Chronicle's story read:

> The Bancroft Library's treasured "plate of brasse," supposedly nailed to a tree on the Marin coast by Sir Francis Drake in 1579, was revealed yesterday by its custodians to be an elaborate scholarly fake.
>
> The plate, inscribed with a proclamation taking possession of "the whole land" in the name of Queen Elizabeth I, was tested by scientists in the United States and England. They found it to be composed of modern metal rolled and cut in ways unknown in Drake's time.
>
> "All of the evidence that has been brought out in the last two years has been negative," said James D. Hart, director of the Bancroft collection on the University of California's Berkeley campus.
>
> "The plate will continue to be displayed at the library," Hart added, "but posted with it will be a two-page account of the scholarly detective work which shows how history can be investigated."

Rebuttal to the 1977 Reports

Hart correctly anticipated that the revelations of July, 1977, would not be "accepted everywhere as ... conclusive."[21] The first dissent appeared in the August, 1978, issue of *California History,* the California Historical Society's periodical. It was by Drake scholar Robert H. Power entitled *A Plate of Brass by me ... C. G. Francis Drake* (with editorial assistance by Donald C. Pike).

After a brief review of the plate's history from 1937 to 1974 when its authenticity was questioned by Admiral Morison, Power charged that Morison's claim that the plate was a hoax was hasty and ill-considered; and offered the further comment that the recent reports of experts announcing the results of their studies present "a mosaic of contradictory opinion." From the reports of Smith of Massachusetts Institute of Technology and Hedges of Oxford University he cited their statements that "evidence from the viewpoint of a materials scientist is not sufficient to form a historical conclusion" and that the test results "do not provide unequivocal proof of the authenticity or the forgery of the plate." As to the conclusions of Michel and Asaro, he conceded that they were definitive, as well as adverse, but suggested that they may have been founded upon insufficient data. He noted that further investigation (a molybdenum X-ray) had been ordered by Bancroft, but that a certain definitive ballistic type study suggested by Smith had never been undertaken.

Power then charged that linguistics and calligraphy of the plate had received only casual attention from *Reexamined 1977,* and from authorities and nonauthorities alike; and asserted that these factors should have received additional study before an "essentially negative"[22] result was announced, in view of the fact that the metallurgical tests were "inconclusive." He added that no unequivocal answer to the plate's age is possible until a radioactive dating system is devised to age-date brass.

The rest of the article was an interesting and detailed discussion of the plate's inscription, and a rebuttal to many of the contentions made by various experts in respect to its spelling, "unknown letter forms," including black letters, superfluous strokes over certain letters, and problems with the letter "J." Also discussed were clarifications in the text disclosed by the 1977 radiograph of the plate, such as that the "C" before Drake's name was actually two letters—a "G" within a larger "C." The text of the plate was analyzed in detail by means of twenty-four annotations covering questionable spelling or other points. The article concluded as follows:

> Additional clues to the authenticity of the plate found in the inscription—and the great unlikelihood of these elements being

forged — are too myriad and complex to be detailed here. Certainly they warrant further study and discussion by experts. Considering that the metallurgical tests on the plate were inconclusive, that evaluations of the engraving tools were not made, that the unusual letter forms have been identified with Elizabethan script, and that the extraordinary radiograph reveals previously unknown Elizabethan elements in the inscription, there should be no doubt that *Reexamined 1977* was only a small first step in a comprehensive investigation into the origin of the Bancroft Plate of Brass signed "C G Francis Drake."[23]

A Final Search for the Plate

It seemed that the year 1978 might see a resolution of the differences on this issue by one means or another, possibly by discovery of the true plate. It was in October, 1977, that Hart received a telephone call from the wife of a prominent Alameda County jurist to the effect that during the early years of the century her family had resided near Bolinas where her father had been engaged in working a copper mine on the Wilkins property. Although the family left the area before she was born, she had been told by her mother that some member of the family, while walking along a Bolinas beach, had picked up a metal plate with the name "Drake" on it, and had brought it home to the cabin where they lived.

When the cabin went up in flames not long after, it was so totally destroyed that the family never went back to salvage anything from the ashes, and she assumed, accordingly, that the plate might still be there. She had seen no need to bring this information to the attention of authorities until she saw the headlines in the summer of 1977 pronouncing the plate at Bancroft a "fake." She then decided that she ought to make her story known.

When Hart soon thereafter discussed the information with Heizer, they both felt that this lead should be investigated. After locating the former Wilkins property through county records, Heizer began, with a capable crew, to reconnoiter the location of the burned cabin itself. They were aided in their efforts by a photograph of the cabin furnished by Hart's informant. With its aid, after two or three days of tramping over Bolinas Ridge, they located the cabin site on a hillside above Copper Mine Creek, about a mile east of Highway No. 1.

The next step was to acquire a metal detector and to cover the site with it, inch by inch, and foot by foot, which was done on December 19, 1977. Nothing of consequence was discovered, but in one corner of the ruins there was a large pile of bricks, remnants of the cabin chimney, on the mantel of which, supposedly, the plate had reposed before the fire. Perhaps the ancient relic lay buried somewhere under these bricks; so it became necessary to undertake the arduous task of removing them, not to mention the necessity for obtaining National Park Service approval to do so.

Between the delays in getting such an approval, and the repeated rains that came in the early months of 1978, Heizer and his crew were unable to undertake the task until April. With five student archaeologists and appropriate tools, Heizer moved into the site energetically and in a single day had moved every brick as well as much of the soil beneath and behind them. The result was total disappointment, and the necessity to return the next day to restore the site, as nearly as possible, to its original condition.

The excavators had only the satisfaction of having fully exhausted the possibilities of what seemed to be a promising clue, one that suggested that the Bolinas area might, after all, have provided the anchorage site. Later it was learned through Thomas Barfield, long-time Bolinas resident and co-author of *Last Stage For Bolinas,* that the cabin had been vacated for some time before it burned, which could explain the paucity of any artifactual findings at the cabin site. For Heizer, it was the last and most promising of several Drake-plate possibilities that had been brought to his attention during a long Drake-oriented career.

One Last Possibility

While one means of disproving the authenticity of the Shinn plate might be to discover the true relic, the last great hope of accomplishing that miracle probably vanished with the contents of the cabin on Bolinas Ridge. Yet there remains, conceivably, still another chance that such a denouement will come about. This is the possibility that if the plate was in the nature of a hoax, some one in the original "know" may be willing to divulge his or her secret of the identity of the master mind and his ingenious handiwork. Hart has shed some interesting light on this subject:

As to why there should be a hoax, Admiral Morison suggested that the enthusiasm of Professor Bolton in telling his students to be aware that the Plate might some day be found (Morison said Bolton "begged his students to keep their eyes open; and if it were found, bring it to him") provided an irresistible temptation for some joker to have fun at the expense of the distinguished professor. . . .

Since the point of a hoax is to show up the person who is gulled and since no one ever came along to reveal a fraud, defenders of the Plate contended that such lack of revelation was in itself an argument against the idea of a hoax. Some skeptics about the Plate have nevertheless even suggested the name of a possible hoaxer or two who died soon after its discovery. Other skeptics have put forward still another reason why, if there was a hoax, it was not revealed by the perpetrators. Professor Barnes suggested that a forgery might have been created by students of Professor Bolton as a prank but that when this great scholar accepted the Plate so completely and enthusiastically, they were too embarrassed to reveal it.[24]

When Hart made reference to the suggestion by "some skeptics" of "the name of a possible hoaxer or two who died soon after" the plate's discovery, he may have been alluding to the statement made in this connection by the late Francis P. Farquhar in his article entitled "Drake in California," which appeared in the *California Historical Society Quarterly* for March, 1957. Farquhar said: "Before leaving the subject of the Plate it should be mentioned that there are those who claim to know that it is a forgery. One story has it that a man named Clark and the late George Barron, one-time curator of the De Young Museum, conspired to produce a forgery and that the plate in question is it."[25]

Despite the naming of specific people, it does not appear that Farquhar pursued, or intended to pursue, the matter further. This would seem to be implicit in his statement that since no proof had been presented, this story, like a number of others, "fails to qualify as evidence." Nevertheless, there is nothing to preclude the possibility that, despite the passage of time, skillful and persistent investigation may yet uncover the true story of how the Shinn plate came into existence.

Incidentally, it is difficult to agree with Morison's characterization of the Shinn plate as a "complete and clumsy hoax." Any practical joke or deception that is able to challenge the abilities of some of the world's greatest scientists as to its genuineness for nearly half a century may be "complete," but certainly not "clumsy." As Hart has so well said: "The ostensible reasons for failure to reveal it [as a hoax] are intriguing, as are all questions concerned with the Plate. It remains a fascinating object. Over forty years after its finding the Plate of Brass still tantalizes all who take an interest in it."[26]

23

CHAPTER

The Departure

*Tenet 15: Drake departed from Nova Albion on July 23,
1579, and* The World Encompassed *reported that "not
farre without this harborough did lye certaine Ilands . . .
[with] one of which we fell July 24." What is the
significance of the dates and apparent time elapsed on this
leg of his journey?*

AFTER thirty-six days at Nova Albion, Drake considered that
everything was in readiness for the transpacific voyage, and
his captured sailing instructions assured him that the season
and the winds were now favorable for that undertaking. Accordingly,
on July 23, 1579, the *Golden Hind* sailed out of the harbor, leaving
behind Rodrigo Tello's frigate and a chorus of wailing natives, not to
mention a dozen or more of Drake's own crew, if the legend of the
Nicasios (discussed in Chapter 5) be given credence.

"Not farre without this harborough," according to *The World Encompassed,* they "fell," as mentioned earlier (see p. 32), with the Farallones, which they called the "Ilands of Saint James" for undisclosed
reasons. Here they found a "plentifull and great store of Seales and
birds," and apparently spent the 24th gathering "such provision as
might competently serve our turne for a while." Having completed

their foray on the wildlife of this continental outpost, they resumed their westward trek on the 25th, now irrevocably committed to a circumnavigation of the globe.

Aerial view of the Southeast Farallon Island. (Courtesy U.S. National Wildlife Service.)

The Ilands of Saint James

The rocky Farallones lie twenty-six miles due west of the Golden Gate Bridge, and not more than twenty miles southwest of the mouth of Drake's Estero. There are three of them, the North, the Middle, and the Southeast Farallones, but only the latter contains enough land to call it much of an island. It is about a mile long by half a mile wide, and has a mountainous backbone broken by steep gorges, one of which practically cuts the island in two. Its highest point above sea level is known as Tower Hill, surmounted at an elevation of 358 feet by a lighthouse completed in 1855. Elevation of the North Farallon is 155 feet, and that of the Middle Farallon, really nothing more than a huge rock, is barely 20 feet above the water.

The islands were probably discovered by Juan Rodriguez Cabrillo in 1542, but they were not mentioned in his report and map of the expedition.[1] Their first mention by any early explorer was by Cermeño in the report which he sent back to Spain in 1596, and their first appearance on any chart was in that of Vizcaino *circa* 1603.[2] Juan Francisco de la Bodega y Cuadro in 1775 named the group Farallones de los Frailes to honor the friars *(frailes)* of the Franciscan order. The name "Farallon" is derived from a nautical Spanish word meaning small, pointed islands of the sea, and fittingly describes the Middle and North Farallones, which are of interest only to scientists.[3]

Comments by Wagner

One of the unusual things about the "Ilands of Saint James" is the fact that they were mentioned in no contemporary account other than *The World Encompassed.*[4] To such a Drake expert as Henry R. Wagner, this was a circumstance that was suspicious as well as unusual.[5] Finding it difficult to understand why they had not been mentioned by Hakluyt in "The Famous Voyage" if they had appeared in his original source material, Wagner wondered if the compiler of *The World Encompassed* could have obtained his information from some other source.

With this in mind, he proceeded to surmise that the author of *The World Encompassed,* having no authentic information about any islands in that vicinity, "thought it would enliven the interest of the narrative to mention them, even adding a little detail about Drake getting a supply of seals and birds there."[6] He then commented: "As seals were plentiful at Point Reyes, no good reason can be assigned for Drake's waiting to go to the southeast Farallon after a supply, especially as there is no certainty that the Point Reyes Indians frequented these islands and consequently may have known nothing about the large herds of sea lions on the southeast Farallon."[7]

Discussion by Other Drake Scholars

No others have shared Wagner's suspicions about the islands of St. James, but several Drake experts have left a record of their thoughts about the islands and how Drake came to visit them. George Davidson, for example, thought that without information on the safety of approaching them, from Indians who frequented them, Drake would have avoided them—as every careful navigator does today. But Davidson surmised that Drake had probably learned from the Indians at Point Reyes that the islets that could be seen from that promontory abounded in sea lions and, accordingly, that "he visited them for fresh provisions without going out of his course."[8]

John W. Robertson was at a loss to understand how Drake became aware that these islands were the habitat of seals and birds, because he felt that Davidson's hypothesis that Drake had learned of them through "the Indians who frequented them," and whose only canoes were grass-built *balsas* unfit for ocean navigation, was an unduly imaginary conclusion. He reasoned, nevertheless, that Drake must have known that the islands were heavily populated with seals and birds; and regarded the fact that Drake left his anchorage "without refilling his larder" and did stop at the Farallones as proof that he "knew he could obtain from them such supplies as he needed for his homeward voyage."[9]

In a more recent discussion of the departure from the anchorage and arrival at the islands, Raymond Aker suggested that the description of the quantities of birds and seals would indicate that the entire group was reconnoitered, either at that time, or perhaps previously by Tello's small bark. The party availed itself of the opportunity to obtain some of the birds, eggs, and seals, which even today abound on the southeast island, but Aker felt that proper victualling had been completed on the mainland before departure, and that these merely supplemented the regular salt provision with enough fresh meat to last a few days.[10]

Comments of the Debaters

Tenet 15 mentioned Drake's departure from Nova Albion, and inquired the significance of the dates and apparent time elapsed on this leg of his journey. In responding to this query, each participant indicated that the trip from his particular anchorage site to the Farallones could have been made by leaving on July 23 and arriving at or near the Southeast Farallon on the 24th.[11] This being so, the 24th could have been given to the harvesting of seals, birds, and eggs, followed by final departure on the 25th. The trip from Bolinas would have covered a distance of less than twenty miles, hence Neasham suggested that there may have been an afternoon departure or possibly a "shakedown" run from that point.

The Guild cited the seamen's practice in the sixteenth century of changing the log date at noon instead of at midnight so that Drake could have left the Estero on the morning of the 23rd, and reached the Farallones before dark, which would have been the 24th on the log. It is also possible that he could have hove-to overnight because of fog or light wind, and so not have reached the islands until the following morning (but still the 24th).

Power stated that *The World Encompassed* account of departure and arrival dates would have correlated with the sailing time from Point San Quentin to the Farallones. As he explained it, these requirements are met by departing from Point San Quentin in the morning, reaching the Golden Gate in time for the afternoon ebb current, and riding this tidal flow through the Golden Gate. It would then be too late to approach the Farallones until the following day.

There was, of course, no harbor at the Southeast Farallon, but the surrounding waters were shallow enough to have permitted Drake to anchor overnight in six to ten fathoms of water within half a mile of the island. From that point, several trips with the ship's tender would have served to complete their foraging objectives.

In the opinion of the Guild, the dates of departure from the anchorage site and arrival at the islands provide no basis for identification of a specific landing location. Neasham took a similar stand, reasoning that since it was no more than a one-day journey from any one of the three sites, it was immaterial whether the reason for that period of travel time was based on the hour of departure, on the making of a date change at noon instead of midnight, on hoving-to for the night, or on giving the *Golden Hind* a major shakedown.

By way of rebuttal to the Guild position, Power commented that *The World Encompassed* was a journal, rather than a log. Journals at sea were always kept on a midnight to midnight basis, according to Lt. Commander D. W. Waters of London, reputedly the world's greatest authority on Tudor navigation, who reviewed the facts of this particular case.

Evaluation of Earlier Comments

Wagner started off on the wrong tack by assuming that since the islands were not mentioned in "The Famous Voyage," the story about them must have been manufactured out of practically whole cloth by the compiler of *The World Encompassed*. In so doing, Wagner revealed his unfamiliarity with Hakluyt's poor track record of errors and omissions in relation to "The Famous Voyage,"[12] and also failed to realize that no one, not even the compiler of *The World Encompassed,* could have had sufficient imagination to invent with accuracy the story of the wildlife on the islands—a story that remained otherwise unknown to the world for another two centuries. Wagner suggested, moreover, that the plentiful supply of seals at Point Reyes would have obviated the need for a stop at the islands to obtain further supplies, overlooking the fact that Drake might be coming from a port where there were mussels and seals,[13] but not a plentiful supply of birds and eggs. The only point on which his conjectures were probably right was that the Indians would not have been likely to know of the food supply on the Farallones.

Davidson's assumptions were equally irrational as to Drake's learning from the natives about the wildlife on the islands. Not only were the islands completely uninhabitable, so far as the natives were concerned, but the California tribes had no means of visiting them or of learning what food sources they might hold.

Robertson abandoned his usual logical approach to such matters, permitting himself to assume that Drake left his anchorage "without refilling his larder," and then treating that entirely unsupported assumption as "proof" that "he knew he could obtain from them [the islands] such supplies as he needed for his homeward voyage."

Advance Information about the Islands

Whether Drake had foreknowledge of the Farallones and of the possibilities for obtaining food supplies there is a good question, and one on which the comments of Raymond Aker make sense, whether the anchorage site was coastal or within San Francisco Bay. Taking everything into consideration, the probabilities would seem to be that (1) Drake's Spanish charts would have contained no information on the subject; (2) he had no opportunity to gain knowledge concerning the islands and their available wildlife at the time of his arrival from the north, no matter which bay he had entered; (3) the natives knew nothing about the situation on the islands; (4) if they did have such information, they would not have realized its importance to Drake, or have been able to communicate it to him if they did; and (5) it is unlikely that the small bark would have been sent on a two-day jaunt (especially from within San Francisco Bay) on the bare possibility of discovering a food supply on these islands.

In any case, whether or not Drake had a plentiful supply of seals at his Nova Albion anchorage, he would hardly have dared to depart on the long transpacific voyage without a full larder. By a process of elimination, one is forced to conclude that, without earlier reconnaissance, Drake's first knowledge of the food supplies on the Farallones was gained as he approached the southeast island; and that despite being already well stocked, he could not resist the opportunity to augment what must already have been an adequate food supply with eggs and fowls that may not have been readily available at the anchorage site, and with perhaps enough more fresh meat to last a few days.

Summary

Native reaction to the impending departure of their visitors began as soon as they recognized what was happening. Depressed by the intensity of their grief, the compiler of the source material for *The World Encompassed* failed to provide posterity with a record of the preparations for take-off and the plan for disposition of the second ship, leaving us instead with a behavioral study of the California Indians, of which the following excerpt is typical:

> And as men refusing all comfort, they onely accounted themselves as cast-awayes, and those whom the gods were about to forsake: so that nothing we could say or do, was able to ease them of their so heavy a burthen, or to deliver them from so desperate a straite, as our leaving of them did seeme to them that it would cast them into.

When the day of departure finally came, the sorrowing natives "ranne to the top of the hils to keepe us in their sight as long as they could, making fires before and behind, and on each side of them, burning . . . sacrifices at our departure." So far as the anchorage site was concerned, the only clue to be derived from this behavior is to be found in the words "to the top of the hils." They tell us not only that there was more than one hill in the vicinity of the careenage site, but that there were headlands in the direction of the sea, to the summits of which they might run for the purpose of keeping the ship in sight as long as possible.

From this standpoint, there would appear to be little to choose between the Estero and Point San Quentin, with Bolinas less favored in this respect due to the distance of any hill from its prospective anchorage location. Viewing the matter of departure generally, it is difficult to see where the debate on this tenet did a great deal to further the claims of any one of the three participants. As the Guild stated: "The historical facts of departure and arrival date at the islands do not give evidence of any specific landing place."

24

The "Portus Novae Albionis"

Tenet 16: The Vera Totius Expeditionis Nauticae map of the world by cartographer Jodocus Hondius (London, 1589), contains in its upper left-hand corner a plan of the Portus Novae Albionis. Discuss the significance of the Portus Plan and its correlation with the proposed landing site.

A S INDICATED in an earlier chapter, the "Portus Novae Albionis" is one of the five marginal insets on Hondius' celebrated Broadside Map. Its width is 2½ inches, its height 1 15/16 inches. Its Latin name, meaning Port of Nova Albion, was presumably coined by Hondius. Because of the belief that it may hold the key to the location of Drake's California anchorage, it is a name which, in Drake circles, may have become almost as well known as that of Sir Francis himself.

The purpose of the "Portus," like that of its companion insets, was to illustrate a memorable occurrence in the course of the voyage, and Drake's dramatic departure from Nova Albion was chosen by Hondius as one of the five incidents. The *Golden Hind* is shown sitting near the inner shore of a cove or apparently small harbor shaped like a seal's

F¡da corporum laceratione & crebris in montibus sacrifieijs, hujus
Novi Albionis portus .incol . Draci. jam bis coronati . deceßum desicnt.

GMC

The "Portus Novae Albionis." An enlargement of one of the insets on the Hondius
Broadside map depicting the California anchorage. It has been cited as supporting evidence by
the advocates of every harbor for which anchorage honors have been claimed.

head. Human figures are shown at several points on shore. At the left
of the harbor is a long, narrow peninsula, and to *its* left, just outside
the harbor, is an island of almost equal length. The name "Portus
Novae Albionis" appears just within the harbor boundaries.

Early Discussion of the "Portus"

Through Bancroft's *History Of California*,[1] we learn that the
"Portus Novae Albionis" first came to the attention of Californians
about 1878 when John W. Dwinelle published a review of Bryant's
History of the United States making reference to it.[2] Dwinelle was
convinced that Bodega Bay was the harbor in which Drake repaired
his ship, and regarded the "Portus" as supporting evidence. He had
obtained from the British Museum a photographic copy of it, enlarged
to the dimension of about 5 by 6 inches, and had visited Bodega Bay

with it in hand. He reported that all the indications called for by Drake's narrative existed there.[3]

Comment by Hale and Bancroft

Two giants in the field of history were among the first to perceive the importance of the "Portus Novae Albionis" as a factor in the search for Drake's California anchorage. They were Edward Everett Hale and Hubert H. Bancroft, both writing in 1884. In a monograph in Winsor, *Narrative and Critical History of America*, Hale stated that after Drake's return, Hondius made a map of the world "in which he tracked both the routes of Drake and Cavendish; and of that portion showing New Albion, as well as of his little plan of Drake's Bay."[4] According to Hale, the sketch of the "Portus" (he did not call it that) had been copied from Bryant's *Popular History of the United States*, and though it had originally appeared on the margin of Hondius' Broadside map, it had been omitted from the reproduction of that map in the Hakluyt Society's edition of *The World Encompassed* published in 1854.[5] It was Hale's conclusion that the "chart of Drake's Bay . . . has, unfortunately, no representation to any bay on the coast, and is purely imaginary."[6] However, he went on to say that "it will not be long, probably, before the question is decided. This writer does not hesitate to say that he believes it will prove that Drake repaired his ship in San Francisco Bay."[7]

Bancroft also included in his *History of California* a sketch of the "Portus Novae Albionis" which he had borrowed from Hale.[8] Disagreeing with Hale, however, Bancroft stated that he found nothing in Hale's maps to change his own opinion about Drake's anchorage, and he added: "These maps like all others represent Drake's port from the current narratives as a good bay in about 38° of latitude; all the rest is purely imaginary."[9] He found himself unable to express any decided opinion as between Drake's and Bodega bays, saying "I find no foundation for such an opinion. It is not probable that there will ever be any means of ascertaining the truth."[10]

Discussion by Davidson

While Hale, Dwinelle, and Bancroft had all discussed the significance of the marginal inset on the Hondius Broadside map, George

Davidson, in his treatise of 1890,[11] was the first to refer to it as the "Portus Novae Albionis." He had obtained from the British Museum an accurate tracing of it, and found himself puzzled by its lack of "geographical position, scale, meridian, soundings or explanatory note"; in fact, he found it "nearly unintelligible."[12] He asserted that there was no harbor like it on the coast, "and the relatively large islet outside the point appears further to complicate the subject." As a matter of fact, he "solved" his problem of trying to reconcile the large islet outside the protecting westerly point of the "Portus" with the fact that no such islet exists at Point Reyes only by persuading himself that a sixty-foot column or pillar just off the Point might serve in lieu of that shown on the "Portus."[13] He translated the Latin legend at the foot of the "Portus" to read as follows: "By horrible lacerations of their bodies and by frequent sacrifices in the mountains, the inhabitants of the port of New Albion deplore the departure of Drake, now twice crowned."[14]

Discussion by Wagner

Before 1926, when Wagner published *Sir Francis Drake's Voyage Around the World*, the only study in some depth of the "Portus" had been that by George Davidson. Consequently, Wagner devoted a good part of his discussion of the "Portus" to a critique of what Davidson had to say, including the following:

> The most important piece of evidence known to us is the plan of the *portus*.[15] ... What appears to be an island off the head has bothered everyone who has investigated this subject, as there is no bay known on the coast which has an island occupying a similar position. The fact appears to be that it is not intended to be an island at all, but simply a part of the head itself, which, on the pen-and-ink sketch from which the engraving was made, was not shown clearly as attached to it. Trinidad Head [North of Eureka] has an excrescence almost exactly like that shown on the plan.... The Hondius plan is good evidence, in fact almost convincing, that Drake anchored in Trinidad Bay.
> Professor Davidson was much worried about the island which appears on the Hondius plan. This, he thought, was intended to represent not an island but a rock some sixty feet in height near the east end of Point Reyes.... This is not at all reasonable, as the so-called island on

the plan is almost as long as the port and could not have been intended to represent this small rock.[16] ... Davidson seems to have developed such a predilection for Drake's Bay that he was unable to appreciate the force of anyone's argument who, dissenting from his view, attempted to prove that Drake might have repaired his ship in some other bay.[17]

Discussion by Robertson

Ever a skeptic, logician, and iconoclast, John W. Robertson did not express an opinion of his own about the Drake landfall, but contented himself with pointing out the defects in the theorizing of others. He noted that Hale had believed that the "Portus" was merely diagrammatic; and that both Bancroft and Hale felt that it was "an imaginary reproduction intended to illustrate the text accompanying the description given in *The World Encompassed*."[18] With respect to the opinions of Dwinelle and Davidson, Robertson commented:

> This sketch map plays queer tricks with those who too fixedly gaze upon its bewitching contour.[19] ... That two such capable men as Dwinelle and Davidson could have based their harbor on a marginal drawing of unknown authenticity, and that each should deduce from it proofs positive of their individual selections, is the best evidence that this, with other cartoons, was intended for, and did fit into these most unprovable generalizations. They were coveralls—not well fitting garments.[20]

Wagner had published his monumental work on Drake only a few months before Robertson's own book was issued. This gave the latter an opportunity to comment on Wagner's opinions of the "Portus," which he did as follows:

> Mr. Wagner seems to have fallen a victim to its protean shape and by diagram and slight alterations he has found the bay that materializes this sketch [i.e., the "Portus"], fitting it as the shoe does the foot. It is true that his "portus" is many degrees north of the location all the narratives have given it, for it [Trinidad Head] is situated about 41° northern latitude, and it is a cove never before dignified with the appellation of "harbor." It is of such small size that our coast maps scarce note the indentation and 200 yards will measure its longest diameter.[21] ... Truly, the shoe and the foot belong to the same individual, merely the left shoe is being fitted to the right foot.[22]

Comments by Sprent

In 1927 the British Museum published a treatise dealing with the Hondius Broadside entitled *Sir Francis Drake's Voyage Round the World 1577–1580: Two Contemporary Maps*. Originally published to mark the 350th anniversary of Drake's departure from Plymouth, a second edition was issued in 1931 with a few minor alterations and the addition of a portrait of Drake. The description of the maps was written by R. P. Sprent, assistant keeper and superintendent of the Map Room, and that dealing with the "Portus" is under the heading of Vera Totius Expeditionis Nauticae Descriptio D. Fran Draci, etc. (Amsterdam ? 1590).[23] Excerpts from it concerning the "Portus" are as follows:

> There are five insets on the map: two are almost identical with the Antwerp (French Drake) map, and may perhaps have been copied from the same source; another is a picture of the *Golden Hind*, which Hondius may himself have seen at Deptford, where she was preserved for many years. The remaining insets, in the upper corners, illustrate events of the voyage: that on the right the visit to Java, and that on the left the stay on the California coast during which Drake took possession of "New Albion." The latter (showing the *Portus Novae Albionis*) is of importance as one of the chief pieces of evidence in identifying the harbour used by Drake on the California coast.[24] ... It is largely on this inset that a recent investigator of the subject bases his argument in favor of Trinidad Bay.[25]

Comments by an Anthropologist

Robert F. Heizer, author of *Elizabethan California* and other treatises dealing with Drake in California, had the following to say about the "Portus":

> This little map has been referred to as the authentic map of the bay in which Drake stayed, but it has been so plausibly compared with six or eight different bays along the Pacific Coast that it is impossible to affirm it is a plan of *the* bay which Drake entered. It may be, but to prove this the bay has got to be first identified on some other basis than the *Portus Novae Albionis* plan, and then its shape compared to that of the *Portus*.[26] ... I would also question Power's statement that the Hondius ... map is "the principal key to locating the site of Drake's anchorage." While the *Portus* sketch is presumably something more than a mere

product of the imagination of the mapmaker, Jodocus Hondius, it is quite unknown what source the latter may have had available, and whether (as seems probable) he embellished the little drawing with scenes of marching men, Indians building fires, and so on.[27]

After referring to several of the harbors which have been likened to the "Portus," Heizer asserted:

It cannot represent every one of these and in my opinion until more is known of its inspiration it should not be classed as a "principal key." Power had to go to considerable effort to explain away three "apparent inconsistencies" with the actual geography in the effort to force it to fit the situation he wishes it to conform to.[28]

Comment by Gilliam

Few people are as knowledgeable in reference to San Francisco Bay as Harold Gilliam, distinguished author of *Island In Time*. He characterized the "Portus" as "the most controversial piece of evidence" in the search for the "lost harbor" of New Albion, saying:

Both amateur and professional historians have tried to fit the Hondius map like a piece of a jigsaw puzzle to various places on the California coastline. George Davidson believed that the map was a portrayal of Drake's Bay and the peninsula was Point Reyes. He was unable to explain the island, however, except as one of the offshore rocks of Point Reyes. . . . Skeptics claim the map does not represent any real location, but is probably a fanciful drawing by Hondius—his own idea of the way the port might have appeared. Historian Robert Becker even finds a new location to which the map could apply—Tom's Point on the east side of Tomales Bay. "The drawing," he concludes, "can be applied to a number of different locations, even to one heretofore overlooked, and . . . the sketch itself is at best only corroborative evidence."[29]

Nevertheless the search for the Hondius harbor goes on . . . the contenders spin out their theories in minute detail, piling elaboration on elaboration in confusing array. . . . The Hondius map must be considered in conjunction with various other clues to the landing place . . . . Conceding possible error in ascertaining latitude, the harbor could be expected to be within a degree of the 38th parallel, which passes through both Drake's Bay and northern San Francisco Bay. Bodega, Tomales, and Bolinas bays would also qualify.[30]

Gilliam might also have mentioned the fact that two coves or inner harbors within the confines of San Francisco Bay lie within a sixth of a latitudinal degree of the 38th parallel, these being San Quentin Cove and a small sub-bay on the Petaluma River near its outlet into San Pablo Bay. As for the latter, Robert C. Thomas, author of an unpublished treatise entitled "Drake at Olompali," believes that Drake's final repair site was on the western shores of this sub-bay, not far from where the McGraw-Hill book warehouse presently stands. Cited in support of his theory is the "Portus Novae Albionis," as well as a map of the upper San Francisco Bay prepared by Don Jose Canizares who came to the area with Lieutenant Don Juan Manuel Ayala on the *San Carlos* in 1775.[31]

Discussion by Aker

While the Drake Navigators Guild was pursuing its search for the exact site of Drake's landing, it made comparisons of the two East Indies geographic insets on the Hondius Broadside Map with the places depicted, acting on a suggestion that if they proved accurate enough for a close correlation to be made, then the chances would be two out of three that the "Portus" was also a faithful representation of Drake's haven as it appeared in 1579; and that the inset could then probably be correlated closely with that haven today, unless major physical changes had occurred.[32]

Preliminary studies of the three geographic insets on the map disclosed certain similarities. Each was basically contrived to make it an aerial perspective view. Each view was probably drawn or constructed from some actual elevation. The draftsman was influenced by a low-angle perspective and attempted to correct for it so that his sketch would more closely resemble a map. The insets were constructed in accordance with the rules of perspective, and the draftsman handled his work with skill. By the time of Drake's voyage, some conventional topographic symbols were in use on maps and charts to denote hills and rolling terrain.

Members of the Guild then undertook extensive research into the East Indian insets. The studies dealing with various phases of their effort to identify the California anchorage on the basis of the Hondius Broadside and its insets ultimately required seventy pages to describe, including those needed for a correlation of the California harbor with results of the study. In addition to the descriptive material, there were twenty-nine pages of maps, charts, and illustrations, many of them dealing with the Java and Molucca insets, as well as that showing the *Golden Hind* aground.[33]

In general, what the author endeavored to uncover and emphasize were those factors in the companion insets and contemporary accounts which might point to or suggest an original source. This required an intensive study of the details of the two East Indies insets, including a first-ever identification of the location of the Java anchorage. Aker is a marine draftsman of considerable experience, and his expertise in the fields of draftsmanship generally, and of sailing vessels in particular, has provided him with a depth of insight into his subject not usually enjoyed by anchorage students.[34]

In seeking a source for the "Portus" among the contemporary accounts, Aker frequently referred to *The World Encompassed,* pointing out that one group in the inset is taking its "farewell as described . . . in *The World Encompassed";* that the act of another group "is very probably the one described in *The World Encompassed";* and that Hondius' Latin description "probably stems from one similar to that in the *World Encompassed.*"[35] The point being made by these references is that Hondius did not really understand what he had engraved, and presumably, therefore, that the inset simply represented a copy of an original Drake drawing or chart.[36]

Conclusions From This Study

According to Aker, two of the Broadside's geographical insets were found to be faithful views of the places depicted, and the inset showing the *Golden Hind* hung up on a reef was determined to be an accurate representation of that incident. Allowing that sources other than Drake's records could have been found for the Moluccas inset, Aker felt it highly improbable that Hondius could have found any such for the "Portus Javae Majoris" inset, which shows only a small part of a very large harbor complex. The grounding inset revealed details that were apparently beyond the scope of Hondius' technical ability in nautical matters.

On the basis of these studies and findings, Aker felt that all these insets, including that showing the ship aground, were derived from

Drake's records. He further believes, on the basis of what they reveal, that the "Portus Novae Albionis" most probably was also derived from Drake's records and correctly portrays the site of his landing in California with the same meticulous draftsmanship displayed by the other insets.[37]

The Other Side of the Coin

Despite the fact that Aker has skillfully marshaled the available evidence, and has drawn therefrom the inferences which he believes it will support, he also conceded that the evidence has its weaknesses. For example, there is no consistency of orientation between the Moluccas and the Java insets, putting them more in the category of a view, rather than a map.[38] He points to what he says are various Hondius errors, such as failing in the Moluccas inset to show the king's canoe, to depict the towline properly, and to depict the canoes in accordance with descriptions of the same in Hakluyt and *The World Encompassed*.[39] In the same inset, details appear to have been invented, such as showing the canoe canopies to be peaked instead of flat, and showing a steering oar where other representations of the scene have none.[40]

Aker has conceded that the inset showing the ship aground on a reef is not susceptible to geographical verification;[41] and that Hondius may have had other than Drake records as a source for the Moluccas inset.[42] He directs attention to the fact that Hondius did not show the *Golden Hind* with its sails furled in the Moluccas inset, contrary to the showing in the French Drake Map, as well as to what would be expected while the ship was being towed.[43] He points out the confusion in the *Portus* where Hondius showed several groups of natives apparently bidding a frantic farewell to a ship that is going nowhere and an encampment that is still in place. In all these various inconsistencies, Aker sees a lack of understanding on the part of Hondius, and therefore a mere copying from some original record.[44] To a disinterested observer, these dissimilarities from the insets on the French Drake Map (from which Hondius apparently borrowed) are evidence that he probably did *not* see an original Drake record, but improvised as he thought best.

One feature of the Hondius Broadside which throws doubt on the claim that its maker had access to original records is its depiction of the track of Drake's voyage, as to which Hondius simply followed the same basic pattern of most of the earlier global maps, showing the same errors and omissions. For example, instead of showing a wide swing to the west and northwest on leaving Guatulco, as described in *The World Encompassed,* and undoubtedly by Fletcher, the track was shown as hugging the coast of the Californias, passing close to the San Francisco Bay area on the way north! No careening stops were pictured in Chile or near the Island of Caño, nor any stop at Guatulco. With access to original records of the voyage, it would seem that Hondius should have been able to avoid this series of flagrant errors.[45]

Opinion of the Guild

Tenet 16 requested discussion of the significance of the "Portus" plan and its correlation with proposed landing sites.

From the standpoint of the Guild, the "Portus" provides the key clues that pinpoint Drake's encampment, carrying vital information even if viewed only as a rough field sketch. Interpreted in a general way, the inset "correlates to a cove inside a sandspit on the west side of the mouth of Drake's Estero," where "hills and bluffs there correspond to the inset." The Guild went on:

> Details on the inset are engraved with care, and the Portus Plan has point-for-point correspondence with the cove, a fair degree of scale relationship, and too many points of agreement for coincidence. Comparative features are the cove's seal-head shape and matching indentations in the crest of the bluff overlooking the cove, including even a small point at the outer end. These are hard geographical features. Hondius' spit matches spits that form at Drake's Cove in shape, location, and angular relationship. The island relates to sandbars that form adjacent to the spit.

Comment on Behalf of Bolinas Lagoon

According to Neasham, the "Portus" is considered one of the basic clues to Drake's landing site, and he interprets it as Bolinas Lagoon

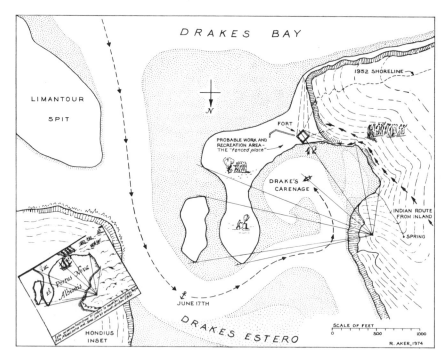

A reconstruction of the "Portus Novae Albionis" at Drake's Estero in which the channel, spit and island correspond in location to the site's features in 1952. (Drawing by Raymond Aker, 1974.)

because the latter corresponds in shape and apparent size to the "Portus" in various respects, including the fact that the hills and gullies to the east are almost exact duplicates of those found today at Bolinas Lagoon. In "Drake's California Landing," written in 1973, Neasham stated:

> Contributing evidence in favor of Bolinas Lagoon includes the Hondius Broadside, which depicts Drake's anchorage and fort. This can be applied to Bolinas Lagoon, perhaps more easily than to San Francisco Bay or Drake's Bay. The island outside would be Duxberry Reef, a hazard to navigation, which Drake would have noted.

Response on Behalf of San Quentin Cove

According to Power, the "Portus Novae Albionis" is definitive evidence that Francis Drake discovered San Francisco Bay:

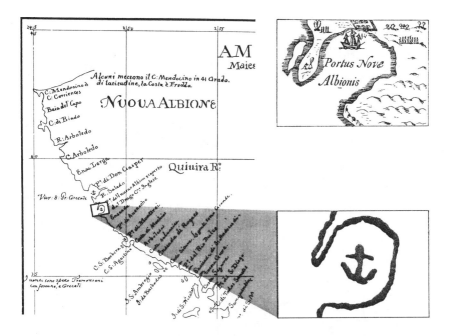

A comparison of the Portus plan, scaled to size, with Drake's anchorage on Dudley's sub-map of the Carta prima Generale. (Drawing prepared for V. Aubrey Neasham by Edmond Gross, 1974.)

It is a plan of the northern portion of this bay and of no other part of the earth. The *Portus* island compares so favorably to the distinctive form of Belvedere Island that this single comparison identifies San Francisco Bay as the anchorage of the *Golden Hinde*. In addition, the *Portus* peninsula has the general form of the Tiburon peninsula, and the shape of the actual bay in the *Portus Novae Albionis* is nearly identical with the shape of northern San Francisco Bay. The latter includes an opening into San Pablo Bay which is depicted as a shoreline on the Elizabethan plan. This may have been intended as an horizon if the vantage point was in the vicinity of Angel Island. In views of this kind, the land to the rear of the cartographer, such as Angel Island, is never depicted, as per the other Hondius inset of *Portus Java* which does not depict the opposite shore of an estuary. (See map reproduced in *California Historical Quarterly*, Summer, 1973, pp. 12–13.)

By way of rebuttal, each debater analyzed the contentions of the other two and pointed out their asserted weaknesses. The Guild set forth in some detail why, in its opinion, Belvedere Island and the

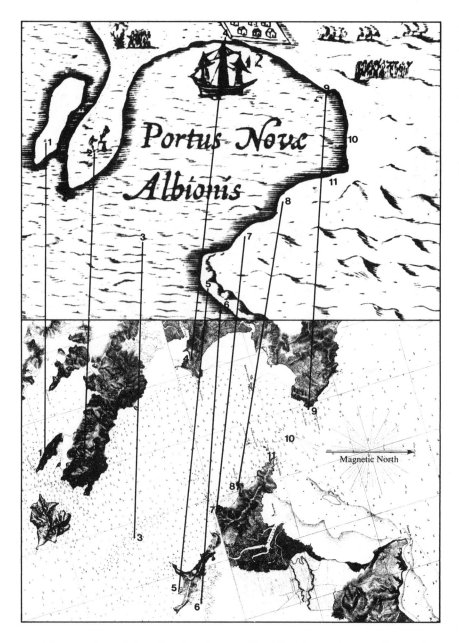

A comparison of San Francisco Bay (1856 U.S.G.S. map) to the Portus plan. (Prepared for Robert H. Power in 1974.)

Tiburon Peninsula did not compare reasonably with the "Portus." It followed this with a similar analysis in reference to Bolinas Lagoon. Neasham offered a nine-point analysis of the deficiencies of the Guild's comparison of the Estero with the "Portus," and a six-point analysis to the same effect in relation to the presentation on behalf of San Quentin Cove.

In one of the lengthiest statements of the entire debate, Power responded to the Guild's comparison of the Estero to the "Portus." In part, he said:

> The Guild tries to make the *Portus* Plan fit their area by creating a non-existent anchorage out of a changeable sand shoreline at the entrance to Drake's Estero and inventing the place name "Drake's Cove." It is a geographical myth and a geological improbability. . . . There is no cove extant today, and the Guild cannot establish that there was an anchorage cove extant at Drake's Estero in 1579 nor can they determine the configuration of the sandspit in that year.

By way of rebuttal to the Neasham position, Power stated:

> As for Bolinas Lagoon, it does not compare with the *Portus Novae Albionis* in any way whatsoever. Because there is no comparative orientation, comment on the orientation of the fort on the *Portus* plan with the levies Dr. Neasham excavated in the Bolinas marsh is, therefore, not possible.

According to Power, the "Portus" is "definitive, like a fingerprint. It could not have been drawn by imagination. There's no way the map could be contradicted."[46]

Decorative or Accurate?

The "Portus Novae Albionis" has been referred to by many names: marginal sketch, border design, ribbon border inset, sketch plan, little map, Hondius sketch, marginal illustration, border inset, inset map, Elizabethan plan, and so on. It has been a popular piece of evidence, receiving attention from most Drake scholars of the past century. During the same period, its value as an anchorage clue has been controversial. The question, of course, is whether it is merely a decorative or illustrative marginal sketch, or represents an attempt to draw an accurate topical chart.

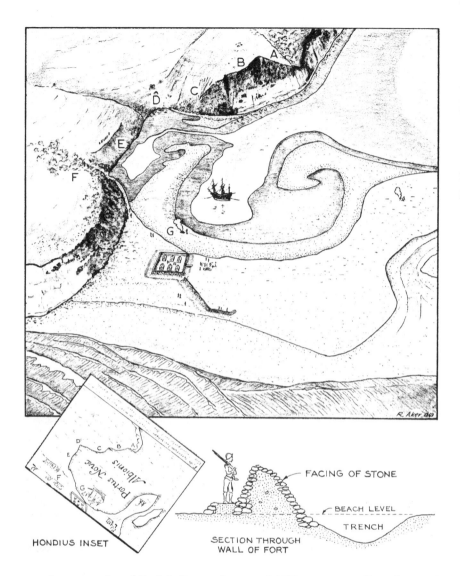

FACING OF STONE

BEACH LEVEL

TRENCH

HONDIUS INSET

SECTION THROUGH
WALL OF FORT

A reconstruction of Drake's Cove and presumed 1579 encampment (low-tide aspect). The letters A to G on the drawing indicate a series of adjacent landscape features that appear to correspond well with similar points on the Portus plan. (Drawing by Raymond Aker, 1974.)

At least eleven sponsors of various anchorage candidates have indicated a belief that the "Portus" fits the location of their particular cove or harbor rather well, and supports their respective claims to the honor of being the true Drake anchorage. To recapitulate, these are Bodega Bay (Dwinelle), Drake's Bay (Davidson), Drake's Estero (the Guild), Bolinas Lagoon (Neasham), Tomales Bay (Becker), San Quentin Cove (Power), the Petaluma River near San Pablo Bay (Thomas), Trinidad Bay, north of Eureka (Wagner), Pirate's Cove, near San Luis Obispo (Pate and Dobson), Half Moon Bay, a few miles south of San Francisco (Brown), and Nehalem Bay in Oregon (Viles and Jensen).

Several Drake scholars are convinced that the source of the "Portus" was Drake's original records. As indicated in an earlier chapter, Power is satisfied that Hondius, through his friendship with Thomas Talbot, keeper of the records at about the time the Drake log was supposedly deposited there by order of Queen Elizabeth, had access to Drake's original records.[47] Speaking of the Hondius Broadside and its inset, Davidson said: "The authority of the Hondius Map cannot be gainsaid." After citing its full title in Latin, he commented: "This explicit statement clearly demonstrates that Hondius had access to the discoveries of Drake, of Cavendish, and surely of the Spaniards."[48] Dwinelle believed "that the Hondius map was furnished him by Fletcher, who made it on the spot."[49]

Others were of the same view. Wagner wrote: "The plan of the "Portus" was unquestionably taken from some record of the expedition, whether Fletcher's account or Drake's log cannot be definitely determined,"[50] and later: "The small views on the Hondius broadside may have been taken from the map of Drake's voyage which in the time of Purchas was still hanging in the gallery at Whitehall."[51] More recently, Aker suggested that "if not copied altogether from similar insets on a source map, such as the one at Whitehall, the views could have been loaned to Hondius long enough for him to make copies for his own use, possibly surreptitiously."[52]

On the other hand, each of these persons expressing such a strong belief that the "Portus" was based on the records of the voyage or on information from some one who had been on the voyage, also entertained a strong opinion in favor of some particular (but in each case different) harbor as Drake's landing site: Power for San Francisco Bay, Davidson for the Point Reyes cove, Dwinelle for Bodega Bay, Wagner for Trinidad Bay, and Aker for Drake's Estero. The others relied on the "Portus" as a part of their proof, but expressed no opinions on its source.

Dissenting Opinions

Wagner considered the "Portus" the most important piece of evidence known to us,[53] but both Hale[54] and Bancroft[55] regarded it as diagrammatic, if not entirely imaginary, and placed no reliance on it in support of their harbor choices. Heizer stated that "it . . . has been so plausibly compared with six or eight different bays along the Pacific Coast that it is impossible to affirm that it is a plan of *the* bay which Drake entered."[56] Robertson wrote:

> The dreams that this "Portus" may induce are past psycho-analysis. For my part, I refuse to gaze into its crystalline depths and, with wax-filled ears, I give no heed to the siren song. Not recognizing the tangible resemblance it bears to any Pacific Coast harbor, I regard the Hondius sketch, not as a serious attempt to carry out a description given either by Drake or by any member of the crew; merely an illustrator's design to accompany the verbiage of the *World Encompassed*.[57]

As a matter of fact, each of the five proponents of "Portus" authenticity has been obliged to make adjustments in his proposed site in an effort to make it fit the specifications of the "Portus." The Guild must assume what the Estero's shape was in 1579, as well as the existence and shape of a parallel sandbar, as it was four centuries ago, in order to match the map inset. San Quentin Cove proponents have to pretend that the extension of the Bay into San Pablo Bay does not exist in order to present a forced and somewhat crude similarity to the "Portus." Dwinelle, Davidson, Wagner, and Neasham were all unable to point to an adjacent island even remotely resembling that delineated on the "Portus."

Another View of the "Portus" Source

For a century Drake scholars, or some of them, at least, have been pointing at Francis Fletcher as the probable source of Hondius' "Portus Novae Albionis." Dwinelle started it in 1878 when he wrote:

The writer of the Dutch account of Drake's voyage, to which the map was prefixed, had access to the papers of Fletcher, the chaplain of Drake's crew, and the historiographer of the expedition. Comparisons of the two narratives show that. Undoubtedly he had personal intercourse with many of Drake's crew, probably with Fletcher himself, certainly with those who furnished him with information for his map. . . . [The "Portus"] is just such a map as a good penman ignorant of linear and aerial perspective would have made on the spot, if he had a taste for pen-and-ink maps, such as Fletcher is known to have had. We have no doubt that Hondius' map was furnished to him by Fletcher, who made it on the spot.[58]

Already noted has been Wagner's comment that the "Portus" plan was taken from "Fletcher's account or Drake's log."[59]

The part possibly played by Fletcher again came to light, although indirectly, in 1971, with the publication of Aker's *magnum opus* dealing with Drake in California. In that section of his book entitled "A New Evaluation of the Evidence," the author pointed out the similarity of the event depicted in the "Portus" to the incidents described in *The World Encompassed*.[60] His references to that account are both accurate and relevant, but the problem with them is that Hondius (1563-1611) had been dead for seventeen years when *The World Encompassed* was published in 1628. It is inconceivable, therefore, if the Broadside was issued *circa* 1595, that Hondius could have been depicting scenes or incidents never described until thirty or more years later. Without further explanation, Aker's references to *The World Encompassed* as the source of Hondius' "Portus" could prove confusing

As a matter of fact, those same circumstances did confuse author Robertson, causing him to take exception to Davidson's assertion that the Hondius Broadside was probably issued in 1595. Robertson reasoned that because the "Portus" depicted a scene described only in *The World Encompassed* in 1628, the Hondius map was necessarily issued after the date of that narrative.[61] What Robertson was unaware of, and Aker did not make clear, was that the Fletcher account of the voyage, on which both Hakluyt and *The World Encompassed* narratives of the Nova Albion visit were largely based, was probably available to Hondius, as it was to Hakluyt, before 1589;[62] although in Hakluyt's case, because of his need to abridge the account to fit the limited space which he had available for it in his 1589 edition, the description of the scene depicted by the "Portus" happened to be a part of the story which he edited out.[63]

The evidence points toward Fletcher as *the* source of Hondius' inspiration for the "Portus" for at least two other reasons: (1) Because that inset seems obviously to have been based on an incident which in 1595 would have been available only through the Fletcher account of Nova Albion used later as its principal source by *The World Encompassed;* and (2) because the language of the inscription below the "Portus" is unmistakably Fletcherese in character, indicating Hondius' intent to depict what Fletcher had so dramatically described.

Plan of the Hondius Sketch

The "Portus" has all the earmarks of having been a two-stage production: (1) A drawing which originally showed only a small harbor with a ship at anchor opposite a group of structures on shore; and (2) the subsequent superimposing upon this placid scene of groups of persons engaged in activities apparently unrelated to ship and encampment. This is precisely what could have been expected if Hondius, having learned from Fletcher's account of Drake's dramatic departure from Nova Albion, decided to use the incident for inset purposes; and then was able to find a sketch of a small harbor, possibly that at Nova Albion, which he could adapt for his purposes by adding the various groups of figures. This could explain the inconsistency in a scene peopled with figures bidding a frantic farewell to a ship at anchor and a camp still fully set up. It seems highly unlikely that such a drawing, complete in all its details, would have been found by Hondius in either Fletcher's or Drake's records.

Assuming it reasonable to believe that Hondius may have had access to original material pertaining to the voyage, this still leaves important questions unanswered: What *was* the probable source of Hondius' material? When did it probably become available to him? Apart from Drake or Fletcher records, was there another potential source of such material available to Hondius? Did Fletcher's account contain maps and illustrations and, if so, what was his skill as a draftsman or illustrator? Is it likely that Drake's log would have contained a sketch which could have served Hondius as a prototype?

Fletcher as a Source

It is known that Francis Fletcher illustrated the earlier and still extant part of his account of the circumnavigation with drawings and an occasional map. Dwinelle left the impression that Fletcher had some talent for map-making,[64] but gave no clue to the source of that impression. On the other hand, Wagner published a number of Fletcher's drawings and two or three of his maps;[65] and from a study of his representations of Great Britain and the lower part of South America, his efforts in that direction were rather crude and primitive.[66] Nevertheless, if Hondius saw the Fletcher account, as he may well have, he also saw whatever maps it included, regardless of their quality.

From the foregoing, it may reasonably be inferred that: (1) Hondius got his material from the same source as did *The World Encompassed* (and Hakluyt), namely, an account prepared by Francis Fletcher; (2) Fletcher's account was available before 1589, because Hakluyt made use of a part of it in "The Famous Voyage" published during that year; (3) this was a period when Hondius was known to be living in London,[67] where he was undoubtedly acquainted with Hakluyt, if not with Fletcher personally; (4) no other account of the Nova Albion visit, apart from *The World Encompassed,* setting forth the incident portrayed by the "Portus" has ever been published, enhancing the probability that Hondius' exclusive source was Fletcher; (5) Fletcher's material did contain maps and illustrations, such as they were, and they would have been available to Hondius if he saw the account itself; and (6) it is highly unlikely that Drake's log would have set forth nonnavigational material of the dramatic kind in which Fletcher specialized, although it may well have contained a simple sketch of the California harbor which could have served as a basis for the embellishments added by Hondius, including the name "Portus Novae Albionis."

While the foregoing may be regarded as reasonable inferences based on noncontroversial facts, to pursue the matter further would necessitate conjecture and theorizing. Nevertheless, two thoughts present themselves, both contrary to the conclusion reached by Aker: (1) It is not unreasonable to believe that Hondius' primary purpose in respect to the "Portus," as with the inset showing the *Golden Hind* on a reef, was to tell a story or to present a dramatic incident, rather than to depict its background with precision or in accurate detail. If the intention was narrative, rather than geographic, it follows that the setting was secondary. (2) If this is so, it does not necessarily follow that Aker's guiding postulate was sound, namely, that if the two East Indies insets were proved accurate, the "chances would be two out of three that the 'Portus' was also a faithful representation of Drake's haven as it appeared in 1589."

As a result of Guild studies and findings, Aker concluded that there was "more than a probability" that the Portus inset was "derived from Drake's records,"[68] although he said nothing to suggest that he was using that term to include those of Fletcher. But, like his surmise with respect to the Whitehall map as a source, his conclusion on this score must also be regarded as no more than conjectural in view of the strong inferences pointing in Fletcher's direction, unless he is willing to expressly include that worthy as a probable source if not, indeed, the prime source of the "Portus."

While we are still in the field of conjecture, it is possible that Hondius had access to both Fletcher and Drake records. Would he have used or needed the log as a source for the "Portus" if he already had what he felt was a usable sketch from Fletcher's account? This is the unanswerable question. While Aker concluded the "Portus" was probably derived from the Drake log, there is much evidence susceptible to a contrary interpretation; and, of course, Aker's conclusion appears to have been reached without consideration of the facts pertaining to Fletcher's undoubted part in the picture.

Value of the "Portus" as a Clue

The "Portus" has been described as "a tiny map that has been twisted and turned to represent every inlet on the coast from Half Moon Bay to Oregon."[69] As a matter of fact, even that seemingly broad assertion represents something of an understatement, because the map has also been used to support a contention that Pirate's Cove near San Luis Obispo in central California was the spot where Drake landed and careened his ship.[70]

In any attempt to evaluate the "Portus" as a clue, it is interesting to realize that the criteria are not quite the same as they were ten years ago. Our amateur anchorage sleuths have done a remarkable job in an all-out effort to connect the "Portus" to original Drake records, not sparing time, effort, or money. Sleuth Robert Power has uncovered information on how, where, and from whom such records may have been obtained by Hondius. Sleuth Raymond Aker has supplied information whether the records that may have been obtained by Hondius were true representations of the places and scenes they purported to show. Between them, they appear to have exhausted most of the possibilities for research in both directions.

None of these recently discovered data were available to Hale or Bancroft in the 1880s when they were surmising, without giving much thought to the subject, that the "Portus" was purely imaginary. Even in the 1920s, when Robertson was describing it as a marginal drawing of bewitching contour and protean shape, but of unknown authenticity, he had little more on which to base a conclusion than Hale and Bancroft. It would be interesting to hear what these earlier scholars might say if they could give us their thoughts today in the light of the Power and Aker discoveries.

Questions and Answers

To a considerable extent the value of the "Portus" as a clue must depend on the answers to a number of questions. Question: Was the "Portus" intended to be decorative or accurate? The answer in the light of present knowledge is that it was not intended to be purely decorative, but that the extent of its accuracy is still uncertain. Question: Was its source a part of the expedition's original records? The answer is "possibly," but that more likely its source was Fletcher, the expedition's historiographer. Question: Was the original drawing on which the "Portus" was based an accurate one drawn to scale on the spot? Again, the answer has to be "possibly," but there is no persuasive evidence to so indicate. Question: Regardless of the source, were details of the "Portus" such as the figures shown, the "texture of the landscape," and the ship itself added by Hondius to give it more interest? The answer is that Hondius almost certainly invented and applied its intriguing title to the "Portus"; and there are indications that he may have added other important details which would have been beyond the technical ability of anyone on the voyage. However, Aker directs attention to features that he believes may have been in the original sketch and which, in his opinion, were merely copied by Hondius without understanding their significance.[71]

Still another question that may be of greater practical importance than any of the foregoing concerns the value of a clue that two such capable men as Dwinelle and Davidson could claim as providing proof positive in support of their respective anchorage choices.[72] The list of names that began with Dwinelle and Davidson has now swelled to eleven, as listed earlier. Only one of the several coves, lagoons, and bays could have been the site of the *Golden Hind*'s anchorage, but which?

Summary

The reader who ponders the foregoing multiplicity of claims will wonder whether it is possible that some one or two anchorage candidates bear a much greater resemblance to the "Portus" than others. To a considerable extent, this is possible because the "Portus" island has proved to be a stumbling block for all contenders except the San Francisco Bay proponents (Belvedere) and the supporters of Drake's Estero (with its phantom sandbar). Nevertheless, special similarity to the "Portus" has been asserted by several of the harbor sponsors, including the three participants in the 1974 debate. Both the Guild and Power claim point-for-point correspondence with the "Portus," the Guild in several respects,[73] Power in ten enumerated particulars.[74] Consequently, the situation remains controversial, and the "Portus" affords no clear-cut answer to the tenet under consideration.

From the standpoint of the disinterested observer, the following conclusions are drawn: (1) although the evidence purporting to authenticate the "Portus" is rather persuasive, it is only circumstantial as well as controversial, and its significance rests upon inferences and conjectures that cannot rise to the level of certainty or proof positive; (2) although there is some basis for the conjecture that Hondius merely copied the details of the "Portus" from some original drawing, this is too slender a reed to serve as fully convincing evidence on the point;

and (3) since the sponsors of almost every harbor on the California and Oregon coasts, as well as some within San Francisco Bay, claim the "Portus" to be probative of their respective candidates for anchorage honors, then entirely apart from any consideration of the authenticity and accuracy of the engraving, we are confronted with a highly controversial situation which reduces the status of the "Portus" to one of corroborative evidence at best.

CHAPTER

The Montanus Illustration

*Tenet 17: What is the significance of Arnold Montanus'
illustration "The Crowning of Drake," which was published in De Nieuwe en Onbekonde Weereld of Beschryvning van Americo en 1 + Zuid-Land ... (Amsterdam, 1671)?*

T HE CLUE of latest vintage in the race for anchorage honors is
an engraving which has existed for more than three centuries. It was entitled "The Crowning of Drake" and was
supposedly prepared by Arnold Montanus, a Flemish craftsman. It
appeared as an illustration in a book published in Amsterdam in 1671,
entitled *De Nieuwe en Onbekonde Weereld: of Beschryvning van Americo
en 1 + Zuid-Land*.[1]

In its foreground the engraving purports to show Francis Drake
standing with hands on hips while a feathered crown is being placed
upon his head by a native chief. In the background are what appear to
be a multitude of Indians at the left, and a small army of soldiers at the
right. In the distant center is a ship carrying full sail. The engraving
has acquired the status of an anchorage clue, at least for the purposes of

the 1974 debate, because the topography in the background of the picture shows a striking similarity to San Francisco Bay, as viewed from near the site above San Quentin Cove where Shinn said he found the brass plate.

When this similarity was first detected and by whom are probably questions that only Power can answer. Obviously it was sometime after he first presented his Point San Quentin anchorage theory in 1954; and of course it had to be before the publication of his 1973 article in the *California Historical Quarterly*[2] in which he suggested that Montanus may have had a concrete source for his drawing, and that the illustration is actually an accurate depiction of the port of Nova Albion.

The Montanus Concept

Regardless of when the theory of the illustration as an anchorage clue was first propounded, it was in his 1973 article that Power stressed its remarkable resemblance to a view from Point San Quentin looking across an arm of San Francisco Bay toward Tiburon and Angel Island. He called attention to the little-known facts that Arnold Montanus was a grandson of the partner and brother-in-law of Jodocus Hondius; that Montanus' grandmother (Hondius' sister) was an author and favorite of Queen Elizabeth who, because of her favored position at the Court, may very well have seen Drake's official portfolio from the voyage and have left other written records which Montanus would have inherited; and that Montanus, therefore, was the intellectual and physical heir of the man who created the "Portus Novae Albionis" and could very well have had Hondius' notes and sketch books from that project. On this basis Power suggested that this dual heritage leads to the speculation that Montanus had a special source for his work, and that the illustration may be something more than a mere imaginative depiction of the port of Nova Albion.

Power added that support for this speculation had been brought forth recently by Alex Cumming, curator of Drake's ancestral home, Buckland Abbey, Devonshire. Cummings identified the coat of arms on the right side of the banner in the illustration as that of the City of Plymouth, from which Drake first sailed. Cummings maintained that this detail must have been taken from actual voyage records, as it is an

A comparison of shorelines at the upper right between the 1671 Montanus engraving of the crowning of Drake by the California Indians (above) and a view from Point San Quentin looking across an arm of San Francisco Bay toward Tiburon (below).

unlikely display of arms for an artist to have conjured up in the 1670s. Power concluded with the observation that the Montanus illustration has never been shown to match any other part of Marin County.

Strange Duplication

The illustration is said to have been the work of Arnold Montanus, but it also appeared in another book about the New World entitled *America*.[3] The latter was also published in 1671, but in English and in London. It was a copiously illustrated tome of 675 pages, by John Ogilby, "His Majesty's Oceanographer, Geographick Printer, and Master of the Revels in the Kingdome of Ireland." Many of the same engravings were used in both books, and some of the textual material was the same, allowing for differences in language. Obviously, use of the Drake engraving was through some arrangement with Montanus, the nature of which has never become known.[4]

The text accompanying the Ogilby illustration describes the Drake visit to Nova Albion. Covering portions of three large pages, it begins with the statement that "Nova Albion was so denominated by Sir *Francis Drake,* when he was there Entertain'd by the King of that Countrey." It appears to have been a rather loosely reworded statement of "The Famous Voyage" version of the same events, but with one interesting deviation. The statement says that at the "coronation" on June 26, 1579, the Indian king, after being assured by Drake that he would be welcome, "came with a Retinue of about twelve thousand Men."[5] Since there is no mention of such a large number of "Men" in "The Famous Voyage," *The World Encompassed,* or any other contemporary account, where did Ogilby secure such a figure? This interesting error has been traced to De Bry's *Americae Pars VIII*, published in 1599, in the appendix of which is an illustration (No. 5) purporting to show Drake being visited by the California Indians. In the short Latin text accompanying the illustration are the words meaning "12,000 men," but the source of this statement is yet to be discovered.[6]

Comment by a Drake Scholar

Robert F. Heizer discussed the Montanus illustration in his *Elizabethan California,* saying that he could see a number of things wrong with the engraving.[7] Among these "wrong things" were Drake being beardless; each of the great crowd of Indians at the foot of the hill is armed with a long spear (not a California Indian weapon); and the anchored, not careened, ship appears to be in full sail.

Heizer felt that the scene was one made up to fit the narrative with some assistance, probably, from De Bry's earlier, and equally imaginative, ideas of what California Indians looked like. He went on to say:

> Surely in Drake's day, no Indian, chief or lesser person, ever dressed the way the Indian 'Hioh' is shown by Montanus. The "banner" (or plate) shown in the engraving bears the coat of arms of the City of Plymouth, and this is considered "as an unlikely display of arms for an artist to have conjured up in the 1670's."[8] Why is it unlikely? I would think since Drake and his voyage were so closely associated with Plymouth, the port from which he sailed and to which he returned in glory, that the arms of the city would be exactly what some inventive artist *would* put in a picture he was creating a century after the voyage.[9]

Comment by the Guild

Tenet 17 asked simply: "What is the significance of Arnold Montanus' illustration, *The Crowning of Drake?*" Presumably, it meant the significance as a clue to the location of the anchorage.

The Guild stated that it did not use the engraving as evidence because of its late date of publication and evident errors; for example, cavalier dress, Indians with spears although they had none, striped tents instead of conical dwellings, the *Golden Hind* shown as a ship of the seventeenth century resting a great distance from the camp. Montanus clearly improvised. What is fact and what is not? Resemblance to the view of the shore on the horizon in this print can be found in numerous instances. This kind of detail can be roughed-in so casually by an artist composing an illustration, even as embellishment, that its value as an identifying feature *alone* is questionable.

Comment on Behalf of Bolinas Lagoon

The 1671 drawing by Arnold Montanus is a fanciful view. Drake is shown in what appears to be cavalier clothing, and his men, far in excess of the number he had with him, are also dressed in the manner of the seventeenth century. The Indians are not reminiscent of the

Coast Miwok in appearance, dress, or habitations. The scene showing the *Golden Hind* at anchor conceivably related to many spots in California, including Bolinas Lagoon. To designate it as a particular spot, however, may be begging the case more than the artist intended.

Further Comment by Power

After restating the position set forth in his 1973 article as a part of his 1974 debate material, Power added that the Montanus illustration provides support for his anchorage theory because it correlates with the discovery site of the plate of brass, with a good careenage site, and with the location of Drake's fort as indicated in the comparison and correlation of the San Francisco Bay map and the "Portus Novae Albionis."

Summary

The engraving represents another of those controversial pieces of circumstantial evidence which seem to provide a clue to the location of the 1579 California anchorage. In the single respect that the physical background of the scene depicted bears a remarkable similarity to a view from near San Quentin Point, the engraving suggests that its maker had authentic information as a basis for his work.

On other scores, however, it is apparent that the engraver was depending largely on his imagination, with some borrowing of both subject and text from an earlier engraver, De Bry. With the possible exception of the background, everything on the engraving is wrong in one way or another: Drake in cavalier garb and without a beard; his men also in seventeenth-century clothing and too numerous; the Indians not reminiscent of the Coast Miwok in appearance, dress, habitations, or weapons; a seventeenth-century ship in full sail, rather than careened, and too far away from the shore; striped tents rather than conical habitations; and the plate shown as a banner with City of Plymouth coat of arms (something not mentioned in the narratives). With all these deviations by the engraver from recorded facts, and the substitution of his imagination instead, it is difficult to believe that he would have given more than casual attention to the mere background of the scene, or have taken the pains to reproduce it from some ancient original sketch, if such were available.

In addition to this array of variances from reality and known fact, other questions are raised by the time lapse of nearly a century. What explanation is there for the source or prototype of the engraving not having appeared sooner in connection with a subject of such great sixteenth-century interest? Despite the impressive familial connections disclosed by Power's prodigious research, the chances of such a prototype having been preserved from one century to another would seem to have been slight.

Unanswerable questions are raised by the simultaneous appearance of the illustration in two different volumes of travel, printed in different languages and countries. All in all, it is doubtful that the resemblance noted by Power, when viewed from a disinterested standpoint, is the result of anything more than coincidence and, therefore, it appears that the engraving provides only a tenuous, if not entirely fanciful anchorage clue.

CHAPTER

The Cermeño Visit

Tenet 18: What is the significance of the Declaration by the Spanish Captain Sebastian Rodriguez Cermeño and others who were with him who were shipwrecked in 1595 in the bay presently known as Drake's Bay?

OF THE many clues to the location of Drake's California anchorage, one of the most significant, or potentially significant, was the visit in 1595 of Captain Sebastian Rodriguez Cermeño and his Manila galleon to the coast of northwest America. Those who assert that Drake landed elsewhere than in the bay that bears his name, regard the Cermeño visit as prime evidence in support of their position. Those espousing the cause of Drake's Estero would brush off Cermeño's visit as neither probative nor conclusive. But the story of the Spanish captain and his adventures in this part of the world represent high drama, apart from any bearing they may have on the Drake controversy.

Cermeño, his name sometimes spelled Cermeñho and Cermeñon,[1] was the first Spanish sea captain to set foot on the soil of northern California, although its shores had been coasted by Spanish explorers more than half a century before.[2] It was in 1565, however, that the first Spanish vessel made the long and lonely voyage from the Philippines to Acapulco, bringing supplies for the colonists of Spanish America, and later transporting silks, spices, and other precious merchandise of the East. Returning, these ships carried Mexican and Peruvian pesos that were to become the standard of value in the Orient.

The western terminus of these vessels was the Philippines, and to the people of New Spain the ships became known as the "Manila galleons." Their numbers varied from one to four a year, and they continued to sail this route regularly until 1815. Their coming was eagerly awaited by both the colonists of Mexico and the buccaneering privateers that attempted to waylay them.[3]

The eastward voyage of the galleons was long and arduous. The customary route took the vessels north to about 40° N, at which level they would encounter the California coast and head south along it to Mexico; however, there were no known ports along that coast where an emergency stop could be made. Luis de Velasco, viceroy of Mexico during the years beginning 1590, became concerned with this situation and, after much correspondence with the Spanish king, obtained authority to arrange a voyage of discovery. He then ordered it to be undertaken by a skilled Portuguese navigator, Sebastian Rodriguez Cermeño.

On July 5, 1595, the *San Agustin*, a galleon under his command, sailed from Cavite in the Philippines, with 130 tons of cargo and a complement of about seventy men. After crossing the Pacific and sighting the American continent at a point above Cape Mendocino, they proceeded slowly southward along the coast, finally rounding Point Reyes and coming to anchor in what is today known as Drake's Bay. This was on November 6, 1595, and on the following day, Cermeño landed and took formal possession of the land and port in the name of the king of Spain. He named it the Bahia de San Francisco because he was accompanied by a friar of the order of St. Francis who took this occasion to thus honor the name of his patron saint.

Cermeño made an official report of his voyage on his return to Mexico, and a translation of that part of it pertaining to his Drake's Bay sojourn will be found in Appendix F. He described the bay as horseshoe-shaped, with a river running into it, over the bar of which (leading into Drake's Estero) there were three fathoms of water at high tide. He added that on entering into the Estero, "you will find fresh water on the right side, which comes from another river with a plentiful supply of water, and where this falls in there are Indians settled."[4]

Details of Cermeño's Sojourn

On the day of his arrival, many Indians appeared on the beach, and one of them came out to the ship in a tule balsa which he propelled with a paddle with a blade at each end. He remained beside the ship for some time talking in his native tongue. Some cotton cloth, silk, and a red cap were given him, all of which he accepted and then returned to shore. Early the next morning four more natives, each rowing a tule balsa, came out to the ship and remained alongside, talking as the man had the previous day. They were also given gifts of cloth and returned to the shore. As soon as they had departed, Cermeño went ashore in the ship's boat with twenty-two men, seventeen of them harquebusiers. This armed party landed on the beach near some Indian habitations. The natives were said to be well built and robust, but inclined to fatness. The men were entirely naked; the women wore grass or skin skirts.

Cermeño and his armed men, arranged in military order, then marched to an Indian village about a harquebus shot from the beach. Here they found about fifty adults who looked upon the Spaniards with great fright. These natives were peaceable and gave their visitors some small seeds. These seeds, wild birds, and elk were said to have been the main dietary resources of the Indians.

On proceeding another mile and a half the Spaniards encountered a band of hostile native men, with faces painted in black and red, who skirmished in a circle and uttered loud howls. Fortunately, two Indians who had accompanied Cermeño from the shore spoke to the hostiles, who then laid down their weapons and approached in a humble manner as if terrorized. After a journey of about nine miles in all, the Spaniards returned to the beach where a camp was being set up and entrenchments for defense were being made.

For about a week the crew were busy, erecting their camp and assembling a launch, for which the parts had been carried from the Philippines on the deck of the *San Agustin*. On November 15, the captain, accompanied by nine other men with arms, went up Drake's Estero in the ship's boat. The main estero had Indian villages along its shores and a settlement near its mouth. One village was situated on a hill about two miles from the estero entrance on the east shore. Exploration of the Limantour Estero was also made, near the entrance to which was another Indian village.

Late in November the *San Agustin* was driven aground by a strong onshore gale. Details of the disaster were not given by the reports but at least two men, including a priest, were lost in the wreck, together with the ship's cargo and food supplies. Thus it became necessary to forage up-country for food. The Spaniards made two or three journeys into the hinterland, a distance of about 3 leagues (between 9 and 12 miles). They found the land fertile, and noted wild birds and deer.

On December 8, 1595, the survivors of the *San Agustin* left the Bahia de San Francisco in their Philippine launch which they had named the *San Buenaventura*.[5] They reached Acapulco after many hardships on January 31, 1596. Several members of the crew and the pilot are reported to have elected to travel overland and eventually to have reached Sombrerete, a mining camp in Mexico.[6] Having been wrecked near Point Reyes, they would necessarily have had to cross the Golden Gate or the Bay of San Francisco at some point. Despite this fact, the inner harbor, now known as the Bay of San Francisco, remained the mysterious "lost port" for another 174 years.[7]

Comments of Drake Scholars

George Davidson felt that when Cermeño and his crew landed in Drake's Bay, they must have learned that Drake's vessel had been there. Only sixteen years had elapsed and the incident was of too wonderful a character to the uncivilized natives to be soon forgotten. From the respect paid by the Indians to Drake, Davidson thought it probable that the post set up by Drake when he took possession still existed; "but as his name was heartily execrated by the Spaniards, they may well have destroyed all vestiges of his visit with pardonable satisfaction; the more especially to obliterate every sign of his having taken possession of the country."[8]

John W. Robertson thought it possible that the reason for the Cermeño survey was the news that Drake had found a good harbor near latitude 38°N.[9] Robertson noted that the reception received was markedly hostile, quite different from the worshipful greetings accorded to Drake and his sailors.[10] He felt that fifteen years could not have wiped out the memory of Drake's visit nor have destroyed all evidence of Drake's stay; that some remains of the ship reported by John Drake as abandoned in the port would have been found; and that while "Cermeño is positive in his statement that they were the first white men that these Indians had seen, he found nothing to excite his curiosity or to arouse his suspicion of Drake's recent visit; for had there been trace of the handiwork of the artisans who repaired Drake's ship, Cermeño would have recorded it."[11]

Comment by Wagner

Henry R. Wagner's ideas were in much the same vein as those of Davidson and Robertson. He conjectured that the Indians must have received many presents from Drake and his crew, and although there was a possibility that they may have hidden these from Cermeño, it was difficult to believe that not a single one remained in view. Wagner noted that Cermeño apparently found no trace of the fort erected by Drake, because the stock instructions to Spanish explorers at that period were to look for signs of civilized people;[12] that the Indians had bows and arrows and that he could find no other kind of iron with which to cut a weapon or anything else, meaning that he found no sign of iron.

In his 1924 treatise "The Voyage to California of Sebastian Rodriguez Cermeño in 1595,"[13] Wagner summed up his views of the Cermeño visit as follows:

> Negative evidence can never be conclusive, and it is always possible, of course, that the objects which probably in great number the Indians had previously obtained from Drake and his party may have been hidden. One of the accounts mentioned the fact that the Indians acted as if they had never seen people like them before; and no doubt the Spaniards interpreted this as evidence that no Europeans had ever been in the bay previously, but Indian actions are easily misinterpreted. Generally speaking, the actions of the Indians were very similar to those described in the *World Encompassed*, with the notable exception, of course, that they did not weep nor lacerate themselves nor try to impose the sovereignty of the country on Rodriguez Cermeño, as they did on Drake in the account of Drake's voyage.

Comments of Debate Participants

Tenet 18 asked "the significance of the Declarations by Cermeño and others who were with him who were shipwrecked in 1595 in ... Drake's Bay."

Drake's Estero looking toward Drake's Bay. (Philip Hyde.)

According to the Guild, the Cermeño account gives a comparative record of navigation into Drake's Bay in 1595 in a ship of similar size and type as Drake's. It gives evidence that Drake could have entered the Estero at high tide since there were three fathoms on the bar outside, about 16.5 feet. The *Golden Hind's* deep draft was 13 feet.

The Guild explained that Cermeño did not enter the Estero because there was no reason to do so. He assumed the bay was safe, for his worst weather had come from the northwest. Actually, nowhere did he deny Drake's prior presence. As for the numbers of Indians seen by each expedition, Drake saw a great number on *one* occasion, because they came from inland to see the English. No such delegation visited Cermeño. On the other hand, Cermeño mentioned, in connection with the bows and arrows of the natives, that "we could find no other kind of iron." Did he, perhaps, see iron arrow points made by Drake's blacksmith?

Comment on Behalf of Bolinas Bay

In Neasham's opinion, the most important fact about Cermeño's visit in 1595 was that he made no mention of Drake whatsoever. In fact, he gave no indication of Europeans ever having been at Drake's Bay. Cermeño would have seen and mentioned Drake's fort, had the latter been at the Estero. As for the mention of "No other kind of iron," this meant that the Indians had bows and arrows, "but not any kind of iron with which to cut weapons or other things." Why did Cermeño not take the ship into the protection of the inner estero, if it was such a good spot for Drake? Instead, he remained at anchor outside the bar until blown ashore in a winter storm from the southwest.

Statement on Behalf of San Quentin Cove

According to Power, the Cermeño account is significant since there are more dissimilarities between it and the English accounts than there are similarities, strongly suggesting that Drake did not visit the Drake's Bay area. Some of these dissimilarities were: Drake's *Golden Hind* safely entered an inner harbor on the day of arrival; Cermeño never did take the *San Agustin* into an inner harbor. Drake experienced complete nautical safety, but the *San Agustin* was wrecked on Drake's Bay beach. Drake saw hundreds of Indians, their king alone having a "guard of about 100 tall and warlike men"; Cermeño apparently never saw more than a hundred adult Indians at one time. Drake took overnight to reach the Farallones, whereas Cermeño in his survival launch passed those islands on the day of departure. *The World Encompassed* made no specific mention of crabs at Nova Albion; Cermeño did so. This is understandable, for crabs are strictly a coastal food.

The Guild's sole evidence that in Drake's time there was sufficient water over the bar at Drake's Estero is Cermeño's report of a depth of 3 fathoms, which the Guild translates as meaning 16.5 feet. The *Golden Hind's* draft of 13 feet would seem to indicate a flotation differential of 3.5 feet. However, 3 fathoms is a rounded figure, as is a "draft of 13 feet," and not a precise reading down to the inch, so that the figures really express depths ranging from 12.5 to 13.5 feet, and 3 fathoms could be any depth between 13.5 and 18.5 feet. The former is too shallow to have permitted the *Golden Hind* to enter Drake's Estero safely. This could explain why Cermeño did not enter it with the *San Agustin,* which the Guild says was similar in type and size to the *Golden Hind.*

Power also suggested that "to keep the record straight, there is no support in the accounts that the Indian delegation 'came from inland' as alleged by the Guild."

Prima Facie *Case*

Strangely enough, one argument against the *Golden Hind* ever having been in Drake's Estero was not mentioned by Power, although Neasham called it "the most important fact about Cermeño's visit in 1595." This is the contention that Cermeño's failure to find any sign of Drake's supposed visit to the Estero virtually forecloses any possibility of his having spent a good part of the summer of 1579 in the same area where Cermeño spent more than 30 days only sixteen years later. Those who share this opinion base it on two grounds:

1. That in view of the number of persons (more than eighty), the length of time (more than a month), and the nature of the multifarious activities (blacksmithing, carpentry, and mere living) in the restricted area concerned, it is difficult to believe that no material sign of Drake's earlier presence in the area would have been reported or noted. The every-day life activities, together with the undoubted abandonment of numerous worn-out and broken items left as no longer useful for the voyage home, should have created a litter that would have been unmistakably present.

2. That the same conclusion must necessarily be drawn from the fact that no Drake artifact was produced by the extensive subsurface explorations (ninety pits and trenches) carried out at the Estero site by the Drake Navigators Guild between 1952 and 1961.

These nonfindings by Cermeño in the sixteenth century and by the Guild in the twentieth at best represent negative evidence. Yet by some they have been regarded as establishing a *prima facie* case, since they are persuasive and difficult to rebut. On the other hand, the marshaling of a variety of contrary contentions, although readily possible, would serve no useful purpose at this time.

Dissimilarities

From Power's standpoint, the importance of the Cermeño account lay in its correlation with Drake's experience in Nova Albion, because it was Power's feeling that the dissimilarities between the Cermeño and Drake accounts exceed the similarities. The dissimilarities he mentioned and the potential rejoinder to each by Estero proponents are as follows:

1. *Drake brought his ship into an inner harbor; Cermeño did not.* The answer to this is that their purposes and needs were different. Drake sought a totally secure harbor where he could beach and repair the *Golden Hind,* rest his men, and reprovision his ship over a period of several weeks. Cermeño intended only to remain long enough to put together his prefabricated launch and make a brief survey of the inner bay. The only purposes (originally, at least) in assembling the launch were to explore the Estero, check the depth of water at its entrance or bar, and thus to determine its feasibility for future galleon use. He may have considered that depth insufficient for entry of the *San Agustin* into the Estero. More significantly, his report made no recommendation of it for that purpose, and there is no record of any Manila galleon having used it in the next 220 years.[14]

2. *Drake experienced complete nautical safety, while the* San Agustin *was wrecked on Drake's Bay beach.* The difference between disaster and "complete nautical safety" probably had little to do with the anchorage site, but rather with two other factors: (a) The dangerous winter season when Cermeño was in the bay, as contrasted with the relatively safe summer season at the time of Drake's visit to the North Pacific coast; and (b) an error in the handling by Cermeño of his vessel.[15] Nautical safety depended rather on the navigational experience, skill and sound judgment of the captain. Drake was one of the era's greatest navigators and ship handlers. Cermeño apparently had no particular experience in other than established ports.

3. *Crabs eaten by the Indians at Drake's Bay* were mentioned by Cermeño, but not by *The World Encompassed* (at Nova Albion, at least). Power contended that this was pertinent because crabs are purely a coastal food, and the lack of mention by *The World Encompassed* could suggest a San Francisco Bay location, such as San Quentin Cove, where no crabs are found. Presumably the rejoinder on behalf of the coastal bays would be that crabs *were* mentioned by *The World Encompassed,* but under the general heading of "mussels."

4. *Drake saw many more Indians than Cermeño.* This was apparently true and reasonably explainable on two grounds:

a) Contrary to Power's assertion that there was no support in the accounts for the statement that many Indians "came from inland" especially to see the English, *The World Encompassed* had this to say: "Against the end of three daies (the newes having the while spread itselfe further, and as it seemed a great way up into the countrie) were assembled the greatest number of people which we could reasonably imagine to dwell within any convenient distance round about."

b) It is also reasonable to infer that large numbers of natives did not frequent the chilly Point Reyes area in the wintertime when Cermeño was there, as opposed to Drake's visit in June.[16]

5. *Drake took overnight to reach the Farallones, while Cermeño in his survival launch passed them on the day of departure.* This reopens a subject dealt with at some length in an earlier chapter, to which reference is made.[17] However, the logical response to this alleged dissimilarity is that there really was none. As Power explained it in that chapter, Drake would have left San Quentin Cove in the morning, passed through the Golden Gate in the afternoon, then have hove-to overnight, approaching the Farallones the next day. Cermeño left Drake's Bay on December 8, "sailed about ten leagues and lay to during the . . . night." But did he leave Drake's Bay at 5 a.m. or at 3 p.m.? If the latter, he too might have hove-to for the night had he wished to try an approach to the Southeast Farallon the next morning.

Further Guild Rebuttal

Power's assertion that the similarities between the Drake and Cermeño accounts are exceeded by the dissimilarities would undoubtedly be challenged by the Guild. They could presumably assert the following similarities:

1. Both Drake and Cermeño came in search of a suitable harbor, but for different reasons.

2. Both came with ships of about the same tonnage, each heavily laden with extraordinarily precious cargo.

3. Both had crews of about the same number.

4. Both arrived after voyages of great length.

5. Both approached the harbor from the north, and reported a somewhat similar latitude.

6. Both saw the white cliffs, although Cermeño did not mention them.

7. Both were given similar welcomes by the Indians, including the lonesome boat approach and the long-winded oration.

8. Both established camps at the rear of the bay visited.

9. Both explored the area in the vicinity of their camps.

10. Both described the weapons and dwellings of the natives.

11. Both described the wildlife and available food.

12. Both made excursions up into the country.

13. Both found the hinterland fertile and fruitful.

14. Both stayed about the same length of time, Drake thirty-six days, Cermeño thirty-two days.

15. Both spent much of their stay getting their vessels ready for departure.

16. Both left a ship in the harbor, Drake his small ship, Cermeño his large one.

17. In both cases, it is believed that at least one member of the expedition walked back to Mexico.[18]

18. In both cases, reports were made concerning their respective visits.

19. In both cases, these reports mentioned the islands that were passed on leaving.

Behavior of The Indians

In what respects did the actions of Cermeño's Indians differ from those of the natives encountered by Drake? Despite the similarity of receptions given the visitors on each occasion, as described by the Cermeño and *The World Encompassed* accounts, there were also points of difference. In this connection, Wagner chose to question whether a "canow" and a tule boat were one and the same.[19] Another Drake expert, however, found no difficulty with this point, saying: "This was undoubtedly the same type of craft seen by Cermeño 16 years later. His description makes it quite certain that it was a tule balsa."[20]

In the welcome itself there were differences toward Cermeño that might be taken as an indication that the Indians he saw had been in contact with white men before, if the two groups of Indians be considered one and the same. In both cases, the Indians on the beach sent one of their number off in a boat, but the caution and reserve shown by the spokesman sent to Drake was in sharp contrast to Cermeño's welcomer, who made only one trip out to the ship, and after delivering a similarly lengthy oration was induced to come alongside. He readily accepted a number of gifts offered to him, and with these he returned to the shore satisfied.[21]

No doubt the less reverential behavior on the part of Cermeño's Indians would have been attributed by Estero proponents to psychological factors; for example, Cermeño put seventeen armed men on shore and probably frightened and antagonized the Indians with this initial show of force. Drake, on the other hand, used psalm-singing and prayer reading, which entranced the natives, particularly when he let them visit his fortified compound to hobnob with members of his party. Cermeño's crew may have caused a reaction entirely different from that by Drake's group, which included several boys, three male blacks, and even a young woman.[22] There may have been other factors which would have made a material difference in the behavior of the natives toward Cermeño,[23] including the fact that the years had brought a different generation of natives into maturity, and that the population residing near the Estero in 1595 may have been a largely, or even entirely, different group than was on hand in 1579.

Semantic Subtlety

It is unwise to underestimate the ingenuity and zeal of a persistent anchorage sleuth, or his ability to find something of seeming significance in even the most minor of clues. Among the ardent supporters of the theory that Drake brought the *Golden Hind* into San Francisco Bay was Walter A. Starr. Now deceased, Starr was an interested participant in California Historical Society activities with respect to the plate found by Beryle Shinn, and one of the contributors to a fund for its purchase.

In an article published in 1962 entitled "Drake Landed in San Francisco Bay in 1579,"[24] Starr offered the usual arguments favoring the San Quentin site, but included a further point that has never been mentioned or given consideration by any Drake scholars, even Power himself. This, tersely stated, was a part of his comparison of the Cermeño account with that of *The World Encompassed:* "The Drake account always refers to the landing place as shore. The Cermeño account always as beach."

The World Encompassed, in that part of it dealing with Nova Albion, used the word "shoare" twice, but makes no reference to "beach." According to Wagner's translation of that part of Cermeño's account pertaining to Drake's Bay, including supporting declarations, the term "beach" was used six times and the word "shore" twice.[25] Whatever the value of this obscure bit of evidence, it is apparent that Starr was convinced that the narrators of these contemporary accounts, between them and unwittingly, of course, had provided a significant clue as to whether the respective anchorages were seaside or bayside.

Summary

Considering the negative character of Cermeño's report and the circumstances of his unfortunate visit to Drake's Bay, it is surprising how much of a tempest our debaters were able to stir up in such a small teapot. In an ordinary discussion, the fact that Cermeño reported nothing about any European having previously visited Drake's Bay would simply have been accepted at face value. But in a controversy, such as the triangular one with which we are dealing, every ambiguous word and statement represents a straw to be grasped at by one or another of its participants.

Obviously, one of two things is true: Either Drake was in the Estero in 1579, or he was not. To prove either on the basis of negative evidence is impossible. The evidence is susceptible to several interpretations, and the differences are incapable of resolution on the basis of reasonable inferences or otherwise.

It does seem clear that, so far as his report is concerned, Cermeño saw nothing to indicate that Drake had been in Drake's Bay; on the other hand, he also saw nothing to deny his earlier presence there. So far as all the explanations and counter-explanations are concerned about the negativity of Cermeño's report, these are entirely speculative, and more or less cancel each other out. From the purely objective point of view, the Cermeño report does not provide substantial support for any one of the three anchorage theories.

27

The Dudley Maps

Tenet 19: Discuss the significance of the cartographic information about the California coast contained in Robert Dudley's 1647 atlas, Arcano del Mare, and manuscript chart.

A PROMINENT cartographer of the early seventeenth century was Robert Dudley, an Englishman born in 1574, a bare three years before Drake's departure on his global voyage. He was the illegitimate son of the Earl of Leicester, who had been a staunch friend of Drake and one of the sponsors of his circumnavigation. His mother was Lady Sheffield, the sister of Admiral Lord Howard. He attended Oxford and inherited his father's estate after the death of his brother, the Earl of Warwick, in 1590. He married the sister of Thomas Cavendish who, in 1586–1588, had emulated Drake by sailing around the world and capturing a rich Spanish treasure ship. He was related to Richard Hakluyt indirectly through the latter's marriage to a cousin of Cavendish.

Dudley became the administrator of the estate of Cavendish, after the latter's death in 1592. Thus he came into possession of two ships which had belonged to Cavendish, and is said to have himself projected a voyage to the South Seas. He was dissuaded from making this trip because of his lack of experience, and changed his plans to a voyage to the West Indies in 1594. There is no record that he had any contact with Drake who was living in London at that time. However, through his kinsmen he may well have had the opportunity to meet and talk with Drake, as he had a keen interest in details of the Pacific phases of the 1577—1580 voyage because of his own South Seas plans. In other words, it is possible that he obtained from Drake personally *circa* 1593 or 1594 some of the data which appeared in maps of the California coast that were published more than half a century later.

Dudley emigrated to Italy in 1605, where he spent the rest of his life. He is said to have begun work about 1630 on an atlas which was posthumously published in 1646 or 1647 under the title of *Arcano del Mare*. Also during those years he prepared a number of manuscript drawings which, although never published, were preserved in the Royal Library at Munich, Germany. Two of these published maps and one of those unpublished purported to depict the coast of northern California.

The Maps of Special Interest

The three maps have been described in some detail in an earlier chapter. The unpublished one, known as Chart No. 85, is an undated manuscript which Davidson located in the Munich Library in the 1880s. Of particular interest on this chart is a round bay at about 38° labeled "B: di noua Albion" outside the mouth of a river or estuary identified as "Il Por:^{to} boniss^{mo}." If drawn to scale, the greatest width of the bay would have been eighteen miles, and the width across its opening would have been around eight or nine miles.

Among the published maps included in the *Arcano del Mare* was the "Carta Particolare, No. XXXIII," hereafter referred to as "Carta Particolare," which modified Chart No. 85 in minor respects; however, "B: di noua Albion" remained much the same in shape and location, but was identified simply as "Po:^{to} di Nuova Albion." No sign of any islands outside the bay is shown on either map.

The second of the published maps from the *Arcano del Mare* is that known as the "Carta prima Generale d'America dell'India Occidentale e Mare del Zur," but usually referred to as the "Carta prima

AMERICA
Maiestrale

NUOUA ALBIONE.

Quijıra Rᵒ

MARE DEL ZUR.

The *Carta prima Generale,* Robert Dudley's chart of the northwest coast of America, 1647.

Generale." It differs substantially from the "Carta Particolare," and appears to have been based to a large extent on the Vizcaino discoveries. It is significant for the fact that Dudley shows both the bay entered by Vizcaino, that is, P. di Don Gaspar, and that entered by Drake, suggesting that Dudley did not associate Vizcaino's bay with that visited by Drake, and apparently considered the two to be distinctly different bays. Of further interest is the fact that Dudley added not one, but two bays, in close association with each other below Vizcaino's bay, a fact that strongly suggests that he had learned from some source that there was another immediately north of Drake's California anchorage.

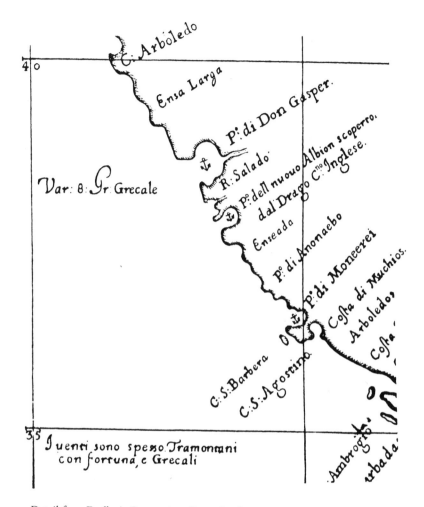

Detail from Dudley's Carta prima Generale, showing two bays below Vizcaino's P°. di Don Gaspar, one of which is identified as the port discovered by Drake, and therefore cited in support of the Bolinas Bay theory.

Dudley Belatedly Discovered

The first California mention of Dudley maps came to light a full century ago in an article by John W. Dwinelle appearing in the *San Francisco Bulletin* for October 5, 1878.[1] Dwinelle held that Drake's California anchorage was in Bodega Bay, and cited as greatly strengthening his view the "map ['Carta Particolare'] from *Arcano del Mare,* edition of 1647." He asserted that the latitude, the coastline, and the topography shown by the map lent support to his anchorage theory.

A more complete treatment of the Dudley maps was that of Edward Everett Hale in Winsor, *Narrative and Critical History of America* (Volume III), published in 1884.[2] Hale had earlier related the romantic story of Dudley and his atlas in an article that appeared in the American Antiquarian Society's *Proceedings* for October 21, 1873.[3] He also evinced an early interest in Drake's California anchorage, and in his treatise on the subject he reproduced the "Carta Particolare" in full-page size,[4] as well as a small sketch from the "Carta prima Generale."[5] In part, he had the following to say:

> In this discussion, the map of Dudley, whose information was nearly at first-hand, plays an important part. His representation of Drake's Bay—a sort of bottle-shaped harbor—so far resembles the double bay of San Francisco, that it would probably decide the question, but that, unfortunately, he gives two such bays. His two maps (the *Carta Particolare* and the *Carta prima Generale*) also, do not very closely resemble each other. It becomes necessary to suppose that one of his bays was that which we know as Bodega Bay, or that both are drawn from the imagination.[6] ... The writer does not hesitate to say that he believes it will prove that Drake repaired his ship in San Francisco Bay.[7]

Comments by Scholars

In the 1880s Davidson began to gather cartographic evidence from various sources: A tracing of the "Portus Novae Albionis" from the British Museum[8] (probably after reading Dwinelle's discussion of it);[9] photographs of the "Carta Particolare" and the "Carta prima Generale" from the Harvard College Library;[10] and, finally, the first photographs ever taken of nine original manuscript charts of the northwest coast of America by Robert Dudley (from the Library at Munich).[11]

Before Davidson received the manuscript charts, he had not been fully satisfied that the "Portus" chart was to be a decisive factor in his search for the Drake anchorage; but when the manuscript photographs arrived, he saw from a glance at unpublished Chart No. 85 that the "Portus" was an almost "exact counterpart of his [Dudley's] 'B: di

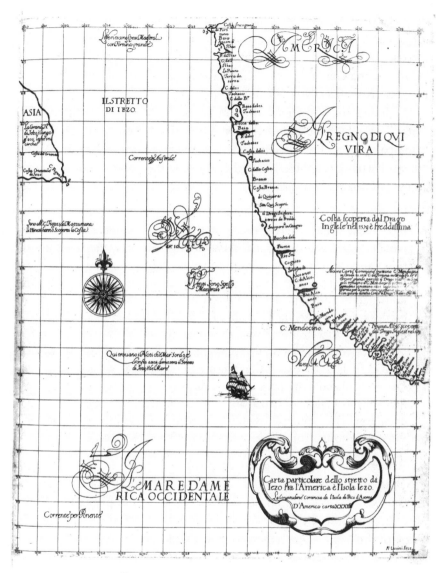

Dudley's Carta Particolare, Chart XXXIII, 1647.

noua Albion,' on a scale twice as large and with the same orientation. It was no longer a small port."[12]

In other words, when Davidson found Chart No. 85, he felt that he had the evidence which established to his satisfaction that Drake had landed in Drake's Bay and had careened his ship in the cove behind

Point Reyes. He then presented his findings to the California Historical Society, which published them in 1890.[13] In the appendix to that treatise, he included copies of fifteen maps and charts, among them the "Carta prima Generale," the "Carta Particolare," and Manuscript Chart No. 85, as well as Nos. 83 and 83 bis.

Included in Wagner's work on Drake is a section entitled "The Maps," in which he devoted four pages to a discussion of Dudley's principal maps. He also included a full-page reproduction of the "Carta Particolare".[14] He was rather unimpressed with Dudley's work, so far as Drake is concerned:

> One of the peculiarities of Dudley's cartographical productions is that they show a bay every twenty or thirty miles along the coast, into which a river is always shown as entering. The bay, the river and the two capes which are necessary adjuncts at the entrance of each bay usually have the same name. . . . It is possible that Dudley had some information about the depth of water in some of the ports but considering his inventive genius as manifested in his manufacture of names, it is more likely that he also invented most of these.
>
> Reviewing the matter, it appears that Dudley took all the knowledge he had of Drake's expedition from Hakluyt's 1600 version, the *World Encompassed* and maps previously published, and in reality his maps bear no evidence that he obtained any geographical information from Drake or anyone else connected with the expedition. He probably, however, did obtain some from his brother-in-law, Thomas Cavendish.[15]

Robertson devoted the greater part of three pages in his 1927 text to the Dudley maps, and he included reproductions of Manuscript Charts No. 83 and No. 85, as well as of the "Carta prima Generale." He expressed doubt that Drake had ever personally communicated the shape of the bay in which he landed to Dudley, who was only six years old when Drake returned from his circumnavigation, and was a mere youth when Drake sailed on his last voyage in 1595.

Robertson was impressed by Chart No. 85, finding it interesting because it contained a pencil marking that would seem to indicate that the real bay extended farther southward than the one originally drawn. He remarked that "evidently some one did attempt to change the original shape of this bay and to enlarge its size." He commented further:

This map with the pencilled corrections has not received the attention at the hands of commentators that has been given to the Hondius "Portus." It would seem that it deserves far more consideration for it is an actual addition to a map intended to represent the Harbor of St. Francis. The date of this addition cannot be conjectured.[16]

Twelve pages of Aker's text dealing with the Drake anchorage question were devoted to the maps of Dudley, including a translation of the legends appearing on each.[17] In addition, Aker reproduced what appear to be full-size copies of Manuscript Charts Nos. 83 and 83 bis,[18] No. 85,[19] the "Carta Particolare,"[20] and the "Carta prima Generale."[21] He also included enlargements of the last three to show their details.

Aker characterized Dudley's charts as among the most important sources for locating Drake's port on the California coast. He felt that Dudley's statements in *Arcano del Mare* and in his charts suggest a faith in Drake that could not have been fostered by mere hearsay or vague references;[22] that Drake had sailed to the North American west coast, had obtained possession of Spanish charts, had made his landfall just as the Spanish galleons had, and had coasted south in their track, therefore he was in an excellent position to give the comparisons of distances and positions that Dudley, in his chart legends and text of *Arcano del Mare,* said Drake and the Spanish pilots found there.

In his 1974 publication *Drake's California Landing: The Evidence for Bolinas Lagoon,* Neasham described the "Carta prima Generale" in some detail.[23] A close examination of it in the area from the Bay of Don Gaspar to Drake's anchorage to the south reveals, he suggested, a surprising similarity in shape to the upper portion of the hole in the plate found by Beryle Shinn; in fact, they are almost identical, with the exception of the inner harbor depicted by a small projection on Dudley's map.[24] The significance of this similarity, according to Neasham, was that Dudley must have had access to information supplied by Drake, "possibly the long-lost 'Drake Log'."[25] Moreover, since the map shows the port of Nova Albion somewhat below a similar harbor labeled Port of Don Gaspar, the name given by Vizcaino in 1603 to the present Drake's Bay, Neasham reasoned that "what Dudley presumably depicted then was the Drake anchorage directly south of Drake's Bay, at the spot now known as the inner lagoon of Bolinas Bay."

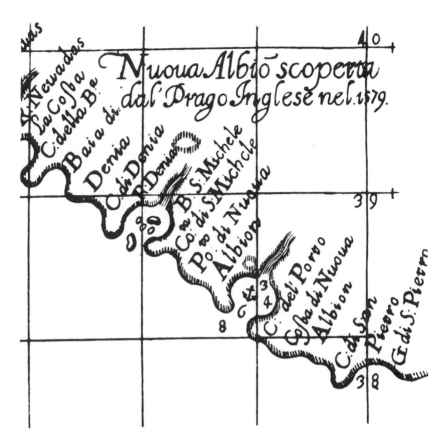

Detail of the Carta Particolare, presented in support of the Drake Navigators Guild theory that B. S. Michele represents Bodega Bay, while Drake's Bay follows logically below showing an anchorage (the anchor) and soundings.

Conclusions of the Participants

Tenet 19 asked for a discussion of the significance of the cartographic information about the California coast contained in Dudley's 1647 atlas, *Arcano del Mare,* and Manuscript Chart No. 85.

The Guild believed that because of Dudley's family connections and plans to emulate Drake's voyage while Drake was still alive, he was likely to have information on Nova Albion from Drake, and therefore that his charts showing Drake's anchorage are important sources for locating it. According to the Guild, the most significant of his maps was his Chart No. 85, precedent for the "Carta Particolare," because on that chart, in the bay named B: di Noua Albion, is a small

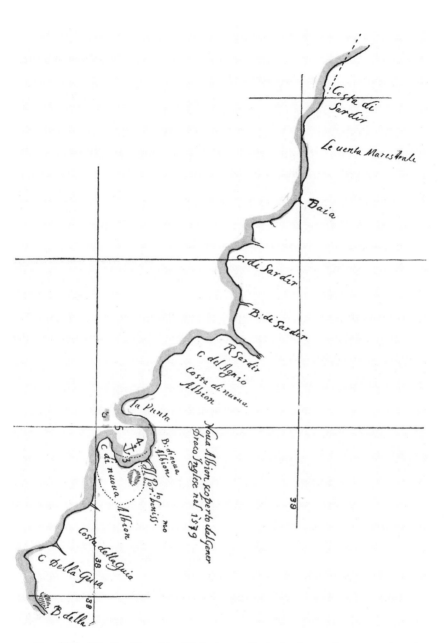

Costa di
Sardir

Le uenta Maestrale

Baia

C: di Sardir

B: di Sardir

R Sardir
C: del Agnio
Costa di nuoua
Albion

la Punta

B: nuoua
Albion

C di nuoua Albion

Il Por: boniss:
jo: mo

Noua Albion scoperta dal Gener
Draco Inglese nel 1579

Costa della Guia

C: Della Guia

B: della:

38

39

Unpublished Dudley Chart No. 85. Its interest lies in the change of contour made in the Drake port which is designated "Il Por^to boniss^mo", meaning "the best of harbors." The date of neither the map nor the pencil markings is known, but would probably have been between 1630 and 1647.

inner waterway corresponding to Drake's Estero named Il Por:^to boniss.^mo, literally "the best of ports." A line on the west side is simply named La Punta, much as Point Reyes today is familiarly referred to as "the point." In the published version, the haven is identified only as Po:^to di Nuoua Albion, port of Nova Albion.

The significance of the "Carta Prima Generale," according to Neasham, is that the port of Nova Albion is placed in an inner harbor below latitude 38°, about 37° 50', at the location of Bolinas Bay. Directly to the north a few miles are the Port of Don Gaspar and the Rio Salado, names given to Drake's Bay and its estero in 1603 by the Vizcaino expedition.[26] Neasham also directs attention to the fact that the "Carta Particolare" shows an anchorage a little above 38°, with fathom depths of 8, 6, 4, and 3 for Drake's anchorage, which essentially agree with the 6, 5, 4, and 3 given on Chart No. 85. Indicated on this manuscript map, in the relative positions of the Port of Don Gaspar and Rio Salado of the "Carta Prima Generale," and San Michele of the "Carta Particolare," are the Bay of Sardir and the Rio Sardir, sometimes called Sardina.

According to Power, Robert Dudley, as a young man, may have been in a position to have gained special knowledge about the Drake voyage, but it has not been established that he did gain such knowledge. Accordingly, there is no demonstrated significance in the two charts he published a half century later. Dudley's material is not a reliable source of evidence for either Drake's Estero, Bolinas, or San Francisco Bay; but if one desires to use his information in favor of one place or another, it would be more positive for San Francisco Bay than any other anchorage.

In rebuttal to Guild and Neasham comments, Power presented a number of contentions: Dudley's maps, published fifty years after Drake's death, would have required half a century of recall of cartographic detail. His efforts in no way resemble Drake's Bay or Estero because they depict a bay two to three times wider than the widest part of Drake's Bay, and because the so-called "inner waterway" seen by the Guild as Drake's Estero is merely a diagrammatic river entrance which Dudley used repeatedly on his numerous maps. Power continued:

> The Guild silently rejects Dudley's other map in his *Arcano del Mare*, the *Carta prima Generale,* for a very good reason. They reject it because,

as noted by Dr. Neasham, it establishes that Dudley believed Drake had not anchored in the bay today called Drake's Bay which he identified in 38° 45′ as *P:* to *di Don Gaspar*. Instead, he created a southerly anchorage in about 37° 50′ which he identifies as *P:* to *dell nuoua Albion . . . .* This not only corresponds in approximate location, as noted by Neasham, to Bolinas Lagoon, but also to the Golden Gate.

There is absolutely no claim Dr. Neasham can make for this map that does not equally apply to San Francisco Bay, and its size makes it far more like San Francisco Bay in nature than Bolinas Lagoon. The legend Il Por:to boniss.mo, literally the "best of ports," fits San Francisco Bay, but certainly not Drake's Estero.

Detail from the Carta prima Generale with inset superimposed by Robert H. Power. According to Power, this proves that Dudley did not believe Drake landed at Drake's Bay (P.º di Don Gaspar) nor in Drake's Estero (R. Salado), but near the Golden Gate. Power also asserts that the map on p. 319 used to support the Bolinas theory is an inaccurate 1890 "pen and ink" copy of the map.

Importance of the Dudley Maps

As with most clues to the Drake anchorage puzzle, this is a category suffused with controversy, more so, perhaps, than is casually evident. From the time that Dudley's maps appeared on the scene as a Drake anchorage source a century ago, they have received much attention from Drake scholars, although never before has an effort been made to summarize and evaluate their conclusions.

Some of those discussing Dudley have characterized his maps as important. Hale was the first to do so, although he found the two published maps confusing because of their lack of resemblance to each other.[27] Dwinelle, Davidson, and Neasham all treated Dudley's cartographic productions as having great significance. Aker described Dudley's maps, both published and unpublished, as "one of the most important sources for locating Drake's port on the California coast."[28] Neither Robertson nor Wagner felt them to be particularly impressive or useful.

On the other hand, because of material inconsistencies between the maps, Drake scholars have only found it possible to rely upon some of them to the exclusion of others. Dwinelle considered his choice of Bodega Bay strengthened by the "Carta Particolare."[29] Davidson drew special inspiration from Chart No. 85, although he did include copies of other Dudley maps of the Pacific northwest coast in the appendix to his 1890 publication.[30] Neasham relied solely on the "Carta Prima Generale,"[31] whereas Aker and the Guild placed their reliance in both Chart No. 85 and the "Carta Particolare."[32]

All Dudley maps depicted coastal bays or harbors, and Power therefore found difficulty in treating them as a source of value. Instead, he pointed out some of the weaknesses in the Guild's reliance on Dudley, namely, their "silent rejection" of the "Carta Prima Generale" because of its conflict with Manuscript Chart No. 85 and the "Carta Particolare"; the fifty years' lapse between the date of Dudley's acquisition of information and that of the publication of his atlas, requiring more than half a century of "recall of cartographic detail"; and the fact that Chart No. 85 depicts a bay eighteen miles in diameter and the "Carta Particolare" twenty-four miles, three times wider than the widest part of Drake's Bay.

Summary

The most persuasive feature in connection with the Dudley maps is the fact that he had extraordinary opportunities to gain authentic information during his early years. On the other hand, the shortcomings of his works have been highlighted by both Wagner and Power. Between them, they make these points: (1) Although Dudley may have had special opportunities to obtain inside information from Drake sources, there is no proof that he did so, and Dudley himself never made such a claim; (2) the belated publication of his atlas and the nonpublication of his manuscript charts detract from their value as a reliable source for the location of Nova Albion; (3) the fact that, except for Chart No. 85 and the "Carta Particolare," there is little resemblance between his various depictions of the California coast; and (4) as Wagner points out, Dudley's inventiveness, as manifested by his manufacture of names, suggests that he may also have invented other features of his maps dealing with the California coast.

At all events, we have another anchorage clue that can be interpreted much as the reader chooses. Hale found both published maps possibly supportive of San Francisco Bay. To Dwinelle, the "Carta Particolare" provided evidence in favor of Bodega Bay. For Neasham, the "Carta prima Generale" indicated that Drake's landfall had been at Bolinas, but Aker and the Guild relied on Chart No. 85 and the "Carta Particolare" as support for Drake's Estero. Davidson saw in Chart No. 85 a definite confirmation of the Hondius "Portus" as showing that Drake's anchorage had been in the cove on the north side of Point Reyes. Even Power asserted that the legend which, translated, means "the best of ports," would have fitted San Francisco Bay, but not Drake's Estero, and insisted that there was no claim that Neasham could make for the "Carta prima Generale" that did not apply with equal force to San Francisco Bay.

From an objective point of view, the Dudley maps are an interesting and, in some respects, possibly an authentic source of information for locating Drake's California anchorage. On the other hand, they

have a number of evidentiary drawbacks, including questionable reliability, conflicting depictions, and the bewildering fact that one or
another of them, like the "Portus," has been used to support nearly
every serious contender for anchorage honors. Like the "Portus," their
controversial situation reduces their status to one of purely secondary
value.

CHAPTER

The de Morena Story

Tenet 20: What is the significance of the account of Drake's pilot, N. de Morena, who claimed that he had been put ashore at an "arm of the sea" which he believed connected with the Gulf of California and the Atlantic Ocean?

AMONG REPORTS about the circumnavigation of 1577–1580 is an apocryphal tale concerning a man, said to have been a pilot with Drake, whose name was N. de Morena or de Morera. The story, it seems, was passed along to Father Jeronimo de Zarate Salmeron by Father Antonio de la Ascension, who had accompanied Vizcaino to California in 1602–1603. It was reported by Father Salmeron in *Documentos Para la Historia de Mexico*,[1] translation of a part of which was published in Los Angeles in a magazine known as *Land of Sunshine* for February, 1900.[2] The full text of the account, brief as it is, will be found in Appendix G. Its substance is as follows:

The story had originally been given to Captain Rodrigo del Rio, the governor of New Spain, in the middle 1580s by its central figure, N. de Morena. The latter was a "foreign" (non-English) pilot who had "steered the Englishman [Captain Francisco Draque]" from the "sea of the north [the Atlantic]" to "that of the South [the Pacific]" through the Straits of Magellan (mistakenly referred to as the Strait of Anian). The pilot asserted that when Drake left his California anchorage to return "to his country," he, Morena, was so sick that it was thought he was going to die, so they put him ashore "to see if the airs of the land would give him life."

Miraculously, he recovered his health within a few days and set forth on foot for Mexico, walking "for the space of four years." He traveled "through divers lands, through many provinces, more than five hundred leagues [approximately 700 miles][3] of mainland, until he had come far enough to catch sight of an arm of the sea which divided the lands of New Mexico from another very great land which is on the side of the West." He told how this arm of the sea ran "from north to south; and that it seemed to him it went on to the north to connect with the harbor where the Englishman had put him ashore. And that on that sea coast he had seen many good harbors and great inlets; and that from the point where they put him ashore he would venture to get to Spain in 40 days in a good ship's tender [presumably via the Sacramento River and east to the Great Lakes]; and that he must go to get acquainted with the Court of England."

De Morena offered to take Governor Rodrigo del Rio to the "arm of the sea which he discovered; and said that he could easily cross him over to the other [west] side. This arm of the sea is held to be an assured thing. It is that of the Gulf of California, called Mar Rojo [Red Sea]; and the land which is on the other [west] side is that of the Californias."

De Morena was apparently anxious to get his story to the ears of the governor in person. He "came forth" to New Mexico, proceeding from there to Santa Barbara in Chihuahua, and finally located del Rio at the mines of Sombrerete. There is no sequel to the tale, nothing to indicate that he ever got to England or his reason for wanting to do so. It does not appear that del Rio paid much attention to the story. He did not accept the offer to be taken to the Gulf of California, he did not appear to have shown any interest in the hypothetical water route that Morena thought could lead to Spain in forty days, and there is nothing to indicate that he had Morena's fascinating tale recorded in the customary way in the annals of New Spain.

An Earlier Version of the Story

Modern knowledge of de Morena's travels appears to date from February, 1900, when the translation of Father Salmeron's Spanish report in his 1626 history of events before that date in California and New Mexico was published in the *Land Of Sunshine*,[4] yet there must have been an earlier translation and publication of which there is no present record. A history of Marin County by J. P. Munro-Fraser, published in 1880, had the following to say:

> The noted English voyager Sir Francis Drake, sailed along the coast in 1579, but historians are doubtful as to whether he discovered the San Francisco Bay. It would appear that this voyage was made from Oregon, where it is said his Spanish pilot, Morera, left him, and thence found his way overland to Mexico, a distance of three thousand five hundred miles.[5]

Similar information appeared in a later section of Munro-Fraser's book, although it indicated that Morera had deserted Drake and "set out upon that unparalleled feat of pedestrianism, traveling alone . . . through . . . miles of unbroken wilderness, inhabited only by savages and wild beasts, the amazement of a hand full of natives who had never seen anything before that approached to a white man."[6]

The source of Munro-Fraser's information concerning Morera was not given, but it antedates the *Land of Sunshine* article by twenty years. The incident was not mentioned in that part of the Munro-Fraser book entitled "The General History and Settlement of Marin County," which strongly contends that Drake's landing was at Drake's Bay.[7]

Comments by Scholars

It is interesting to find the story discussed by Henry R. Wagner, in his account of the circumnavigation, and to see that he felt the tale may have some foundation in fact[8] because Drake did have a pilot named Morera. According to Wagner, a letter by Gaspar de Vargas from Guatulco, dated April 13, 1579,[9] indicated that some of the sailors of the vessel anchored at that port thought the name of Drake's pilot was Morera, a name that could hardly be mistaken for Silva, Drake's other pilot. Wagner felt that the similarity of names, Morena and Morera, together with the fact that both were referred to as pilots was more than a coincidence. Whether or not there was any truth in the story, it may have been responsible for the impression, which became current in the early seventeenth century, that California was an island, and that in some way Drake was responsible for "placing on the maps the extension of the Gulf of California to the Strait of Anian," that is, to San Francisco Bay.

Raymond Aker seemed to be the only other Drake scholar who took notice of the de Morena account. Like Wagner, he was inclined to think that the story was genuine,[10] and that if Morena had been put ashore anywhere, it would have been at the California anchorage. His comments were very interesting:

> Morena may have been a deserter from Drake's camp, but if so, it seems hardly likely that he would want to go on to the Court of England, nor would there be any good reason for concealing desertion from the Spanish. As an aside, it is evident that Morena would have discovered the Golden Gate and San Francisco Bay, and from his description it is clear that the point where Drake had left him was close to the "stopping place" or terminus of what Morena assumed to be the Strait of Anian from which he judged that he could reach Spain in 40 days. It may have been a mistake for him to mention this to the Spanish, as in the final analysis this was exactly what they did not want.

The concluding tenet of the 1974 debate was No. 20,[11] asking the significance of the story of de Morena "who claimed that he had been put ashore at an 'arm of the sea' which he believed connected with the Gulf of California and the Atlantic Ocean."

Responses by Participants

Morena's account indicates that he had discovered an arm of the sea (San Francisco Bay) which he interpreted to have both a passage to the Atlantic and an inland connection with the Gulf of California. The Guild felt, therefore, that after being put ashore at Drake's Bay, Morena inadvertently came upon the Golden Gate and San Francisco Bay. He probably thought that its northern end led to a shortcut across the continent, since he said he "would venture to get to Spain in 40 days in a good ship's tender." After being ferried across the bay by the Indians, he probably journeyed south without seeing the lower end of the bay.

Being greatly impressed with his discovery, he sought out the highest available official to make it known to him. This information may have become known to Cermeño and have furnished at least a part of the motivation for his 1595 visit to Drake's Bay. Since Morena was a pilot, the latitude of this "arm of the sea" would have been known to him, and perhaps have been passed on to Cermeño. His story may also have been the basis for the early belief that California was an island.

It was Neasham's opinion that Morena's account must be regarded as secondary information, possibly hearsay. It is doubtful that it ever reached official ears, because the rigid Spanish colonial system required that an accurate record be made of all such activities and accounts; however, no such record of the Morena story has ever been found. Had it been recorded and the existence of the present San Francisco Bay been known, then Portola, the official Spanish discoverer of San Francisco Bay, would not have been so astonished in 1769 to find the great inland estuary (present San Francisco Bay) blocking his way in his attempt from Monterey to reach the Bahia de San Francisco, as Drake's Bay was then called, having been so named by Cermeño in 1595.

According to Power, there is no other explanation of de Morena's story than to assume that in his mind he linked San Francisco Bay and the Gulf of California. The viewing of the San Francisco peninsula as an island is a fair observation from southern Marin County because there is no visible end to San Francisco Bay from that vantage point. The "arm of the sea" refers to San Francisco Bay, and the harbor correlates to an anchorage at Point San Quentin. It is probable that Morena crossed the Strait of San Pablo and not the Golden Gate, so San Francisco remained an island in his mind. If Morena saw San Francisco Bay, it was because Drake left him in a harbor on the "arm of the sea" we call San Francisco Bay.

Considerations of Authenticity

Neasham pointed out that the Morena account must be regarded as secondary information. As a matter of fact, it appears to be at least fourth-hand hearsay—Morena to Governor del Rio to Father Ascension to Father Salmeron to (or through) the translator whose version of it appeared in the pages of the *Land of Sunshine*. It contains obvious errors, and no doubt acquired some of its vagueness as it went from listener to listener. If Morena left Nova Albion in 1579, his four-year trek would have brought him to New Spain in 1583, after which more than forty years elapsed before his story finally reached the pages of Father Salmeron's book.

Several considerations militate against its authenticity. As Neasham, an eminent historian in his own right, has also pointed out, the fact that no record of this remarkable tale of travel and adventure has ever been found in the official archives of Mexico casts doubt upon its authenticity. The archives of Mexico are full of accounts from New World explorers, among which Morena's story about San Francisco Bay has never appeared. Against it also is the fact the Spaniards let one hundred seventy years go by before really checking out Morena's important information. Moreover, if that information had reached Cermeño, he should have been fully aware of the "arm of the sea" that is the present San Francisco Bay.

On the other hand, the story does seem to have a curious ring of truth. The similarity of names seems more than a coincidence, and the accuracy of its basic data, though crude in various respects, could hardly have been manufactured out of whole cloth. More than word of Drake's visit to the area, it may have been responsible for the successive visits of Cermeño and Vizcaino to the same vicinity, as well as for the erstwhile belief that California was an island. And finally, as the Guild has pointed out, the fact that Morena's account has not come to light in the archives of Mexico or Spain does not arbitrarily make it untrue or dubious. It may simply have been too dangerous to the interests of New Spain to have been put in writing.

Reasonable Inferences

Assuming for the purposes of discussion that Morena's story did have a factual foundation, what bearing does it have on the location of Drake's California landfall? Some inferences might reasonably be drawn from the account:

1. From any Marin County anchorage, Morena would have seen San Francisco Bay on his pedestrian way to Mexico. He would have had to cross the bay at some point, whether at the Golden Gate, at the

Strait of Carquinez, or in between, because he spoke of his point of departure as an "arm of the sea."

2. Although such a crossing was necessary to get to Mexico on foot, it is understandable, in the light of Portola's subsequent experience, that Morena may never have seen either end of the bay.

3. That he never saw the lower end is a reasonable inference from his belief that it may have been connected with the Gulf of California.

4. That he never saw or explored the upper end is likewise a reasonable inference, because he was a pilot familiar with latitudes and maritime theories, believed it possible to get to Spain in forty days by ship's tender, and therefore was convinced that through the north end of the bay must lie the long-sought short route across mid-continent to the Atlantic.

Summary

No wonder that Morena was so excited about his discoveries that he had to bring them to the attention of the highest official in Spanish America! But the question posed by Tenet 20 asks for comment on the significance of the Morena account to the search for Drake's California anchorage. This question answers itself if the account had no foundation in fact, as Neasham believes.

If, however, it was authentic, as the Guild and Power believe, then neither of them sees anything in it adverse to their respective positions on the anchorage site. Why was Morena so anxious to reach the English court? There could have been two reasons: Because Drake did *not* see San Francisco Bay and therefore he, Morena, wanted to bring to the court the astounding news of how close Drake had been to this remarkable body of water without seeing it; or, more likely, to collect two years of back pay for his services as a pilot on what he understood was a royal-sponsored voyage.[12] Whatever his reason, he never made it back to England.

Returning, accordingly, to the four inferences listed above, and granting their reasonableness, what do they tend to prove or disprove with referencee to the location of Drake's anchorage? Precisely nothing, apart from the fact that it was not far from San Francisco Bay. The debaters have not said it quite so emphatically, but they have pointed to nothing to suggest that the Morena account has any particular value as a clue for identification of the anchorage site.

29

CHAPTER

An Overview of the Evidence

WENTY-ONE chapters of evidence have been presented, four of them comprising contemporary accounts and maps. The other seventeen include comprehensive discussions of each factor and feature that could conceivably provide a clue to the location of Drake's California anchorage. Now it is time to summarize and analyze the conclusions reached in those seventeen chapters, and to see where they have brought us in our search for the locale where Sir Francis spent the summer of 1579.

The Approach. — Clearly Drake's brief and abortive quest for the Northwest Passage was without significance so far as the discovery or location of the port of Nova Albion some two weeks later was concerned. Nor does it appear that his approach from the north provided any clue of value to the problem under consideration. Each proponent of a principal anchorage site was able to envision the *Golden Hind* sailing south along the coast and into his particular harbor, but there is no evidence which, from the purely approach standpoint, suggests that one harbor, rather than another, was *the* port of Drake's choice. No score for any contestant.

The Latitudes. — This issue really should have been controversial, but actually was not. The sponsors of the three leading candidates for the anchorage site had no difficulty in concluding that the harbor where the *Golden Hind* was careened was in latitude 38°, because the harbor sponsored by each is situated close to that line. The considerations supporting a 38° 30′ latitude, with an appropriate allowance for computational error, have been given little attention by Drake scholars. Be that as it may, the fact that the three leading harbors are all situated very near the 38th parallel nullifies its value as a specific clue to any one of the three. Again no score.

The White Cliffs. — This is a clue with definite significance, because both of the principal contemporary accounts refer to the "white bankes and cliffes, which lie towards the sea." This is a test of anchorage location which could fit all three harbors equally if based on the premise that the cliffs face the sea, irrespective of their direction from or relation to the harbor of refuge. If based on the location of the cliffs in relation to the harbors, that is, how they "lie toward the sea" from each, then the score would have to be 3 for the Estero, 1 for San Quentin Cove, and 0 for the Lagoon.

The Harbor. — The type of harbor for which Drake had been searching for hundreds of miles depended on a number of factors, such as its suitability for "careening and graving," for "watering and victualling," and for the location and construction of a fort. Whether Hakluyt's "faire and good Baye" and *The World Encompassed*'s "conuenient and fit harborough" were one and the same is also a factor to be considered, because it might have a bearing on whether Drake's vessel entered an inner harbor for its careening.

So far as "watering and victualling" and suitability for fort construction were concerned, the evidence does not favor any one of the three sites over the other two. With respect to suitability for careenage the evidence is controversial, but San Quentin Cove, with its record of use for careenage purposes in the nineteenth century, seems to present the stronger claim. However, in reference to whether the phrases "faire and good Baye" and "fit and conuenient harborough" were intended to be synonymous, the argument on behalf of San Quentin Cove was not persuasive. On the whole, however, in the "harbor" category, while honors were about evenly divided between the Estero and San Quentin Cove, the latter must be given a slight edge, with Bolinas Lagoon a distant third. Score 3 for San Quentin Cove, 2 for the Estero, and 1 for the Lagoon.

The Weather. — The weather so dramatically described in *The World Encompassed* as having been encountered at Nova Albion matches rather well the summer weather on the Point Reyes peninsula and, to a lesser extent, that of Bolinas Bay. Unquestionably, the evidence on this issue favors the Drake's Estero position. Score 3 for the Estero, 2 for the Lagoon, 0 for San Quentin Cove.

The Hinterland. — One of the highlights of Drake's Nova Albion sojourn was his trip up into the country, as reported by both "The Famous Voyage" and *The World Encompassed*. From the standpoint of having any relation to the anchorage location, this was a rather slender clue, turning primarily on the statement in *The World Encompassed* that "the inland we found to be *farre different* from the shoare." Of course, in each case the inland would have been found different from the shore, the degree of difference depending on how far away from the shore the "inland" lay. Nevertheless, since the journey went far enough into the hinterland to encounter elk and "conies" by the thousands, it is difficult to believe that the differential, so far as the Estero was concerned, was not somewhat greater than in the case of its rival harbors. Score 2 for the Estero and 1 for each of the other harbors.

The Flora. — It is hard to believe that the plant life described in *The World Encompassed* could be so thoroughly controversial, but it is. The opinions of the proponents of the principal harbors are hopelessly divided about the identity of the main tree and plant thus described, with their opinions having some bearing on the location of the anchorage. The result is that with such controversial contentions, the conclusions to be reached afford no assistance toward a solution. No score.

The Fauna. — In the course of his visit to the hinterland, Drake encountered thousands of "very large and fat Deere," as well as a "multitude of a strange kinde of Conies." Since the latter were unfamiliar animals, the authors of the principal contemporary accounts described them in detail. Unfortunately, in parts of Marin County there were, until recent times, at least, not only two kinds of elk (large deer), but also two kinds of burrowing rodents (conies), to wit, pocket gophers and ground squirrels, thus making it possible for the sponsors of contending harbors to engage in a heated but not too conclusive debate, in which the weight of the evidence seems, to a disinterested observer, to favor the proponent of San Quentin Cove. Score 3 for the Cove, 1 for the Estero, 0 for the Lagoon.

The Indians. — There are two principal pieces of evidence concerning the Indians Drake encountered: (1) The ability of ethnologists to identify, on the basis of linguistic clues, the Indians seen by Drake as members of the Coast Miwok tribe, inhabitants of the Marin County peninsula; and (2) the fact that an Indian village is known to have been situated, as reported by *The World Encompassed,* within three-quarters of a mile of Drake's supposed camp, at each of the three contending harbors. Unfortunately, neither of these clues assists in pinpointing the particular harbor where Drake repaired his vessel, or in providing support for the claims of any of the three anchorage contenders.[1] Nor do considerations of political history or "sense of destiny" provide any assistance in solving the landing site riddle. The contentions urged in this regard are merely argument, and rest on no evidence of any kind.

Artifactual Evidence. — No physical evidence that can be conclusively related to Drake's presence in California has been turned up. Even if the recently discovered Elizabethan sixpence of pre-Drake mint date[2] could be archaeologically authenticated, it would at most tend to confirm that the *Golden Hind* was careened somewhere in Marin County which, of course, we already know. Having reportedly been found at the site of the former Indian village of Olompali, it could provide no identification of a particular harbor.

None of the hundreds of sixteenth-century artifacts found among the middens of the Point Reyes peninsula can be positively connected with the Drake visit. The search for the foundations of Drake's fort in the Bolinas area and at Drake's Estero has turned up nothing of value. Other supposed sixteenth-century relics from Marin County, such as the ancient anchor, the mortar, and the Javanese halberd tip, provide no help in the anchorage search. Consequently, there is a total lack of physical evidence of Drake's presence. No score for any contestant.

The Shinn Plate. — This artifact is the one piece of evidence which, under the proper conditions, could have led to the anchorage site. Unfortunately, from the day of its discovery, this fascinating piece of brass has been controversial. Early doubts as to its authenticity were lulled somewhat by the results of tests conducted by disinterested experts, only to have their conclusions contradicted by similar tests four decades later. Although these recent studies have not conclusively

Prince Philip and Admiral Nimitz viewing the plate of brass at the Bancroft Library in Berkeley in 1956.

established that the plate, as claimed by historian Samuel Morison, is "a complete and clumsy hoax,"[3] they have reduced its credibility to the point where its value as one of the more significant clues to the anchorage location has been virtually nullified. Taken in conjunction with the original controversy about the circumstances surrounding the finding of this "portable artifact," it is apparent that the Shinn plate has lost its value as supporting evidence for any anchorage candidate. No score for any contestant.

The Departure.—Proponents of San Quentin Cove contend that the circumstances attending the departure of the *Golden Hind* for the long voyage across the Pacific favored a San Francisco Bay anchorage, because it alone of the three principal harbors would have required an overnight trip to the Farallones, in contrast to the less-than-full-day trip from either coastal harbor. But it does not appear that this is necessarily a significant clue to the anchorage location. Such edge as there is, however, would favor the claim of San Quentin Cove. Score 1 for the Cove.

The "Portus".—This most controversial of all potential clues has turned out to be of little assistance in the effort to pinpoint a particular harbor. Extensive research on the part of Drake scholars tends to relate the "Portus Novae Albionis" to original records of Fletcher or Drake, but without certainty in the matter. However, the fact that the proponents of eleven different anchorage sites have used the "Portus" as a part of the evidentiary support for their claims deprives it of much value as a means of what the doctors refer to as "differential diagnosis." No score.

The Montanus Illustration. — This is really a one-harbor clue, that is, a clue which, could it be confirmed, would support the claim of San Quentin Cove as Drake's anchorage, but that of no other harbor. It is a drawing showing the "coronation" of Drake by the California Indians published nearly a century after his Pacific coast visit, and featuring a remarkable resemblance to a view looking across San Francisco Bay from a hill back of Point San Quentin. Apart from the physical background, however, every other part of the picture is inconsistent with known and recorded facts. Accordingly, from an objective point of view, it represents an interesting but tenuous, if not entirely fanciful clue. No score.

Cermeño. — This is another one-harbor clue, because it concerns only the visit of a Spanish sea captain to Drake's Bay in 1595, a mere sixteen years after Drake's summer in Nova Albion. When Cermeño filed his official report, it contained no mention of finding any signs of Drake, but commented that the Indians encountered there acted as though they had never seen white men before. This is a fact for which Drake's Estero proponents could offer many conjectural explanations. However, little can be proved by negative evidence, and the Cermeño report does not provide substantial support for any one of the three anchorage theories. No score.

The Dudley Maps. — The situation concerning the maps of the California coast drawn by Robert Dudley in the seventeenth century is the same as with respect to the "Portus." Unquestionably, they have some basis of authenticity in Dudley's family connections with Cavendish and possibly with Drake himself, but proof is lacking. Unfortunately, these maps have several shortcomings, when considered as a group; besides, most of the proponents for particular harbors cite Dudley maps in support of their respective positions, thereby depriving them of probative value so far as a particular harbor is concerned. No score.

Pilot de Morena. – Though not mentioned by the English accounts of the voyage, this Drake pilot was reputed to have left Nova Albion in July, 1579, and to have walked to Mexico. Since it is apparent that he would have had to cross San Francisco Bay or the Golden Gate in order to reach Mexico from any of the three Marin County harbors under consideration, it is also apparent that his adventure has no particular value as a clue for identification of a specific anchorage site. No score.

From this review, it is evident that eleven of the seventeen discussional chapters provide insufficient evidence to entitle any of the competing harbors to a score. For the other six chapters, a very rough total score for the three contestants might be 11 for Drake's Estero, 4 for Bolinas Lagoon, and 9 for San Quentin Cove.[4] Such a result will manifestly please no proponent of any of the three anchorage candidates, nor will it settle the question of where Drake repaired his vessel; but it does represent, from an unprejudiced point of view, an approximate evaluation of the indications provided by the available clues. Moreover, it demonstrates the inefficacy of most of the so-called anchorage clues as significant contributors to the solution of a great controversy. As one Drake expert put it:

> The identification of any place depends upon multiple factors that converge at a specific point. Similarities of contour, the discovery of an artifact, or tenuous reasoning based upon personal assumptions are not adequate to establish exact location—no matter how inviting they may be for pure speculation.[5]

After four hundred years of mystery, including nearly two hundred years of controversy, we still have no solution to the Drake anchorage riddle. Another Drake scholar has summarized the situation thus:

> As of this moment we still do not know where Drake spent his five weeks in California, and despite the various arguments, each of which is equally persuasive since we lack any real proof, the problem remains one which continues to attract new theories. Every person who has addressed the question, despite the fact that he might be formally labelled as historian, anthropologist, climatologist, or geographer, has worked under the restriction of having available the same limited documentary information. Thus far, no specialist knowledge has succeeded

The Prayer Book Cross. Now situated on a knoll in San Francisco's Golden Gate Park, this 57-foot sandstone symbol of an ancient form of punishment was originally unveiled on the opening day of the Midwinter Fair, January 1, 1894, the gift of George W. Childs, a Philadelphia editor and philanthropist. It is inscribed with the message that it is a memorial to the prayer service which Chaplain Francis Fletcher held gratefully on St. John's Day, June 24, 1579, after the Golden Hind *had put safely into its California anchorage. That service was the first to use the English book of Common Prayer, handbook of the Anglican Church, in North America.*

in discovering the solution to the problem . . . . But opinions have not and never will solve the question — only some kind of archaeological or documentary evidence can resolve the problem. Some new discovery in the archives of England, or some archaeologist's find, or an accidental discovery some where along the California shore within the lands once held by the Coast Miwok Indians may yet provide the answer.[6]

In the meantime, the topic of "Drake" arouses interest wherever San Francisco Bay Area residents get together. As one writer has said delightfully:

> One's favorite bay is to be defended in the same sporting spirit with which he would cheer for the football teams of Stanford or the University of California at the Big Game. Around countless firesides on long winter nights, during innumerable trans-bay ferry rides and bridge crossings, partisans of each bay have argued their claims for decades.[7]

A surprising amount of new information has been developed within the past two decades, and additional clues will undoubtedly continue to turn up in the years to come. On a Marin County beach or somewhere in the British archives may be found the key that finally unlocks the mystery. On the other hand, there are those who secretly hope that the riddle will remain unsolved, leaving it to each of us to dream about where Sir Francis may have pitched his tents and caulked his ship, rather than to have a challenging mystery solved and a monument erected, after which we are left with nothing to contemplate on long winter evenings but the dreary prospect of gas shortages, galloping inflation, and politics as usual.[8]

The reader is invited to review the evidence for himself, study the clues, and fill in his own score card. There are still a few small harbors between San Luis Obispo and Seattle which have been overlooked in the long and intensive search for the true anchorage. There is no entry fee, and the clues are spelled out, in a general way, at least, in these pages. Perhaps you, too, can hope to solve the puzzle of the centuries, and you will enjoy it thoroughly whether you succeed or not.

IV

PART

DOCUMENTS

APPENDIX A

Excerpt from
"The Famous Voyage," 1589,
Covering the California Sojourn

FOLLOWING is a reproduction of that part of the 1589 edition of
"The Famous Voyage" which is concerned with the California visit,
including the description of the trip from Central America:

This Pilot brought us to the hauen of Guatulco, the town whereof as
he told us, had but 17. Spaniards in it.[1] Assoone as we were entred this
hauen wee landed, and went presently to the towne, and to the Towne
house, where we found a Judge sitting in judgement, he being associate
with three other officers, vpon three Negroes that had conspired the
burning of the Towne: both which Judges, and prisoners we tooke, and
brought them a shipboord, and caused the chiefe Judge to write his
letter to the Towne, to command all the Townesmen to auoid, that we

might safely water there. Which being done, and they departed, we ransaked the Towne, and in one house we found a pot of the quantitie of a bushell, full of royals of plate, which we brought to our shippe.

And here one Thomas Moone one of our companie, tooke a Spanish Gentleman as he was flying out of the towne, and searching him, he found a chaine of golde about him; and other jewels, which he tooke, and so let him goe.

At this place our Generall among other Spaniards, set a shoare his Portingall Pilot, which he tooke at the Islands of Cape Verde, out of a shippe of S. Marie porte of Portingal, and hauing set them a shoare, we departed[2] hence, and sailed to the Island of Canon, where our Generall landed, and brought to shoare his owne ship, and discharged her, mended, and graued her, and furnished our shippe with water and wood sufficiently.

And whiles we were here, we espied a shippe, and set saile after her, and tooke her, and founde in her two Pilots, and a Spanish Gouernour, going for the Islands of the Philippinas: we searched the shippe, and took some of her marchandizes, and so let her goe. Our Generall at this place, and time, thinking himselfe both in respect of his private iniuries receiued from the Spaniards, as also of their contempts and indignities offered to our countrey and Prince in generall, sufficiently satisfied, and revenged: and supposing that her Maiestie at his returne would rest contented with this seruice, purposed to continue no longer upon the Spanish coasts, but began to consider and to consult of the best way for his Countrey.

He thought it not good to returne by the Streights, for two speciall causes: the one, least the Spaniards should there waite, and attend for him in great number and strength, whose hands he being left but one shippe, could not possibly escape. The other cause was the dangerous situation of the mouth of the Streights in the south side, where continuall stormes raining and blustering, as he found by experience, besides the shoales, and sands upon the coast, he thought it not a good course to aduenture that way; he resolued therefore to auoide these hazards, to goe forward to the Islands of the Moluccaes, and therehence to saile the course of the Portingals by the Cape of Bona Speranza.

Upon this resolution, he began to thinke of his best way to the Moluccaes, and finding himselfe where he nowe was becalmed, he sawe, that of necessitie he must be forced to take a Spanish course, namely to saile somewhat Northerly to get a wind. We therefore set saile, and sailed in longitude 600.[3] leagues at the least for a good winde, and thus much we sailed from the 16. of Aprill, till the 3. of June.

The 5. day of June, being in 42.[4] degrees towards the pole Arctike, we found the aire so colde, that our men being greeuiously pinched with the same, complained of the extremitie thereof, and the further we went, the more the cold increased vpon vs. Whereupon we thought it best for that time to seeke the land, and did so, finding it not mountanous, but lowe plaine land, & clad, and couered ouer with snowe, so that we drewe backe againe without landing, till we came within 38. degrees towards the line.[5] In which heigth it pleased God to send vs into a faire and good Baye, with a good winde to enter the same.

In this Baye we ankered,[6] and the people of the Countrey, hauing their houses close by the waters side, shewed themseues vnto vs, and sent a present to our Generall.

When they came vnto vs, they greatly wondred at the things that we brought, but our Generall (according to his naturall and accustomed humanitie) curteously intreated them, and liberally bestowed on them necessarie things to couer their nakedness, whereupon they supposed us to be gods, and would not be perswaded to the contrarie: the presents which they sent to our Generall were feathers, and cals of networke.

Their houses are digged round about with earth, and haue from the uttermost brimmes of the circle, clifts of wood set vpon them, ioyning close together at the toppe like a spire steeple, which by reason of that closenes are very warme.

Their beds is the ground with rushes strowed on it, and lying about the house, haue the fire in the middest. The men goe naked, the women take bulrushes, and kembe them after the manner of hempe, and thereof make their loose garments, which being knit about their middles, hang downe about their hippes, hauing also about their shoulders, a skinne of Deere, with the haire upon it. These women are very obedient and seruiceable to their husbands.

After they were departed from vs, they came and visited vs the second time, and brought with them feathers and bags of Tabacco for presents: And when they came to the top of the hill (at the bottome whereof we had pitched our tents) they staied themselues: where one appointed for speaker, wearied himselfe with making a long oration, which done, they left their bowes vpon the hill, and came downe with their presents.

In the meane time, the women remaining on the hill, tormented themselues lamentably, tearing their flesh from their cheekes, whereby we perceiued that they were about a sacrifice. In the meane time, our Generall, with his companie, went to praier, and to reading of the Scriptures, at which exercise they were attentiue, & seemed greatly to be affected with it: but when they were come vnto vs, they restored againe vnto vs those things which before we bestowed vpon them.

The newes of our being there, being spread through the Countrey, the people that inhabited round about came downe, and amongst them the King himselfe, a man of goodly stature, & comely personage, with many other tall, and warlike men: before whose comming were sent two Ambassadors to our Generall, to signifie that their King was comming, in doing of which message, their speech was continued about halfe an howre. This ended, they by signes requested our Generall to send some thing by their hand to their King, as a token that his comming might be in peace: wherein our Generall having satisfied them, they returned with glad tidings to their King, who marched to vs with a princely maiestie, the people crying continually after their manner, and as they drewe neere vnto vs, so did they striue to behaue themselues in their actions with comelines.

In the fore front was a man of a goodly personage, who bare the scepter, or mace before the King, whereupon hanged two crownes, a lesse and a bigger, with three chaines of a maruelous length: the crownes were made of knit worke wrought artificially with fethers of diuers colours: the chaines were made of a bonie substance, and few be the persons among them that are admitted to weare them: and of that number also the persons are stinted, as some ten, some 12. etc. Next vnto him which bare the scepter, was the King himselfe, with his Garde about his person, clad with Conie skins, & other skins: after them followed the naked comon sort of people, euery one hauing his face painted, some with white, some with blacke, and other colours, & hauing in their handes one thing or another for a present, not so much as their childre, but they also brought their presents.

In the meane time, our Generall gathered his men together, and marched within his fenced place, making against their approching, a very warlike shewe. They being trooped together in their order, and a general salutation being made, there was presently a generall silence. Then he that bare the scepter before the King, being informed by another, whome they assigned to that office, with a manly and loftie voice, proclaimed that which the other spake to him in secret, continuing halfe an howre: which ended, and a generall Amen as it were giuen, the King with the whole number of men, and women (the children excepted) came downe without any weapon, who descending to the foote of the hill, set themselues in order.

In comming towards our bulwarks and tents, the scepter bearer began a song, obseruing his measures in a daunce, and that with a stately countenance, whom the King with his Garde, and euery degree of persons following, did in like manner sing and daunce, sauing only the women which daunced, & kept silence. The Generall permitted them to enter within our bulwarks, where they continued their song and daunce a reasonable time. When they had satisfied themselues, they made signes to our General to sit downe, to whom the King, and divers others made seuerall orations, or rather supplications, that he would take their prouince & kingdome into his hand, and become their King, making signes that they would resigne vnto him their right and title of the whole land, and become his subiects. In which, to perswade vs the better, the King and the rest, with one consent, and with great reuerence, joyfully singing a song, did set the crowne vpon his head, inriched his necke with all their chaines, and offred vnto him many other things, honouring him by the name of Hioh, adding thereunto as it seemed, a signe of triumph: which thing our Generall thought not meete to reiect, because he knewe not what honour and profite it might be to our Countrey. Wherefore in the name, and to the vse of her Maiestie, he tooke the scepter, crowne, and dignitie of the said Countrey into his hands, wishing that the riches & treasure thereof might so conueniently be transported to the inriching of her kingdome at home, as it aboundeth in ye same.

The common sorte of people leauing the King, and his Garde with our Generall, scattered themselues together with their sacrifices among our people, taking a diligent viewe of euery person: and such as pleased their fancie, (which were the yongest) they inclosing them about offered their sacrifices vnto them with lamentable weeping, scratching, and tearing the flesh from their faces with their nailes, whereof issued abundance of bloode. But wee vsed signes to them of disliking this, and staied their hands from force, and directed them vpwards to the liuing God, whome onely they ought to worshippe. They shewed vnto vs their wounds, and craued helpe of them at our hands, whereupon wee gaue them lotions, plaisters, and ointments agreeing to the state of their griefes, beseeching God to cure their diseases. Euery thirde day they brought their sacrifices vnto vs, vntill they vnderstoode our meaning, that we had no pleasure in them: yet they could not be long absent from us, but daily frequented our companie to the houre of our departure, which departure seemed so greeuous vnto them, that their ioy was turned into sorrow. They intreated vs, that being absent we would remember them, and by stelth prouided a sacrifice, which we misliked.

Our necessarie busines being ended, our Generall with his companie trauiled vp into the Countrey to their villages, where we found heardes of Deere by 1000. in a companie, being most large, and fat of bodie.

We found the whole Countrey to be a warren of a strange kinde of

Connies, their bodies in bignes as be the Barbarie Connies, their heads as the heads of ours, the feete of a Want, and the taile of a Rat being of great length: vnder her chinne on either side a bagge, into the which she gathereth her meate, when she hath filled her bellie abroad. The people eate their bodies, and make great accompt of their skinnes, for their Kings coate was made of them.

Our Generall called this Countrey, Noua Albion, and that for two causes: the one in respect of the white bankes and cliffes, which lie towards the sea: and the other, because it might haue some affinitie with our Countrey in name, which sometime was so called.

There is no part of earth here to be taken vp, wherein there is not a reasonable quantitie of gold or siluer.[7]

At our departure hence our General set vp a monument of our being there, as also of her Maiesties right and title to the same, namely a plate, nailed vpon a faire great poste, whereupon was ingrauen her Maiesties name, the day and yeare of our arriuall there, with the free giuing vp of the prouince and people into her Maiesties hands, together with her highnes picture and armes, in a peece of sixe pence of currant English money vnder the plate, where vnder was also written the name of our Generall.

It seemeth that the Spaniards hitherto had neuer bene in this part of the Countrey, neither did euer discouer the lande by many degrees, to the Southwards of this place.

"The Course"

Pages 440–442 of Volume III of Hakluyt's 1600 Edition

The course which Sir *Francis Drake* held from the hauen of *Guatulco* in the South sea on the backe side of *Nueua Espanna,* to the Northwest of *California* as far as fourtie three degrees: and his returne back along the said Coast to thirtie eight degrees: where finding a faire and goodly hauen, he landed, and staying there many weekes, and discouering many excellent things in the countrey and great shewe of rich minerall matter, and being offered the dominion of the countrey by the Lord of the same, hee tooke possession thereof in the behalfe of her Maiestie, and named it *Noua Albion.*

Wee kept our course from the Isle of Cano (which lyeth in eight degrees of Northerly latitude, and within two leagues of the maine of Nicaragua, where wee calked and trimmed our ship) along the Coast of Nueua Espanna, untill we came to the Hauen and Towne of Guatulco, which (as we were informed) had but seuenteene Spaniards dwelling in it, and we found it to stand in fifteene degrees and fiftie minutes.

Assoone as we were entred this Hauen we landed, and went presently to the towne, and to the Towne house, where we found a Judge sitting in judgement, he being associate with three other officers, upon three Negroes that had conspired the burning of the Towne: both which Judges and prisoners we tooke, and brought them a shippeboord, and caused the chiefe Judge to write his letter to the Towne, to command all the Townesmen to avoid, that we might safely water there. Which being done, and they departed, wee ransaked the Towne, and in one house we found a pot of the quantitie of a bushell full of royals of plate, which we brought to our ship.

And here one Thomas Moone one of our companie, took a Spanish gentleman as he was flying out of the Towne, and searching him, he found a chaine of Gold about him, and other iewels, which we tooke and so let him goe.

At this place our Generall among other Spaniards, set a shore his Portugall Pilote, which he tooke at the Island of Cape Verde, out of a ship of Saint Marie port of Portugall, and hauing set them a shoore, we departed thence.

Our Generall at this place and time thinking himselfe both in respect of his private iniuries received from the Spaniards, as also of their contempts and indignities offered to our Countrey and Prince in generall, sufficiently satisfied, and revenged; and supposing that her Maiestie at his returne would rest contented with this seruice, purposed to continue no longer upon the Spanish coastes, but began to consider and to consult of the best way to his Countrey.

He thought it not good to returne by the Streights, for two speciall causes: the one, least the Spaniards should there waite, and attend for him in great number and strength, whose handes he being left but one ship, could not possibly escape. The other cause was the dangerous situation of the mouth of the Streights of the South side, with continuall stormes raining and blustring, as he found by experience, besides the shoals and sands upon the coast, wherefore he thought it not a good course to aduenture that way; he resolued therefore to auoide these hazards, to goe forward to the Islands of the Malucos, and therehence to saile the course of the Portugales by the Cape of Bona Speranza.

Upon this resolution, he began to thinke of his best way for the Malucos, and finding himselfe, where hee now was, becalmed, hee sawe that of necessitie hee must bee enforced to take a Spanish course, namely to saile somewhat Northerly to get a winde. Wee therefore set saile, and sayled 800 leagues at the least for a good winde, and thus much we sayled from the 16 of Aprill after our olde stile till the third of June.

The fift of June being in fortie three degrees towardes the pole Arcticke, being speedily come out of the extreame heate, wee found the ayre so colde, that our men being pinched with the same, complayned of the extremitie thereof, and the further we went, the more the colde increased vpon us, whereupon we thought it best for that time to seeke land, and did so, finding it not mountainous, but low plaine land, & we drew backe againe without landing, til we came within thirtie eight degrees towardes the line. In which height it pleased God to send vs into a faire and good Bay, with a good winde to enter the same.

In this Bay wee ankered the seuententh of June, and the people of the Countrey, having their houses close by the waters side, shewed themselues vnto vs, and sent a present to our Generall.

When they came vnto vs, they greatly wondred at the things which we brought, but our Generall (according to his naturall and accustomed humanitie) curteously intreated them, and liberally bestowed on them necessarie things to couer their nakednesse, wherevpon they they supposed vs to be gods, and would not be perswaded to the contrary; the presentes which they sent vnto our Generall were feathers, and cals of net worke.

Their houses are digged round about with earth, and haue from the vttermost brimmes of the circle clifts of wood set vpon them, ioyning close together at the toppe like a spire steeple, which by reason of that closenesse are very warme.

Their bed is the ground with rushes strawed on it, and lying about the house, they have the fire in the middest. The men goe naked, the women take bulrushes and kembe them after the manner of hempe, and thereof make their loose garments, which being knit about their middles, hang downe about their hippes, having also about their shoulders a skinne of Deere, with the haire vpon it. These women are very obedient and seruiceable to their husbands.

After they were departed from vs, they came and visited vs the second time, and brought with them feathers and bags of Tabacco for presents: And when they came to the toppe of the hil (at the bottome whereof wee had pitched our tents) they stayed themselues, where one appointed for speaker wearied himselfe with making a long oration, which done, they left their bowes vpon the hil, and came downe with their presents.

In the meane time the women remaining on the hill, tormented themselues lamentably, tearing their flesh from their cheekes, whereby we perceiued that they were about a sacrifice. In the meane time our

Generall, with his companie, went to prayer, and to reading of the Scriptures, at which exercise they were attentive and seemed greatly to be affected with it: but when they were come vnto vs they restored vnto vs those things which before we had bestowed vpon them.

The newes of our being there being spread through the countrey, the people that inhabited round about came downe, and amongst them the king himself, a man of goodly stature, and comely personage, with many other tall and warlike men: before whose comming were sent two Ambassadours to our Generall, to signifie that their king was comming, in doing of which message, their speech was continued about halfe an howre. This ended, they by signes requested our Generall to send something by their hand to their king, as a token that his comming might bee in peace: wherein our Generall hauing satisfied them, they returned with glad tidings to their king, who marched to vs with a princely Maiestie, the people crying continually after their maner, and as they drewe vnto vs, so did they striue to behaue themselues in their actions with comelinesse.

In the forefront was a man of a goodly personage, who bare the scepter, or mace before the king, wherevpon hanged two crownes, a lesse and a bigger, with three chaines of a merueilous length: the crownes were made of knit work wrought artificially with feathers of diuers colours: the chaines were made of a bony substance and few be the persons among them that are admitted to weare them: and of that number also the persons are stinted, as some ten, some twelue, etc. Next vnto him which bare the scepter, was the king himselfe, with his Guarde about his person, clad with Conie skinnes, and other skinnes: after them followed the naked common sort of people, euery one hauing his face painted, some with white, some with blacke, and other colours and hauing in their hands one thing or another for a present, not so much as their children, but they also brought their presents.

In the meane time, our Generall gathered his men together, and marched within his fenced place, making against their approaching, a very warlike shewe. They being trooped together in their order, and a general salutation being made, there was presently a generall silence. Then he that bare the scepter before the king, being informed by another, whome they assigned to that office, with a manly and loftie voice, proclaimed that which the other spake to him in secret, continuing halfe an houre: which ended, and a generall Amen as it were giuen, the king with the whole number of men and women (the children excepted) came downe without any weapon, who descending to the foote of the hill, set themselues in order.

In comming towards our bulwarks and tents, the scepter bearer began a song, obseruing his measures in a dance, and that with a stately countenance, whom the king with his Garde, and euery degree of persons following, did in like manner sing and dance, sauing onely the women which daunced and kept silence. The General permitted them to enter within our bulwark, where they continued their song and daunce a reasonable time. When they had satisfied themselues, they made signes to our Generall to sit downe, to whom the king, and diuers others made seueral orations, or rather supplication, that he would take their prouince and kingdom into his hand, and become their king, making signes that they would resigne vnto him their right and title of the whole land, and become his subjects. In which to perswade vs the better, the king and the rest, with one consent and with great reuerence, ioyfully singing a song, did set the crowne vpon his head, inriched his necke with all their chaines, and offered vnto him many other things, honouring him by the name Hioh, adding therevnto as it seemed a signe of triumph: which thing our Generall thought not meete to reiect, because hee knewe not what honour and profite it might bee to our countrey. Wherefore in the name, and to the use of her Maiestie, he tooke the scepter, crowne and dignitie of the said Countrey in his hands, wishing that the riches and treasure thereof might so conveniently be transported to the inriching of her kingdome at home, as it aboundeth in the same.

The common sort of the people leauing the king and his Guarde with our Generall, scattered themselues together with their sacrifices among our people, taking a diligent viewe of euery person; and such as pleased their fancie, (which were the youngest) they inclosing them about offred their sacrifices vnto them with lamentable weeping, scratching and tearing the flesh from their faces with their nayles, whereof issued abundance of blood. But wee used signes to them of disliking this, and stayed their hands from force, and directed them vpwardes to the liuing God, whom onely they ought to worshippe. They shewed vnto vs their wounds, and craued helpe of them at our handes, wherevpon wee gaue them lotions, plaisters, and ointments agreeing to the state of their griefes, beseeching God to cure their deseases. Euery thirde day they brought their sacrifices vnto vs, vntil they vnderstoode our meaning, that we had no pleasure in them: yet they could not be long absent from vs, but daily frequented our company to the houre of our departure, which departure seemed so grieuous vnto them, that their ioy was turned into sorrow. They intreated vs, that being absent wee would remember them, and by stelth prouided a sacrifice, which we misliked.

Our necessarie businesse being ended, our Generall with his companie traueiled vp into the Countrey to their villages, where we found heardes of Deere by a thousand in a companie, being most large and fat of body.

We found the whole countrey to bee a warren of a strange kinde of Conies, their bodyes in bignes as be the Barbary Conies, their heads as the heades of ours, the feet of a Want, and the taile of a Rat being of great length: vnder her chinne on either side a bagge, into the which shee gathereth her meate when she hath filled her belly abroad. The people eate their bodies, and make great account of their skinnes, for their Kings coate was made of them.

Our Generall called this countrey, Noua Albion, and that for two causes: the one in respect of the white bankes and cliffes, which ly towardes the sea; and the other, because it might haue some affinitie with our Countrey in name, which sometime was so called.

There is no part of earth here to bee taken vp, wherein there is not some speciall likelihood of gold or siluer.

At our departure hence our Generall set vp a monument of our being there; as also of her Maiesties right and title to the same, namely a plate nailed vpon a faire great poste, wherevpon was ingrauen her Maiesties name, the day and yeere of our arrivall there, with the free giuing vp of the Prouince and people into her Maiesties hands, together with her highnes picture and armes, in a peice of sixe pence of current English money vnder the plate, where vnder was also written the name of our General.

It seemeth that the Spaniards hitherto had neuer bene in this part of the countrey, neither did euer discouer the land by many degrees to the Southwards of this place.

Comparison
of Hakluyt's Three
Accounts of the
California Sojourn

Differing Versions of Corresponding Paragraphs from the
California Sojourn Accounts Appearing in Hakluyt's 1589
and 1600 Editions of the Principall Navigations

Original 1589 Edition

Vpon this resolution, he began to thinke of his best way to the
Moluccaes, and finding himselfe where he nowe was becalmed, he saw,
that of necessitie he must be forced to take a Spanish course, namely to
saile somewhat Northerly to get a winde. We therefore set saile, and
sailed *in longitude 600.* leagues at the least for a good winde, and thus
much we sailed from the 16. of Aprill, till the 3. of June.

The 5. day of June, being in *42.* degrees towards the pole Arctike, we found the aire so colde, that our men being *greeuously* pinched with the same, complained of the extremitie thereof, and the further we went, the more the colde increased vpon vs. Wherevpon we thought it best for that time to seeke the land, and did so, finding it not mountan-ous, but lowe plaine land, *& clad, and couered ouer with snowe, so that we drewe back againe without landing,* till we came within 38. degrees towards the line. In which heigth it pleased God to send vs into a faire and good Baye, with a good winde to enter the same.

In this Baye we ankered, and the people of the Countrey, hauing their houses close by the waters side, shewed themselues vnto vs, and sent a present to our Generall.

Volume III, 1600 Edition, pages 736-737

Vpon this resolution, hee began to thinke of his best way to the Malucos, and finding himselfe where he now was becalmed, he saw that of necessitie hee must be forced to take a Spanish course, namely to sayle somewhat Northerly to get a winde. Wee therefore set saile, and sayled *600.* leagues at the least for a good winde, and thus much we sailed from the 16. of April, till the 3. of June.

The 5. day of June, being in *43.* degrees towards the pole Arctike, we found the ayre so colde, that our men being *greeuously* pinched with the same, complained of the extremitie thereof, and the further we went, the more the colde increased vpon vs. Wherevpon we thought it best for that time to seeke the land, and did so, finding it not mountain-ous, but lowe plaine land, till wee came within 38. degrees towards the line. In which height it pleased God to send vs into a faire and good Baye, with a good wind to enter the same.

In this Baye wee anchored, and the people of the Countrey hauing their houses close by the waters side, shewed themselues vnto vs, and sent a present to our Generall.

Volume III, 1600 Edition, page 440

Vpon this resolution, he began to thinke of his best way for the Malucos, and finding himselfe, where hee now was, becalmed, hee sawe that of necessitie hee must bee enforced to take a Spanish course, namely to saile somewhat Northerly to get a winde. Wee therefore set saile, and sayled *800* leagues at the least for a good winde, and thus much we sayled from the 16 of Aprill *after our olde stile* till the third of June.

The fift day of June being in *fortie three* degrees towardes the pole Arcticke, being speedily come out of the extreame heat, wee found the ayre so colde, that our men being pinched with the same, complayned of the extremitie thereof, and the further we went, the more the colde increased vpon vs, whereupon we thought it best for that time to seeke land, and did so, finding it not mountainous, but low plaine land, *& we drew backe againe without landing,* til we came within thirtie eight degrees towardes the line. In which height it pleased God to send vs into a faire and good Bay, with a good winde to enter the same.

In this Bay wee ankered *the seuententh of June,* and the people of the Countrey, hauing their houses close by the waters side, shewed themselues vnto vs, and sent a present to our Generall.

In comparing the three versions, differing language has been italicized. The differences can be summarized as follows:

1. "in longitude 600." in the 1589 edition becomes simply "600." in the 1600 edition, at page 737, and "800" in the 1600 edition at page 440.

2. "42." in the 1589 edition becomes "43." in the 1600 edition at page 737, and "fortie three" in the 1600 edition at page 440.

3. "greeuously" in the 1589 edition remains the same in the 1600 edition at page 737, but is omitted in the latter at page 440.

4. "& clad, and couered ouer with snowe, so that we drewe back againe without landing" in the 1589 edition was deleted entirely in the 1600 edition at page 737, but appeared as "& we drew backe againe without landing" in the 1600 edition at page 440.

5. "the sevententh of June" was inserted in the 1600 edition at page 440, but did not appear in the 1589 edition or in the 1600 edition at page 737.

6. The clause "after our olde stile" was inserted in the 1600 edition at page 440, but did not appear in the 1589 edition or in the 1600 edition at page 737.

Excerpt from
The World Encompassed
Covering the
California Sojourn

From Guatulco we departed the day following, viz. April 16, setting our course directly into the sea, whereon we sayled 500 leagues in longitude, to get a winde: and betweene that and Iune 3, 1400 leagues in all, till we came into 42 deg. of North latitude, where in the night following we found such alteration of heate, into extreame and nipping cold, that our men in generall did grieuously complaine thereof, some of them feeling their healths much impaired thereby; neither was it that this chanced in the night alone, but the day following carried with it not onely the markes, but the stings and force of the night going before, to the great admiration of vs all; for besides that the pinching and biting aire was nothing altered, the very roapes of our ship were stiffe, and the raine which fell was an vnnatural congealed and frozen substance, so that we seemed rather to be in the frozen Zone than any way so neere vnto the sun, or these hotter climates.

Neither did this happen for the time onely, or by some sudden accident, but rather seemes indeed to proceed from some ordinary cause, against the which the heate of the sun preuailes not; for it came to that extremity in sayling but 2 deg. farther to the Northward in our course, that though sea-men lack not good stomaches, yet it seemed a question to many amongst vs, whether their hands should feed their mouthes, or rather keepe themselues within their couerts from the pinching cold that did benumme them. Neither could we impute it to the tendernesse of our bodies, though we came lately from the extremitie of heate, by reason whereof we might be more sensible of the present cold: insomuch as the dead and sencelesse creatures were as well effected with it as ourselues: our meate, as soone as it was remooued from the fire, would presently in a manner be frozen vp, and our ropes and tackling in a few dayes were growne to that stiffnesse, that what 3 men afore were able with them to performe, now 6 men, with their best strength and vttermost endeauour, were hardly able to accomplish: whereby a sudden and great discouragement seased vpon the mindes of our men, and they were possessed with a great mislike and doubting of any good to be done that way; yet would not our general be discouraged, but as wel by confortable speeches, of the diuine prouidence, and of God's louing care ouer his children, out of the Scriptures; as also by other good and profitable perswasions, adding thereto his own cheerfull example, he so stirred them vp to put on a good courage, and to quite themselues like men, to indure some short extremity to haue the speedier comfort, and a little trouble to obtaine the greater glory, that euery man was throughly armed with willingnesse and resolued to see the uttermost, if it were possible, of what good was to be done that way.

The land in that part of America, bearing farther out into the West than we before imagined, we were neerer on it then wee were aware; and yet the neerer still wee came vnto it, the more extremitie of cold did sease vpon vs. The 5 day of Iune, wee were forced by contrary windes to runne in with the shoare, which we then first descried, and to cast anchor in a bad bay, the best roade we could for the present meete with, where wee were not without some danger by reason of the many extreme gusts and flawes that beate vpon vs, which if they ceased and were still at any time, immediately upon their intermission there followed most uile, thicke, and stinking fogges, against which the sea preuailed nothing, till the gusts of wind againe remoued them. which brought with them such extremity and violence when they came, that there was no dealing or resisting against them.

In this place was no abiding for vs; and to go further North, the extremity of the cold (which had now vtterly discouraged our men) would not permit vs; and the winds directly bent against vs, hauing once gotten vs under sayle againe, commanded vs to the Southward whether we would or no.

From the height of 48 deg., in which now we were, to 38, we found the land, by coasting alongst it, to bee but low and reasonable plaine; euery hill (whereof we saw many, but none verie high), though it were in Iune, and the Sunne in his neerest approch vnto them, being couered with snow.

In 38 deg. 30 min. we fell with a conuenient and fit harborough, and Iune 17 came to anchor therein: where we continued till the 23 day of Iuly following, During all which time, notwithstanding it was in the height of Summer, and so neere the Sunne; yet were wee continually visited with like nipping colds as we had felt before; insomuch that if violent exercises of our bodies, and busie employment about our neces-sarie labours, had not sometimes compeld us to the contrary, we could very well haue been contented to haue kept about us still our Winter clothes; yea (had our necessities suffered vs) to haue kept our beds; neither could we at any time, in whole fourteene dayes together, find the aire so cleare as to be able to take the height of Sunne or starre.

And here hauing so fit occasion (notwithstanding it may seeme to be besides the purpose of writing the history of this our voyage), we will a little more diligently inquire into the causes of the continuance of the extreame cold in these parts, as also into the probabilities or vnlikeli-hoods of a passage to be found that way. Neither was it (as hath form-erly been touched) the tendernesse of our bodies, comming so lately out of the heate, whereby the poores were opened, that made vs so sensible of the colds we here felt: in this respect, as in many others, we found our God a prouident Father and carefull Physitian for vs. We lacked no outward helpes nor inward comforts to restore and fortifie nature, had it beene decayed or weakened in vs: neither was there wanting to vs the great experience of our Generall, who had often himselfe proued the force of the burning Zone, whose aduice alwayes preuailed much to the preseruing of a moderate temper in our constitutions; so that euen after our departure from the heate wee alwayes found our bodies, not as sponges, but strong and hardned, more able to beare out cold, though we came out of excesse of heate, then a number of chamber champions could haue beene, who lye on their feather beds till they go to sea, or

discovery was announced, William Caldeira claimed to have previously discovered this same plate near Drake's Bay in 1933 and to have discarded it near the Greenbrae hillside where Shinn found it. What is the significance of the plate to the landing site controversy?

XV. Drake departed from Nova Albion on July 23, 1579, and The World Encompassed reported that "not farre without this harborough did lye certaine Ilands . . . one of which we fell *(sic)* July 24." What is the significance of the dates and apparent time elapsed on this leg of his journey?

XVI. The Vera Totius Expeditionis Nauticae map of the world by cartographer Jodocus Hondius (London, 1589) contains in its upper left-hand corner a plan of the Portus Novae Albionis. Discuss the significance of the Portus Plan and its correlation with the proposed landing site.

XVII. What is the significance of Arnold Montanus' illustration, "The Crowning of Drake," which was published in De Nieuwe en Onbekonde Weereld of Beschryvning van America en 1 + Zuid-Land . . . (Amsterdam, 1671)?

XVIII. What is the significance of the Declaration by the Spanish Captain Sebastian Rodriguez Cermeno and others who were with him who were shipwrecked in 1595 in the bay presently known as Drake's Bay?

XIX. Discuss the significance of the cartographic information about the California coast contained in Robert Dudley's 1647 atlas, Arcano del Mare, and manuscript chart.

XX. What is the significance of the account of Drake's pilot, N. de Morena, who claimed that he had been put ashore at an "arm of the sea" which he believed connected with the Gulf of California and the Atlantic Ocean?

Notes

Chapter 1

1. Fletcher, *The World Encompassed*, p. 64. See Appendix D.

2. Stow, *Chronicles*, reprinted in Wagner, *Drake's Voyage*, describing Drake's popularity on his return to England. Wagner, *Drake's Voyage*, pp. 317–323, reprinted Darcie's translation (1625) of a French version of Camden's 1615 Latin account of Drake's life, saying at p. 323: "The Commons nevertheless applauded him with all praise and admiration, esteeming he had purchased no lesse glory in advancing the limits of the English, their honor and reputation, than of their Empire."

3. Blundeville, *M. Blundeville, His Exercises, containing sixe Treatises*, p. 244, reprinted by Wagner, *Drake's Voyage*, p. 313.

4. These were Richard Hakluyt's "The Famous Voyage" in 1589, and extremely brief accounts in Stow, *Chronicles*, in 1592, and Blundeville, *M. Blundeville, His Exercises containing sixe Treatises*, in 1594.

5. For a discussion of the plate of brass, see Chapter 22.

6. Greenhow, *History of Oregon and California*, pp. 72–73.

7. For an excellent account of this situation, see Wagner, *Drake's Voyage*, pp. 194–203.

8. Raleigh, *The English Voyages of the Sixteenth Century*, Vol. 12, p. 54. Raleigh states flatly that Drake's object was to drive England to war.

9. This phrase was coined by Bernardino de Mendoza, Spanish ambassador to England during the circumnavigation years. It was repeated in the 1615 edition of Stow, *Chronicles* (see Wagner, *Drake's Voyage*, p. 305, and Barrow, *Life of Drake*, p. 163).

10. In his reference to Drake's "plundering of Spanish possessions on the western coast of the South American continent," Winston Churchill (see bibliography) leaves the impression that this took place in 1577. The voyage started in 1577, but the plundering was done in 1579.

11. Churchill, *History*, Vol. 2: *The New World*, p. 120.

12. Twiss, *Oregon Territory*, p. 186.

13. Ibid., pp. 183–187.

14. Venegas, *History of California*, Vol. 2, p. 162.

15. Nuttall, *New Light on Drake*, p. xlv, where it is stated that this was the term applied to Drake by his Spanish enemies.

16. See Chapter 7. Spanish agents in England may have picked up the same information from members of Drake's crew at an earlier date, i.e., before 1589.

17. Wagner, "The Voyage of Cermeño," *California Historical Society Quarterly*, Vol. III, pp. 3–24, 1924. See, also discussion in Bancroft, *History of California*, Vol. I, pp. 96–97. (Note: The name of the *California Historical Society Quarterly* was changed in 1971 to *California Historical Quarterly*, and to *California History* in 1978.)

18. Bancroft, *History of California*, Vol. I, pp. 97–105; Wagner, *Cartography*, Vol. I, pp. 111–116. Cermeño may have been instructed to look for evidence of Drake's camp, but Vizcaino's principal order was probably to relocate Monterey Bay, which had been reported earlier by Cabrillo.

19. Griffin, "Letters Translated from the Spanish," in *Publications of the Historical Society of Southern California*, Vol. II, pp. 15–19. See Wagner, *Cartography*, Vol. I, p. 91.

20. See Wagner, "Voyage of Cermeño," for the text of Cermeño's report; also see the comment by Wagner, *Drake's Voyage*, p. 168. For the reports of the Vizcaino expedition, see Rinn, "The Voyages of Vizcaino"; also Robertson, *Francis Drake*, p. 225.

21. Cermeño's vessel, the *San Agustin*, was wrecked in Drake's Bay in 1595. See Wagner, "Voyage of Cermeño." Vizcaino's two vessels became inadvertently separated just before reaching Drake's Bay, and were never reunited. Venegas, *History of California*, Vol. II, Appendix II, pp. 288–289.

22. Robertson, *Francis Drake*, p. 50.

23. Ibid., p. 237.

24. Notably W. S. W. Vaux's edition of *The World Encompassed by Sir Francis Drake*, published by the Hakluyt Society in 1854. This work collected in a single volume all then known narratives about the circumnavigation. Corbett's *Drake and the Tudor Navy* (1898) was also a valuable contribution to the nineteenth-century literature on Drake.

25. The plate was discovered on a hillside near San Quentin Cove; its authenticity has never been fully established. See Chapter 22.

26. Northings of 40° and 44° were reported to have been made by Cabrillo and Ferrelo respectively, but the accuracy of these latitudes is questioned by modern authorities. See Wagner, *Cartography*, Vol. I, pp. 41–42; Robertson, *Francis Drake*, pp. 42–48; Bancroft, *History of California*, Vol. I, pp. 76–80.

27. This course was followed to take advantage of the favorable winds and currents usually encountered in latitudes 40° to 43°. See Wagner, *Cartography*, Vol. I, p. 90; Robertson, *Francis Drake*, p. 49.

28. The controversy that surrounds every phase of the Drake visit to California extends even to the name of his flagship. Was it the *Golden Hinde* or the *Golden Hind*? As some one has quipped: "To 'e' or not to 'e,' that is the question."

Those who feel it should be *Hinde* undoubtedly do so because this was the spelling, not only in the original 1628 edition of *The World Encompassed*, but also in an account of the voyage published in Stow's *Chronicles* in 1592. These include George Davidson, John W. Robertson, Robert F. Heizer, and Robert H. Power, all eminent Drake scholars. This spelling was used for the written debate sponsored in 1974 by the California Historical Society, presumably by agreement of all concerned as a matter of uniformity.

On the other hand, in the 1653 edition of *The World Encompassed*, the spelling was *Hind*. Those who have adopted that spelling include biographers John Barrow, Julian S. Corbett, E. F. Benson, A. E. W. Mason, Ernle Bradford, and George M. Thomson, as well as the distinguished Drake scholars Henry R. Wagner, Miller Christy, Raymond Aker, and Pulitzer-prize-winning historian Samuel Eliot Morison. It was also the spelling used by two authors with a familial interest in the matter. One was Lady Eliott-Drake, the other T. W. E. Roche, author of *The Golden Hind*. Roche was a descendant of Sir Christopher Hatton, from whose heraldic crest, with its "hind trippant or" (meaning: golden hind), Drake took the name.

Since there is no authoritative form, we have chosen the simpler *Hind*, reflecting the usage of the Drake and Hatton families, as well as that of the majority of biographers and Drake scholars.

Chapter 2

1. Thomson, *Sir Francis Drake*, pp. 101–103.
2. Nuttall, *New Light on Drake*, p. 162.
3. Andrews, "The Aims of Drake's Expedition," p. 740.
4. Taylor, "More Light on Drake," pp. 141–142, discussing a "draft plan" of the voyage, from which this list of supplies and provisions has been taken.
5. Drake confiscated da Silva's navigational equipment, including his charts, astrolabe, and log. See Wagner, *Drake's Voyage*, p. 339. When Drake put da Silva ashore at Guatulco, Mexico, in April, 1579, he was permitted to keep his log. However, it was confiscated when he was made a prisoner almost immediately in New Spain and is now preserved in the Archives of the Indies at Seville.
6. Magellan required thirty-seven days, Cavendish forty-nine days, and Richard Hawkins forty-six days. Wright and Rapport, *The Great Explorers*, p. 18.
7. See Chapter 1, n. 15.
8. Meaning "shitfire" in rude sailors' English.
9. The Palau Islands are about 600 miles west of the Philippines in latitude 9° N.
10. Wagner, *Drake's Voyage*, p. 202.
11. Fletcher was probably allowed to keep the journal of the voyage which *he* had prepared.
12. Wagner, *Drake's Voyage*, p. 229.
13. Ibid., p. 230.
14. Robertson, *Francis Drake*, p. 165; Wagner, *Drake's Voyage*, pp. 229, 231.

Chapter 3

1. See Appendix A.
2. Ibid.
3. These diacritical marks appeared in Hakluyt's 1589 edition of "The Famous Voyage."
4. For a summary of the rather meager comments in the principal contemporary accounts with respect to fortification of their encampment, see Chapter 15.
5. See Appendix A.
6. According to "The Famous Voyage," the name was Nova Albion, but *The World Encompassed* showed it as merely Albion.
7. *The World Encompassed* called it a "plate of brasse."
8. This is "The Famous Voyage" version.
9. According to the Julian, or old-style, calendar.
10. See Chapter 23.
11. Nutall, *New Light on Drake*, p. 51. See also Chapter 9.
12. This affords an illuminating glimpse of what was *not* related in the principal accounts of the English writers.

Chapter 4

1. See language of *The World Encompassed*, Appendix D.
2. While Hakluyt gave the name as Nova Albion, a term which has been universally

accepted, it is perplexing to find the name reported by *The World Encompassed*, published in 1628, to have been simply Albion. One can only surmise that Albion (Latin for England) was the name appearing in Fletcher's original manuscript, principal source of *The World Encompassed*, but that Hakluyt, working from the same manuscript and perceiving that Nova Albion would be more appropriate, simply added "Nova" on the basis of his rather freely exercised editorial prerogatives. See Appendix H.

3. This included such early maps as the French Drake, the Dutch Drake, the Silver Map, the Molyneux Globe of 1592, the Blagrave Map of 1596, and even the Molyneux Map of 1600. See Chapter 10.

4. These included the Hondius Broadside, the De Bry Map of 1599, and the Dudley maps (see Chapter 10). This diversity seems to have depended upon the account relied upon and the interpretation by the particular mapmaker.

5. As one Drake authority has pointed out, people are not "aware of the fact that the soil of California was divided between a large number of small tribes, whose territorial boundaries were nearly as well fixed as those of a modern county." Wagner, *Drake's Voyage*, p. 495, n. 67.

6. Kroeber, *Handbook of the Indians of California*, pp. 273–274; Heizer, *Francis Drake and the California Indians, 1579*, p. 254.

7. Kroeber, *Handbook of the Indians of California*, p. 274, Figure 22; Heizer, *Francis Drake and the California Indians, 1579*, p. 254, Figure 1; Barrett, *Ethnogeography*, Vol. 6, No. 1, map facing p. 332. Recent students in this field assert that the territory occupied by the Coast Miwok was not necessarily limited to the boundaries depicted above.

8. In his run down the coast, Drake must have passed up one or more bays through oversight or design, including such harbors as Crescent City, Trinidad Bay, and Humboldt Bay.

9. This would assume that the harbors of the sixteenth century are still extant. It is possible, of course, that Drake anchored in a cove which has subsequently disappeared through topographic changes. Such a theory has been espoused by the Drake Navigators Guild in reference to Drake's Estero.

10. As its enthusiastic inhabitants fondly refer to it.

11. Mourelle, *The Voyage of the Sonora in 1775* (Russell edition), pp. 55–57.

12. Rinn, "The Voyages of Vizcaino," pp. 62–63.

13. Wagner, *The Last Spanish Exploration*, pp. 337 ff.

14. Bancroft, *History of California*, Vol. II, pp. 294–320, and 628–652; Vol. IV, pp. 158–159.

15. Ibid., Vol. IV, pp, 395–396. For a more complete account of the activities of Stephen Smith and his associates at Bodega, see the *Oakland Tribune* ("The Knave") for June 15, 1956.

16. Davidson, *The Coast Pilot*, p. 251.

17. Ibid., p. 252.

18. Ibid., p. 254. Davidson indicates that it was the Russian writer Tebenkoff (Tebenkov), who included this observation in his work of 1848.

19. Davidson, *The Coast Pilot*, p. 252.

20. Wagner, *The Last Spanish Exploration*, p. 337.

21. Rinn, "The Voyages of Vizcaino," pp. 62, 63, 82, and 83. See also, Fig. 31, following p. 81.

22. Mourelle, *Voyage of the Sonora in 1775*, Russell edition, pp. 54–55.

23. Wagner, *The Last Spanish Exploration*, p. 340.

24. Rinn, "The Voyages of Vizcaino." At p. 63, the depth "at the mouth" of this "very large river" is given as seven fathoms, although this sounding may not have been taken precisely at the entrance bar.

25. Wagner, *The Last Spanish Exploration*, p. 340.

26. Davidson, *The Coast Pilot*, p. 250, reported ten feet. Cronise, *The Natural Wealth of California*, p. 85, reported eleven feet.

27. U.S. Coast & Geodetic Survey Chart No. 5603 (1956).

28. Munro-Fraser, *History of Marin County*, p. 307; Davidson, *The Coast Pilot* places the date in 1852.

29. Shell, *Marin's Historic Tomales and Presbyterian Church*, p. 12.

30. Stillman, *Seeking the Golden Fleece*. In a footnote at p. 298 of that work, the author states that General Vallejo, in an address delivered at the centennial celebration of the founding of the Mission of San Francisco, asserted positively that it was Tomales Bay that Drake entered.

31. Shell, *Marin's Historic Tomales*, at p. 8, speaks of the commencement of regular service by the steamers *John Hancock* and *Cassie Telfair* in 1867.

32. Cronise, *The Natural Wealth of California*, p. 86.

33. Shell, *Marin's Historic Tomales*, p. 4.

34. Ibid.

35. Kneiss, *Redwood Railways*, p. 50.

36. Shell, *Marin's Historic Tomales*, p. 11.

37. Ibid.

38. Wagner, "The Voyage of Cermeño."

39. Rinn, "The Voyages of Vizcaino," pp. 61–63.

40. Bancroft, *History of California*, Vol. I, pp. 86–87 and 157–159.

41. Soule, Gihon and Nisbet, *The Annals of San Francisco*, pp. 32–33.

42. Munro-Fraser, *History of Marin County*, p. 304.

43. Davidson, *The Coast Pilot*, p. 193.

44. Hale, "Critical Essay on Drake's Bay," p. 75 of Vol. III of Winsor, *Narrative and Critical History of America*.

45. Rinn, "The Voyages of Vizcaino," pp. 62 and 82. Of this anchorage, Vizcaino said: "It is well protected from all winds and may be safely entered. It has an abundance of wood and water." He anchored overnight, but did not land there.

46. Bolanos, *Derotero*.

47. Davidson, *Identification*, pp. 32 and 33. See also, his *The Coast Pilot*, p. 193.

48. Davidson, *Identification*, p. 32.

49. Davidson, *The Coast Pilot*, p. 194.

50. Ibid., p. 193.

51. This is from the *Derotero* with translation by Wagner, *Drake's Voyage*, p. 498, n. 19. The same information is set forth almost verbatim in Admiral Cabrero Bueno's *Navigacion Especulativa Y Practica*, published in Manila in 1734 and cited by Davidson, *Identification*, p. 34.

52. Meighan and Heizer, "Archaeological Exploration" at pp. 73–81, *The Plate of Brass*. For an earlier discussion of the same subject, see Heizer, "Archaeological Evidence of Sebastian Rodriguez Cermeño's California Visit in 1595."

53. Davidson, *The Coast Pilot*, p. 194.

54. Ibid.

55. In 1878, steamers of three times the tonnage of Drake's ship were visiting the Estero weekly, according to the writer of a review of Bryant, *History of the United States*, published in the *San Francisco Bulletin* for October 5, 1878. Bancroft thought that this writer was John W. Dwinelle (see Vol. I, Bancroft, *History of California*, p. 89). As late as 1890, small "butter schooners" were regularly picking up cargoes at several points within the Estero, according to *Nova Albion Rediscovered*, Appendix V, p. 167.

56. Davidson, *The Coast Pilot*, p. 191.

57. Hussey, "Site of the Lighter Wharf at Bolinas," p. 1.

58. Ibid. See also, Robertson, *Francis Drake*, p. 182.

59. Davidson, *The Coast Pilot*, p. 191.

60. Hussey, "Site of the Lighter Wharf at Bolinas," pp. 2 and 3.

61. Davidson, *The Coast Pilot*, p. 180.

62. Galvin, ed., *The First Spanish Entry into San Francisco Bay, 1775*. His information was taken from the *Journal of Manuel de Ayala*, containing the story of the Bay of the Carmelite.

63. Ibid.

64. Davidson, *The Coast Pilot*, p. 180.

65. Ibid.

66. Molera, *The March,* pp. 58, 60, and 64. The report of Don Jose de Canizares on his "reconnaissance of the port of San Francisco" will be found at pp. 65–68.

67. Ibid., p. 66.

Chapter 5

1. See Lady Eliott-Drake, *The Family,* p. 14, in which the author states that Drake was born in 1542 or 1543. In a study of the subject of Drake's age, Wagner indicates that the date could have been as early as 1538 or as late as 1544. *Drake's Voyage,* p. 457.

2. Nuño da Silva, deposition given on May 23, 1579, as reported by Nuttall, *New Light on Drake,* p. 302.

3. Francisco Gomez Rengifo, deposition given on February 18, 1580, as reported by Nuttall, *New Light on Drake,* p. 355.

4. Sometimes referred to as "gentlemen cadets," or "second sons" of noblemen. In a deposition given by San Juan de Anton, reported by Nuttall, *New Light on Drake,* p. 161, they were referred to as "gentiles hombres caballeros," or cavaliers. See also, Roche, *The Golden Hind,* p. 167.

5. For a discussion of Fletcher's narrative, see Wagner, *Drake's Voyage,* p. 289. See also, Chapter 8.

6. The incident is fully described in the "Anonymous Narrative" as reported by Wagner, *Drake's Voyage,* p. 282.

7. Wagner, *Drake's Voyage* p. 32.

8. Ibid.

9. See Chapter 28.

10. San Juan de Anton, deposition given March 16, 1579, as reported by Nuttall, *New Light on Drake,* p. 171.

11. Ibid., p. 172.

12. Ibid., p. 171.

13. See Appendix A.

14. Wagner, *Drake's Voyage,* quoting a part of the "Anonymous Narrative," p. 271. Davidson, at p. 48 of his 1908 treatise on Drake, speaks of "the young negress of 15 years, 'a Pper negro wench,' who was with child to Drake and his officers" but does not give the source of his information about her age.

15. Wagner, *Drake's Voyage,* pp. 124, 271, and 335.

16. Another illuminating glimpse of what was not disclosed by the principal English accounts.

17. "The Famous Voyage" and *The World Encompassed.*

18. The "Anonymous Narrative," as reported by Wagner, *Drake's Voyage,* p. 271.

19. John Drake's "First Declaration," as reported by Nuttall, *New Light on Drake,* p. 32.

20. The "Anonymous Narrative," as reported by Wagner, *Drake's Voyage,* p. 281.

21. Camden, as translated by Abraham Darcie, *The True and Royall History of the Famous Empresse Elizabeth.* See Wagner, *Drake's Voyage,* p. 322.

22. Corbett, *Drake and the Tudor Navy,* Vol. I, p. 300, fn.

23. J. P. Munro-Fraser, in his *History of Marin County,* p. 96, speaks of "an old Indian legend which came down through the Nicasios." Since Kroeber, in his *Handbook of the California Indians,* makes no reference to a tribe or sub-tribe by that name, it must be assumed that Munro-Fraser was speaking of members of the Coast Miwok tribe living in the village of Nicasio.

24. Munro-Fraser, pp. 96 and 97.

25. Ibid, p. 98.

26. The sole source of the legend is Munro-Fraser and every writer's discussion of it relates back, directly or indirectly, to that source.

27. Davidson, *Identification,* p. 35.

28. Robertson, *Francis Drake,* pp. 221, 222, and 226.

29. Wagner, *Drake's Voyage,* pp. 148, 167.

30. Heizer, *Elizabethan California,* pp. 78–79.

31. Wagner, *Drake's Voyage,* p. 148.

32. Ibid.

33. Aker, "Report of Findings," p. 330.

34. Ibid., p. 331.

35. Nuttall, *New Light on Drake,* p. 137. Nicolas Jorje was a prisoner on the *Golden Hind* from February 5 to March 5, 1579.

36. Ibid., pp. 181, 186. In addition to the two thus mentioned, a third black, a young woman named Maria, was subsequently made a captive.

37. If there were 86 or 87 on board, having in mind the prior loss of 5 to enemy action and 8 in an open boat in a storm in September, 1578, Drake would have had to have 100 on board the *Golden Hind* when it arrived in the Pacific. For this reason as well as the tendency of prisoners to exaggerate, such estimates do not check out with the arithmetic of the personnel of the three ships.

38. Nuttall, *New Light on Drake,* p. 32.

39. Ibid., p. 52. Nuttall mistakenly translated John Drake's first deposition to mean that Drake had lightened his ship in the Moluccas "by reducing their company to sixty men." Fortunately, Wagner, *Drake's Voyage,* p. 181, corrected this error by pointing out that "all John Drake said was that they were only sixty in number" and that there was no "evidence that Drake left any men at Ternate." To the same effect as Wagner was the translation given by Lady Eliott-Drake in her *The Family and Heirs of Drake,* Vol. 2, p. 357.

40. Nuttall, *New Light on Drake,* p. 32.

41. For a discussion of this discrepancy, see Wagner, *Drake's Voyage,* p. 148; also, Aker, "Report of Findings," pp. 330–342.

42. Drake Navigators Guild, "Nova Albion Rediscovered," p. 15, which states "we may readily believe there was suppressed and even open discontent in the incongruous, closely packed company on his ship, only to be understood and appreciated by those who have made long sea voyages."

43. Cermeño was the captain of a Spanish ship, the *San Agustin* assigned to explore the California coast for harbors that might be suitable for the use of Spanish vessels plying between the Philippines and Acapulco. While in the present Drake's Bay in November, 1595, the *San Agustin* was wrecked.

44. The story of de Morena's adventures was reported in the February issue of *Land of Sunshine,* XII:3 See Chapter 28, *infra.*

45. Davidson, *Identification.*

46. Ibid., p. 35.

47. Ibid., p. 57.

48. Munro-Fraser, *History of Marin County,* p. 97.

49. The map was reproduced in color in Robertson, *Francis Drake,* p. 256 f.

50. Ibid., p. 255.

51. Ibid., p. 255.

52. Ibid., p. 221.

53. Ibid., p. 222.

54. Ibid., p. 222.

55. Ibid., p. 226.

56. Ibid., p. 226.

57. Ibid., p. 226.

58. Ibid., p. 255.

59. Stanger and Brown, *Who Discovered San Francisco Bay?,* p. 137.

60. Ibid., p. 141.

61. On the basis of the information available to him, Robertson implied that the legend might have had credibility if the blond natives seen by Crespi had been encountered near Point

Reyes. In effect, one of his reasons for rejecting the legend was because the mestizos were encountered elsewhere than in certain parts of Marin County.

There are several responses to this view of the evidence: (1) The legend, as reported by Munro-Fraser, did not limit the area where the Drake crewmen finally came to rest as being near Point Reyes or Nicasio; it stated that they made their way "into the county" which could have been anywhere on the Marin peninsula or in the Bay area. (2) Even from Nicasio, the airline distance to San Francisco is less than 25 miles, not too great a distance for the Drake crewmen and their offspring to have migrated in the course of two centuries. (3) There is recent evidence to suggest that the Costanoan Indians, who peopled the San Francisco area when the Spaniards first arrived there, may also have occupied a part of the eastern shores of Marin County in pre-mission days, thus possibly accounting for crewmen's descendants having moved to the area south of the Golden Gate. (4) In any event, what other explanation of the Crespi-Palou encounters is there? Apart from the Cermeño visit in 1595, no other white men are known to have set foot on northern California soil prior to 1769. None of the Cermeño crew remained behind, and there is really no other way to account for the mestizos seen by Crespi and Palou except on the basis of the legend of the Nicasios.

62. Wilson, *The World Encompassed*, p. 211, giving the author's estimate that the survivors of the voyage were probably about half of the original complement of 164. A careful computation, however, based upon the arithmetic outlined elsewhere herein, places the number of survivors at about 104.

63. Penzer, ed., *The World Encompassed*, p. 139, indicating that Francis Fletcher had reported the number lost on the *Marigold* at "28 Soules," in addition to Captain Edward Bright.

64. These were John Fry, captured off the coast of Morocco but later returned to England; Peter Carder, who made his way over land and sea from the vicinity of the Straits of Magellan to England, finally arriving in 1586 (see Wagner, *Drake's Voyage*, pp. 83–84); and pilot de Morena, who made it on foot from Nova Albion to Mexico, arriving there about 1583 (see Chapter 28).

65. There is no record of the number or identity of those who returned to England on the *Elizabeth* with Captain Winter, nor do the accounts of his return shed any light on the subject of Drake survivors. On returning to England, he had the distinction of having been the first to negotiate the Straits of Magellan from west to east; and the dubious distinction of being charged with desertion. According to John Drake (see Nuttall, *New Light on Drake*, p. 27), Winter was imprisoned for deserting Drake and would have been hung but for the latter's intervention.

66. This was the count made surreptitiously by Nicolas Jorje during the month when he was a prisoner on the *Golden Hind*.

67. Since 58 was the last total of those on board mentioned by *The World Encompassed*, it is believed to be the number that returned to England. See Penzer, ed., *The World Encompassed*, p. 78.

68. See page 56.

69. See n. 67.

70. These five instances were as follows: (1) The eight men ordered into an open boat in October, 1578, as described hereinafter. (2) The pilot, Nuño da Silva, put ashore at Guatulco. (3) The dozen or more men ordered to man Rodrigo Tello's frigate for the journey from Mexico to California. (4) The pilot, N. de Morena, who was said to have left the ship at Nova Albion and to have walked back to Mexico. (5) The three blacks captured on the coast of South or Central America who were put ashore on Crab Island in the East Indies. These five instances do not take into account the other crew members who appear to have been left at Nova Albion.

71. The explanation given by John Drake for the marooning of the three blacks was to "found a settlement." Rather obviously, the purpose was to avoid the problems involved in having an infant on board for the final nine months of the voyage.

72. The accounts do not explain how the personnel of these two ships were reassigned. The indications are that Drake transferred most of them to the *Golden Hind*, and that the latter may

have had 90 or more persons on board when it emerged from the Straits of Magellan in September, 1578.

73. Nuttall, *New Light on Drake*, p. 42, tells of this incident as reported in *Purchas, His Pilgrimes*, London, 1625, Part IV.

74. Ibid. Among the eight men thus left to their fate, Peter Carder was the only one who succeeded in returning to England. The others perished after enduring unbelievable privation and hardship.

75. This was the frigate or bark taken from Rodrigo Tello near the island of Caño in March, 1579. Its carrying capacity has been estimated at 14.

76. As a matter of fact, da Silva was subjected to four depositions during the years 1579 and 1580, while a Spanish prisoner, two of them before the infamous Spanish Inquisition. As a Portuguese who had been associated with Drake for more than a year, his reception by the Spaniards was not a friendly one.

77. The "Anonymous Narrative," as reported by Wagner, *Drake's Voyage*, p. 271, reported that Maria had been "gotten with childe between the captaine and his men pirates" and by the time they reached Celebes in November, 1579, she had become "very great."

78. See Aker, "Report of Findings," pp. 333–334, for a discussion of why "there is good reason to conjecture that the missing members of Drake's crew remained at Nova Albion."

Chapter 6

1. San Luis Obispo Bay, sponsored by Robert W. Pate and Richard Dobson, also by Mrs. G. O. Sagen; a small sub-bay on the Petaluma River near its outlet into San Pablo Bay, sponsored by Dr. Robert C. Thomas; and Nehalem Bay in Oregon, sponsored by Donald Viles and Wayne Jensen.

2. Actually, some of the early information indicated that the repair of the *Golden Hind* took place in latitude 48°, which would have been near the Strait of Juan de Fuca and Vancouver Island. See Nuttall, *New Light on Drake*, p. 31 and 50.

3. Vancouver, *Voyage of Discovery*, published 1798.

4. Bancroft, *History of California*, Vol. I, p. 87.

5. Burney, *Chronological History*, Part I, p. 355.

6. Arrowsmith was undoubtedly confused, however, by the fact that the early name for the Point Reyes harbor was Bay of San Francisco, a name conferred by Cermeño in 1595.

7. Colnett, *Journal of Captain James Colnett*, p. 174.

8. Bancroft, *History of California*, Vol. I, p. 87, fn.

9. Heizer, *Elizabethan California*, p. 13.

10. Bancroft, *History of California*, Vol. I, p. 87 fn.

11. See *American Historical Review* for August, 1874.

12. Verne, *The Exploration of the World*, 1879.

13. Cronise, *The Natural Wealth of California*, pp. 5 and 6.

14. Vol. II, p. 76.

15. Stillman, *Seeking the Golden Fleece*, p. 298.

16. Dating it, that is, from 1798 when Captain James Burney published his *Voyage of Discovery*.

17. Lewis, *George Davidson, Pioneer West Coast Scientist*, p. v.

18. Wagner, *Drake on the Pacific Coast*, published in 1970 after his death in 1959.

19. According to the San Rafael *Independent-Journal* for February 23, 1967. According to the Bakersfield *Californian* for October 7, 1971, their views were shared by Mrs. G. O. Sagen of Bakersfield. For a more detailed report on Mrs. Sagen's opinions on the subject of Drake, see Heizer, *Elizabethan California*, p. 16.

20. Gilliam, *Island in Time*, p. 16.

21. See *Vanguard*, a publication of Portland State University for November 16, 1971, and pamphlet entitled *The Northern Mystery* by Don M. Viles and M. Wayne Jensen, Jr.

22. Vol. 42, No. 3, pp. 251-302.

23. Ballena Press, P. O. Box 711, Ramona, California 92065.

24. Drake Navigators Guild, "Nova Albion Rediscovered," p. 25.

25. Starr, Chickering, and Farquhar are now deceased.

26. Edward P. von der Porten, *Our First New England,* originally published in the U.S. Naval Institute Proceedings for December, 1960. See, also, Gilliam, *Island in Time,* pp. 27–30.

27. Morison, *The European Discovery,* Vol. II, p. 677.

Chapter 7

1. Froude, *History of England from the Fall of Wolsey to the Defeat of the Spanish Armada,* Vol. XI, p. 341.

2. Among the nineteenth-century writers who have given lip service to this legend are Robert Greenhow in *History of Oregon and California,* p. 73, Henry S. Burrage, in *Early English and French Voyages,* p. 84, Edward Everett Hale in Justin Winsor's *Narrative and Critical History of America,* Vol. III, p. 79, and Julian S. Corbett, in *Drake and the Tudor Navy,* Vol. I, p. 426.

3. Greenhow, *History of Oregon and California,* p. 73, fn.

4. Corbett, *Drake and the Tudor Navy,* Vol. I, p. 426.

5. Twiss, *Oregon Territory,* pp. 33–34. Twiss concluded that Hakluyt's own preface warranted the supposition that he prepared the narrative and that there is not the slightest ground for attributing it to Francis Pretty. In accord with the foregoing are Wagner, *Drake's Voyages,* p. 238, and Robertson, *Francis Drake,* at p. 260, Appendix.

6. These are *Harleian MSS No. 540, Folio 93,* and *Harleian MSS No. 280, Folio 23.* A full description of these narratives is given by Wagner, *Drake's Voyage,* pp. 241–245, in which he refers to the second account as the "Anonymous Narrative." That portion of the latter which pertains to the California visit is set forth in Chapter 9.

7. The results of this checklist are found at pages liv to lx of the introduction to the facsimile edition of *The Principall Navigations Voiages and Discoveries of the English Nation,* published in 1965 by the Cambridge Press for the Hakluyt Society and the Peabody Museum of Salem.

8. The one copy which has its leaves pasted in is owned by the Newberry Library in Chicago. An earlier census made from New York in 1940 by Willis Holmes Kerr had shown a total of fifty-five known copies, all but seven of which had the Drake leaves. Thus, in both surveys, approximately 85 percent were found to have the Drake leaves. The Kerr data will be found in his article "The Treatment of Drake's Circumnavigation," *Papers of the Bibliographical Society of America,* Vol. 34, pp. 300–302.

9. This excludes from consideration defective copies and other irrelevant deviations. It also excludes any reference to the collateral problem of the Bowes Leaves discussed by Kerr at pp. 285–288 of his article "The Treatment of Drake's Circumnavigation," or to their discussion at pages liii–lx of the 1965 Hakluyt edition of *The Principall Navigations.*

10. The only known exception to this general rule occurs in one of the copies owned by the Huntington Library in Pasadena, the Drake leaves therein being found between pages 649 and 650.

11. This is a logical deduction from the sequence of signatures; and Wagner in *Drake's Voyages,* p. 238, remarks the fact that the book is bound in "sixes." Certainty on the point is obtainable only through inspection of a copy in its original binding, that is, an inspection that would disclose the size of the sets originally bound into the book.

12. This must be inferred from the apology for its omission in Hakluyt's preface. Note the interesting comments by Taylor in her *Late Tudor and Early Stuart Geography,* pp. 18–19, and in *The Original Writings and Correspondence of the Two Richard Hakluyts,* Vol. 2, p. 407.

13. Careful comparison of "The Famous Voyage" with the sources referred to (note 6) has been made by Wagner in *Drake's Voyages,* pp. 245–285.

14. Taylor, *Late Tudor and Early Stuart Geography,* pp. 18–19, and *The Original Writings and Correspondence of the Two Richard Hakluyts,* Vol. 2, p. 407; Wagner, *Drake's Voyage,* pp. 232 and

238–239; Burrage, *Early English and French Voyages,* p. 427, and Sabin, *Dictionary of Books Relating to America,* Vol. 7, p. 543.

15. For a discussion of the Hondius Broadside, see Chapter 10.

16. For the texts of "The Famous Voyage," see Appendixes A, B, and C.

Chapter 8

1. See discussion of the "Anonymous Narrative," p. 105.

2. Sloane Manuscript No. 61.

3. Wagner, *Drake's Voyage,* p. 288.

4. Robertson, *Francis Drake,* p. 169.

5. Wagner, *Drake's Voyage,* p. 494, n. 58.

6. Ibid., p. 288.

7. Ibid., p. 290.

8. These really represent variances, rather than contradictions, and are probably attributable to editorial changes made by Hakluyt in the course of adapting or editing the Fletcher manuscript to meet his own needs.

9. Bancroft, *History of California,* Vol. I, p. 85.

10. Ibid., p. 91.

11. Robertson, *Francis Drake,* p. 167.

12. Wagner, *Drake's Voyage,* p. 489.

13. For an analysis of defects and shortcomings of "The Famous Voyage," see Appendix H.

14. Aker, "Report of Findings," p. 248.

15. Wagner, *Drake's Voyage,* p. 488.

16. The third part of the volume is itself divided into two sections. The first, of 41 pages, discusses the 1585 voyage. The second discusses the 1595 voyage, including Drake's death, and is entitled *A Full Relation of Another Voyage Made by Sir Francis Drake and others to the West Indies.*

17. See Chapter 10.

Chapter 9

1. Nuttall, *New Light on Drake,* p. 31.

2. Ibid., pp. 50 and 51.

3. Wagner, *Drake's Voyage,* pp. 329–334.

4. This is the *Harleian MSS No. 280, Folio 23,* referred to in Wagner, *Drake's Voyage,* pp. 243–245.

5. See Chapter 5. See, also, Wagner, *Drake's Voyage,* pp. 271, 281.

6. Wagner, *Drake's Voyage,* p. 277.

7. Ibid., pp. 303–304.

8. This is a date which appears in no other account, whether it be through inadvertence or for lack of factual foundation; but see Bishop's article "Drake's Course in the North Pacific," *British Columbia Historical Quarterly,* July, 1939, p. 170.

9. Wagner, *Drake's Voyage,* p. 312.

10. Ibid., pp. 316–323.

11. Ibid., pp. 324–326.

12. Heizer, *Elizabethan California,* pp. 76–77. See also, p. 217.

13. Chapter 10.

14. Ibid.

15. See Appendix E.

16. De Bry probably had no access to original manuscripts, and this account by Camden, the only other early history, was not published until 1615.

17. See Chapter 28, and full text in Appendix G.

18. See Chapter 26, and full text in Appendix F.

Chapter 10

1. *Webster's International Dictonary* tells us that "map" is a term which most commonly applies to a representation of the surface of the earth, or a section of it, whereas "chart" usually refers to a marine map, including any adjacent land surfaces. Under such definitions, "chart" may be a more accurate bit of terminology in reference to our study centering about the California coastline. Nevertheless, we are using the more generic term "map" to apply rather loosely to all of the cartographic material discussed or presented in this chapter.

2. Wagner, *Cartography.*

3. Wagner, *Cartography,* Vol. I, p. 80, and Vol. II, p. 287; also *Drake's Voyage,* p. 405. The map is also discussed in Christy, *The Silver Map of Drake's Voyage,* pp. 29 and 38. The map itself is reproduced in the latter volume at Plate VII; also in *Drake's Voyage,* p. 404, and in Winsor, *Narrative and Critical History of America,* Vol. III, p. 40.

On this map, above California, is the legend: "Hucusque navigationes Lusitanorum 1520. Hispanorum 1540. Anglorum 1580." Wagner suggests that these are approximations of the dates of Portuguese, Spanish, and English voyages into the region of the Pacific northwest coast, the English voyage being that of Drake, of course. The latter is not mentioned by name, nor is there any mention of Nova Albion.

4. Reproduced by Wagner, *Drake's Voyage,* p. 406; by Christy, *Silver Map,* at Plate VIII; and by Winsor, *History of America,* Vol. III, p. 42. Wagner discussed it in *Drake's Voyage,* pp. 407–408, and in his *Cartography,* Vol. I, p. 82 and Vol. II, p. 288. Christy, in his *Silver Map,* at pp. 30, 41, and 42, and Winsor, in *History of America,* Vol. III, pp. 41–42. The 1587 map was published in Paris, but the legend referred to was in Spanish.

5. The date in each instance should have been 1579.

6. For a partial reproduction of this globe as it pertains to California, see Wagner, *Drake's Voyage,* p. 139. For discussion of it, see the same text at pp. 87, 137–138, 142, 310–311, 413–416, and 430; also Wagner, *Cartography,* Vol. I, pp. 83, 84, and 103, and Vol. II, p. 290; also Winsor, *History of America,* Vol. III, p. 212. Hakluyt, in the preface to his 1589 *Principall Navigations,* describes it as "a very large and most exact terrestriall Globe, collected and reformed according to the newest, secretest, and latest discoveries, both Spanish, Portugall, and English, composed by M. Emmerie Mollineux of Lambeth, a rare gentleman in his profession."

7. Reproduced by Wagner, *Drake's Voyage,* p. 415, and discussed at pp. 87, 137, 142, and 416, as well as in Wagner, *Cartography,* Vol. I, p. 83 and Vol. II, p. 292.

8. See discussion by Wagner, *Drake's Voyage,* p. 416.

9. Such a map was that of Molyneux of 1600 pictured herein at p. 131; another was the John Daniel Map of 1637, reproduced in Wagner, *Cartography,* Vol. I, p. 120, discussed therein at pp. 119–121, and described in Vol II, p. 308. The Dutch maps were usually of this type, including those of Hondius and that of Laet, dated 1630. The latter was reproduced in Wagner, *Cartography,* Vol. I, p. 95, and discussed therein at p. 94 as well as in Vol. II, p. 306.

10. For example, the Briggs Map of the North Part of America, appearing in *Purchas, His Pilgrimes,* Vol. III, pp. 852–853, London, 1625. This is reproduced in Wagner, *Cartography,* Vol. I, p. 117, showing a "P⁰ Sʳ Francisco Draco" in 38° N, and has been described in the same volume at p. 114, and in Vol. II, p. 304. A rather similar Dutch map was issued in 1624 by Abraham Goos, as illustrated in Wagner, *Cartography,* Vol. I, p. 115, and discussed therein at p. 114, as well as in Vol. II, p. 304. The French map issued in 1650 by Nicolas Sanson showed a "P. de S. Francisque Drac" below Cape Mendocino. See Wagner, *Cartography,* Vol. I, pp. 130–131, and Vol. II, p. 312.

11. Prime example of such an arrangement is the map issued with Ogilby's *America,* published in 1671. A French version will be found in the DeLisle Map of 1700 which shows "Nouv. Albion," "P. de Drak," in 38° of latitude, together with the Drake sailing track, this map having been reproduced in Wagner, *Cartography,* Vol. I, p. 141, discussed therein at pp. 131 and 140, and listed in Vol. II, p. 322. Another French version is the Pierre Mortier Map of 1705, showing

both "N. Albion" and "Port de Drak," reproduced in Wagner, *Cartography,* Vol. I, p. 161, and discussed in the same volume at p. 160, and in Vol. II, p. 324.

12. This is the name given to this "very rare and interesting medallion" by Miller Christy in his geographical essay *The Silver Map of Drake's Voyage,* p. 1.

13. In his treatise mentioned in the preceding note, Christy contends, at pp. 2, 7, and 37–39, that the medallions were struck in 1581, or at least not later than 1582. Disagreement with this view is expressed by Wagner, *Drake's Voyage,* p. 409.

14. There is no conclusive evidence to establish the place of issuance. The probabilities point toward Holland on the basis of information outlined by Wagner, *Drake's Voyage,* pp. 408–409.

15. The device of showing a globe-girdling sailing track on a world map has also been employed by the designers of the French Drake Map, the Dutch Drake Map, and the Hondius Broadside, which are the next three maps to be treated herein.

16. According to Wagner, *Drake's Voyage,* p. 412, two of the medallions are in the British Museum, and another is in the possession of the Drake family in England. Two are also known to be in the collection of the National Maritime Museum.

17. Christy, *The Silver Map,* p. 6.

18. Ibid., pp. 4–6.

19. Ibid., p. 2. Also, see Davidson, *Francis Drake,* p. 54.

20. Christy, *The Silver Map,* pp. 3 and 4; also, see Davidson, *Francis Drake,* p. 54.

21. For a complete description of the map on the medallion, see Christy, *The Silver Map,* pp. 8–14; see, also, Davidson, *Francis Drake,* pp. 55–63.

22. Errors in the map are discussed by Davidson, *Francis Drake,* pp. 56–58. See comment by Wagner, *Drake's Voyage,* p. 412, and by Christy, *The Silver Map,* p. 21.

23. Robertson, *Francis Drake,* p. 150.

24. Lady Eliott-Drake, *The Family and Heirs,* Vol. I, pp. 73–74; Wagner, *Drake's Voyage,* p. 408.

25. Davidson, *Francis Drake,* p. 71 (see n. 19 above); Christy, *The Silver Map,* pp. 44–45.

26. Many have believed that Hondius was the engraver. For this view, see Christy, *The Silver Map,* p. 39; also Davidson, *Francis Drake,* p. 71. Wagner, *Drake's Voyage,* p. 408, cites authority indicating that the engraver was Michael Mercator. Christy, in *The Silver Map,* pp. 41–45, leans to the theory that the engraving was done at the instance of Hakluyt, possibly by the same man who engraved the "Peter Martyr Map" of 1587, described herein at p. 114.

27. See discussion by Wagner, *Drake's Voyage,* p. 409.

28. Reproduced herein at p. 118. Copies will be found in the appendix to *Sir Francis Drake's Voyage Round the World: Two Contemporary Maps,* published by the British Museum, 1931 edition; also, in Wagner, *Drake's Voyage,* opposite p. 427; in Robertson, *Franicis Drake,* p. 159; and in Nuttall, *New Light on Drake,* opposite p. lvi of the introduction.

29. This was published in Paris in 1641 under the name *Le Voyage Curieux faict autour du Monde par Francois Drach,* the original edition having been issued in 1913 under a slightly different title. For details, see Wagner, *Drake's Voyage,* p. 430.

30. Wagner, *Drake's Voyage,* p. 432; also the edition of the British Museum publication mentioned in n. 28 above, pp. 8 and 9. It is not clear whether the name was "van Sijpe" or "van Sype."

31. Wagner, *Drake's Voyage,* p. 427.

32. Ibid.

33. The significance of these boundary lines is uncertain. For a discussion, see Nuttall, *New Light on Drake,* pp. lv and lvi of the introduction, also Robertson, *Francis Drake,* p. 158, and Wagner, *Drake's Voyage,* pp. 427–430.

34. Nuttall, *New Light on Drake,* p. lv of the introduction, see, also, Wagner, *Drake's Voyage,* p. 427, and p. 9 of the British Museum publication mentioned in n. 28, above.

35. This is the British·Museum publication mentioned in n. 28 above.

36. See pp. 7-8 of the British Museum publication mentioned in n. 28 above.

37. Wagner, *Drake's Voyage,* p. 434; see, also, his *Cartography,* Vol. I, p. 88, and Vol. II, p. 310.

38. Wagner gives this point a rather full treatment in *Drake's Voyage*, pp. 431–434.

39. See authorities cited in n. 34, above.

40. See discussion in the British Museum publication mentioned in n. 28 above, at p. 9. See also, Wagner, *Drake's Voyage*, p. 430, and Robertson, *Francis Drake*, p. 158.

41. See discussion in the British Museum publication mentioned in n. 28 above, p. 8.

42. See reproduction at p. 120 herein. Reproduced also in Wagner, *Drake's Voyage*, p. 425, and discussed at pp. 137 and 424–426; also mentioned in Robertson, *Francis Drake*, p. 158, and in the British Museum publication described in n. 28, p. 9. It is not listed or mentioned in Wagner, *Cartography*.

43. Wagner, *Drake's Voyage*, p. 424.

44. Robertson, *Francis Drake*, p. 158; also, the British Museum publication mentioned in n. 28 above, p. 9.

45. See the British Museum publication mentioned in n. 28 above, p. 9.

46. Ibid. Note also, Wagner's comment at p. 426 in *Drake's Voyage*.

47. Ibid., p. 424.

48. Ibid.

49. Ibid., p. 426.

50. Ibid.

51. See endpapers and page 122 for reproductions of this map, which was entitled "Vera Totius Expeditionis Nauticae Descriptio D. Franc. Draci qui 5. navibus probe instructis, ex Anglis solvens 13 Decembris anno 1577. terrarum orbis ambitus circum navigans, unica tantum navi, ingenti cum gloria, ceteris partim flammis, partim fluctibus correptis, in Angliam redijt 27 Septembris 1580."

52. In 1928, another copy, but without the printed text, came into the possession of the Royal Geographical Society of London. Reproductions of the map have appeared in the 1854 edition of *The World Encompassed* published by the Hakluyt Society; in Wagner, *Drake's Voyage*, facing page 417; in the appendix to *Sir Francis Drake's Voyage Round the World: Two Contemporary Maps*, published by the British Museum; and as front and rear endpapers of Benson, *Sir Francis Drake*. In recent years two specimens of the original map came into the possession of Robert H. Power, of the Nut Tree, California, one of which he presented in 1977 to the Bancroft Library, Berkeley.

53. See the text of the British Museum publication mentioned in the previous note, p. 11. Wagner, at p. 417 of *Drake's Voyage*, points out that the map on the Drake portrait (in the Broadside text) erroneously shows the Cavendish circumnavigation route rather than that of Drake, and he concludes for this and other reasons that the map and text were not simultaneously issued.

54. Wagner, *Drake's Voyage*, p. 417. See also the text of the British Museum publication mentioned in n. 52 above, p. 11.

55. The portrait shows a different date of return to England than does the title of the map, a curious error showing that the map and the small one on Drake's portrait were not engraved by the same person. See Wagner, *Drake's Voyage*, p. 417.

56. The portrait, according to the text of the British Museum publication mentioned in note 52 above, is a reversed and slightly reduced copy of an engraving signed by Hondius and derived from an engraving by Thomas de Leu after the painting by Jean Rabel.

57. The British Museum publication mentioned in note 52 above, p. 10, suggests a publication date of 1590. Davidson, *Identification*, pp. 38 and 41, suggests 1595. Wagner stated that he was unable to find confirmation of such dates, commenting on this fact both in *Drake's Voyage*, p. 417, and in *Cartography*, Vol. I, p. 87. However, in the last-mentioned volume at the same page, he stated that the copy of the map obtained by the Royal Geographical Society in 1928 has the portraits of Drake and Cavendish pasted on the back marked "fecit Londini" and signed by Hondius. If this means anything, it could indicate that the map was published in London before 1595, probably sometime between 1590 and 1593 while Hondius was still living in that city.

58. Wagner, *Drake's Voyage*, p. 417.

59. Something of the life of Hondius will be found in Wagner, *Cartography,* Vol. I, pp. 103–112.

60. The map is generally supposed to have been issued in Amsterdam, but that fact has never been established. See note 57, above, concerning London as a possible place of publication.

61. About this dotted line, Wagner says in *Drake's Voyage,* pp. 418–419: "The dotted line showing his route continues to about 48°.These dots are part of the engraving and are much more distinct on the map in the British Museum than on that belonging to the Royal Geographical Society. On the one in the British Museum there is a blur above the star as if some one had tried to remove the dots.As the dotted line stands, it corresponds to the account given in *The World Encompassed,* whereas if it had stopped at the star in 42°, it would correspond to that in the original version of "The Famous Voyage." On the map as reproduced in 1854 by the Hakluyt Society in its edition of the *The World Encompassed,* the dotted line ends at the star, there being no appearance of any extension beyond. As a result of this omission, Davidson was misled into basing on this map his principal argument that Drake had not gone up to 48°. In this regard, Wagner refers to the argument advanced by Davidson in *Francis Drake,* pp. 90–91.

62. See the text of the British Museum publication referred to in note 52 above, p. 10.

63. The insets on each of the two lower corners of the map are very similar to those on the French Drake Map and the Dutch Drake Map, reproduced herein respectively at page 118 and page 120.

64. Wagner, *Cartography,* Vol II, pp. 296–312.

65. Reproduced in Wagner, *Cartography,* Vol. I, p. 105, and in *Drake's Voyage,* opposite p. 424. Discussed in the latter volume at p. 423, and in *Cartography,* Vol. I, p. 104, and Vol. II, p. 296.

66. Wagner, *Cartography,* Vol. I, p. 104, According to Vol. II, p. 296 of the same work, others are (or were) in the possession of Mrs. James Flood, of San Francisco, and of Count Rocco Gianinni, of Lucca, Italy.

67. Wagner, *Cartography,* Vol. I, pp. 109–110, and Vol. II, pp. 300, 302, and 305.

68. Davidson, *Identification,* pp. 41–42.

69. Wagner, *Cartography,* Vol. I, p. 110, and Vol. II, p. 305.

70. See Plate No. 11 in Davidson, *Identification;* also Robertson, *Francis Drake,* p. 103.

71. I found a copy of this map in Paris. Although not listed among the maps in Wagner, *Cartography,* it corresponds substantially to Map No. 314 on p. 307 of Vol. II of that work.

72. As to the legend that California was an island, see Wagner, *Cartography,* Vol. I, pp. 114–117, 125–129, and particularly 144–147.

73.See Chapter 27.

74. Wagner, *Cartography,* Vol. II, p. 311. Reproduced by Wagner, *Drake's Voyage,* page 435; by Davidson, *Identification,* Plate 13; by Bancroft, *History of California,* p. 87; and by Winsor, *Narrative and Critical History of America,* Vol. III, p. 78. For a detailed description of this map, see Davidson, *Identification,* pp. 48–51.

75. The *Arcano del Mare* was first published in 1630, in the opinion of J. G. Kohl (see Wagner, *Cartography,* Vol. I, p. 122). Kohl, a German librarian and scholar of the middle nineteenth century, was given a congressional appropriation to enable him to make copies of his maps for the United States government. The results of that work are in the Library of Congress. He also left a memoir with maps on the discovery of the western coast of America, now in the library of the American Antiquarian Society (see Winsor, *Narrative and Critical History of America,* Vol. III, p. 209).

76. See Appendix E.

77. Listed and fully described in Wagner, *Cartography,* Vol. II, pp. 310–311; also described in Davidson, *Identification,* p. 48.

78. Reproduced by Davidson, *Identification,* as Plate 12; by Robertson, *Francis Drake,* p. 199; by Bancroft, *History of California,* Vol. I, p. 88; and by Winsor, *Narrative and Critical History of America,* Vol. III, p. 77.

79. The relationship of this chart to maps showing the results of the Vizcaino expedition of 1602–1603 is discussed at length in Wagner, *Cartography,* Vol. I, pp. 119–121, and Vol. II, pp. 310–311. The subject has also been treated by Wagner, *Drake's Voyage,* pp. 436–437, and by Davidson, *Identification,* p. 48.

80. Davidson, *Identification,* p. 45.

81. Ibid.

82. See Appendix E.

83. Davidson, *Identification,* p. 47.

84. Ibid., pp. 42–44. See, also, Chart 7 of the foregoing.

85. Ibid., p. 43.

86.Reproduced by Wagner in *Drake's Voyage* p. 420, and discussed therein at p. 421. Also described in Wagner, *Cartography,* Vol. II, p. 294.

87. Wagner, *Drake's Voyage,* p. 421.

88. Wagner, *Cartography,* Vol. I, p. 133, and Vol. II, p. 316.

89. The title page also carried the interesting information that the books were "Printed by the Author and are to be had at his House in White Friars."

90. Wagner, *Cartography,* Vol. II, p. 316, with discussion of the similarity of both the text and map to those appearing in the Dutch text on America, also published in 1671, by Arnold Montanus.

91. The exact name given in the dedicatory inscription is Anthonio D° Ashley, Baroni Athley de Wimburne.

92. The seventeenth-century belief in California's insularity has been discussed by Wagner in *Cartography,* Vol. I, pp. 114–117, 125–129, and particularly 144–147.

93. Described by Wagner in *Cartography,* Vol. II, p. 297. Reproductions of it will be found in Vol. I of the same work, opposite p. 86; in Wagner, *Drake's Voyage,* opposite p. 422; in Robertson, *Francis Drake,* p. 143; and in Winsor, *Narrative and Critical History of America,* Vol. III, p. 80.

94. Quaritch was a noted London bookseller in the nineteenth century. His theory as to the *Twelfth Night* map was set forth in his 1879 catalogue, No. 321, Book No. 11919. As usual, there was no unanimity of opinion on the subject. Henry Stevens (History Collections, i. 200) believed that Shakespeare's reference was to the "curious little round-face shaped map" in Wytfliet's *Ptolemaeum Augmentum* of 1597. The latter is undoubtedly one of those listed by Wagner in *Cartography,* Vol. II, pp. 292–293.

95. See discussion of the Molyneux Map of 1600 in Winsor, *Narrative and Critical History of America,* Vol. III, p. 217.

96. Ibid. See, also, Twiss, *The Oregon Territory,* p. 45.

97. See discussion in this chapter at page 114.

98. Robertson, *Francis Drake,* p. 242. See also, Jonathan Swift, *Gulliver's Travels,* p. 72 (1977 text based on 1735 edition).

Chapter 11

1. Drake had with him during his California visit four blacks, three men and a woman. See Chapter 5, pp. 52–54.

2. Bancroft, *History of California,* Vol. I, pp. 81–94.

3. "The Francis Drake Controversy," by J. S. Holliday, director of the California Historical Society, in the Society's *Quarterly,* Vol. LIII, p. 200 (1974).

4. Trumbull, "Man with a Mission: Where Did Drake Land?" *San Francisco Chronicle,* June 19, 1959.

5. The twenty tenets are listed in Appendix I.

Chapter 12

1. See Chapter 2, p. 19.

2. Ibid.

3. Wagner, *Drake's Voyage,* p. 4, and map following p. 38.

4. The most significant statement in any contemporary account in reference to the North-west Passage is set forth in *The World Encompassed* as follows:

> The time of the yeare now drew on wherein we must attempt, or of necessitie wholly give over that action, which chiefly our Generall had determined, namely, the discovery of what passage there was to be found about the Northerne parts of America, from the South Sea, into our owne Ocean (which being once discovered and made known to be navigable, we should not onely do our country a good and notable service, but we also ourselves should have a nearer cut and passage home; where otherwise, we were to make a very long and tedious voyage of it, which would hardly agree with our good liking, we having been so long from home already, and so much of our strength separated from us), which could not all be done if the opportunity of time were now neglected: we therefore all of us willingly harkened and consented to our Generalls advice, which was, first to seek out some conve-nient place wherein to trimme our ship, and store ourselves with wood and water and other provisions as we could get, and thenceforward to hasten on our intended journey for the discovery of the said passage, through which we might with joy returne to our longed homes.

5. The term "Spanish course" was used in "The Famous Voyage" to refer to the sailing routes which the Spaniards had discovered in the Pacific, the exact language being: "Upon this resolution, he began to thinke of his best way to the MOLUCCAS, and finding himselfe where he nowe was becalmed, he sawe, that of necessitie he must be forced to take a Spanish course, namely to sail somewhat Northerly to get a winde."

6. Davidson, *Identification,* p. 10.

7. Aker, "Report of Findings," pp. 257–259.

8. Ibid., p. 261.

9. Ibid., p. 264.

10. A latitude taken at sea, that is, by dead reckoning.

11. Aker, "Report of Findings," pp. 227, 257.

12. See Chapter 6, p. 70.

13. Ibid., p. 78.

14. Morison, *The European Discovery of America,* Vol. 2, p. 676.

15. See discussion of these maps in Chapter 10.

16. Aker, "Report of Findings," p. 108.

17. This would seem to confirm the latitudes given by *The World Encompassed* for entry into the bay and the anchorage.

Chapter 13

1. For example, *The World Encompassed* as well as John Drake, in both his depositions, stated that the most northerly latitude reached was 48°. This was at variance with the latitudes given by Hakluyt of 42° and finally 43°.

2. Chapter 15, pp. 172–176.

3. Chapter 8, p. 99.

4. Chapter 8, pp. 98, 100.

5. This subject is discussed in some detail in Appendix H.

6. Samuel Johnson, in his 1741 biography of Drake, placed the latter "in 38° and his anchorage in 38° 30′," cited in Davidson, *Francis Drake,* p. 27. Other biographers placing the anchorage at 38° 30′ included Corbett in 1898 (Vol. I, p. 307) Mason in 1941, p. 178, and Thomson in 1972, p. 141, all undoubtedly relying on *The World Encompassed.*

7. Referring to the 1589 edition, ultimately corrected in one of the two 1600 edition ac-counts.

8. Aker, "Report of Findings," p. 449.

9. The series of arguments and counterarguments that follows is presented for the purpose of providing a broader and more balanced perspective on the subject of anchorage latitude than could be made available within the limits of the 1974 debate format. It serves also to support other aims of the chapter as a whole, that is, to demonstrate not only that this is a problem to which there can be two viable approaches, but also, conforming to the request of Tenet 2, that they may be capable of being reconciled with each other. There is no intent to quarrel or take issue with, much less to denigrate, the statements or theories of any of the distinguished debate participants. It should not be assumed that any of the views expressed necessarily represents or reflects the opinion of the author.

10. Chapter 9, p. 105.

11. Aker, "Report of Findings," p. 223.

12. Eighty-five percent of all presently known copies of the 1589 Hakluyt contain the so-called "Drake leaves" in permanently bound form. See Chapter 7, pp. 88, 90.

13. See discussion of Hakluyt errors and omissions in Appendix H.

14. Ibid.

15. Aker, "Report of Findings," p. 218.

16. Chapter 10, p. 105.

17. Aker, "Report of Findings," pp. 227 and 257.

18. Ibid., pp. 226–227.

19. Ibid., p. 227.

20. Wagner, *Drake's Voyages,* p. 161. But see Wagner, *Cartography,* Vol. I, p. 117, which reproduces the Purchas map of 1625 showing Pº Sʳ Francisco Draco in 38° rather than 38½°.

Chapter 14

1. "Punta de barrancas blancas" (Promontory of the White Cliffs) appears on the Vizcaino chart of his anchorage at "Puerto de los Reyes" in 1603. See Oko, "Francis Drake," *California Historical Society Quarterly,* Vol. XLIII, No. 2, June, 1964, pp. 137 and 153.

2. This phrase was used by the Guild to describe the entry of the *Golden Hind* into Drake's Bay. It is based upon the words of Hakluyt "it pleased God to send us into a faire and good Baye, with a good winde to enter the same."

3. In honor of Daniel Bernoulli (1700–1782), author of *Hydrodynamia* (1738), which dealt with the motion of fluids and gases. *Encyclopedia Britannica,* III, 458 (1961).

4. Sea birds congregated in immense numbers on every islet and cliff along the coast inaccessible to their enemies. The whiteness of the cliffs will decrease or disappear with the extermination of the birds, or when they are driven to more remote shores. Stillman, *Seeking the Golden Fleece,* p. 289.

5. White cliffs are a marked feature of the California coast. Gold Bluffs immediately north of Trinidad are the most conspicuous "white cliffs" along the entire coast. There are also white cliffs at Bodega Bay, and Dwinelle advanced this as an argument in support of his landing-site theory. Alcatraz was called White Island in the sailing directions used by many in entering the Bay in 1849.

6. Named "Punta del cantel blanco" (Point of the Steep White Rock) by the early Spanish explorers.

7. Power, "Drake's Landing in California," *California Historical Quarterly,* Vol. LII, p. 116, 1973.

Chapter 15

1. Aker, "Report of Findings," p. 269.

2. The catalogue entry for "The Course" was as follows: "The Voyage and course which Sir Francis Drake held from the haven of Guatulco, on the backside of Nueua Espanna, to the

Northwest of California, as far as 43 degrees, & from thence backe againe to 38 degrees, where in a very good harbour he graved his shippe, entrenched himselfe on land, called the countrey by the name of Noua Albion, and took possession thereof on the behalfe of her Maiestie."

3. The contemporary lexicon referred to was *Seaman's Dictionary* by Sir Henry Mainwaring, published in 1623.

4. The comment of the Guild on the suitability of the Bolinas Lagoon for careenage purposes was as follows: "Channel depths are governed by the lagoon's tidal prism, the volume of water enclosed between planes of mean higher high water and mean lower low water, which is the average volume of water that flows in and out during the tidal cycle. A constant ratio exists between the cross-sectional area of the entrance and the volume of the tidal prism. Because of geographical configuration, Bolinas Lagoon was not likely to have ever had a significantly greater tidal prism, despite the adverse effects [mining, lumbering, farming operations] postulated by Dr. Neasham, which cannot be verified."

5. See Chapter 2.

6. Heizer, *Elizabethan California*, p. 9. As he viewed the situation: "Drake had little to fear by deciding to make a stopover and get his ship ready for the long voyage home. He must have been aware of how few warships the Spaniards had in the Pacific, he knew from experience what poor gunners they were, he was fully aware that he was in an empty ocean and on a coast unknown to his enemies, and he also knew that they did not know his plans. Everything considered, Drake in 1579 had every reason to believe that the Spanish either would not follow him, or if they did, they were not likely to find him. Drake's account gives no hint that he anticipated pursuit and discovery while he was re-fitting his ship, and in part this may be due to his being in a well-hidden spot where a cruising ship could not possibly see him."

Chapter 16

1. Second edition, p. 73.

2. Vol. XV, p. 431, under the heading of "Sir Francis Drake." Cited by Davidson, *Francis Drake*, 1908, pp. 97 and 104.

3. Davidson, *Identification*, p. 13, n. 33.

4. Referred to by Davidson, *Francis Drake*, pp. 104–105.

5. McAdie, "Nova Albion—1579," p. 11.

6. Chapman, *A History of California*, p. 103.

7. Holmes, *New Spain to the Californias by Sea*, p. 166.

8. Robertson, *Francis Drake*, p. 232.

9. Power, "Drake's Landing in California," p. 117.

10. Wagner, *Drake's Voyage*, p. 488.

11. Thomas, "Drake at Olompali," p. 41, citing "What's Happening to Our Climate?" by Samuel W. Matthews.

12. Dyson, *The World of Ice*, p. 179.

13. Ibid., pp. 170–171.

14. Aker, "Report of Findings," p. 305.

15. McAdie, "Nova Albion—1579," p. 11.

Chapter 17

1. "The Famous Voyage" account of the inland visit was much shorter than that of *The World Encompassed*. In respect to the native habitations, *The World Encompassed* said: "Their houses were all such as we have formerly described, and being many of them in one place, made seuerall villages here and there." Power interpreted this to mean "a good-sized Indian village in each valley from San Rafael north."

2. See Chapter 19.

Chapter 18

1. See Harrington, "Tobacco among the Karuk Indians," Bureau of American Ethnology, Bull. 94 (1932), pp. 17–18, 40.
2. Heizer, *Elizabethan California*, p. 63.
3. Wagner, *Drake's Voyage*, p. 492, n. '26.
4. Kroeber, *Handbook of the Indians of California*, p. 277.
5. Heizer, *Elizabethan California*, p. 63.
6. Aker, "Report of Findings," pp. 318–319.
7. In each of his three versions of the Nova Albion visit, Hakluyt not only spelled "Tabacco," instead of "Tobacco," but he printed it in different type in each instance.
8. Wagner, *Drake's Voyage*, p. 492, n. 26.
9. Hale, article in Winsor, *Narrative and Critical History of America*, Vol. III, p. 69, n. 2.
10. Aker, "Report of Findings," p. 318. But the English would not necessarily have seen it smoked under the conditions of their meetings with the Indians.
11. See Chapter 19.

Chapter 19

1. According to Power, the Barbary cony is more closely related to the rhinoceros than it is to any member of the rodent family. It has small hoofed feet, no tail, and no oral pouches, but its over-all color and body form are very similar to the California ground squirrel. Scientists presume that this look-alike phenomenon is due to environmental adaptation to similar living conditions in rocks and grassland.
2. Stillman, *Seeking the Golden Fleece*, pp. 295–297.
3. Eschscholtz, *Zoologischer Atlas*.
4. Stillman, *Seeking the Golden Fleece*, p. 297.
5. Beechey, *Narrative of a Voyage to the Pacific*, p. 390.
6. Robertson, *Francis Drake*, pp. 185–186.
7. Wagner, *Drake's Voyage*, p. 492, n. 42.
8. Aker, "Report of Findings," p. 310.
9. North of San Rafael.

Chapter 20

1. Barrett, "The Ethnogeography of the Pomo," and especially n. 7 beginning on p. 36. The historical material which he quoted on Nova Albion was taken from a composite account based on both "The Famous Voyage" and *The World Encompassed* entitled "Early English Voyages to the Pacific Coast of America."
2. Edition of 1953, pp. 275–278. At p. 273 of his text, Kroeber said: "Point Reyes peninsula seems to have been uninhabited." This statement was not true of the sixteenth century, in view of the experience of Cermeño, and the archaeological findings of Heizer and others.
3. See Chapter 6 in reference to Heizer and his contributions to the literature on Drake in California.
4. Heizer, *Elizabethan California*.
5. Ibid., p. 31. See also Stanger and Brown, *Who Discovered the Golden Gate?* p. 163.
6. Heizer, *Elizabethan California*, p. 22.
7. Pp. 350–351.
8. Forbes, *California: A History of Upper and Lower California*, p. 5.
9. Davidson, *Francis Drake*, p. 31.
10. Wagner, *Drake's Voyage*, p. 147.
11. Ibid., p. 495, n. 67.

12. Wilson, *The World Encompassed,* p. 159.

13. In the next sentence, after that describing the placing of the crown on Drake's head, *The World Encompassed* explained the "song and dance" of the natives by saying that "they were not only visited of the gods (for they still judged us to be), but the great and chiefe God was now become their God, their king and patron, and themselves were the onely happie and blessed people in the world."

14. See Power's statement as set forth at p. 220.

15. A major miracle would be required in view of the fact that the Indians had no means of written communication.

16. From an unpublished treatise entitled "Drake at Olompali," by Dr. Robert C. Thomas, of San Francisco, a descendent of Coast Miwok chiefs Marin and Ynitia.

17. Thomas,"Drake at Olompali," p.65. Presumably Drake's Estero proponents would, in the light of this statement, feel that the natives followed a different pattern of behavior when Cermeño appeared because they had learned from the Drake experience that such visitors were neither evil spirits nor gods, but simply another tribe of human beings invading their territory.

18. Thomas, "Drake at Olompali," p. 64.

Chapter 21

1. Deposition of John Drake reported in Nuttall, *New Light on Drake,* p. 51; also see p. 104.

2. Heizer, "Archaeological Evidence of Sebastian Rodriguez Cermeño's California Visit in 1595."

3. Von der Porten, *Drake-Cermeño.* At p. 65, the author said: "Despite searches, no group of sixteenth-century artifacts has been found elsewhere," i.e., other than in the Drake's Bay area.

4. Heizer, *Elizabethan California,* pp. 18–19. For a report on the earlier excavations, see "Nova Albion Rediscovered," pp. 21–31. See, also *Drake-Cermeño,* by Von der Porten, pp. 62–64, indicating possible, but not positive, Drake findings.

5. Heizer, *Elizabethan California,* p. 19.

6. *San Francisco Chronicle,* Nov. 9, 1974.

7. North served for many years as port collector for San Francisco.

8. *San Rafael Independent* for Jan. 10, 1974.

9. *San Francisco Chronicle* for April 5, 1955.

10. Of interest from both a historical and an archaeological standpoint is the recent discovery of the remains of a small town established within the Straits of Magellan as a defense against Drake. This was the little settlement of Rey don Felipe, also known as Port Famine, founded in 1584, and completely abandoned by 1590. Its virtually unmarked site was rediscovered in 1955, despite near eradication through predatory activities of Indians. Archaeological excavations between 1969 and 1971 revealed the stone foundations of a chapel, several large iron nails, pieces of lead shot, and many fragments of pottery, in addition to 11 skeletons. *See* Omar R. Ortiz, "A Sixteenth Century Hispanic Harbor in the Strait of Magellan, South America." *Nautical Archaeology,* 5.2, 1976, pp. 176–179.

Those who doubt a landing by Sir Francis at Drake's Bay point to the Port Famine findings as an indication of what, after the lapse of an equal period of time, the Guild should have discovered in their search for a fort at Drake's Estero, instead of the essentially negative discovery of a few boulders in a questionable pattern. The Guild, on the other hand, would deny the validity of any comparison between the two situations on grounds that Port Famine was an established settlement for several years, rather than a temporary encampment of only a few weeks' duration; also because of a lack of data as to type of ground involved and distance of structures from the water, as well as differing weather and tidal conditions, not to mention the fact that discovery of the Magellan site was facilitated by the visibility of a portion of the chapel's walls still standing above ground.

11. Nuttall, *New Light on Drake,* p. 51; also, p. 104 above.

12. Drake had done this twice earlier in the voyage. *See* Aker, "Report of Findings," p. 330.

Chapter 22

1. See Chapter 3.
2. See Appendixes A, B, and D.
3. Chapter 9, p. 105.
4. *California Historical Society Quarterly,* Vol. XVI, pp. 10–11, 1937.
5. Heizer, *Elizabethan California,* p. 18.
6. *The Plate of Brass,* special publication No. 25 of the California Historical Society, 1953, pp. 48–64.
7. *California Historical Society Quarterly,* Vol. XVI, pp. 271–274, 1937.
8. Ibid., pp. 275–281.
9. *Saturday Evening Post,* April 3, 1943, pp. 32–36.
10. These other experts included Professor Vincent T. Harlow, of Oxford University, Professor Earle R. Caley, of the Frick Chemical Laboratory, Princeton University, and the Deputy Keeper of Manuscripts at the British Museum, Dr. Robin Flower.
11. There is evidence to indicate that Allen Chickering found Caldeira to be evasive, and that he did not believe Caldeira's story, Chickering having vouchsafed that conclusion to Heizer in the course of conversations on several occasions. For an up-to-date review of the Caldeira matter, see article by Doerr and Dunn entitled "Drake's California Harbor: Another Look at William Caldeira's Story" in *Terrae Incognitae,* Vol. IX, pp.49–59, 1977. The Caldeira find was but the first of a series of "Drake" plates "found" at various places in California, as reported by Heizer in *Elizabethen California,* pp. 34–40. For recent reports of such finds in the Bolinas area, see page 259 of this chapter and story in the *San Rafael Independent-Journal* for Sept. 25, 1978 captioned "A New Twist in Drake Tale."
12. Morison, *The European Discovery of America,* Vol. II, p. 680. So far as his California visit is concerned, Admiral Morison's research was rather superficial and his narrative concerning it contains a number of inaccuracies, as well as conclusions not altogether justified by the information available to him.
13. Wagner, *Drake on the Pacific Coast,* pp. 6–7 and 17–18.
14. The commission was appointed by Governor Reagan in 1972 and includes among its membership of twenty-four Drake scholars Power, Aker, and Neasham.
15. Hart, *The Plate of Brass Reexamined,* 1977, pp. 15–16.
16. Ibid., pp. 12–14.
17. Ibid., pp. 18, 37.
18. Ibid., pp. 21–22, 69 and 75.
19. Michel and Asaro, *Chemical Study of the Plate of Brass,* p. 23.
20. Hart, *The Plate of Brass Reexaamined,* 1977, p. 25.
21. Ibid., p. 25.
22. Ibid.
23. Power, "A Plate of Brass by Me—C. G. Francis Drake."
24. Hart, *The Plate of Brass Reexamined,* 1977, p. 24.
25. Farquhar, "Drake in California," *California Historical Society Quarterly,* Vol. XXXVI, p. 28, 1957.
26. Hart, *The Plate of Brass Reexamined,* 1977, p. 25.

Chapter 23

1. Wagner, *Drake's Voyage,* p. 166.
2. Ibid.
3. Gleason, *The Islands and Ports of California,* p. 56.
4. Wagner shared with a number of other Drakophiles the impression or illusion that information appearing in *The World Encompassed,* but not in "The Famous Voyage," must represent additions to the original source, despite the fact that everything we know about

Hakluyt and his need to condense Fletcher's narrative into his available space indicates that he omitted anything which to him did not seem essential.

5. Wagner, *Drake's Voyage*, p. 164.

6. Ibid., p. 167.

7. Ibid.

8. Davidson, *Identification*, p. 57.

9. Robertson, *Francis Drake*, p. 219.

10. Aker, "Report of Findings," pp. 328 and 329.

11. The Guild inadvertently used the dates "August 23" and "August 24," instead of "July 23" and "July 24."

12. See discussion of Hakluyt's errors and omission in Appendix H.

13. Nuttall, *New Light on Drake*, p. 50, and at p. 104 above.

Chapter 24

1. Bancroft, *History of California*, Vol. I, pp. 81–94.

2. Ibid., pp. 88–89, footnotes.

3. Ibid., giving the page numbers in *Bryant's History* dealing with the Hondius map at pp. 570–577. Dwinelle's review was published in the *San Francisco Bulletin,* October 5, 1878.

4. Vol. III, p. 80.

5. Ibid.

6. Vol. III, p. 75.

7. Ibid., p. 78.

8. Vol. I, p. 88.

9. Ibid., p. 89.

10. Ibid., p. 94.

11. Davidson, *Identification*, p. 38.

12. Ibid.

13. Ibid., p. 39.

14. Ibid.

15. Wagner, *Drake's Voyage*, p. 134.

16. Ibid., p. 164.

17. Ibid., p. 496. Interestingly, Wagner's characterization of Davidson was equally applicable to himself. To his dying day (in 1957), Wagner insisted that Drake's anchorage was in Trinidad Bay, as indicated by his posthumous treatise, *Drake on the Pacific Coast,* published in 1970.

18. Robertson, *Francis Drake*, p. 210.

19. Ibid., p. 205.

20. Ibid., p. 235.

21. Ibid., p. 205.

22. Ibid., p. 206.

23. Sprent, *Sir Francis Drake's Voyage Round the World,* pp. 10–11.

24. Ibid., p. 10.

25. Ibid.

26. Heizer, *Elizabethan California,* p. 6.

27. Heizer, *Elizabethan California,* p. 25.

28. Ibid.

29. Gilliam, *Island in Time,* p. 16.

30. Ibid., pp. 16, 25.

31. Thomas, "Drake at Olompali," pp. 31–34.

32. Aker, "Report of Findings," p. 186.

33. The portions of Aker's book, "Report of Findings," dealing with this subject include pp. 102–121, "The Hondius Broadside," pp. 186–209, "The Message of the Insets," pp. 210–217, "The Portus Novae Albionis," and pp. 274–291, covering "Identification of the Portus Novae Albionis" and "The Careening Basin."

34. Davidson, on the other hand, had no peer in his knowledge of sailing conditions and the California coast.

35. Aker, "Report of Findings," p. 212.

36. Ibid., p. 213.

37. Ibid., p. 211.

38. Ibid., p. 187.

39. Ibid., p. 192.

40. Ibid., p. 194.

41. Ibid., p. 207.

42. Ibid., p. 211.

43. Ibid., p. 192.

44. Ibid., p. 209.

45. The Broadside did contain one interesting deviation from the general pattern. It appears to show Drake's track as having originally been engraved at 48° or higher, presumably in conformity with such earlier charts as the Silver Map and the Molyneaux Globe, as well as the Fletcher account, since that was the most northerly latitude reached according to *The World Encompassed*. It was then corrected to extend only to a star engraved at about 43°, possibly representing a compromise between the 44° of the French Drake map and the 42° reported by Hakluyt in his 1589 edition.

46. Story in the *Redwood City Tribune*, April 3, 1971, quoting Power to this effect.

47. See *California Historical Quarterly*, Vol. LII, p. 111, 1973.

48. Davidson, *Sir Francis Drake*, p. 91. Incidentally, Hale in Winsor, *Narrative and Critical History of America*, Vol. III, p. 80, states that Kohl (who prepared the Catalog of Maps in Hakluyt) thought that "Hondius may have used Drake's own charts in this little marginal sketch."

49. Bancroft, *History of California*, Vol. I, p. 89.

50. Wagner, *Drake's Voyage*, p. 154.

51. Ibid., p. 291.

52. Aker, "Report of Findings," p. 109.

53. Wagner, *Drake's Voyage*, p. 154.

54. Hale in Winsor, *Narrative and Critical History of America*, Vol. III, p. 75.

55. Bancroft, *History of California*, Vol. I, p. 89.

56. Heizer, *Elizabethan California*, p. 6.

57. Robertson, *Francis Drake*, p. 207.

58. See article in the *San Francisco Bulletin* by John W. Dwinelle, October 5, 1878. The last two sentences quoted may also be found in the footnote on p. 89 of Bancroft, *History of California*, Vol. I.

59. Wagner, *Drake's Voyage*, p. 154.

60. Aker, "Report of Findings," p. 212.

61. Robertson, *Francis Drake*, pp. 192, 194.

62. Aker, "Report of Findings," pp. 150–151. See, also, Wagner, *Drake's Voyage*, pp. 245, 288.

63. Aker, "Report of Findings," p. 151.

64. See Dwinelle's statement, quoted at p. 289.

65. Wagner, *Drake's Voyage*. For examples of Fletcher's maps and drawings, see pp. 43, 45–47, 52 and 54.

66. Ibid., p. 58.

67. During 1584–1593, according to Aker, "Report of Findings," pp. 104, 107.

68. Aker, "Report of Findings," p. 211.

69. Pike, "The Historiography of the Drake Controversy," *California Historical Quarterly*, Vol. LII, p. 128, 1973.

70. "Pirate's Cove" in *True West Magazine*, December, 1967, pp. 6 and 48.

71. Aker, "Report of Findings," p. 213.

72. Robertson, *Francis Drake*, p. 235.

73. *California Historical Quarterly*, Fall, 1974, p. 251.

74. *California Historical Quarterly*, Vol. LIII, pp. 253–255, 258, 1974. See, also, Power, *A Study of Two Historic Maps*, June 1, 1978, which sets forth a proportional tangent comparison between the "Portus Novae Albionis" and an 1856 United States Coast Survey map of northern San Francisco Bay. Revised edition issued September, 1978.

Chapter 25

1. Montanus, p. 213.

2. Vol. LII, pp. 117–119, 1973.

3. Ogilby, *America*, p. 303.

4. Ibid.

5. This error in the number of men is traceable to De Bry's *Americae Pars VIII*, and particularly to the text accompanying Illustration No. 5 of the Appendix of that book.

6. The maximum number of members of the Coast Miwok tribe, according to Kroeber, was 1500.

7. Heizer, *Elizabethan California*, p. 27.

8. The quotation is from Power, "Drake's Landing in California," *California Historical Quarterly*, Vol. LIII, p. 122, 1973. Power was quoting a statement by Alex Cumming, curator of Buckland Abbey, Drake's ancestral home.

9. Wagner, *Cartography*, Vol. II, p. 316, indicated a belief that there was some relationship between the Montanus and Ogilby tomes, since they were of a similar size and date of issuance. Many plates which appeared in Montanus were used by Ogilby, as well as some of the maps. Obviously, there was some kind of arrangement between them, but this provides no helpful information whether the engraving was entirely a project of the imagination or had, to some extent, an authentic source or background.

Chapter 26

1. Also as Zermenyo and Sermeño.

2. The first such voyage was by Juan Rodriguez Cabrillo in 1542–1543.

3. The British captured four of them: The *Santa Ana* in 1587, the *Encarnacion* in 1709, the *Cavadonga* in 1743, and the *Santisima Trinidad*, largest ship of her time, in 1762.

4. See Appendix F.

5. Holmes, *New Spain to the Californias by Sea*, p. 207.

6. Robertson, *Francis Drake*, p. 56, directs attention to a "letter written by Costanso, the well-known pilot who accompanied Portola (published in *Out West*, January, 1902, p. 59). The letter, dated Oct. 9, 1772, itself quotes from Cabrero Bueno's book of sailing instructions a statement about the wreck of the *San Agustin* in 1595: "But some Mariners of its Crew, with the Pilot, saved themselves, who, traversing the immense country which intervenes between said port and New Biscay, arrived at the end of many days at Sombrerete, a Mining Camp of that Government, bordering on New Galicia." A footnote to the report in *Out West* says that Sombrerete is near Zacatecas, adding that "the tramp of these shipwrecked men must rank as one of the most remarkable journeys ever recorded."

The story is believable, since it is difficult to understand how the entire crew of the *San Agustin* (70 men) could have managed the voyage to Mexico in a launch. On the other hand, one is impelled to wonder, from the similarity of circumstances involving in each instance a pilot and a return to the mining town of Sombrerete, whether Cabrero Bueno may not have confused the story with that of Morena, the Drake pilot. The subject is not mentioned in the official reports of Cermeño and his aides.

7. Robertson, *Francis Drake*, p. 50.

8. Davidson, *Identification*, p. 34.

9. Robertson, *Francis Drake*, p. 50.

10. Ibid., p. 224.

11. Ibid., p. 225.

12. Wagner, *Drake's Voyage*, pp. 168–169.

13. *California Historical Society Quarterly*, Vol. III, p. 8, 1924.

14. Admiral Cabrero Bueno, in his *Coast Pilot*, published *circa* 1743, mentions the Estero, saying: "On the northeast are three white rocks very near the sea, and opposite the middle one an *estero* makes in from the sea with a good entrance and no breakers." There is nothing to indicate that he recommended its use or that it was used by passing galleons.

15. Wagner, "The Voyage to California of Sebastian Rodriguez Cermeno in 1595," published in the *California Historical Society Quarterly*, Vol. II, April, 1924, also separately as a monograph (see p. 6 of the latter). He quotes Francisco de Bolanos, a pilot with Cermeño, as saying "that the loss was more the fault of the captain than of the bad weather."

16. Aker, "Report of Findings," p. 361, where in speaking of the elk that roamed the Point Reyes peninsula, he stated that they could have visited the site in the winter when it "was temporarily abandoned by the Indians for less inclement inland villages."

17. See Chapter 23.

18. In the case of Drake, it was N. de Morena whose story will be found in Chapter 28. In the case of Cermeño, several were involved, as set forth in note 6, this chapter.

19. Wagner, *Drake's Voyage*, p. 169.

20. Aker, "Report of Findings," p. 270.

21. Ibid., p. 271.

22. Davidson, *Francis Drake*, p. 48, speaks of "the young negress of 15 years, a 'Pper negro wench,' who was with child to Drake or his officers," but does not give the source of his information as to her age.

23. For still another suggested explanation, see Heizer, *Elizabethan California*, p. 26.

24. *California Historical Society Quarterly*, Vol. XLI, p. 27, 1962.

25. *California Historical Quarterly*, Vol. LIII, p. 287, 1974, and in Appendix F. The word count shown herein is based on his original statement and supporting statements as set forth on pp. 13, 14 and 23 of Wagner, "The Voyage to California of Sebastian Rodriguez Cermeño in 1595."

Chapter 27

1. Bancroft, *History of California*, Vol. I, p. 90, footnote.

2. Hale, in Winsor, *Narrative and Critical History of America*, pp. 74–78.

3. Ibid., p. 74.

4. Ibid.

5. Ibid., p. 76.

6. Ibid., p. 77.

7. Ibid., pp. 74--78.

8. Davidson, *Identification*, p. 35.

9. Bancroft, *History of California*, Vol. I, p. 89.

10. Davidson, *Identification*, p. 35.

11. Ibid.

12. Ibid., p. 38.

13. The full title of this treatise is *Identification of Sir Francis Drake's Anchorage on the Coast of California in the Year 1579*. It was read before the California Historical Society on March 12, 1889, and published by the Society in 1890.

14. See page 321. Also reproduced by Wagner, *Drake's Voyage*, opposite p. 435.

15. These excerpts are from pp. 434–437 of Wagner, *Drake's Voyage*.

16. Robertson, *Francis Drake*, pp. 207–208.

17. Aker, "Report of Findings," pp. 173–185.

18. Ibid., pp. 176 f.
19. Ibid., pp. 174 f, with detail at pp. 178 ff.
20. Ibid., pp. 176 ff, with detail at pp. 178 ff.
21. Ibid., at pp. 178 f, with detail at pp. 178 ff.
22. Ibid., p. 173.
23. Neasham, *Drake's California Landing*, pp. 8 and 10.
24. Ibid., p. 10.
25. Ibid.
26. Ibid., p. 8.
27. Hale, in Winsor, *Narrative and Critical History of America,* p. 75.
28. Aker, "Report of Findings," p. 173.
29. Bancroft, *History of California*, Vol. I, pp. 89–90, footnotes.
30. Davidson, *Identification*, p. 38.
31. Neasham, *Drake's California Landing*, p. 8.
32. Aker, "Report of Findings," pp. 177–178, and 226. See also statement by the Guild at p. 324.

Chapter 28

1. Father Salmeron's story was originally contained in a book entitled *Documentos para la historia de Mexico*, Series III, Tomo IV, published *circa* 1626.
2. A translation of that part of Father Salmeron's story dealing with de Morena was published in the February, 1900 issue of *Land of Sunshine*, XII: 13.
3. Based on the short land league used by Cermeño for his inland measures of distance (approximately 2400 yards per league).
4. See notes 1 and 2, this chapter.
5. Munro-Fraser, *History of Marin County,* p. 18.
6. Ibid., p. 309.
7. Ibid., pp. 95–98.
8. Wagner, *Drake's Voyage,* pp. 148 and 494.
9. Nuttall, *New Light on Drake,* p. 214.
10. Aker, "Report of Findings," pp. 337–340.
11. See Appendix I, page 391.
12. When another member of the Drake contingent became stranded in South America, but managed to get back to England in 1586, he was given an audience by Queen Elizabeth, who rewarded him with "twenty-two angels and many gracious words." Nuttall, *New Light on Drake,* p. 42, n. 2. According to *Webster's Unabridged Dictionary,* an "angel" was an English gold coin issued 1465–1634, and valued after 1553 at 10 shillings.

Chapter 29

1. At least one Drake expert believes that any edge in this category should go to Drake's Estero and Bolinas Lagoon, rather than to the San Quentin site, because of the possibility that Costanoan Indians may have held the San Quentin area in 1579. See Heizer, *Elizabethan California,* pp. 31–33.
2. Although the Olompali sixpence is a genuine English coin, its authenticity as a Drake artifact is suspect. From an archaeological standpoint, it is not adequately authenticated. It is said to have been found at an Olompali site, but other sixpences have also been said to have been found in Marin County. Archaeologists raise a question whether this coin may be a plant, as it now appears may have been the case with the Shinn plate.
3. Morison, *The European Discovery of America,* Vol. II, p. 688.
4. Depending on the weight to be assigned to the categories of "white cliffs" and "Indians," the score could vary from the given figures.

5. Oko, "Francis Drake and the California Indians," *California Historical Society Quarterly,* Vol. XLIII, p. 149, 1964.

6. Heizer, *Elizabethan California,* pp. 11 and 12. Heizer suggests that there are still possibilities of archival research in England. For example, the second half of Fletcher's journal may yet come to light, because Conyers said that he was making an exact copy of it. Another possibility is that the Drake or Fletcher originals may have been filed with the papers of Sir Joseph Banks or Charles Darwin, since they rummaged through such items in preparing material for publication on the voyage of the *Beagle.* A written document might tell us little, but the possibility of finding sketches, such as Fletcher's, could possibly settle the matter.

7. Gilliam, *San Francisco Bay,* p. 43.

8.The California Historical Resources Commission has undertaken to identify, if possible, the location of Drake's California anchorage, holding hearings for that purpose on October 21–23, 1978. Following the presentation of extensive evidence, the Commission voted 3 to 1, with 1 abstention, that a decision could not be made on the available evidence. At its meeting of March 2, 1979, the subject was considered further and three votes were taken: (1) Adversely to the authorization of a plaque by a 2 to 2 vote, with 1 abstention; (2) Favorably, by a 3 to 2 vote, on a resolution to the effect that Drake probably landed at Drake's Estero; and (3) Finally, in favor of a motion rescinding all action taken and postponing the matter until its next meeting to be held May 4, 1979, at Torrance.

Appendix A

1. This first sentence of the excerpt from the 1589 edition was omitted from page 440 of the 1600 edition, hence the latter began with "Assoone as we were entered, etc." The latter was prefixed, however by a new paragraph as follows:

> Wee kept our course from the Isle of Cano (which lyeth in eight degrees of Northerly latitude, and within two leagues of the maine of Nicaragua, where wee calked and trimmed our ship) along the Coast of Nueua Espanna, untill we came to the Hauen and Towne of Guatulco, which (as we were informed) had but seuenteene Spaniards dwelling in it, and we found it to stand in fifteene degrees and fiftie minutes.

2. At page 440 of the 1600 edition, the word "hence" was changed to "thence," and the rest of the paragraph and the first sentence of the next were omitted.

3. The words and figures "in longitude 600" were omitted from page 440 of the 1600 edition, and were replaced by only the figure "800."

4. The figure "42" was changed on page 440 of the 1600 edition to "fortie three."

5. The words "& clad, and couered ouer with snow, so that" were omitted from page 440 of the 1600 edition, being replaced by the word "and."

6. The words "In this Baye we ankered" were changed at page 440 of the 1600 edition to read "In this Bay wee ankered the seuententh of June."

7. The words "reasonable quantitie of gold or silver" were changed at page 442 of the 1600 edition to "some speciall likelihood of gold or silver," and at page 738 of the 1600 edition to "some probable shew of gold or silver."

Appendix F

1. Translation by Henry R. Wagner published in *California Historical Society Quarterly,* Vol. III, pp. 12–15.

Appendix G

1. Lummis, ed., Translation of excerpt from Salmeron, *Documentos para la historia de Mexico* containing an "Account of N. de Morena," published in *The Land of Sunshine,* Feb. 1900, Vol. XII, p. 13.

2. The brackets in the text are those of the original translator who assumed that the word

"paraje" in the text, meaning place or residence, was a misprint for "pasaje," meaning passage or strait.

Appendix H

1. Wagner, *Drake's Voyage*, p. 405 and map opposite the same page. Actually his error goes back to 1582 when he published *Divers Voyages* containing a map of the world by Michael Lok with a cryptic legend over the northwest coast of America in obvious reference to the Drake voyage reading "Anglorum 1580," showing that even then Hakluyt was confused.

2. Wagner, *Cartography*, Vol. I, p. 82.

3. Twiss, *Oregon Territory*, p. 49.

4. Wagner, *Drake's Voyage*, p. 264, n. 21.

5. Ibid., p. 192. Wagner stated: "It is said in the 'Famous Voyage' that England was reached November 3, and this was repeated even in 1600 when Hakluyt reprinted the account. The only way to account for the discrepancy is to suppose that November 3 may have been the day the ship reached London." Of course, such an explanation was not "the only way to account for the discrepancy." In the first place, Wagner himself conceded (at p. 505) that this could not have been correct. In the second place, a more likely explanation is that failure to make a correction in the 1600 edition was due to the fact that no one had called the mistake to his attention. At all events, it represents another in Hakluyt's record of errors with reference to "The Famous Voyage."

6. Wagner, *Drake's Voyage*, p. 253, n. 9.

7. Schurz, *The Manila Galleon*, p. 304.

8. Schurz obtained his information from Antonio de Morga's *History of the Philippines*, published in 1609.

9. Nuttall, *New Light on Drake*, p. 50.

10. Wagner, *Drake's Voyage*, p. 253, n. 11.

11. Ibid., p. 263, n. 20.

12. Twiss, *Oregon Territory*, pp. 37–38, as the result of which Twiss commented: "This is a very striking instance of the truth of Captain W. Burney's remark 'that the author of the Famous Voyage seems purposely, on some occasions, to introduce confusion as a cloak for ignorance'."

13. Wagner, *Drake's Voyage*, p. 240.

14. Ibid., p. 262, n. 16.

15. Ibid., p. 264, n. 23.

16. Ibid., p. 74.

17. Ibid., p. 167.

18. Ibid., p. 263, n. 17.

19. Ibid., p. 263, n. 18; also p. 270, n. 36.

20. See discussion at p. 363.

21. Referring to such inferences as that Hakluyt had "rejected '38 deg. 30.' in favor of '38. degrees towards the line,'" see Aker, "Report of Findings," p. 227.

22. Wagner, *Drake's Voyage*, p. 288.

23. Ibid., p. 164.

24. Robertson, *Francis Drake*, p. 194.

25. In his prefatory letter entitled "Richard Hakluyt to the Favourable Reader," the author said "being of late (contrary to my expectation) seriously delt withall, not to anticipate or preuent an other mans paines and charge in drawing all the seruices of that worthy Knight into one volume, I have yielded vnto those my friendes which pressed me in the matter, referring the further knowledge of his proceedings, to those intended discourses."

26. Bolton, *Drake's Plate of Brass*, pp. 9–10.

27. Bishop, "Drake's Course in the North Pacific," p. 153.

28. Aker, "Report of Findings," p. 125.

29. Twiss, *Oregon Territory*, p. 38.

Bibliography

Aker, Raymond. "Report of Findings Relating to Identification of Sir Francis Drake's Encampment at Point Reyes National Seashore" (typescript). Point Reyes, Calif.: Drake Navigators Guild, 1970.

———. "Sir Francis Drake at Drake's Bay: A Summation of Evidence Relating to the Identification of Sir Francis Drake's Encampment at Drake's Bay, California" (typescript). Point Reyes, Calif., 1978.

———. "The Cermeno Expedition at Drake's Bay, 1595" (typescript). Point Reyes, Calif., 1965.

Allen, Robert W. and Robert W. Parkinson. "Identification of the Nova Albion Conie: A Research Report of the Drake Navigators Guild" (typescript). Point Reyes, Calif.: Drake Navigators Guild, 1971.

Andrews, Kenneth R. *Drake's Voyages: A Reassessment of Their Place in Elizabethan Maritime Expansion.* New York: Charles Scribner, 1967.

———. "The Aims of Drake's Expedition of 1577–1580." *American Historical Review,* Vol. LXXIII, pp. 724–741.

"Anonymous Narrative." British Museum Harleian MS No. 280, Folio 23. Printed by the Hakluyt Society in *The World Encompassed by Sir Francis Drake* (1854), pp. 174–186, under the title "A discourse of Sir Francis Drakes iorney and exploytes after he had passed yᵉ Straytes of Megellan." Cited as the "Anonymous Narrative" by Wagner, *Drake's Voyage,* pp. 271, 281, 289.

Arcano del Mare. See Dudley, Robert.

Arrowsmith, Aaron. *Chart of the Pacific Ocean Drawn from a Great Number of Printed and Ms. Journals.* London, 1798.

Ascension, Father Antonio de la. *The Voyage of Sebastian Vizcaino.* English translation, London, 1759, from a part of Venegas, *Noticias de la California.*

Bancroft, Hubert H. *History of California,* Vol. I. San Francisco: A. L. Bancroft, 1884.

Barrett, Samuel A. "The Ethnogeography of the Pomo and Neighboring Indians." *University of California Publications,* American Archaeology and Ethnology, Vol. 6, No. 1, 1908.

Barrington, Daines, ed. *Miscellanies.* London, 1781.

Barrow, John. *The Life, Voyages and Exploits of Admiral Sir Francis Drake, Knt.* London: John Murray, 1843.

Beechey, Frederick W. *Narrative of a Voyage to the Pacific in 1825 – 1828.* London, 1831. 2 vols.

Benson, E. F. *Sir Francis Drake.* London: John Lane, 1927.

Bishop, R. P. "Drake's Course in the North Pacific." *British Columbia Historical Quarterly* (Vancouver, B.C.), July, 1939.

Blagrave, John. *Astrolabium Uranicum Generale.* London, 1596.

Blundeville, Thomas. *M. Blundeville, His Exercises containing Sixe Treatises.* London, 1594.

Bolanos, Francisco de. *Derotero* (1603). Preserved in the Biblioteca Nacional in Madrid; cited by Wagner, *Drake's Voyage,* p. 161.

Bolton, Herbert E. and others. *Drake's Plate of Brass: Evidence of his Visit to California in 1579.* Special publication No. 13 of the California Historical Society, 1937.

————. *The Plate of Brass: Evidence of the Visit of Francis Drake to California in the Year 1579.* Special publication No. 25 of the California Historical Society, 1953.

Bradford, Ernle. *Drake.* London: Hodder and Stoughton, 1965.

Brereton, R. M. *Did Sir Francis Drake Land on Any Part of the Oregon Coast?* Portland: J. M. Gill, 1907.

Brown, Alan K. "Did Drake Land Here?" *La Peninsula: Journal of the San Mateo County Historical Association,* Feb. 1960, Vol. X, No. 4, pp. 3–5.

————. *See* Stanger, Frank M. and Alan K. Brown.

Brown Library, John Carter. *Annual Report of Management Committee* (containing information bearing on the date of the Hondius Broadside). Providence, R.I., 1958.

Bryant, William Cullen. *Popular History of the United States.* New York: Scribner, Armstrong & Co., 1876. 4 vols.

Bueño, Admiral Cabrero. *Navigacion Especulative y Practica.* Manila, 1734.

————. *The Coast Pilot* (English translation). Manila, 1743.

Burney, Captain James. *Chronological History of the Discoveries in the South Seas or Pacific Ocean, Part I.* London: Luke Hansard, 1803.

Burrage, Henry Sweetser. *Early English and French Voyages, Chiefly from Hakluyt, 1534 – 1608.* New York, 1906.

Burton, Robert T. *The British Heroe, or Sir Francis Drake Revived.* London, 1687.

Camden, William. *Annales Rerum Anglicarum, et Hibernicarum, regnante Elizabetha, ad Annum Salutis MDLXXXIX.* London, 1615. From a French translation issued in London in 1624, Abraham Darcie made the first English version, published in London in 1625 as *The True and Royall History of the Famous Empress Elizabeth.*

Caughey, John Walton. *California.* New York: Prentice-Hall, 1940.

Cermeño, Sebastian Rodriguez. "Report of Visit to California in 1595." Translated by Henry R. Wagner in *California Historical Society Quarterly,* Vol. III, pp. 3–24, 1924.

Chapman, Charles E. *History of California: The Spanish Period.* New York: McMillan, 1921.

Chickering, Allen L. "Some Notes with Regard to Drake's Plate of Brass." *California Historical Society Quarterly,* Vol. XVI, pp. 275–281, 1937.

Christy, Miller. *The Silver Map of Drake's Voyage.* London: Henry Stevens, 1900.

Churchill, Awnsham. "Sir William Monson's Naval Tracts." *A Collection of Voyages and Travels,* Vol. 8. London: 1704. 8 vols.

Churchill, Winston. *History of the English-Speaking Peoples: The New World.* Vol. 2. New York: Dodd, Mead, 1956.

Clarke, Samuel. *The Life and Death of Sir Francis Drake.* London: Simon Millay, 1671.

Cleland, Robert Glass. *From Wilderness to Empire.* New York: Knopf, 1944.

Colnett, Captain James. *The Journal of Captain James Colnett Aboard the Argonaut from April 26, 1789 to November 3, 1791.* Toronto: The Champlain Society, 1940.

Cooke, John. *British Museum Harleian MS No. 540, Folio 93. Circa* 1580–1585.

Coote, C. H. *Shakespeare's "New Map" in Twelfth Night.* London, 1878.

Corbett, Julian S. *Drake and the Tudor Navy.* London: Longmans, Greene, 1898. 2 vols.

Costanso, Michael. "Letter of October 9, 1772." *Out West,* Vol. 16, Jan., p. 59, 1902.

Cronise, Titus Fey. *The Natural Wealth of California.* San Francisco: H. H. Bancroft, 1868.

Darcie, Abraham. *The True and Royal History of the Famous Empress Elizabeth.* London, 1625, representing a translation into English of the French version of Camden's 1615 work in Latin.

Davidson, George. *Examination of Some of the Early Voyages of Discovery and Exploration on the Northwest Coast of America from 1539 to 1603.* Washington: U.S. Government Printing Office, 1887.

———. *Francis Drake on the Northwest Coast of America from 1539 to 1603.* Washington: U.S. Government Printing Office, 1887.

———. *Francis Drake on the Northwest Coast of America in the Year 1579.* San Francisco: Printed by F. F. Partridge for the Geographical Society of the Pacific, Vol. V. Series II, 1908.

———. *Identification of Sir Francis Drake's Anchorage on the Coast of California in the Year 1579.* Printed for the California Historical Society by Bacon & Company, 1890.

———. *The Coast Pilot.* Washington: U.S. Government Printing Office, 1889.

Dawson, Giles E. and Laetitia Yeandle. *Elizabethan Handwriting, 1500–1600.* Washington, D.C., 1966.

De Bry, Theodore. *Americae Pars VIII.* Frankfurt, 1599.

———. *Grande et Petit Voyages.* A series of volumes, Frankfurt, 1590–1634.

Dillingham, Matthew P. "A Review of the Findings of Dr. Adan E. Traganza Relative to the Site of Drake's Landing in California" (typescript). Point Reyes, California: Drake Navigators Guild, 1960.

Dixon, James Main. "Drake on the Pacific Coast," *Publications of the Historical Society of Southern California (Los Angeles),* Vol. IX, pp. 86–96 (1912). Also, *The Overland Monthly,* Vol. LXIII, pp. 537–545, 1914.

Documentos para la historia de Mexico, Series III, Tomo IV. Excerpt translated and published in *The Land of Sunshine,* Feb. 1900. *See* Salmeron.

Doerr, Albert E. "Drake's California Harbor: Another Look at William Caldeira's Story," *Terrae Incognitae.* Vol. IX, pp. 49–59, 1977.

Drake Navigators Guild. "Nova Albion Rediscovered" (typescript). Point Reyes, California: Drake Navigators Guild, 1956.

Drake, Sir Francis (a nephew). *The World Encompassed*. London: 1628. Reprinted 1635; also in 1653 as part of a collection of voyages, *Sir Francis Drake's Voyages*. Reprinted 1854 by the Hakluyt Society, London: W. S. W. Vaux, ed.; and in 1926, by the Argonaut Press, London, N. M. Penzer, ed.

———. *Sir Francis Drake Revived*. London: Nicholas Bourne, 1626.

Dudley, Robert, *Arcano del Mare* (an atlas of maps). Florence, Italy, 1647.

Dunn, Oliver, ed. *See* Doerr, whose article was completed by Dunn after Doerr's death in 1972.

Dyson, James L. *The World of Ice*. New York: Knopf, 1962.

"Early English Voyages to the Pacific Coast of America from their Own and Contemporary Accounts. Chapter: Sir Francis Drake," *Out West*. Vol. XVIII, pp. 73–80, 1903.

Eliot, Charles W., ed. *Voyages and Travels: Ancient and Modern,* includes "The Famous Voyage." New York: P. F. Collier & Sons, Harvard Classics, Vol. 33, 1910.

Eliott-Drake, Lady. *The Family and Heirs of Sir Francis Drake*. London: Smith, Elder, 1911. 2 vols.

Ellison, Joseph W. "True or False?" *Saturday Evening Post,* April 4, 1943, pp. 32, 35–36.

Eschscholtz, Johann Friedrich. *Zoologischer Atlas*. Berlin: G. Reimer, 1829–1833.

Farquhar, Francis P. and Walter A. Starr. "Drake in California," *California Historical Society Quarterly,* Vol. XXXVI, pp. 21–34, 1957.

Fink, Colin and E. P. Polushkin. *Drake's Plate of Brass Authenticated*. Special publication No. 14 of the California Historical Society, 1938.

Fletcher, Francis. *The World Encompassed*. *See* Drake, Sir Francis (a nephew).

———. Manuscript in the British Museum, Sloane No. 61.

Forbes, Alexander. *California: A History of Upper and Lower California*. London, 1839. Reprinted by John Henry Nash, San Francisco, 1937.

Froude, James Anthony. *History of England from the Fall of Wolsey to the Defeat of the Spanish Armada*. London: 1872–1875, Vol. XI, 12 vols.

Galvin, John, Ed. *The First Spanish Entry into San Francisco Bay, 1775*. San Francisco: John Howell Books, 1971.

Gerhard, Peter. *Pirates of the West Coast of New Spain*. Glendale, Calif.: Arthur Clark, 1960.

Gilliam, Harold. *Island in Time*. San Francisco: Sierra Club, 1962.

———. *San Francisco Bay*. Garden City, N.Y.: Doubleday, 1957.

Gleason, Duncan. *The Islands and Ports of California*. New York: Devin-Adair, 1958.

Greenhow, Robert. *The History of Oregon and California*. Boston: Charles C. Little and James Brown, 1845.

Griffin, George B. "Letters Translated from the Spanish." *Publications of the Historical Society of Southern California,* Vol. II, pp. 15–19.

Hakluyt, Richard. *Divers Voyages*. London, 1582. Reprinted for the Hakluyt Society, London, 1850.

———. *Peter Martyr's Decades*. Paris, 1587.

———. *The Principall Navigations, Voiages and Discoveries of the English Nation*. London, 1589. Contains "The Famous Voyage." Same, 1600 edition (3 vols). Vol. III contains "The Famous Voyage" and "The Course." For French editions of "The

Famous Voyage," see *Le Voyage de L'Illustre Seigneur et Chevalier Francis Drach* (1613) and *Le Voyage Curieux faict autour* (1641). A facsimile of the 1589 edition was printed by Cambridge University Press for the Hakluyt Society, 1965, 2 vols.

Hale, Edward Everett. "Dudley and the Arcano del Mare," *American Antiquarian Society's Proceedings,* Oct. 21, 1873.

————. "Critical Essay on Drake's Bay," in Winsor, *Narrative and Critical History of America,* Vol. III. Boston: Houghton Mifflin, 1884. 8 vols.

Harper, J. and J. *Lives and Voyages of Drake, Cavendish and Dampier.* New York, 1832.

Harrington, John P. *Tobacco Among the Karuk Indians of California.* Bureau of American Ethnology, Bulletin 94. Washington, D.C.: U.S. Government Printing Office, 1932.

Hart, Francis Russell. *Admirals of the Caribbean.* Boston: Houghton Mifflin, 1922.

Hart, James. *The Plate of Brass.* Berkeley: Bancroft Library, 1977. 4 pp.

————. *The Plate of Brass Reexamined, 1977.* Berkeley: Bancroft Library, 1977.

Haselden, R. B. "Is the Drake Plate of Brass Genuine?" *California Historical Society Quarterly,* Vol. XVI, pp. 271–274, 1937.

Heizer, Robert F. "Archaeological Evidence of Sebastian Rodriguez Cermeño's California Visit in 1595." *California Historical Society Quarterly,* Vol. XX, pp. 315–328, 1941.

————. *Elizabethan California.* Ramona,Calif.: Ballena Press, 1974.

————. *Francis Drake and the California Indians, 1579.* Berkeley: University of California Press, 1947.

————, ed. *Handbook of North American Indians,* Vol. 8: *California.* Washington, D.C.: Smithsonian Institution, 1978.

Heizer, Robert F. and William W. Elmendorf. "Francis Drake's California Anchorage in the Light of the Language Spoken There," *Pacific Historical Review (San Francisco),* Vol. XI, pp. 213–217, 1942.

Herrera, Antonio de. *Historia General del Mundo.* Valladolid, 1606. 3 vols.

Hittell, Theodore H. *History of California,* Vol. 1. San Francisco: N. J. Stone, 1885.

Holliday, J. S. "The Francis Drake Controversy." *California Historical Quarterly,* Vol. LIII, pp. 197–202, 1974.

Holmes, Maurice G. *New Spain to the Californias by Sea.* Glendale, Calif.: Arthur Clark, 1963.

Howay, Judge F. W. *Journal of Captain James Colnett Aboard the Argonaut from April 26, 1789 to November 3, 1791.* Toronto, Canada: The Champlain Society, 1940.

Howell, John Thomas. *Marin Flora.* Berkeley: University of California Press, 1970.

Humboldt, Alexander von. *Essai Politique sur de Royaume de Nouvelle Espagne.* Paris, 1811. 2 vols. Translated by John Black as *Political Essay on the Kingdom of New Spain.* London, 1811. 4 vols.

Hussey, John Adam. "Site of the Lighter Wharf at Bolinas." Berkeley: Typewritten treatise prepared under the auspices of the Works Progress Administration, 1936.

Hutchinson, William Henry. *California.* Palo Alto, Calif.: American West, 1969.

Kelly, I. T. Article entitled "The Coast Miwok," appearing in Vol. 8, *California,* Robert F. Heizer, ed., of the *Handbook of North American Indians,* William C. Sturtevant, general ed. Washington: Smithsonian Institution, 1978.

Kerr, Willis Holmes. "The Treatment of Drake's Circumnavigation in Hakluyt's

'Voyages,'" *Papers of the Bibliographical Society of America.* Portland, Maine, 1940, Vol. 34, pp. 283–300.

Kinniard, Lawrence. "Nova Albion," a chapter in *History of the Greater San Francisco Bay Region.* New York: Lewis Historical Publishing Co., 1966, pp. 22–36.

Kneiss, Gilbert H. *Redwood Railways.* Berkeley: Howell-North, 1956.

Kraus, Hans P. *Sir Francis Drake.* Amsterdam: N. Israel, 1970.

Kroeber, A. L. *Handbook of the Indians of California.* Berkeley: California Book Co., 1923; 2d ed. 1953.

Land of Sunshine, The. Charles F. Lummis, ed. *See* Salmeron, Father Jeronimo.

Lewis, Oscar. *George Davidson, Pioneer West Coast Scientist.* Berkeley: University of California Press, 1954.

Lummis, Charles F., ed. of *The Land of Sunshine* and its successor magazine, *Out West.*

Mainwaring, Sir Henry. *Seaman's Dictionary.* London, 1623.

Markham, Captain. *Davis's Voyages.* London: Hakluyt Society edition, 1850. Cited in Winsor, *Narrative and Critical History of America,* Vol. III, p. 217.

Mason, A. E. W. *The Life of Francis Drake.* London: Hodder and Stoughton, 1941.

Mason, Jack, with Thomas J. Barfield. *Last Stage for Bolinas.* Petaluma, California: North Shore Books, 1973.

Mathes, W. Michael. *Vizcaino and Spanish Expansion into the Pacific Ocean, 1580–1630.* Special publication No. 44 of the California Historical Society, 1968.

Matthews, Samuel W. "What's Happening to Our Climate?" *National Geographic Magazine,* November 1976.

McAdie, Alexander G. "Nova Albion–1579." *American Antiquarian Society Proceedings,* New Series, 1918, Vol. 28, pp. 189–198.

McClellan, R. Guy. *The Golden State: A History of the Region West of the Rocky Mountains.* Philadelphia: William Flint, 1872.

Meighan, Clement W. "Excavations in Sixteenth Century Shellmounds at Drake's Bay, Marin County." *Reports of the University of California Archaeological Survey,* No. 9, Paper 9. Berkeley, 1950.

———. "Report on the 1949 Excavations of Sixteenth Century Sites of Drake's Bay." *University of California Archaeological Survey* Ms. No. 79, 1949.

———, and Robert F. Heizer. "Archaeological Exploration of Sixteenth Century Indian Mounds at Drake's Bay." *California Historical Society Quarterly,* Vol. XXXI, pp. 98–100, 1952.

Michel, Helen V. and Frank Asaro. *Chemical Study of the Plate of Brass.* Berkeley, 1977.

Mofras, N. Duflot de. *Exploration of Oregon and California,* Paris, 1844. 2 vols.

Molera, E. J. *The March of Portola and the Log of the San Carlos.* San Francisco: California Promotion Committee, 1909.

Monson, Sir William. "Sir William Monson's Naval Tracts," in Awnsham Churchill, *A Collection of Voyages and Travels,* London, 1704.

Montanus, Arnoldus. *Die Nieuwe en Onbekonde Weereld: Beschryvning van Americo en 1 + Zuid-Land . . .* Amsterdam, 1671.

Morison, Samuel Eliot. *The European Discovery of America: The Southern Voyages.* New York: Oxford University Press, 1974.

Mourelle, Francisco Antonio. "Voyage of the Sonora," in Daines Barrington, ed., *Miscellanies,* London, 1781, pp. 469–534.

————. *The Voyage of the Sonora*. Reprinted from the above, with annotations by Thomas C. Russell, San Francisco, 1920.

Munro-Fraser, J. P. *History of Marin County.* San Francisco: Alley, Bowen, 1880.

Neasham, V. Aubrey and William E. Pritchard. *Drake's California Landing: The Evidence for Bolinas Lagoon.* Sacramento: Western Heritage, 1974.

Nichols, Philip. *Sir Francis Drake Revived.* London, 1626.

Nuttall, Zelia. *New Light on Drake.* London: Hakluyt Society, 1914, New Series, XXXIV. Includes translation of many Spanish documents dealing with Drake, such as depositions of John Drake, Nicolas Jorje, and San Juan de Anton.

Ogilby, James. *America, being the latest, and most accurate description of the New World.* London, 1671.

Oko, Captain Adolph E. "Francis Drake and Nova Albion," *California Historical Society Quarterly,* Vol. XLIII, pp. 135–150, 1964.

Out West, Charles F. Lummis, ed. Successor magazine to *The Land of Sunshine.*

Palou, Father Francisco. "Journal of Father Palou," excerpts from, as translated by Stanger and Brown, eds., *Who Discovered the Golden Gate?* pp. 132–146.

Parks, George Bruner. *Richard Hakluyt and the English Voyages.* New York: American Geographical Society, 1930.

Penzer, N. M., ed. *The World Encompassed.* London: The Argonaut Press, 1926.

Phillips, P. Lee. *List of Geographical Atlases in the Library of Congress.* Washington: U.S. Government Printing Office, 1909.

Pike, Douglas G. "Historiography of the Drake Controversy." *California Historical Quarterly,* Vol. LII, pp. 128–130, 1973.

"Pirate's Cove." *True West Magazine,* Dec. 1967, pp. 6, 48.

Plate of Brass, Drake's. See Bolton.

Plate of Brass, The. See Bolton: also, Hart.

Power, Robert H. "A Plate of Brass by Me . . . C. G. Francis Drake." *California History,* Vol. LVII, pp. 172–185, 1978.

————. *A Study of Two Historic Maps.* Vacaville, Calif.: Ulatis Creek Printing, 1978; revised and reprinted in September, 1978, by Paragraphics, San Rafael.

————. "Drake's Landing in California, a Case for San Francisco Bay." *California Historical Quarterly,* Vol. LII, pp. 101–128, 1973.

————. "Portus Novae Albionis Rediscovered?" San Francisco: *Pacific Discovery,* Vol. VII, pp. 10–12, 1954.

Pritchard, William E. *See* Neasham, V. Aubrey and William E. Pritchard.

Purchas, Samuel. *Purchas, His Pilgrimes, in Five Bookes,* London: William Stansby, 1625.

Quinn, D. B. and R. A. Skelton, *The Principall Navigations Voiages and Discoveries of the English Nation.* Cambridge, England: published for the Hakluyt Society and the Peabody Museum of Salem at the University Press, 1965, 2 vols.

Raleigh, Walter. *The English Voyages of the Sixteenth Century.* Glasgow: James McLehose, 1906.

Rinn, Ida Louise. "The Voyages of Vizcaino." Berkeley: Thesis prepared for M.A. degree at University of California, Dec. 1926.

Robertson, John W. *Francis Drake and other Early Explorers Along the Pacific Coast.* San Francisco: Grabhorn Press, 1927.

————. *The Harbor of St. Francis.* San Francisco: Grabhorn Press, 1926.

Roche, T. W. E. *The Golden Hind.* New York: Praeger, 1973.

Rolle, Andrew P. *California: A History.* New York: Crowell, 1969.

Rowse, A. L. "The Elizabethans and America." *American Heritage* (New York), April, 1959.

Russell, Thomas C. *See* Mourelle, Francisco.

Sabin, Joseph. *Dictionary of Books Relating to America.* New York: Bibliographical Society of America, 1869–1874. 11 vols.

Salmeron, Father Jeronimo de Zarate. *Documentos para la historia de Mexico,* Series III, Tomo IV, published *circa* 1626, a part of which was translated as "Relation of Events in California and New Mexico up to 1626," an excerpt from which was published in *Land of Sunshine,* Vol. XII, p. 13, Feb. 1900.

Santamaria, Father Vicente de. "Father Santamaria on Angel Island," in Frank M. Stanger and Alan K. Brown, eds., *Who Discovered the Golden Gate?* p. 163.

Schurz, William Lytle. *The Manila Galleon.* New York: Dutton, 1939.

Shell, Elton E. *Marin's Historic Tomales and Presbyterian Church.* Tomales, Calif., 1949.

Silva, Nuño da. "Composite Account." From Wagner, *Drake's Voyage,* pp. 338–349.

Sir Francis Drake Revived. See Nichols, Philip.

Soule, Frank, J. H. Gihon and J. Nisbet. *The Annals of San Francisco.* New York: D. Appleton, 1850.

Sprent, F. P. *Sir Francis Drake's Voyage Round the World: Two Contemporary Maps.* London: British Museum, 2d. ed., 1931.

Stanger, Frank M. and Alan K. Brown, eds. *Who Discovered the Golden Gate?* Menlo Park, Calif.: San Mateo County Historical Association, 1969.

Starr, Walter A. "Drake Landed in San Francisco Bay in 1579: The Testimony of the Plate of Brass." *California Historical Society Quarterly,* Vol. XLI, pp. 1–29, 1962.

———. "Evidence of the Visit of Sir Francis Drake to California in the Year 1579." *California Historical Society Quarterly,* Vol. XXXVI, pp. 31–34, 1957.

Stillman, J. D. B. "Did Drake Discover San Francisco Bay?" *The Overland Monthly* (San Francisco), Vol. 1, pp. 332–337, 1968.

———. *Seeking the Golden Fleece.* San Francisco: A. Roman, 1877.

Stow, John. *Chronicles* (containing an account of "Francis Drake His Voyage Round About the World"). London, 1592, reprinted London, 1615 and 1635.

Taylor, E. G. R. "Francis Drake and the Pacific: Two Fragments." *Pacific Historical Review,* Vol. I, pp. 360–369, 1932.

———. *Late Tudor and Early Stuart Geography.* London: Methuen, 1934.

———. "More Light on Drake." *The Mariner's Mirror, Journal of the Society for Nautical Research* (Cambridge, England), Vol. 16, 1930.

———. "The Missing Draft Project of Drake's Voyage of 1577–80," *Geographical Journal of the Royal Geographical Society* (London), Vol. LXXV, 1930.

———. *The Original Writings and Correspondence of the Two Richard Hakluyts.* London, 1930. 2 vols.

———. *Tudor Geography, 1485–1583.* London: Methuen, 1930.

Tebenkov, M. *Gidrograf ceskia zamecamia* (translated as *Hydrographic Observations Accompanying the Atlas of the Northwestern Shores of America*). St. Petersburg: The printing house of the Naval Cadet Corps, 1852. Cited by Davidson, *The Coast Pilot,* p.254; also, Davidson, *Identification,* p. 36.

Thomas, Robert C. Unpublished manuscript entitled "Drake at Olompali." San Francisco, 1978.

Thomson, George Malcolm. *Sir Francis Drake.* New York: William Morrow, 1972.

Treganza, Adan E. "The Examination of Indian Shellmounds in the Tomales and Drake's Bay Area with Reference to Sixteenth Century Historical Contacts." Manuscript on file at the State of California Department of Parks and Recreation, History Section.

——. *The Examination of Indian Shellmounds within San Francisco Bay with Reference to the Possible 1579 Landfall of Sir Francis Drake*. Vacaville, Calif.: Nova Albion Explorations, 1957.

Tuthill, Franklin. *History of California*. San Francisco: H. H. Bancroft Co., 1866.

Twiss, Sir Travers. *The Oregon Territory: Its History and Discovery*, sometimes cited as *The Oregon Question Examined*. London, 1846.

Vancouver, Captain George. *Voyage of Discovery to the North Pacific Ocean, 1790–1795*. London, 1798. 3 vols.

Varley, F. J. "Drake's Plate of Brass." *Geographical Review*, Vol. 95, pp. 159–160.

Vaux, W. S. W., ed. *The World Encompassed by Sir Francis Drake*. London: Hakluyt Society, 1854.

Venegas, Miguel. *Noticias de la California*, Madrid, 1757. 3 vols. Translated as *A Natural and Civil History of California*, London, 1759.

Verne, Jules. *Exploration of the World: Famous Travels and Travelers.* (Translation from the French). New York, 1879.

Viles, D. M. and M. W. Jensen, Jr. "The Northern Mystery." Portland, Ore.: *Vanguard*, a publication of Portland State University, Nov. 16, 1971. 8 pp.

Villiers, Alan. "Sir Francis Drake." Washington: *National Geographic Magazine*, Feb. 1975, pp. 216–253.

Vizcaino, Sebastian. "Diary of Sebastian Vizcaino, 1602–1603," in *Spanish Exploration in the Southwest*. New York, 1916. (Translated from the Spanish by Herbert E. Bolton.)

Von der Porten, Edward P. *Drake-Cermeño: An Analysis of Artifacts*. Point Reyes, Calif.: Drake Navigators Guild, 1965.

——. "Our First New England." *U.S. Naval Institute Proceedings,* Dec. 1960. Reprinted as pamphlet, Annapolis, Md., 1960.

Le Voyage Curieux faict autour du Monde par Francois Drach. Paris, 1641. See Hakluyt.

Le Voyage de L'Illustre Seigneur et Chevalier Francis Drach. Paris, 1613. See Hakluyt.

Wagner, Henry R. *Cartography of the Northwest Coast of America to the Year 1800*. Berkeley: University of California Press, 1937. 2 vols.

——. "Creation of Rights of Sovereignty Through Symbolic Acts." *Pacific Historical Review*, Vol. VII, 1938.

——. *Drake on the Pacific Coast*. Printed for the Zamorano Club of Los Angeles, with an introduction and notes by Ruth Frey Axe, 1970.

——. "George Davidson, Geographer of the Northwest Coast of America." *California Historical Society Quarterly*, Vol. XI, pp. 299–320, 1932.

——. *Sir Francis Drake's Voyage Around the World*. San Francisco: John Howell, 1926.

——. "The Last Spanish Exploration of the Northwest Coast and the Attempt to Colonize Bodega Bay." *California Historical Society Quarterly*, Vol. X, pp. 313–345, 1931.

——. "The Voyage to California of Sebastian Rodriguez Cermeño in 1595." *California Historical Society Quarterly*, Vol. III, pp. 3–24, 1924.

Wilbur, Marguerite Eyer, ed. *Vancouver in California*. Los Angeles: Glen Dawson, 1953. 2 vols.

Williamson, James A. *The Age of Drake*. London: A. & C. Black, 1938.

Wilson, Derek. *The World Encompassed*. New York: Harper & Row, 1977.

Winsor, Justin. *Narrative and Critical History of America*. Vol. III: *English Explorations and Settlements in North America, 1497–1689*. Boston and New York: Houghton Mifflin, 1884.

World Encompassed, The. See Drake, Sir Francis (a nephew) and Wilson, Derek.

Wright, Helen and Samuel Rapport. *The Great Explorers*. New York: Harper & Brothers, 1957.

Wroth, Lawrence C. *Early Cartography of the Pacific*. Portland, Maine: Bibliographical Society of America, 1944. Vol. 38, No. 2.

Yeandle, Laetitia. *See* Dawson, Giles E. and Laetitia Yeandle.

Ziebarth, Marilyn, ed. for California Historical Society. "The Francis Drake Controversy: His California Anchorage, June 17–July 23, 1579," *California Historical Quarterly*, Vol. LIII, pp. 197–292, 1974. The entire number is devoted to Drake and includes "An Introductory Perspective" (J. S. Holliday); "Point Reyes Peninsula/Drake's Estero" (Drake Navigators Guild); "Bolinas Bay/Bolinas Lagoon" (V. Aubrey Neasham); "San Francisco Bay/San Quentin Cove" (Robert H. Power).

Newspaper Articles

"The Brass Mortar, 1570." *San Rafael Independent*, Jan. 10, 1974.

Dwinelle, John W. Review of Bryant's *Popular History of the United States*. *San Francisco Bulletin*, Oct. 5, 1878.

Gilliam, Harold. "Elizabethan Sixpence Discovered." *San Francisco Chronicle*, Nov. 9, 1974.

"Javanese Halberd Discovered by Bernie Roth." *San Francisco Chronicle*, April 3, 1955.

"Pirate's Cove as Drake's Landing Site." *San Rafael Independent*, Feb. 23, 1967.

"Robert H. Power." *Redwood City Tribune*, June 18, 1959.

Smith, Ed. "A New Twist in Drake Tale." *San Rafael Independent-Journal*, Sept. 25, 1978.

Trumbull, Marjorie. "Man with a Mission: Where Did Drake Land?" *San Francisco Chronicle*, June 19, 1959.

INDEX

A

Acapulco, 19, 142, 143, 304, 306
Africa, Drake's visit to, 21
Aguire, Martin, 143
Aker, Raymond, xvi, 396; charts by, 144, 282, 284; conclusions from study of insets on the Hondius Broadside Map, 278–280, 287, 289, 292; de Morena's story interpreted by, 334; on discrepancy in Drake's crew size before and after Nova Albion, 55; on Drake's arrival time to the Farallones, 266, 268; Drake's Estero defended by, xvi, 81, 165; on latitude for Drake's anchorage site, 158; navigational studies and expertise of, 79, 81, 279; as president of the Drake Navigators Guild, 79, 80–81, 188–189; reports by, 80–81; on source of the "Portus Novae Albionis," 279–280, 287, 289, 291–292, 294; on the "*Tobah*-tobacco" controversy, 204; on weather at Nova Albion, 188–189; and the white cliffs as a clue, 165
Alexander, Wallace M., 246
Alexandria, Egypt, 14, 46
Allie I. Algar, the sealing schooner, 236, 237
American Antiquarian Society, 320
Anchor, found at Drake's Bay, 236–238
Anchorage mystery, 3–12; censorship of information on Drake's voyage, 23, 228; and length of "The Famous Voyage," 90–93
Anchorage sleuths, xvi, 5, 66–82; zeal of, 314
Angel Island, 42, 283, 297; theory of Drake's anchorage near, 168
Anglican Church, 345
Anglo Saxon, the, 38
"Anonymous Narrative," 88, 98, 101, 105, 173; Drake's California visit reported by, 105; and the plate of lead, 242; text of, 105
Antarctic Ocean, 13
Anthony, Nicholas, 48
Approach to Nova Albion, 142–151; California Historical Society's debate on, 142, 149–151, 338; no clue to Drake's anchorage site provided by, 338; opinions of navigational experts, 78–82, 148–149; and search for the Northwest Passage, 19, 142, 143, 145, 146–147, 149–150. *See also* Mexico-to-California voyage
Arcano del Mare (R. Dudley), 316, 317, 319, 323, 326
Archaeological and artifactual evidence, 231–241; anchor found at Drake's Bay, 236–238; debated by the California Historical Society, 238–240, 241, 341; described in contemporary accounts, 231–232; Drake's Estero searched for, 80, 310; for

Drake's fort, 233–234; and the missing Elizabethan sixpence, 234–236, 240–241, 243, 341; from Indian sites, 80, 232–233, 235; mortar and halberd discovered, 238; Point Reyes searched for, 75–76; value as a clue, 341; vestiges from Drake's visit not found by Cermeño, 306–307, 310, 315, 343. *See also* Plate of brass

Argentina: hostile natives in, 181; John Drake captured in, 55, 103

Argonaut, the, 68

Argonaut Press of London, 102

Arrowsmith, Aaron, 68

Artifacts. *See* Archaeological and artifactual evidence

Asaro, Frank, 255, 258

Ascension, Father Antonio de la, 331, 335

Asclepias mexicana, 201

Ashley, Lord, 129

Atlantic Ocean, 334

Audley, John, 51, 52

Ayacheco, the, 41

Ayala, Don Juan Manuel de, 42, 44, 278

B

"Bad bay," location of, 146

Bahia de las Calaveras, 177

Bahia de San Francisco, name for Drake's Bay, 39, 304, 306, 335

Baker, Chistopher, 87

Bancroft, Hubert H., 67, 69, 138; opinion on Drake's California anchorage site, 69, 73, 273; "Portus Novae Albionis" discussed by, 272, 273, 275, 288, 293; on veracity of Fletcher's notes, 100

Bancroft Library, 243; plate of brass in, 246, 254; report on tests and studies of the plate of brass, 254, 257–259

Barfield, Thomas J., 74, 260

Barnes, Thomas G., 254, 255

Barrett, Samuel A., 73; ethnological approach to Drake's California anchorage, 70–71, 215

Barron, George, 261

Bay: defined, 175; vs. harbor as an anchorage clue, 172–177

Bays in Nova Albion, 36–44: contenders for Drake's anchorage site, 44; inner, 42–44; oceanward, 36–42

Beads, 235

Beardsley, R. K., 232

Becker, Robert, 73, 277, 287

Beechey, Captain Frederick W., 43, 68, 71, 148

Belvedere Cove, 42

Belvedere Island, 42, 283, 294

Bernoulli wind, 168

Bible, 28

Birds, 206–207

Bishop, George, 87

Black, James R., 246

Black people: Drake's friendly attitude toward, 52; left by Drake in the Celebes, 53, 54, 63, 408 n. 71; in Nova Albion, 52–54, 112, 314, 416 ch. 11, n. 1; and size of Drake's crew, 55, 56, 406 n. 36

Black woman named Maria, 61, 65, 105; captured during Drake's voyage, 19, 52–53, 112, 407 n.36; pregnancy of, 53, 406 n.14; fate of, 53–54, 65

Blagrave, John, map and book by, 114, 130

Blundeville, Thomas, 6; comment on Drake's California voyage, 106, 158

Blyth, Charles R., 246

Bocqueraz, Leon, 246, 247, 248, 251, 252

Bodega Bay, 34, 39; Captain James Colnett's visit to, 68; J. W. Dwinelle's theory on, 272–273, 319; Humboldt's theory on, 67, 68; latitude of, 36; navigability of lagoon in, 37; as northern oceanward harbor in Nova Albion, 36–37; not a strong contender for Drake's California anchorage, 44; A. F. Rolle's opinion on, 73; visibility of, 147

Bodega, Juan Francisco de la, 36, 38; Farallones named by, 265

Bolanos, Francisco de, 40, 41, 167

Bolinas, 259–260

Bolinas Bay, 32; Cermeño's description as evidence for, 308–309; and Drake's departure from Nova Albion, 270; illustration of, 178; latitude of, 157; as oceanward harbor in Nova Albion, 41–42; navigability of, 41–42; as contender for Drake's California anchorage site, 44; trees near, 42; visibility of, 167; weather of, 189, 190, 340. *See also* Bolinas Lagoon

Bolinas Lagoon: archaeological investigations at, 75–76, 234, 239; conclusion from the summarized evidence, 344; defended by V. Aubrey Neasham, 74–76, 141, 167, 178, 189, 195, 197, 201, 251–252, 281–282, 287, 323, 326, 327, 328, 329; differences between inland environment and, 195, 197;

Dudley's chart cited as evidence for Bolinas
Bay and, 323, 326, 327; fauna and flora at,
201, 341; illustration of, 178; latitude of, 157;
minimal evidence on suitability as a harbor,
339; and the Montanus illustration, 300–
301; navigability of, 41–42, 178–179;
"Portus Novae Albionis" used in defense
of, 281–282; suitability for careening of the
Golden Hind, 177–178, 419 n.4; and white
cliffs as a clue, 339

Bolinas Ridge, 195, 201; ground squirrels on,
211, 212; search for the plate of brass on,
259, 260

Bolton, Herbert E., 246, 248, 253; comment
on the abridgment of "The Famous Voyage," 394; opinion on the plate of brass,
243, 244, 246; and plate of brass as a hoax,
253, 261

Bozarth, Captain A. J., 237

Brace, F. Richard, 79

Brass, Elizabethan, characteristics of, 255,
256–257

Brazil, 15

Briggs, Henry, map by, 161

British Empire, among the Coast Miwok Indians, 220–221, 222–228 *passim*

British Museum, 72, 87, 98, 119, 123, 272,
274; "Anonymous Narrative" in, 105;
Madox diary discovered in, 109

Brodiaea species, 217

Brown, Everett J., 246

Brown, Richard, 200

Bryant, William Cullen, 69, 272, 273

Buckland Abbey, England: curator of, 297;
purchased by Drake, 22

Bueno, Cabrera, 163, 425 n.6, ch. 26

"Bulrushes," 203, 215

Burney, Captain James, 409 n.16; analysis of
Drake's coronation, 224; opinion on
Drake's California harbor, 67, 68, 148

Burrage, Henry S., 402 n.2

C

Cabot, John, 13, 14

Cabot, Sebastian, 13, 14

Cabrillo, Juan Rodriguez: voyage along
northern California coast by, 11, 69; and
discovery of the Farallon Islands, 264

Cacafuego, the, 18

Caldeira, William: plate found and tossed
away by, 246–248, 251; veracity of, 251–
252

Caley, Earle R., 254, 255

California, 4; British Empire established in,
7, 31, 33, 220–221, 222–228 *passim;* eras of
controversy on Drake's anchorage in,
68–72; ice age in, 188; as an island, 125,
129, 334, 335, 336. *See also* California,
northern

California Heritage Preservation Commission, 78, 234

California Historical Resources Commission,
428, n.8

California Historical Society, xvi, 11, 72, 75,
76, 78, 139–140, 237; initial role in Drake's
controversial anchorage site, 70; and the
plate of brass, 244, 246; report of the Drake
Navigators Guild to, 80–81; research
sponsored by, 75, 137

California Historical Society debate, xvi,
141–346 *passim,* 396–398; on accessibility
of the harbor, 178–179, 183, 339; ambiguity and phrasing of the tenets, 165–
166, 168–169, 218; on archaeological evidence, 231, 238–241, 341; on the "bay vs.
harbor issue," 171, 172–177, 339; on Cermeño's declaration, 303, 307–312, 315,
343; on the Caldeira plate, 251–252; conclusions from the evidence presented during, 338–344; debaters and their theories,
141; on the de Morena account, 331, 334–
336, 337, 344; on differences between the
anchorage site and the inland area, 192,
193–198, 340; and Drake's search for the
Northwest Passage, 142, 149–150, 338; on
Dudley maps and charts as clues, 316,
323–327, 343; on flora in Nova Albion,
199–205, 340; on food and water available
at Drake's anchorage site, 179–180, 339; on
the fort built at Nova Albion, 180, 182–
183, 339; on identification of conies, 206,
209–213, 340–341; on identification of
large and fat "deere," 209, 340; on latitude
of Drake's landing site, 152, 157, 162,
338–339; published account of, 141, 253,
397; on significance of Drake's contacts
with the Indians, 214, 218, 220–223, 226,
227–228; on significance of the Montanus
illustration, 296, 300–301, 343; on
significance of the plate of brass to Drake's
landing site, 242, 251–253, 341–342; on
correlation of the "Portus Novae Albionis"
to Drake's anchorage site, 271, 281–285,
294, 342–343; on suitability of the harbor

for careenage, 177–178, 183, 339; on time lapse between Drake's departure from Nova Albion and arrival at the Farallones, 263, 266–267, 270, 342; on the weather as a clue, 184, 188–191, 340; on the white cliffs as a clue, 163, 165–170, 339

California Historical Society Quarterly, (later California Historical Quarterly), 141, 186, 250, 253, 297, 397; Cermeño's account published in, 111; references to the forgery of the plate of brass in, 261

California Maritime Academy, 81

California, northern: Drake as first European explorer on mainland of, 11; first black woman in, 54; first viewed by Spanish explorers, 11; first Spanish sea captain to set foot in, 303. *See also* Marin County; Nova Albion

California sojourn by Drake, xv, 25–32; accounts of, 85–112; "Anonymous Narrative" account of, 105; dates of, 5, 25, 32, 392; described by W. Camden, 106–107; described by John Drake, 103–104; described in "The Famous Voyage," 93–95 (*see also* "Famous Voyage"); described in the Madox diary, 109–110; described by John Stow, 105–106; described in *The World Encompassed,* 153–154, 159–160, 364–379; inland journey during, 192–198; maps pertaining to, 110, 113–133, 271–295, 316–330; maps in fiction pertaining to, 130–133; original source material for, 88, 99–100, 153, 159, 242. *See also* Indians, California

Camden, William, 95, 158; translated account on Drake's California sojourn by, 106–107

Canizares, Don J., 44; map by, 278

Caño, Island of. *See* Island of Caño

Cape Horn, South America, 17

Cape of Good Hope, 21, 143

Cape Mendocino, 147, 304; in Dudley map, 126, 128; in *Gulliver's Travels* map, 133; in the Hondius Globe map, 125

Carder, Peter, 408 n.64, 409 n.74

Careening, defined, 177. *See also Golden Hind*

Carmelo River, 69

"Carta Particolare," 318, 320, 322, 323; compared to Chart No. 85, 128, 317, 329; described, 126; illustration of 127, 319, 321; and Dwinelle's defense of Bodega Bay, 319–320, 328; used by the Drake Navigators Guild in defense of Drake's Bay

and Drake's Estero, 319, 324, 326, 328, 329

"Carta prima Generale," 126, 128, 317–318, 320, 322, 323; compared to "Carta Particolare," 318, 320; cited in support of Bolinas Bay anchorage theory, 323, 324, 326, 327; illustration of, 283, 318, 324, 327; Neasham's reliance on, 323, 326, 328, 329; Power's discussion of, 326–327; rejected by the Drake Navigators Guild, 326–327, 328; shape of the Shinn plate correlated with, 323; two bays below Vizcaino's bay shown in, 318, 324; Vizcaino's and Drake's bays distinguished in, 318

Cary, Gregory, 51

Cathay, 14

Caughey, John W., 73

Cavendish, Thomas: R. Dudley's family connections with, 316, 322, 343; voyage by, 87, 102, 114, 119, 123, 124, 273

Ceanothus thyrsiflorus, 202

Celebes, 20; blacks left by Drake in, 53, 63, 408 n.71

Censorship of information on Drake's voyage, 23, 228

Centennial of Drake's California visit. *See* quadricentennial.

Central America, 9, 53, 64

Cermeño, Captain Sebastian Rodriguez, 9–10, 39, 56, 61, 69, 147, 158, 303–315; account of his visit to Drake's Bay, 111, 303–315; account compared to early Drake accounts, 309, 310–315; artifacts left by, 232, 233, 238, 239; bar at Drake's Estero described by, 304; California inland journey of, 306, 313; California visit reported by, 304–306, 384–386; debate on his report, 303, 307–315, 343; in Drake's Bay, 39, 67, 167, 304, 335, 343; Farallon Islands mentioned in report by, 264–265; Indians reaction to, 305, 306, 307, 308, 313–314; and information in the de Morena story, 335, 336; number of Indians seen by, 308, 311–312; Olema Valley described by, 194; overland journey to Mexico by crew members of, 306; ship wrecked on Drake's Bay beach, 306, 307, 309, 311; substantial evidence for Drake's anchorage site not provided by, 343; Wagner's translation of his account, 111, 315; vestiges of Drake's visit not found by, 306–307, 310, 315, 343

Chapman, Charles E., 70, 71, 186

Chart No. 85, 128, 317, 322; changes in, 127,

322; cited by the Drake Navigators Guild in support of Drake's Estero, 324, 326, 328, 329; cited by Davidson, 320–322, 328, 329; compared to "Portus Novae Albionis," 320–321; discovery of, 317; illustration of, 325; unpublished and undated, 127, 317

Chester, John, 48, 51

Chetco Cove, Oregon, 146

Chickering, Allen, 78, 237; and the plate of brass, 244, 246, 248, 250, 251

Chickering, Sherman, 246

Chief Marin, 74

Chief Ynitia, 74

Chile, 17, 181, 390

China, 14

Chinese porcelain, in Drake's Bay area, 232, 233, 238

Christopher, the, 15, 48–49

Christy, Miller, 413 n.12, n.13, n.20

Churchill, Awnsham, 107

Churchill, Sir Winston, 8

Cimarrones in Panama, 52

Circumnavigation (1577–1580) by Drake, 5–6, 7–8, 10, 13–24; casualties and survivors of, 62–63; danger encountered during, 17, 20–21; distribution of the Spanish treasure after, 22; Dutch maps of, 115–117; early published accounts of, 85–112; English maps of, 114–115; first published account of, 85–95; impact of, 5–8, 23; most complete and detailed account of, 96; mutiny during, 17, 51, 56; pilots for, 15, 19, 52 (*see also* de Morena, N.); proclaimed destination and underlying motives for, 14–15; royal bans on published accounts of, 23, 228; significance of, 23–24; around South America, 15–18; Spanish accounts of, 111–112; and theory of Drake's men left at Nova Albion, 54–65; through the Straits of Magellan, 7, 11, 14, 17; syndicate formed for, 14–15, 22. *See also* Crew for the circumnavigation; Northwest Passage; Ships for the circumnavigation.

Cline, J. M., 248

Clues to Drake's California anchorage, 141, 142–337 *passim;* conclusions and summary of, 338–346; future sources of, 346; insufficient evidence in, 338–339, 340, 341–342, 343–334; results based on analysis of, 344

Coast Miwok Indians, xvi, 72, 178; British Empire established among, 220–221, 222–228 *passim;* descendants of, 74; Elizabethan sixpence found on site of, 235, 341; identification of, xvi, 74, 78, 217, 341; language of, 73–74, 110, 204; legends among, 54–55, 59, 60–62, 406 n.23; and the Montanus illustration, 301; territory of, 34, 35, 341 *See also* Indians, California

Colchero, Alonso, 19, 143, 391

Colnett, Captain James, 68

"Conies" (small rodents), 29, 69, 107, 180, 205, 340; "barbarie," 207, 210; described in early accounts, 207; ground squirrels vs. pocket gophers, 207–209, 210–213; identification of as a clue to Drake's California anchorage site, 31, 206, 207–213

Contemporary accounts, 85–112; on artifacts left by Drake in Nova Albion, 231–232, 242–243; comparison between Cermeño and Drake accounts, 309, 310–315; reconciliation of latitudes reported in, 152–162; source of the two major early accounts, 88, 98–100, 153, 159, 242; use of the words "baye" and "harborough" in, 172–177; use of the words "shore" and "beach" in, 314–315. *See also* California sojourn; "Famous Voyage"; *World Encompassed*

Controversy over Drake's California anchorage site, 4–5, comprehensive review of, xvi, 66–82, 137, 141, 328; impact of the brass plate discovery on, 68, 73, 77, 232, 237; insufficient evidence to resolve, 344, 346; intensity of, 137, 139–140

Cooke, John, 87, 391

Coos Bay, Oregon, 146, 147

Coote, C. H., 130

Copper Mine Creek, 259

Coronation of Drake by the Indians, 29–30, 53, 57, 224–227, 228–229, 296–302 *passim*

"Corsair," Drake known as, 9, 18, 111, 402 n.15

Corte Madera Creek, 43

Costanoan Indians, 218, 427 n.1

Costanso, Michael, Portola's pilot, 425 n.6

Costa Rica, 18, 32

Cotati, 34

"Course, The," 94–95

"Crab Island," 54

Crabs, 311

Crespi, Father, 65; fair-skinned natives found in San Francisco Bay Area by, 59–60, 62, 407–408 n.61; map by, 59, 60

Crew for the circumnavigation, 17, 45,

47–49, 50–52; desertion of malcontents, 56, 61; discrepancy in size before and after Nova Albion visit, 55–57; original size of, 50, 62; size of which returned to England, 63, 408 n.67; theory of men left behind in Nova Albion, 54–65, 263

Cronise, Titus Fey, 69

Cummings, Alex, 297

Cuttill, Thomas, 47

Cyprus, 48

D

Darcie, Abraham, 106–107

da Silva, Nuño, 333; left by Drake in Mexico, 65, 111, 409 n.76; account on Drake's voyage by, 111; captured by Drake, 15, 19, 55; *Golden Hind* described by, 49; log book of, 111, 403 n.5; navigational charts and equipment of, 403 n.5

Davenport, Charles B., 71

Davidson, George, 41, 42, 68, 146, 167, 224, 306; on depth of bar at Drake's Estero, 41, 179; Drake's Bay theory of, 54–55, 58, 60, 70, 275, 277, 287, 321–322; on Drake's visit to the Farallones, 265–266, 268; Dudley maps studied by, 317, 320–322, 328, 329; harbor at Drake's Bay described by, 40; Hondius Broadside Map discussed by, 287–289; illustration of, 71; navigational expertise of, 70, 79, 148; Point Reyes cove theory of, 71, 75, 148, 149, 169–170, 321–322, 329; "Portus Novae Albionis" discussed by, 273–274; on the weather at Drake's Bay, 185, 186, 190; on visibility of Drake's Estero, 168

Dawson, Giles E., 255

Debate on Drake's anchorage site. *See* California Historical Society debate

De Bry, Theodore, 110–111; *Americae Pars VIII* by, 95, 110, 124, 154, 219, 299; "Famous Voyage" used by, 95, 111, 129; maps, 128–129; and the Montanus illustration, 299, 301

de Morena, N., 52; alternative name of, 331, 333; as Drake's pilot, 52, 331–332, 333; left in Nova Albion, 52, 58, 332, 334, 336; overland journey to Mexico by, 52, 58, 332, 333, 336–337, 344, 408 n.64

de Morena, N., story of, 111, 331–337, 344; not found in Mexican archives, 332, 335, 336; "arm of the sea" mentioned in, 331,

332, 334, 335, 336, 337; authenticity of, 333, 334, 335–336, 337; debate on, 331, 334–337; as a clue to Drake's anchorage site, 336–337, 344; and the hypothetical route to Spain, 332, 334, 337; and de Morena's desire to reach the English court, 332, 334, 337; Munro-Fraser's account of, 333; and possibility that de Morena discovered San Francisco Bay, 333, 334, 335, 336; published in the *Land of Sunshine,* 331, 334, 336; related by N. de Morena, 331–332, 387–388; H. R. Wagner's interpretation of, 333–334

Departure from Nova Albion, 263–270; evidence slightly favors San Quentin Cove theory, 342. *See also* Farallon Islands

Deptford, England, *Golden Hind* at, 22, 23, 125, 276

De Young Museum, 261

Dictionary of National Biography, London, 185

Diego, personal retainer of Drake, 52, 54

Dillingham, Matthew P., 80

Discovery, the, 67

Dixon, James W., 70

Dobson, Richard, 73, 287, 409 n.1

Doctors, 50, 51

Doughty, John, 51

Doughty, Thomas, 14, 107, mutiny fostered by, 17, 51, 56; executed by Drake's orders, 17, 21, 49, 51

Drake, Edmund, 46

Drake, Sir Francis, 5–8, 11–12, 21, 22–23, 117, 223; apprenticed to a sea captain, 46; birth of, 46; character of, 23–24, 65; chests of porcelains brought to California by, 238–239; childhood of, 46; as commander of the *Golden Hind,* 4; concept of Nova Albion's territorial extent, 33–34; crew members banished or abandoned by, 63, 64, 65, 408 n.70; crowned by the California Indians, 29–30, 53, 57, 224–227, 228–229, 296–302 *passim;* death of, 6; fame of, 5, 6, 46; as first European to explore northern California's mainland, 11, 223; as first sea captain to circumnavigate the globe in his own ship, 11; heir to estate of, 98; illustrations of, 2, 48, 216; legacy in San Francisco, 12; knighted, 22; log and documents of, 98, 150, 151, 289, 290, 291, 323; map seen and corrected by, 118, 119; navigational skills of, 147–148, 156, 159, 160, 161, 311; nephew of, 98, 204–205; Protestant services on Pacific Coast held by, 12, 28, raids on Spanish ships and colonies, 6, 7–8, 9, 14, 15, 18–19, 47, 181; source of his hatred for the king of Spain, 47

Drake, Sir Francis, the younger, account of Drake's voyage published by, 96, 98, 101

Drake, John, 32, 51; accounts of Drake's California sojourn by, 103–104, 112; captured in Argentina, 55, 103; and frigate left at Nova Albion, 232, 306; latitude reported by, 409 n.1

Drake, S. G., 69

Drake, Thomas, 51, 98

Drake Navigators Guild, xvi; archaeological evidence and surveys by, 232, 233–234, 238–239, 310; on authenticity of the plate of brass, 252; on bay vs. harbor issue, 172–74, 176; conies identified by, 209–210, 211, 212; de Morena story interpreted by, 334–335, 337; on Drake's arrival time to the Farallones, 267, 270; Drake's Bay theory of, 80, 173–174, 238–239, 319, 334; Drake's Estero site defended by, 78–80, 141, 149, 166–167, 174, 177, 179, 193–194, 239, 267, 281, 287, 326; on Drake's fort, 183, 233–234, 239; and Drake's search for the Northwest Passage, 149; Dudley maps and charts interpreted by, 79, 174, 176, 319, 324, 326, 328, 329; and entrance bar at Drake's Estero, 167, 179, 308, 309; on evidence from Cermeño's account, 308; on flora at Nova Albion, 200, 202, 205; formation and purpose of, 78; on latitude of Drake's anchorage, 157, 162; on location of Drake's Oregon anchorage, 146; and the Montanus illustration, 300; Olema Valley as Drake's inland area, 193, 194, 196; on "Portus Novae Albionis," 278–280, 281, 285, 294; and possibility of Drake's inland journey made by two small boats, 196, 197–198; potential comments on similarities in the Drake and Cermeño accounts, 312–313; on Power's political interpretation, 222; reports by, 80–81; research by, 78–81, 148; on suitability of Drake's Estero for careenage, 177; on veracity of Caldeira's account, 251, 252; on weather and winds at Drake's Bay, 188; and white cliffs as a clue, 166–167

Drake's Bay, 9, 32, 39, 67, 69, 167, 311, 304, 335, 343; and accuracy of Drake's reading of latitudes, 147–148; anchor found at,

236–238; archaeological investigations at, 232, 233, 239; Caldeira plate found near, 246, 251; Cermeño's account of, 111, 303–315, 384–386; Chinese porcelain fragments found near, 232, 233, 238; G. Davidson's opinion of, 40, 54–55, 58, 60, 70, 275, 277, 287, 321–322; defended by the Drake Navigators Guild, 80, 173–174, 238–239, 319, 334; in the Dudley maps and charts, 319, 320, 321, 323, 326, 328; English sea captains' opinions of, 67, 68, 148, 149; flora at, 202; Heizer's initial decision on, 217; Indian legend evidence for, 54, 55, 58; Indian villages near, 220, 239; Kroeber's opinion on, 217; S. E. Morison's theory on, 82; Munro-Fraser's theory on, 333; as oceanward harbor in Nova Albion, 39–40; Vizcaino's name for, 323, 326; weather and winds at, 185, 186, 188, 190, 193; white cliffs around, 40, 80, 147, 163, 164, 165–166, 168

"Drake's Cove," 239, 281, 284, 285

Drake's Estero, 44, 73, 303; basin at, 239; Cermeño's exploration of, 305, 308, 311; defended by the Drake Navigators Guild, 78–80, 141, 149, 166–167, 174, 179, 193–194, 239, 267, 285, 287, 308, 309, 326, 404 n. 9; differences between inland country and, 193–194, 197, 198, 340; Drake artifacts not found in, 310; and Drake's arrival at the Farallones, 270; and Drake's fort, 183, 233–234, 239; entrance bar and depth of water in, 167, 179, 304, 308, 309, 311; and fauna evidence, 341; as harbor in Nova Albion, 40–41; illustration of, 308; Indian villages near, 80, 305; latitude of 147–148, 157; S. E. Morison's support of, 148; and the "Portus Novae Albionis," 281; suitability as a harbor, 41, 177, 178, 339; weather of, 191, 340; visibility of, 168; white cliffs as a significant clue to, 80, 169, 170, 339

Dudley maps and charts, 76, 110, 126–128, 174, 176, 316–330; R. Aker's view on importance of, 323, 328, 329; authenticity and reliability of, 322, 326, 328, 329, 330, 343; California Historical Society debate on, 316, 323, 324–330, 343; as a clue to Drake's anchorage site, 319, 321, 323, 324, 328, 329–330, 343; controversy over, 328, 320; dissimilarities in, 317, 320, 328, 329; and Drake as a source of, 317, 322, 323, 324, 326, 329, 343; Drake Navigators Guild's study and interpretation of, 79, 174, 176,

319, 324, 326–327, 328, 329; evidence from cited by nineteenth-century scholars, 319–322; first reference to in California, 319; legends on, 110, 323, 329, 381–383; port of Nova Albion in, 317, 319, 320, 323, 326, 327; "Portus Novae Albionis" compared to, 320, 329; shape of Shinn plate correlated with, 323; Vizcaino's discoveries as basis for, 126, 128, 317–318; weaknesses of, 322, 326, 328, 329, 343. See also "Carta Particolare"; "Carta prima Generale"; Chart No. 85

Dudley, Robert, 76, 173; Arcano del Mare atlas by, 110, 316, 317, 319, 323, 324, 326; birth of, 316; family connections of, 316–317, 324, 343; latitude used by, 158; and possibility of Drake as a source for information given to, 317, 322, 323, 324; probable errors by, 322, 329

Duncan's Point, 34

Dutch Drake Map, 120, 121, 123; compared to the French Drake Map, 119, 123; date of, 121

Dutch maps, 115–117

Duxbury Reef, 41, 282

Dwinelle, John W., 272–273, 287, 291; Bodega Bay theory of, 70, 287, 319, 320, 328, 329; Dudley maps cited by, 319, 320, 328, 329; on source of the "Portus Novae Albionis," 288–289

Dyson, James L., 188

E

Earl of Leicester, 14, 316

Earl of Lincoln, 14

East Indies, 54, 55, 142, 143; geographic insets on the Hondius Broadside Map, 278–279, 280

Ebright, Katherine, 238

Egypt, 14

Ehrman, Sidney M., 246

Eliot, Lawrence, 51

Elizabeth, the, 15, 17, 56; captain and master of, 48; return to England by, 52, 62, 63

Elizabeth I of England, 3, 5, 16, 243; and creation of the Silver Map, 117; distribution of the Spanish treasure by, 22; Drake knighted by, 22; and Drake's log, 98; Drake's possession of Nova Albion on behalf of, 5, 7, 33; and prohibition of published accounts on Drake's voyage, 23; role in syndicate and

purpose of Drake's voyage, 14, 15

Elizabeth II of England, 77, 223

Elizabeth Island, naming of, 17, 392

"Elizabeth Islands," 390

Elk, 215, 305; and identification of fauna in Nova Albion, 209, 211, 340

Ellison, Joseph W., 250–251

Elmendorf, William W., 74

England: alternative routes for Drake's return to, 142–143, 145; anniversary of Drake's circumnavigation in, 77, 223; British Empire related to Drake's coronation and California anchorage, 220–228 passim; date of Drake's return to, 5, 390; Drake's popularity after his return to, 5, 6, 23, 401 n.2; interest in location of Nova Albion harbor, 10; N. de Morena's desire to contact the English court, 332, 334, 337; rivalry with Spain, 8, 114; "sense of destiny," 23, 220, 222, 228

Ensenada del Consolación, 43

Eschscholtz, Johann, 208, 213

Espirito Santo, the, 19, 52

Estero Limantour, 40, 163

Esteros, north of Drake's Bay, 40. See also Drake's Estero

Ethnological approach to Drake's California harbor, 70–71, 73–74, 215, 217, 313–314

Eyre, Edward L., 246

F

Fair, Harry H., 246

"Famous Voyage, The," xvi, 29, 85–95, 349–354; compared to The World Encompassed, 99–100, 152–155, 163, 242–243, 389, 392; condensation of, 91, 93, 156, 159, 160, 184, 289–290, 393–394; "The Course" excerpt in, 94–95, 355–360; T. De Bry's version of, 111, 129; duplicated by Samuel Purchas, 107; errors in, 154–155, 155–56, 159, 160, 176, 268, 389–391; Farallon Islands not mentioned in, 265, 267–268, 392–393; as first published account of the circumnavigation, 85, 88, 159; French seventeenth-century editions of, 117; Hondius' Dutch text of, 95, 110, 111, 123–124; included in only some copies of Principall Navigations (1589 edition), 88, 90, 93; identity of author of, 87–88, 99–100, 242; latitude of Drake's California harbor reported in, 152, 155, 158, 161, 175; length of

1589 edition, 90, 93, 393; Nova Albion specific descriptions in, 33, 172, 174–175, 182, 199, 203, 207, 211, 218, 234, 242, 243; omissions in, 156, 159, 160, 184, 265, 267–268, 392–393; results from condensation of, 393–394; the 1600 edition of, 93–95, 107, 156, 394–395; source used by William Camden, 106; source used by William Monson, 109; the "Spanish course," 417 n.5

Farallon Islands, 20, 32, 149, 263–270; advance information on prior to Drake's arrival, 265–266, 268–269; called "Ilands of Saint James," 32, 263, 264–265; Cermeño's arrival time, 312; Drake's arrival time debated, 266–267, 270, 342; Drake's arrival time from San Quentin Cove, 267, 312, 342; not mentioned in "The Famous Voyage," 265, 267–268, 392–393; seals and birds obtained for food, 32, 263, 265, 266, 269; weather conditions, 189, 191

Farquhar, Francis P., 78, 244; on forgery of the plate of brass, 261

Fauna in Nova Albion, 25–26, 206–213; conclusions based on evidence favors San Quentin Cove, 340–341; debate on, 199–205, 340–341; elk, 209, 211; ground squirrels vs. pocket gophers to identify conies, 207–213; of the inland area, 207–213

Fenton, Edward, expedition by: diary kept by chaplain, 72–73, 109–110; John Drake in, 51, 103

Ferrelo, Bartolomé, 11

Fink, Colin G., 249, 250, 251, 252, 253

Fink-Polushkin report, 249–250, 252, 253, 254, 255, 256

Fish, 206

Fletcher, Francis, 170, 175, 204, 207, 215, 225; account of Drake's voyage by, 51, 88, 98–100, 153, 159, 287, 289; chaplain during Drake's voyage, 20, 51, 61; conflict between Drake and, 20–21; and controversy over Tobah plant, 204, 205; latitudes reported by, 153, 155, 156; notes of as source for two early accounts, 88, 98–100, 153, 159; as probable source for Hondius' "Portus Novae Albionis," 288–292, 293; prayer service held in California by, 345; topics avoided in notes of, 61; veracity in notes of, 100–101; on the weather at Nova Albion, 184, 185, 186, 189, 190–191; The World Encompassed from notes of, 96, 98,

99, 153, 159–160

Flood, Thomas, 51

Flower, Robin, 254

Flora, as clue to the anchorage site, 199–205, 340; near Bolinas Lagoon, 195; blue blossom, 203; buckeye tree, 202, 205; controversy on Tobah, 204–205; coyote bush, 203; inconclusive evidence from, 205, 340; lettuce-like plant with soft down, 199–201; trees without leaves, 201–202. See also Indians, California, plants used by

Folger Shakespeare Library, 254–255

Food acquired in Nova Albion, 30, 104, 179–180, 311

Forbes, Alexander, 68, 224

Fort in Nova Albion, 27, 28, 29; archaeological search for, 233–234, 239; debate on, 180, 182–183, 339; Indian middens near, 220, 221; and San Francisco Bay theory, 252; vestiges not found by Cermeño, 307, 309

Fortescue, George, 51

French Drake Map, 102, 117–119, 121; compared to the Hondius Broadside Map, 118, 119, 280; "corrected" by Drake, 118, 119; date of, 119; Golden Hind in, 118; latitude of Nova Albion in, 160; as source for the Hondius Braodside Map, 151, 280

Frigate captured by Drake, 64. See also Tello, Rodrigo

Frobisher, Martin, 13, 14

Fry John, 408 n.64

Fry, Wayne L., 255

G

Gihon, J. H., 26, 69

Gilbert, Sir Humphrey, 13, 14, 221

Gilliam, Harold: articles on the Elizabethan sixpence, 235–236; "Portus Novae Albionis" discussed by, 277–278

Glen Ellen, California, 34

Globe-maps, 114, 130

Golden Gate, 41, 42, 140: bernoulli wind peculiar to, 168; discussion on Drake's possible discovery of, 149–150; possibly discovered by N. de Morena, 334

Golden Gate National Recreation Area, 41

Golden Gate Park, 345

Golden Hind, the, 3, 4, 5, 12, 19, 22, 32, 78, 106, 152, 338; careening and repair of, 3–4, 20, 25, 31, 69, 76, 104, 138, 177–179, 192,

239, 311, 339, 409 n.2; captain of, 4; crowded condition of, 57, 63–64; depth of water required for, 37, 179, 308, 309; description of, 49; in early maps, 118, 124–215, 129, 271–272, 276, 279, 280, 292; leak in, 57–58, 143, 171, 177; name of, 15, 17, 49; not mentioned in "The Famous Voyage," 392; spelling of, 402–403 n.28; as a spirit ship, 228; stuck on a reef, 20–21, 125, 279, 280, 292; suitability of the California harbor for careening of, 177–179; unloaded in California, 27

Golden Hind II, 18

Gophers, and identification of conies, 208–213

Greenbrae, California, 252

Greenhow, Robert, 7–8, 185, 410 n.2

Gross, Edmund, 283

Ground squirrels, 208–213

Guatulco, Mexico: Drake's departure from, 19, 52, 55, 57, 95, 99, 104, 142, 281; and errors in "The Famous Voyage," 391; pilot left by Drake in, 19, 111

Gulf of California, 331, 332, 334, 335, 337

Gulliver's Travels, map in, 130, 132–133

Gun powder, 15

Guns, on Drake's vessels, 47–48, 49

H

Hakluyt, Richard, 322; as compiler of "The Famous Voyage," 87; and creation of the Silver Map, 117; *Divers Voyages* by, 23, 114; and Theodore De Bry, 110, 111; R. Dudley related to, 316; latitude stated by, 9, 158

Hakluyt, Richard, editorial problems with "The Famous Voyage," 363, 389–395; comparison of California sojourn accounts, 361–363; condensation, 91, 93, 156, 159, 160, 184, 289–290, 393–394, 395; editorial changes by, 204, 363, 404 n.2; errors, 154–155, 155–156, 159, 160, 176, 268, 389–391; omissions, 156, 159, 160, 184, 265, 267–268, 392–393

Hakluyt, Richard, *The Principall Navigations* by, 9, 85–95, 361–363

Hakluyt Society, 88, 101–102, 130

Halberd, Javanese, 238

Hale, Edward Everett, 69; Dudley maps cited by, 320, 328, 329; "Portus Novae Albionis" discussed by, 273, 275, 288, 293; San Francisco Bay theory of, 273, 320, 329

Half Moon Bay, 287, 292

Hall, Christopher, 109

Hall, William, 80

Hallam, Henry, 130

Hanna, Warren L., xvi

Harbor, defined, 175

Harbor of refuge, 38, 171–183; accessibility of, 178–179; bay vs. harbor in description of, 172–177, 339; debate on, 171, 183; conclusion based on evidence presented at the debate, 339; safety from Spanish reprisal, 172, 181–182; suitability for careening of the *Golden Hind,* 177–178

Harbors and bays in Nova Albion, 36–44

Hardison, O. B., 255

Harlow, Vincent T., 254

Harquebus, 51

Harrington, John P., 204

Harrison, George E., 249

Hart, James D., 259; report on the plate of brass, 254, 257–259; on possibility of the plate of brass as a hoax, 260–261, 262

Harvard College Library, 320

Haselden, R. B., 250, 251, 253, 254

Hatton, Christopher, 14; *Golden Hind* named in honor of, 49

Hawkins, John, 14, 46–47

Hedges, R. E. M., 255, 258

Heil, Walter 236

Heizer, Robert F., xvi, xvii, 35, 73–74, 78, 217–218; archaeological investigations by, 232, 233; conclusions on Drake's California anchorage, 74, 217, 218; and Elizabethan sixpences in Marin County, 234, 235, 236; Indians identified by, xvi, 72, 74, 217–218; Indian legend evidence rejected by, 55, 59; Montanus illustration discussed by, 299–300; "Portus Novae Albionis" discussed by, 276–277, 288; on possibilities of future archival research, 428 n.6; on safety from Spanish reprisal, 182, 419 n.6; search for the plate of brass by, 259, 260; on Tobah identification, 204

Herrera, Antonio de, 104

Hildebrand, Joel E., 248

Hinterland, 192–198; Cermeño's description of, 306, 313; debate on, 192, 193–198, 340; evidence favors Drake's Estero, 198, 340; identification of fauna, 207–213

Hioh, and the California Indians, 28–29, 372–373, 375; linguistic study of, 215

Hittell, Theodore H., 69

Holmes, Maurice G., 186
Hondius Broadside Map, 121, 122, 123–125, 129, 150, 151, 160, 276; compared to the De Bry map, 129; compared to the Dutch Drake map, 121; compared to the French Drake Map, 118, 119, 121, 151; compared to the Silver Map, 151; date of publication, 110, 124; described, 123–125; Dutch text of "The Famous Voyage" with, 95, 110, 123–124; East Indies geographic insets in, 278–279, 280; engraver of, 124; errors in, 280, 281; *Golden Hind* shown in, 124–125, 279, 280, 292; illustration of, 122; 150–mile inlet shown in, 150; sources of, 151, 280, 281, 287, 288–292. *See also* "Portus Novae Albionis"
Hondius Globe, 125
Hondius, Jodocus, 2, 110, 117, 124, 271, 277; errors by, 280, 281; maps by, 74, 78, 79, 102, 122, 123–125; A. Montanus related to, 297; sons of, 124; sources of, 150, 151, 287, 293
Hord, Thomas, 51
Horseshoe Bay, California, 42
Hospital Cove on Angel Island, 42
Houve, Paul de la, 216
Howard, Admiral Lord, 316
Howell, John, 77
Howell, John Thomas, 201
Howell, Warren, xvii, 77
Howes, Edmund, 105
Hulsius, Levinus, 95
Humboldt, Alexander von, 67, 68
Huntington Library, 121, 125
Hutchinson, W. H., 73

I

Ice age, during the Drake era, 188
"Ilands of Saint James," 32, 263, 264–265
"Ile Francisca," 54
Ile of Canoes, 106
Illness, 57, 58
Indians, California, xvi, 4, 26–31, 99, 104, 214–230, 232; baskets of, 29, 215; behavior compared during Cermeño and Drake visits, 305, 306, 307, 313–314; boats used by, 305, 313; as clue to Drake's anchorage site, 110, 214, 218, 220, 221–222, 229–230, 341; conies used by, 207; coronation of Drake by, 29–30, 53, 57, 224–227, 228–229, 296–302; debate on, 214, 220–230, 341; Drake's initial contact with, 26–28;

dress of, 27, 28–29, 31, 200, 203, 214–215, 305; effect of psalm singing on, 28, 314; English viewed as gods by, 28, 226–227; fair-skinned and bearded, 59–60, 62; food of, 206, 214, 215, 305, 311; friendliness of, 30–31, 57, 181, 214, 215, 229; houses of, 27, 192, 197, 214; identity of, xvi, 34, 72, 110, 214, 215–218, 221; and information on the Farallon Islands, 265–266, 268–269; and iron, 308, 309; king of, 28–29, 199–200; language of, 109–110; legend of Drake's men remaining in Nova Albion, 54–55, 58, 60–62, 65, 406 n.23; and the Montanus illustration, 299, 300, 301; number of seen by Cermeño and Drake, 311–312; plants used by, 27, 28, 29, 199–201, 203–205, 217; political interpretation of Drake's contact with, 220–221, 222–228; reaction to Drake's departure, 32, 104, 269–270, 274; territory of, 34, 35; weeping and wailing by, 27, 28, 30, 104, 220; Yurok, 72. *See also* Coast Miwok Indians
Indians, California, villages of, 27; archaeological investigations, 232–233; Elizabethan sixpence found in 235; near Drake's Bay, 220; near Drake's Estero, 80; near each proposed anchorage site, 221, 222, 229, 341; in Olema Valley, 194, 195, 196; seen during Drake's California inland journey, 192, 193, 195, 197, 419 n.1; visited by Cermeño, 305
Indians, South American, 99; Drake's hostile encounters with, 51, 180–181, 229
Inverness Ridge, 193, 194
Iron, 308, 309
Island of Caño, 18, 32, 143, 177, 281, 391

J

Jack's Harbor, 39, 69
Java, 21; artifact from, 238; insets in the Hondius Broadside Map, 125, 279, 280, 283
Jenkins, O. P., 249
Jensen, Wayne, 73, 287, 409 n.1
Jorje, Nicolas, 55–56, 408 n.66

K

Kelly, I. T., 35
Kinniard, Lawrence, 73
Knight, Max, xvii
Kroeber, Alfred L., 70, 73, 406 n.23;

ethnological approach to Drake's California anchorage, 215–216, 217; and plants used by the Indians, 204, 217

L

Laguna Ranch, 246, 252

Lamb, F., 129

Lamont, Donald Y., 246

Latitude: of Bodega Bay, 36; of Drake's Bay, 39, 80; miles equivalent to one degree, 153; of the Northwest Passage, 145; of Point Reyes, 147; of San Quentin Cove, 43; "sea latitude," 148, 161; of Tomales Bay, 38

Latitude(s) of Drake's California anchorage, 9, 10, 33, 69, 78, 104, 152–162; and accuracy of Drake's reading of, 147–148, 156, 159, 160, 161; of the contested harbors, 339; debate on, 152, 157–162, 338–339; discrepancy in early accounts of, 152–153, 155–156; in Dudley map, 126, 326, 327; pros and cons for latitude 38°, 69, 78, 106, 107, 124, 125, 129, 158–159, 339; pros and cons for latitude 38°30 ', 159–161, 339; reconciliation in reported discrepancy of, 152, 156–157, 160, 162; and repair of the *Golden Hind,* 409 n.2; value as a specific clue, 338–339

Lawrence Berkeley Laboratory, 255; metallurgical tests on the plate of brass by, 256–257

Leighly, John, 249

Lima, Peru, 104

Limantour: estero, 40, 305; spit, 233, 239

Lime Rock, 168

Lok, Michael, map by, 114, 117

Lucini, Antonio Francesco, 126

M

McAdie, Alexander G., 70, 185–186, 190

McKerron, R. B., 255

Madox, Richard: chaplain during Fenton's voyage, 51, 72, 109; diary of, 72–73, 109–110, 112

Magellan, Fernando, 11, 20, 56; chart of, 14. *See also* Straits of Magellan

Mainwaring, Henry, 174

Manila galleons, 9, 143, 303, 304

Maps and charts, 68, 113–133, 271–295, 316–330; by John Blagrave, 114, 130; of Coast Miwok territory, 35; and competition between Spain and England, 114; by Father Crespi, 59; by D. J. Canizares, 278; in De Bry's atlas, 128–129; Drake's age in, 118, 121; early English, 114–115; errors in, 113, 117, 121, 126, 280, 281, 390; in literature, 130–133; by Michael Lok, 114, 117; Molyneux Globe, 106, 114, 130; of the Northwest Passage, 143, 145; by John Ogilby, 129; the Peter Martyr Map, 114, 117, 390. *See also* "Carta Particolare"; "Carta prima Generale"; Chart No. 85; Dudley maps; Dutch Drake Map; French Drake Map; Hondius Broadside Map; "Portus Novae Albionis"; Silver Map

Marco Polo, 14

Mare Island, 44

Maria. *See* Black woman named Maria

Marigold, the, 15; captain and master of, 48; destroyed in a storm, 17, 62, 392

Marin County, 12, 67, 78, 299; archaeological investigations in, 232; artifacts found in, 11, 235, 238, 243, 244 (*see also* Plate of brass); bays and estuaries in, 42–44, 158; coextensive with Coast Miwok territory, 34, 221; ethnological proof of Drake's visit to, 34, 72, 110, 221, 229, 341; fauna of, 206, 208, 209, 210, 212, 340; flora in, 201, 203; history of, 54, 333; Nova Albion in, 34, 36; possibility of Costanoan Indians in, 218; 38th parallel through, 36, 158

Marin, the, 38

Markham, William, 48

Marshall, Robert, 78

Martyr, Peter, map by, 114, 117, 390

"Master Thief of the unknown world," 8, 18

Medallions, as maps, 115–117

Meighan, Clement W., 232

Mendocino, 106. *See also* Cape Mendocino

Mendoza, Bernardino de, 22, 401 n.9

Merriam, C. Hart, 70

Mestizos, 59, 62

Metallurgical tests of the plate of brass: initial series of, 249–250, 252, 253, 254, 255, 256; sponsored by the Bancroft Library, 255–257

Mexico, 9; archives in, 111–112, 332, 335, 336; overland journeys from California to, 306, 332 (*see also* de Morena, N.); Spanish governors of, 11

Mexico-to-California voyage by Drake, 19, 64, 142–147, 391; and alternative routes for Drake's return to England, 142–143, 145;

anchorage along Oregon coast during, 19, 146; bad weather encountered during, 19, 146; chart of, 144; difficulty of, 145, 146; need for and requirements of a harbor during, 171–183; search for the Northwest Passage during, 19, 143, 145, 146–147, 149

Mexicana, the, 38

Michel, Helen V., 255, 258

Milkweed, 201

Mindanao coast, 20

Miwok Indians. *See* Coast Miwok Indians

Mocha Island, 181

Moffitt, James K., 246

Mofras, Eugene Duflot de, 68

Molucca islands, 32, 143; Drake's departure for, 20, 56, 104, 109; in French Drake Map, 118; in the Hondius Broadside Map, 279, 280

Molyneux, Emery, 130

Molyneux Globe, 106, 130; described, 114

Molyneux Map of 1600, 130, 131

Monson, William, account of Drake's voyage by, 107, 109

Montanus, Arnold: "Crowning of Drake" illustration attributed to, 196, 299; related to Jodocus Hondius, 297

Montanus illustration, 296–302; California Historical Society debate on, 296, 300–301, 343; Drake Navigators Guild opinion on, 300; interpreted as a depiction of Nova Albion port, 297; Power's interpretation of, 297, 299, 301, 302; value as a clue, 301–302, 343

Moone, Thomas, 49

Morena, N. de. *See* de Morena, N.

Morison, Samuel Eliot: anchorage theory of, 82, 149; plate of brass viewed as a hoax, 253, 258, 261, 342

Morocco, 15

Mortar, found at Drake's Bay, 238

Munich, library at, 317, 320

Munro-Fraser, J. P., 333; on Indian legend of Drake's men remaining in Nova Albion, 54, 58, 60, 406 n.23, 408 n.61

Mussels, 30, 104, 180, 311

Mutiny, 17, 51, 57

N

National Park Service, 260

Nautical Safety, 311

Navigational charts and equipment, seized by Drake, 19, 143, 145, 403 n.5

Navigational experts, opinions of, 137, 78–82, 148–149. *See also* Aker, Raymond; Davidson, George

Neasham, V. Aubrey, xvi, 168, 285, 396; on accessibility of Bolinas Lagoon, 178; archaeological tests made by, 75–76; on bay vs. harbor issue, 172, 176; Bolinas Lagoon defended by, 74–76, 141, 167, 178, 189, 195, 197, 201, 203, 251–252, 281–282, 285, 287, 308–309, 323, 326, 327, 328, 329; and the British Empire concept, 222; and the Caldeira discovery, 251–252; Cermeño evidence cited by, 308–309, 310; conclusion on conies, 210–211, 212; de Morena story questioned by, 335, 335, 337; on Drake's departure from Nova Albion, 266, 267; Dudley maps cited by, 323, 326, 327, 328, 329; Indian descriptions cited by, 220, 222; on flora at Bolinas Lagoon, 201, 202, 203; illustration of, 75; on importance of Drake's search for the Northwest Passage, 149; on latitude of Drake's California anchorage, 157; Nicasio as possible location of Drake's inland journey, 193, 195; Olema defended as the inland site, 193, 195, 197; "Portus Novae Albionis" interpreted by, 281–282; on weather conditions at Bolinas Bay, 189

Nehalem Bay in Oregon, as Drake's California harbor, 67, 73, 287, 409 n.1

Nelson, Alan, 255

Newberie, Ralph, 87

New England: name of Nova Albion meaning, 7, 100, 104, 164; originally located in California, 7

New Mexico, 332, 333

New Spain, annals of, 332, 336

New York Public Library, 121

Nicasio, California: Indian villages in, 195, 196, 220; as possible site for Drake's inland journey, 193, 195

Nicasio Indian legend, 58, 60, 65, 263, 406 n.23

Nichols, Henry D., 246

Niebaum, Gustav, 125

Niel, Padre, 69

Nimitz, Admiral Chester W., 66, 78, 148, 342

Nisbet, J., 26, 69

Nombre de Dios, Panama, 47

North, Hart H., 236, 237

Northwest Passage, 13, 19, 138; as a clue to

Drake's California anchorage, 142, 143, 145, 149–150, 338 Drake's search for, 19, 146, 147, 149; latitude of, 145; map of, 143, 145; significant reference to in contemporary accounts, 417 n.4 ch.12

Nova Albion, 5, 10, 31, 33, 34; artifactual evidence for Drake's visit to, 231–262; blacks in, 52–54; Cermeño's account compared to Drake's experience in, 310–314; as coextensive with Coast Miwok territory, 34; as a conquest of the British Empire, 220–221, 222–228; dates of Drake's arrival and departure from, 5, 20, 25, 32, 263, 392; delay in debarking from, 181; Fletcher's notes as source for two accounts of, 99–100; harbors and bays in, 36–44; Indians of, 26–31; 214–230; latitude of, 33, 34, 36, 102, 104, 130, 155, 159, 161; name meaning New England, 7, 104, 106, 164, 403–404 n.2; named by Drake, 5, 31, 33, 45, 106, 107, 163, 164; port of, 297, 317, 319, 320, 323, 326, 327 (see also "Portus Novae Albionis"); San Francisco as capital of, 12. See also California sojourn; Plate of brass

Nova Albion, theory of Drake's men remaining in, 54–65, 263; carrying capacity of frigate related to, 64; crowded conditions on Golden Hind related to, 57, 63–64; discrepancy in crew size before and after Nova Albion visit, 55–57; examples of crew members abandoned or banished by Drake, 63–64, 65, 408 n.70; fair-skinned natives, 59–60; frigate left in, 57; Indian legend evidence, 54–55, 58, 60–62, 407–408 n.61; motivations of crew to remain, 56–58

Novato, California: as location of Drake's inland journey, 193, 195–196, 197; fauna in, 209, 211, 212, 213; name of, 58

Nuttall, Zelia, 112

O

Ogilby, John, 129, 299

Okell, Jack, 246

Oko, Adolph S., 78, 148

Olema, California, 42

Olema Valley: identification of flora in, 200; Indian villages in, 194, 195, 220; as location of Drake's inland journey, 193, 194, 195, 197

Olompali, 278; Elizabethan sixpence found at, 235, 240–241, 341, 427 n.2

Oregon, 8; Drake's anchorage along coast of, 19, 146; and Drake's search for the Northwest Passage, 142; and location for Drake's California harbor, 67, 73, 287, 409 n.1; weather during voyage to Nova Albion from, 187, 189, 191

Orient, 13, 304

Ortelius, map by, 143, 145

Oxford, the, 38

Oxford University, 255, 256, 258

P

Pacific Coast: as "backe side of America," 3–4, 45, 106; Drake as a pioneer explorer of, 11–12; impact of Drake's exploration of, 7–8, 9

Pacific Historical Review, 74, 109

Palau Islands, 20

Palou, Father Francisco: fair and bearded Indians seen by, 62, 408, n.61; and location of England's first colony in the new world, 65

Panama, 46, 391; raided by Drake, 47, 52

Parkinson, Robert W., 79, 80

Patagonian Indians, 181

Pate, Robert W., 73, 287, 400 n.1

Pelican, the, 47; renamed the Golden Hind, 15, 49, 392

Penzer, N. M., 102

Peru, 17, 390

Petah root, 29, 203; bread made from, 180; identification of, 203–204, 217

Petaluma River, 44; sub-bay proposed as Drake's anchorage site, 74, 278, 287, 409 n.1

Philip II, king of Spain, 9, 23

Philippines, 11, 19, 20, 303–304; typhoon season, 143

Pike, Donald C., 258

Pilots for the circumnavigation, 15, 19, 52, 143. See also da Silva, Nuño; de Morena, N.

Pirate's Cove, in San Luis Obispo Bay, 73, 287, 292

Plants. See Flora; Indians, California

Plate of brass, 6–7, 33–34, 77, 242–262; authenticity of, 240–241, 248–251, 252–259, 260–262, 341–342; Bancroft Library report on, 254, 257–259; Bolinas Ridge searched for, 259–260; and the British Empire, 31, 33, 224; the Caldeira plate, 246–248, 251–252; described in contemporary accounts, 31, 105, 107, 231, 234, 242–243; discovery and impact of, 11, 43, 68, 73, 77, 78, 177, 232, 237, 243–244, 402 n.25; Elizabethan sixpence missing from, 234–236, 240–241, 243, 341; given to the University of California, 246; and J. P. Hart, 257–259, 260–261, 262; as a hoax and forgery, 253–254, 255, 256, 258, 260–261, 262, 342; lettering on, 254–255, 258; metallurgical tests on, 249–250, 252, 253, 254, 255–257, 258, 259; Power's opinion of, 239–240, 252, 258–259; San Quentin Cove location of, 43, 78, 243, 297, 402 n.25; shape of the hole chiseled on corner of, 76, 323; the Shinn plate, 243–246; significance as a clue to Drake's anchorage site, 242, 251–253, 341–342; wording on, 245, 251

Plymouth, England, 77; Drake as mayor of, 22; Drake's departure from, 15, 62; Drake's return to, 5–6, 22

Point Arago, Oregon, 146

Point Reyes, 9, 39, 40, 193–194; archaeological tests in, 75–76; cove theory supported by Davidson, 71, 75, 148, 149, 169–170, 321–322, 329; illustration of, 187; latitude of, 147, 157; pocket gophers in, 210; visibility of, 147; weather at, 185–186, 188, 189, 190, 191, 193, 340

Point Reyes National Seashore, 200

Point San Quentin, 43, 177, 182–183, 196, 243; evidence to support theory of Drake's anchorage at, 195–196, 197, 297, 298, 301, 335. *See also* San Quentin Cove

Polushkin, E. P., 249, 250, 252

Pomo Indians, 215

Port of Nova Albion, in Dudley maps and charts, 317, 319, 320, 323, 326, 327

"Port Sir Francis Drake," 125, 130, 133, 161

Port St. Julian, 52; hostile Indians encountered by Drake at, 15, 180–181

Port Townsend, 237

Portola, San Francisco Bay discovered by, 7, 10, 335, 337

"Portus Novae Albionis," 74, 76, 78, 80, 102, 125, 271–295; R. Aker's study of, 279–280; H. Bancroft's comment on, 273, 288, 293; clue to Drake's fort provided by, 182; compared to Dudley's Chart No. 85, 320; compared to a U.S. Geological Survey map, 78, 286; G. Davidson's comment on, 273–274; debate on significance and corre-

lation to Drake's landing site, 271, 281–285, 292–295; Drake Navigators Guild study of, 278–280; Dwinelle's opinion on, 272–273, 287; H. Gilliam's comment on, 277–278; *Golden Hind* in, 271–272, 276; E. Hale's comment on, 273, 288, 293; R. Heizer's comment on, 276–277, 288; illustration of, 272; inserted in the Hondius Broadside Map, 74, 78, 80, 102, 124–125, 150, 271, 273; origin and sources of, 150, 279, 287, 288–292, 293; J. Robertson's discussion of, 275, 288, 293; R. P. Sprent's comments on, 276; R. C. Thomas' theory based on, 74, 278, 287; value as an anchorage clue, 285, 287–288, 292–295, 342–343; Wagner's discussion on, 274–275, 287, 288, 289

Power, Robert H., xvi, 140, 286, 414 n.52; on accessibility of San Quentin Cove, 179; as an anchorage sleuth, 76–78; on the "bay vs. harbor" issue, 172, 174, 176–177; Caldeira account questioned by, 252; conies identified by, 211, 212, 213; the de Morena story interpreted by, 335, 337; on dissimilarities between the Cermeño and early Drake accounts, 309, 310–312; on Drake's arrival time to the Farallones, 267, 312; and Drake's fort, 182–183; Dudley charts viewed as unreliable by, 326–327, 328, 329; on the Elizabethan sixpence, 234–235; and elk identification, 209; flora identified by, 200–201, 202, 205; on the fourteen days of bad weather, 187; on harbor suitable for careening, 177–178; on latitude of Drake's anchorage, 78, 157; library of, 77, 140, 223; Montanus illustration interpreted by, 297, 299, 301, 302; Novato defended as the inland area, 193, 195–196, 197; on 150–mile inlet in the Hondius Broadside Map, 150; plate of brass discussed by, 239–240, 252, 258–259; political interpretation of Drake's contact with the Indians, 220–221, 222–228; "Portus Novae Albionis" evidence cited by, 282–283, 285, 287; on safety from Spanish reprisal, 181–182; San Francisco Bay theory of, 78, 149–150, 167–168, 169, 177, 182, 222, 223, 228, 239–240, 282–283, 287, 301, 326, 327; San Quentin Cove defended by, 77, 141, 177, 179, 182–183, 282–283, 309–310, 311, 312; and secrecy of the discovery of San Francisco Bay, 149–150, 151–152; on significance of the

Northwest passage as a clue, 149; on sources of the Hondius Broadside Map, 150, 151, 287, 293; as unofficial ambassador to England, 223; on weather and visibility as clues to the anchorage site, 186–187, 189–190, 190–191; white cliffs discussed by, 168, 169

Prayer Book Cross, 345

Prayer Book Rebellion, 46

Preston's Point, 38

Pretty, Francis, 87

Principall Navigations, The (Hakluyt), 9, 85–95, 361–363. *See also* "Famous Voyage, The"

Pritchard, William, 76, 234, 239, 396

Protestant services, first on the Pacific Coast, 12, 28

Purchas, Samuel, 95, 107, 161, 287

Q

Quadricentennial of Drake's California visit, xv, 254

Queen Elizabeth I. *See* Elizabeth I

Quivira, 45, 138; Location of, 106, 138; port of, 128

R

Raccoon Strait, 168

Rafinesquia californica, identification of, 200, 201

Raleigh, Sir Walter, 117

Randolph, Edmund, 69

Rawlings, Stuart L., 246

Raymond, Gregory, 51

Raynor, Captain Charles E., 236, 237

Richardson's Bay, 42–43, 44

Rio, Rodrigo del, 331, 332, 335

Robertson, John W., xv, xvi, 68, 393; Cermeño's visit discussed by, 306–307; on conies, 209; critical review of proposed harbors, 71; on Drake's arrival at the Farallones, 266, 268; Dudley maps discussed by, 322–323, 328; on facts exaggerated by Fletcher, 100; Indian legend and fair-skinned natives discussed by, 55, 59–60, 60–62; on map in *Gulliver's Travels,* 130, 132; "Portus Novae Albionis" discussed by, 275, 288, 289, 293; on similarity between two early published accounts of Drake's voyage, 99; on Spanish expeditions to

California, 10; on weather at Nova Albion, 186; on white cliffs as a clue, 165, 166, 169

Rodents. *See* "Conies"

Rolle, Andrew F., 73

Ronquillo, the Spanish governor, 391

Roth, Bernie, 238

Rundel, Philip W., 255

Russia, 8, 37

Russian River, 34

S

Sacramento River, 332

Sagen, Mrs. G. O., 409 n.1

St. Francis, 304

Salmeron, Father Jeronimo de Zarate, 111, 331, 333, 335, 336

San Agustin, 304, 305; survivors of, 306, 425 n.6; wrecked in Drake's Bay, 232, 240, 309, 311

San Andreas Fault, 39

San Bruno, California, 62

San Buenaventura, 306

San Carlos, California, 62

San Carlos, the, 42, 43, 278; in San Francisco Bay, 42, 44, 218

San Francisco, 38; capital of Nova Albion, 12; Drake's anchorage site north of, 4, 9; Drake's legacy in, 12

San Francisco Bay as contender for Drake's anchorage, 36, 39, 42, 43, 58, 215, 306; and accuracy of Drake's reading of latitudes, 148; and Britain's sense of destiny, 222, 228; H. Bancroft's opinion, 69, 73; Crespi's exploration of, 59, 60; G. Davidson's initial theory on, 70; and the de Morena story, 333, 334, 335, 336, 337; fair-skinned natives discovered near, 59–60, E. Hale's opinion, 273, 320; R. Heizer's opinion, 74, 218; latitude of Golden Gate entrance to, 156–157; and the Montanus illustration, 297, 301; opinions in favor of, 67, 68, 69; R. Power's theory of, 78, 149–150, 167–168, 169, 177, 182, 222, 223, 228, 239–240, 282–283, 287, 301, 326, 327; J. Robertson's opinion, 71; and secrecy about Drake's discovery of, 149–150, 150–151; W. A. Starr's theory, 314, 315; and weather encountered by Drake, 187, 189

San Francisco *Chronicle,* 257

San Juan de Uloa, Mexico, 47

San Luis Obispo Bay, as location for Drake's

anchorage, 67, 73, 409 n.1
San Pablo Bay, 34, 36, 42, 44, 278, 283; fauna near as a clue to Drake's anchorage site, 211, 213; as inner bay in Nova Albion, 44
San Quentin Cove as a candidate for Drake's anchorage, 196, 267, 311; accessibility of, 179; and "bay vs. harbor" issue, 176–177; and the Caldeira plate, 251, 252; Cermeño account as significant evidence for, 309, 311; conclusion based on the summarized evidence, 344; defended by Power, 76–78, 141, 177, 179, 182–183, 195–197, 282–283, 309–310, 311, 312; and differences between inland area and, 195–196, 197; and Drake's arrival time at the Farallones, 270, 342; and Drake's fort, 182–183; excavation of Indian sites, 238; fauna evidence in favor of, 213, 340–341; as inner bay in Nova Albion, 43; latitude of, 43, 278; map evidence for, 282–283; Montanus illustration used as evidence for, 297, 298, 301, 343; opinions in favor of, 78; plate of brass discovered near, 43, 78, 243, 297, 402 n.25; Starr's evidence in support of, 314–315; suitability for careenage, 177, 339; and weather encountered by Drake, 189, 190, 340; white cliffs as a clue to, 339. See also Point San Quentin
San Rafael Bay, 43, 44
Santamaria, Father Vicente de, 218
Sausalito, 42, 43
Schilling, Rudolph, 246
Sea lions, 206, 265
Seals, 30, 32, 180, 206, 268
Seamen's Dictionary, 174
Seville, archives at, 111
Shakespeare, William, map in Twelfth Night, 130
Shinn, Beryle: plate of brass found by, 11, 43, 177, 243–244, 297, 402 n.25; plate of brass sold by, 246; story of his discovery, 243–244. See also Plate of brass
Ships for Drake's circumnavigation, 47–49, 392; blacks on board, 52–54; captains and masters of, 47–48; casualties and survivors, 62–63; doctors on board, 50, 51; fate of, 17, 62, 63, 392; gentlemen on board, 50–52; provisions of, 15, 21; provisions for the Golden Hind at Nova Albion, 178–180; theory of crew members remaining in Nova Albion, 54–65; which reached Nova Albion, 49. See also Tello, Rodrigo, Spanish frigate of

Shumaker, Wayne, 255
Sierra Leone, 21
Sijpe, Nicola van, 117
Silting, 39, 42, 43
Silva, Nuño da. See da Silva, Nuño
Silver Map: described, 115–117; illustration of, 116; origins of, 117; references to Drake's California visit in, 117; as source for the Hondius Broadside Map, 151
Simons, A. C., 237
Sir Francis Drake Association, 12
Sir Francis Drake Commission, 75, 78, 79; formation of, 254, 422 n.14
Sixpence, Elizabethan, 234–236, 240–241, 243; authenticity of, 240–241, 427 n.2; discovered in Marin County, 234–236, 241; found at Olompali, 235, 240–241, 341, 427 n.2
Slaymaker, Charles, 234–235
Small, Captain Adrian, 18
Smith, Cyril Stanley, 255, 256, 258
Sombrerete, Mexico, 306, 332
Sonoma County, 34, 36
Sonora, the, 36
Sorocold, John, 48, 51, 52
Soule, Frank, 26, 69
South America, 7, 304; Asian earthenware acquired by Drake near, 232; Drake's voyage below tip of, 17; hostile Indians in, 51, 180–181, 229
South Seas, 7
Spain, 11, 31; de Morena's hypothetical route to, 332, 334, 337; first entry into the Golden Gate, 42; king of, 47, 304
Spanish: accounts of Drake's voyage, 111–112; ambassador to England, 8, 22, 401 n.9; Armada, 8, 23, 138; capture of John Drake, 55, 103; colonies and ships raided by Drake, 6, 7–8, 9, 14, 15, 18–19, 47, 181; knowledge of the California coast, 69; Main, 47, 49, 98; navigational charts, 114; reprisal and Drake's harbor of refuge, 172, 181–182; sixteenth-century voyages to seek Drake's California harbor, 9–10
"Spanish course," 144–145, 417 n.5
Spanish frigate captured by Drake, 64, 104, 306. See also Tello, Rodrigo
Spanish treasure acquired by Drake, 3, 5, 18, 19, 64; distribution of, 22
Sprent, F. P., 119, 276
Sproul, Robert G., 248
Starr, Walter: activities related to the Shinn

plate, 244, 246, 247, 314; and San Quentin Cove theory, 78, 314–315
State Historical Resources Commission, 428 n.8
Stillman, J. D. B., 69, 208–209, 213
Strait of Anian, 13, 143, 332, 334
Straits of Magellan, 15, 62; archaeological remains in, 421 n.10; Drake's passage through, 7, 11, 14, 17, 142, 332; in the Hondius Broadside Map, 124
Stow, John, account of Drake's voyage, 105–106, 158
Sturtevant, William C., 35
Swan, the, 15; captain and master of, 48
Swift, Jonathan, map in *Gulliver's Travels,* 130–132, 133

T

Talbot, Thomas, 150, 151, 287
Taylor, Alexander S., 69
Taylor, Miss E. G. R., report on the Madox diary, 72–73, 109–110, 112
Tello, Rodrigo, Spanish frigate of: captured by Drake, 19, 27, 32, 49, 64, 143, 266, 409 n.75; carrying capacity of correlated with number of men left in Nova Albion, 64; fate of, 240; follows *Golden Hind,* 145; items transferred to, 192; left at Nova Albion, 32, 104, 232, 240, 263, 306, 311; need for, 64, 240; vestiges not found by Cermeño, 306
Temple, Sir Richard Carnac, 102
Ternate, Sultan of, 20
Thomas, John, 48
Thomas, Robert C.: Drake's coronation ceremony discussed by, 228–229; Petaluma River sub-bay theory of, 74, 278, 287; theory on ice age in California, 188
Tiburon, 42, 43, 283, 285; Javanese halberd found near, 238
Tobacco, 204, 205
Tobah, Indian uses and identification of, 27, 28, 29, 203, 204–205
Tomales Bay, 170, 206; entrance into, 38; General Vallejo's opinion on, 38, 70; as harbor in Nova Albion, 37–39, 44; visibility of, 147
Tom's Point, 73, 277
Tower of London, 22, 150
Trees, 42; and identification of Drake's landing site, 201–202

Treganza, Adan E., 75, 233, 238
Tres Reyes, the, 36, 38
Trinidad, 72, 73, 274, 276, 287, 288
Trumbull, Margaret, 139–140
Tuthill, Franklin, 69
Twelfth Night, map in, 130
Twiss, Travers, 225

U

University of California, 243, 254, 255; archaeological investigations sponsored by, 232, 233; tests on the plate of brass facilitated by, 248–250
U.S. Coast Survey, 41, 70, 179
U.S. Geological Survey, 178
U.S. National Wildlife Service, 264

V

Vancouver, Captain George, opinion on Drake's anchorage site, 67, 68, 71, 148
Vargas, Gaspar de, 333
Vaux, W. S. W., 101
Velasco, Luis de, 304
Vallejo, California, 34
Vallejo, General Mariano, Tomales Bay theory of, 38, 70
Ventura, California, 11
Verne, Jules, Drake's anchorage theory of, 69
Vicary, Leonard, 51
Viles, Donald, 73, 287
Vizcaino, Juan Sebastian, 69; in Drake's Bay, 39, 40, 167; chart of his California anchorage, 418 n.1; cold weather encountered in Monterey, 186; Dudley maps based on discoveries of, 126, 128, 317–318; expedition to survey northern California harbors, 9–10, 36–37, 158, 331; Farallon Islands in chart made by, 265; and information in the de Morena story, 336; name given to Drake's Bay by, 39, 323, 326; no record of Tomales and Bodega bays made by, 147
Von der Porten, Edward, 233, 410 n.26

W

Wagner, Henry R., 68, 71, 105, 392; and authenticity of the plate of brass, 252, 253–254; Cermeño account translated by, 111, 315; on Cermeño's failure to find vestiges of Drake's visit, 307; comparison of the two major accounts by, 99; conclusion on conies, 209; definitive work on Drake's voyage by, 72, 77; the de Morena story discussed by, 333–334; on Drake's arrival time at the Farallones, 265, 267–268; on Drake's coronation by the Indians, 225; illustration of, 72; Indian legend evidence rejected by, 55, 59; on maps of Drake's voyage, 113, 119, 125, 129, 322, 328, 329; "Portus Novae Albionis" discussed by, 274–275, 287, 288, 289; and *Tobah* identification, 204; Trinidad Head defended by, 73; on weather conditions, 100, 101, 188; on the white cliffs issue, 164–165, 166, 169

Walsingham, Sir Francis, 14

Water supply, 171; needed at the California landing site, 179–180, 398

Waters, D. W., 267

Wattkyns, Emanuell, 51

Weather conditions as a clue, 25–26, 100, 101, 104; California Historical Society debate on, 184, 188–191, 340, 398; described by John Drake, 104; evidence favors Drake's Bay and Estero, 185–186, 190, 340; fourteen days of bad, 26, 187, 189, 191; northwest wind as a factor, 186, 188, 189; opinions of scholars on, 185–188

Whaling vessels, careened at San Quentin Cove, 177, 179

White cliffs as a clue, 40, 41, 163–170; California Historical Society debate on, 163, 165–170, 397; along Drake's Bay, 80, 82, 147; in England, 164, 169; numerous locations of, 168; role in Drake's naming of Nova Albion, 163, 164, 165, 168–169, 170; significance of as a clue, 339; varying opinions on, 164–165; visibility of, 80, 82

Whitehall map, 292

Wildlife. *See* Fauna

Wilkins property, 259

Wilson, Norman L., 75

Winter, George, 14

Winter, John: captain of the *Elizabeth,* 48, 52, 391; and mutiny, 56; return to England, 62, 408 n.65

Winter, William, 14

Winterhey, Robert, 51

World Encompassed, The, 48, 96–102, 105, 129, 146, 193, 311, 364–379; accuracy and reliability of, 100–101, 153–154, 160; compared to "The Famous Voyage," 99–100, 152–153, 242–243, 389, 391, 392–393; compiler of, 98; on Drake's arrival to the Farallones, 263, 265; Fletcher's notes as source of, 98–100; Fletcher's journal used for narrative of Drake's California visit, 98, 153–154, 159–160, 389; "harborough" used to describe Drake's anchorage site, 172, 173, 174–175, 366; later editions of, 101–102; latitude of Drake's anchorage reported by, 152–153, 155, 157, 160, 161, 175; as most complete and detailed account of the circumnavigation, 96; and the name Albion, 404 n.2

Worrall, John, 51

Y

Yeandle, Laetitia, 255

Yurok Indians. 72

Z

Zarate, Don Francisco de, 19

Zayas, Martinez y, 38

Designer: Jim Mennick
Compositor: Lehmann Graphics
Printer: Publishers Press
Binder: Mountain States
Text: VIP Bembo
Display: Hadriano Stonecut & Weiss Series I
Cloth: Holliston Crown Linen 13344